CONCERT PIANO REPERTOIRE

*A Manual of Solo Literature
for Artists and Performers*

by

Albert Faurot

The Scarecrow Press, Inc.
Metuchen, N.J.   1974

Library of Congress Cataloging in Publication Data

Faurot, Albert.
   Concert piano repertoire.

   1. Piano music—Bibliography. I. Title.
ML128.P3F39   016.7864'05   73-15567
ISBN 0-8108-0685-1

for

RICHARD CANTERBURY

Mentor and Friend

CONTENTS

INTRODUCTION

The need for a handy source of up-to-date information about piano music is felt by all who play the instrument, whether as professional performers, private teachers and pupils, or classroom lecturers and music majors. Though many fine histories of keyboard music exist, no tabulated compendium of the repertoire has appeared for over twenty years.

This book hopes to fill that need by providing quick and accurate data for program-making, teaching and research. New ideas for performance or study will be found in the complete listing of standard composers, including both popular and less familiar titles, with brief evaluations. Forgotten and obscure composers, many of whom are now being rediscovered, are included. Special attention has been given to modern and contemporary works in order to encourage exploration and induce wider performance of new music.

To facilitate speedy research, all composers have been listed in alphabetical order. Dates and places have been listed under each composer. Thus the pianist is saved the tedious task of reference to an index to track down information in separate categories, according to historical period, geographic location, musical form, etc. Further, a chronological chart is provided for relating composers in time. A bibliography of general histories of keyboard music, studies and biographies of important composers, and some reference books, has been added for those wishing to do further research.

Though the piano did not come into general use until the period of Haydn, Mozart and the sons of Bach--roughly 1750--music written for the fully developed harpsichord is still played with pleasure by pianists, and enjoyed by audiences. Works for the concert harpsichord or cembalo, dating from the end of the 17th century and continuing through the first three quarters of the 18th century, have therefore been included in the list.

vii

Earlier works, written for the virginals and spinet, the clavichord or the one-manual cembalo have not been included. These are seldom effective on the piano. Though of great importance historically, and often of real musical merit, they are best heard on the authentic instruments. Fortunately, with the revival of the harpsichord and its family as home and concert instruments, and with the proliferation of fine recordings, the rich literature of early English, Spanish, French and German keyboard music can now be enjoyed as originally conceived. This revival has also inspired a new repertoire of contemporary works, conceived for the harpsichord. Though these can also be played on the piano, they too lose much of their quality in such performance. Since a book devoted to contemporary harpsichord literature is in preparation, these titles have not been included. A recent book on the piano duet covers that field very thoroughly (see Lubin, in the Bibliography). Many fine studies of the classical and standard concertos already exist; and since these works belong properly to the field of ensemble or symphonic literature, they have also been omitted.

A book of this nature cannot hope to be up-to-the-minute, since new piano solos continue to come out week after week, if not day after day. I have not, in fact, attempted to be comprehensive in the listings of music for the last twenty years, since a recent book is devoted specifically to contemporary piano music, though aimed at teachers (see Butler, in Bibliography). Selection herein has been of works which seem to be trend-setting, or outstanding in other ways. A few of the author's enthusiasms (and antagonisms) --heroes and villains--also make an appearance.

Since the 1950s a new type of avant-garde piano music has appeared (the reader may decide to which of the author's "ism" categories it belongs.) Some of these works are large-scale sonatas; others, suites of miniatures, sets of variations, or single brief sketches. It is perhaps unfortunate that many of them were ever published, for though they are exceedingly handsome scores, printed in facsimile, and may one day end up in glass museum cases, they represent, in most cases, isolated early works for piano by composers who have become highly successful in other contemporary musical media.

One applauds the desire for a complete break with the past, and a completely new musical creation. Unfortunately, in writing for the piano this is impossible; the instrument is too strongly anchored in the past, and so intransigent in its demands and limitations. The result has been that many avant-garde composers have turned their backs on the keyboard and closed their ears to the piano sound and, working at the drawing-board, have produced intellectual, scientific, highly technical works that are purely ideal and totally impracticable. These scores are in an elegant, complex, minuscule calligraphy, cramped and crowded, cluttered with a prose text of instructions and mathematical specifications for each note on the page. It is hard to believe that the composers were ever able to sit down at the piano and play, with joy--as Mozart, Chopin, Liszt and Schumann must so often have done--a finished piece. Nicolas Slonimsky has dubbed this kind of writing glossolalia; it is for the initiated. One is tempted to quote St. Paul: "Wherefore let him that speaketh in an unknown tongue pray that he may interpret." Many composers do, but the interpretation is often in an even stranger tongue. Example: "This piano work is in quaquaversal vigesimosecular radical, servicing the titular paranomasia in the ambience of total musical action" (Matriano, Cocktail Music), which, being interpreted, meaneth: "This piano work is in universal 20th-century style, illustrating the pun of the title with all the musical means available."

At the other extreme are "disestablishmentarian verbalizationist" composers (Slonimsky's glossolalia) like Harold Budd, whose piano solo, Lovely Thing, consists of a page with the single sentence, "Select a chord--if in doubt call me (in lieu of performance) at 213-662-7810 for spiritual advice" (premiered at Memphis, Tennessee, October 23, 1969); and like John Cage, whose famous tacit piano solo, 4'33", has the pianist sit silently at the keyboard for that length of time (premiered at Woodstock, New York, August 29, 1952).

A handful of industrious and devoted pianists have laboriously deciphered and mastered the obfuscations of some of these works for performance, with minimal audience response. I remember in the 1960s hearing a chamber recital at Saint-Martin-in-the-Fields participated in by Elisabeth Lutyens, one of the most original and successful of the post-World War II innovational composers in England. First came two classical trios. When Miss Lutyens' own composition appeared on the program, the audience filed silently out of the church.

Some of the disestablishment titles have been included here for those interested. Serious pianists will be pleased to learn that the trend in piano composing is away from the cerebral and the serial, toward an audience and keyboard-oriented type of writing. Herbert Fromm, in an interview with the New York Times at the time of the transfer of the Fromm Music Foundation's headquarters, expressed the fear that without an audience, music as a communicative art would atrophy. Twenty-five years ago, Thomas Mann prophesied that the best servitors of the new might well be those who know and love the old and carry it over into the new.

Another reaction against the scientific technological composition of music for piano is represented by the current repertory revolution being waged by some pianists to reinstate neglected 19th-century "also-rans," overshadowed by the giants of their day and since forgotten. Though many of these seem, on revival, to deserve the oblivion they have suffered, a few have been included here that offer living, challenging keyboard work, and rewarding if not electrifying listening. Some may well remain to enrich the permanent repertoire.

My many years in the Orient have induced in me a profound respect for the indigenous musics of Asia; also a high regard for the performance skills of Asians at the keyboard. Along with this is a never-ceasing wonder at their capacity for enjoyment of things so disparate as a zarzuela, a Noh drama, a gamelan performance, or a piano recital. Though considerable piano music is written, so far few Asians have produced anything outstanding enough for international performance. The highly advanced Japanese, who attract world-wide attention with their avant-garde mixed-media happenings, write rather derivative and unimpressive piano music. A few titles have been included for the armchair traveller. A handsome illustrated biographical catalog, including piano music, was published in 1972 by Ongaku No Tomo Sha Corp., whose music is available through TP. (It is unfortunately neither complete nor accurate, for ONTSC, and there are three other important publishing houses.) A more comprehensive listing of Japanese piano music has been compiled by Eleanor Dornon, who has also translated a series of articles on the development of piano composition in Japan (available from Ms. Dornon).

While a comprehensive listing of piano solo literature has been the aim of this book, it is of course inevitable that there should be "sins of omission and sins of commission"--some valuable music and important composers overlooked, and some included who will eventually prove unworthy or insignificant. For these, my sincere apologies.

For the opinions expressed I do not apologize, but take entire responsibility. It is impossible to be impersonal and objective about music, if one really cares for it. Attractions and aversions are as profound and unfathomable in music as they are in human relations. The truism that one man's cup of tea is another's vial of poison is unfortunately true. Regarding the length and form of the pieces, the categories and periods, and the levels of difficulty, I have tried to give objective, accurate and helpful information. For the opinions expressed, I have been guided by the belief that the awakening of a shared enthusiasm in another is a teacher's finest task. Sometimes antagonism is aroused instead of enthusiasm. If the reader finds that my cup of tea is his poison, he can easily locate those at whom I take pot-shots, and build his program around them.

Thanks are sincerely extended to my colleagues, Isabel Dimaya-Vista, Eleanor Dornon, Lily Chou, and Clara Denny, and to my former student, Frederic Chang, for help generously given; and especially to my student, Ernesto Isagan, for patient, painstaking preparation of the manuscript.

Sharing and interpreting my favorite piano music-- as well as much that has not remained in favor--has been my greatest joy for almost half a century. It is now an added pleasure to be able to extend this to a wider public in printed form.

Albert Faurot

TABLE OF ABBREVIATIONS

General Terms

dim	diminished
ed	edition
F-S-F	fast-slow-fast [also, S-F-S-F]
G [A, B, etc.]	G major [A major, etc.]
g [a, b, etc.]	g minor [a minor, etc.]
LH	left hand
meas	measure
min	minutes
movt	movement
MM	metronome
P&F	prelude(s) and fugue(s)
pub	publisher; published by
RH	right hand
sec	seconds
v	voice [as in 3-v]
var	variation(s)

Levels of Difficulty

Dif	difficult
E	easy
Mod	moderate
Mod (Dif) (E)	moderately (difficult) (easy)
V	virtuoso
V Dif	virtuoso-difficult

Countries (Composers' birthplaces)

Arg	Argentina	Chi	Chile
Aus	Austria	Chin	China
Ausl	Australia	Cu	Cuba
Bel	Belgium	Czech	Czechoslovakia
Bra	Brazil	Den	Denmark
Boh	Bohemia (Czech.)	Egy	Egypt
Can	Canada	Est	Estonia

Fin	Finland	Nor	Norway
Fr	France	Phil	Philippines
Ger	Germany	Pol	Poland
GB	Great Britain	PR	Puerto Rico
Gr	Greece	Rou	Roumania
H	Hungary	Rus	Russia
Isr	Israel	S Af	South Africa
It	Italy	Sp	Spain
Jap	Japan	Swi	Switzerland
Lith	Lithuania	Tur	Turkey
Mex	Mexico	USA	United States of
Neth	Netherlands		America
		Y	Yugoslavia

Music Publishers*

ACH	A. C. Hernandez Establishment, Manila, Philippines
AMP	Associated Music Publishers, Inc., New York
A Tem	Alec Templeton, Canada
Aug	Augener Ltd., London (Gal dist)
B&H	Boosey and Hawkes, Inc., New York
BM	Belwin Mills Publishing Corp., New York
BMI	Broadcast Music, Inc., Canada
BSS	B. Schott Söhne
Ch	Chappell & Co., Inc., New York
CF	Carl Fisher, Inc., New York
CFP	C. F. Peters Corp., New York
EBM	E. B. Marks Music Corp., New York
ECS	E. C. Shirmer Music Co., Boston
EMdM	Ediciones Mexicana de Musica (AMP dist)
EV	Elkan-Vogel Co., Inc., Pa.
Gal	Galaxy Music Corp., New York
GHeD	G. Henle, Munich, Germany (Novello, N. Y.)
GMP	General Music Publishers, New York
GR	G. Ricordi, Milan, Italy (Colombo dist)
GSch	G. Schirmer, Inc., New York
HE	Hinrichson Edition, London (CFP dist)
HHA	Hallische-Handel Ausgabe, Kassel
JF	J. Fisher & Bros., New Jersey
JHI	Joseph Haydn Institute, Heugel, Paris
LPS	Lea Pocket Scores, New York
MCA	Music Corporation of America, New York

---

*Names in parentheses are those of U. S. distributors for foreign publishers.

MEs	Max Eschig, France (AMP dist)
Mills	Mills Music Inc., New York
ONT	Ongaku No Tomo Sha, Tokyo (TP dist)
OxU	Oxford University Press, London
PIC	Peer International, Inc., New York
SMP	Southern Music Publishing Co., New York (Peer dist)
SMF	Silliman Music Foundation, Dumaguete City, Philippines
TP	Theodore Presser Co., New York
UME	Union Musical Española, Madrid (AMP dist)
UNC	University of North Carolina Press, Chapel Hill
Uni	Universal Edition, Austria (TP dist)
Wein	Weintraub Music Co., New York

CONCERT PIANO REPERTOIRE

AITKEN, HUGH (USA), 1924- .

Piano Fantasy in Two Movements (1969). Large-scale virtuoso work of phenomenal difficulty. Uses experimental notation for accidentals, irregular measures without meter, but with numerous metronomic marks. Frequent dynamic shifts and pedalling for sonal effects are indicated. Unmitigated dissonance; the musical rewards seldom match the enormous effort required for reification. V Dif

ALBENIZ, ISAAC (Sp), 1860-1909.

A composer important in the modern renaissance of classical Spanish music. Though a brilliant pianist and an impeccable and prolific composer, (the opus numbers run into the hundreds), he has left only a few works that are viable for the pianist today.

Suite Espagnol: Serenade (Granada), Saeta (Cadiz). Those seeking more music in the style of the popular Tango, may try these two. Mod

Seguidillas, Op 232:5. Brilliant, pianistic encore number, with a lyric interlude. Mod Dif

Iberia, Books I-IV. Bk I: Evocation, El Puerto, Corpus Christi in Sevilla. Bk II: Rondena, Almeria, Triana. Bk III: El Albaicin, El Polo, Lavapies. Bk IV: Málaga, Jerez, Eritana. Here IA has created a major work of 10 separate pieces on regional dance rhythms and styles. The titles are often toponyms, intelligible only to a Spaniard. Unfortunately they give little pleasure to any but an ardent afficionado of Spanish music because of the insistence on a single rhythmic figure in each piece, their length (from 7 to 10 min), their enormous technical demands in ornamentation, octave playing, interpretation. The most accessible are Evocation, El Puerto, Triana, and Corpus Cristi in

Sevilla.   Alicia de la Rocha has made a stunning recording
of the set.   For specialists.

Navarra.   Single late work in IA's best style.   Dif

ALBENIZ, MATTEO (Sp), 1760-1831.

Sonata in D.   One of several Spanish successors to
D. Scarlatti, who wrote for harpsichord, organ, and the
early piano.   The Sonata in D is included in Nin's collection
of 16.   Its thin operatic melodies, dance rhythm and trumpet effect have a faded charm.   Mod E

ALBERTI, DOMENICO (It), 1710-1740.

Eight Sonatas for Gravicembalo.   This short-lived
Venetian composer won fame both as a singer and as a
harpsichord player, and immortality (or possibly notoriety)
for his invention of the "Alberti bass," so boringly used by
generations to come.   Though rather pale and uninspired,
his sonatas have qualities (he is said to have written 38).
The singer expresses himself in well-phrased melodic lines.
DA was ahead of his time in his use of a two-movt form,
and in the ternary (A-B-A) structure of his first movts,
which anticipate the sonata allegro of Bach's sons.

ALEXANDER, HAIM (Isr), 1915- .

Six Israeli Dances.   The Israeli Dances exist in both
an orchestra and a piano version.   Whichever came first,
they are pianistic and attractive, making effective use of
six dance rhythms, and of Middle Eastern modal scales.
Mod

ALEXANDROV, ANATOLY N. (Rus), 1888- .

Sonatas I-XII.   Little known outside the USSR, the
numerous piano works of this pianist-composer follow the
taste and ideology of the country, from a lush romantic

19th-century Slavic style to an innocuous popular style incorporating native folk song and dance rhythms. Sonata No 2, in the early Scriabinesque style, has been recorded. Mod. Eight Pieces on USSR folk songs are late proletarian style.

ALKAN, CHARLES (Fr), 1813-1888.

12 Etudes in Major Keys, Op 35. 12 Etudes in Minor Keys, Op 39; 1 Comme le Vent; 3 Scherzo diabolique, a Symphony; 7 Finale, A Concerto; 10 Allegro alla Barbaresca; 12 Le Festin d'Aesop. Charles Henri Valentin Morhange, the "Berlioz of the Piano," active in Paris at the time of Liszt, still being excavated by musical archeologists. His monolithic works are still intact and almost untouched. The reason is soon obvious, as the pieces are of phenomenal difficulty, minimal musical content, and interminable length (No 7, Finale, alone is 122 pages). There are attractive melodic and rhythmic motifs, occasional passages of unusual figuration, some imaginative development. The harmonic poverty, and mammoth "blow-up" soon pall, and it is easy to understand why they have remained buried, while a 50-sec piece of Chopin is immortal. The Etudes in Minor Keys listed offer a sample of exhibits in the museum. These horrendous marathons are for pianists with unflinching endurance, fabulous technic, unlimited leisure, and preferably with tone-deafness. Dif

ALLANBROCK, DOUGLAS (GB), 1921- .

Forty Changes (1971). Too many, and too little change. Thirty-six pages of variations, laboriously worked out, but undistinguished in content and unoriginal in their development. Prevailingly non-tonal, with a few tonal cadences (for humor?). Dif

AMRAM, DAVID (USA), 1930- .

Sonata (1960). An autobiographer and one-time would-be enfant terrible, DA offers a three-movt piano work, completely atonal, but using many traditional devices. The rhythmic Overture ends quietly. A Lullaby has lyric and

and reposeful moments. Six variations on a pleasing folk-
like theme offer wide and original treatment, subsiding after
a powerful climax. Dif

ANGERER, PAUL (Aus), 1927- .

Stimmung [Moods]. Five well-structured works by
this Viennese serial-expressionist composer written on tone-
rows, evoking various sensations and emotions by contrasted
keyboard figures based on dissonant counterpoint. For the
avant-garde player. Mod Dif

ANTHEIL, GEORGE (USA), 1900-1959.

One-time Bad Boy of American music, who later
settled in Hollywood to write for films, and reformed.
Though he shocked Europe in the 20's and 30's with the
violence of his Sonata Sauvage and Airplane Sonata, the
later works, now available, are more sober, eclectic and
traditional, with occasional flashes of originality.

Sonata No 4 (1948). Something of the "bad boy" is
still to be heard in the first movement's rambunctious drive
and acerbic harmony. The second is almost romantic in
its lushness and ardor. Bi-tonality gives color to the
closing toccata. Mod

Two Toccatas (1948). A rather tame "bad boy"
wrote these. The second is a hoe-down, with an old-
fiddler's tune, rather mild "wrong-note" harmony, one
brief "tantrum" and another bi-tonal octave coda. Mod

APOSTEL, HANS ERIC (Aus), 1901- .

Disciple of Schönberg and Berg, writing in serial
technic.

Kubiniana (1947). These ten "cubist" pieces are
predictably angular, severe and complex. Dif

Suite "Concise" (1965).   Good-humored musical
travelog (Concise is an Alpine village in Switzerland).   Tone-
rows used in a lean and lyric style to evoke pastoral scenes.
Mod

ARCHER, VIOLET (Can), 1913- .

Distinguished educator and composer of chamber
music and choruses, has two concertos and seven sonatas.
VA has moved from a tonally anchored style in early works
to free use of dissonance and the serial technic in later
compositions.

Sonatina No 2.   Three-movt early work, already
exploring new harmonies in a classic structure.   Mod

Sonatas 5, 6, 7.   Not just a one-time-only "duty"
sonata writer, VA has mastered the form in a series of
works developing a distinctive style, pianistic yet demanding.
Four-movt extended works.   Mod Dif

ARDEVOL, JOSE (Sp-Cu), 1911- .

Spanish-born music promoter and composer who
settled in Cuba, composed numerous symphonies and chamber sonatas, as well as three for piano.

Sonata No 3:   Moderato, Invenciones en Rondo,
Diferencias sobre la cantiaga "Entre Ave et Eva."   Neo-
classic three-movt work, well-structured, pianistic, and
with attractive musical content, freely dissonant.   A folkloric tune harmonized alternates with toccata-passages in
the 1st movt.   Light 3-v linear writing characterizes the
middle rondo.   Quiet variations on a modal folk-tune explore
various keyboard motifs, homophonic and polyphonic.
Mod Dif

Sonatina (1934).   Two-movt work, similar to the
above in its use of dissonance; a flowing cantabile followed
by a driving staccato allegro.   Mod

ARENSKY, ANTON (Rus), 1861-1906.

Teacher and mentor of many greater than he, AA wrote music which is of slight importance. The two-piano suites are the best, and deserve to survive. Beside the familiar Op 15 (containing the famous Valse, as well as an attractive Romance and Polonaise), there is a less familiar but attractive set called Silhouettes, Op 23.

Basso Ostinato, Op. 5:5. Pleasing set of variations on a ground bass, continuous in the manner of a passacaglia. Mod

Près de la Mer, Op 52: 4, 5. Set of melodious sketches, of which the best are Nos 4 and 5, with fluent, pianistic figuration and broad cantilena. Mod

Etude in f#, Op 36: 3. Rapid scales in the RH are the technical problem of this study; the LH melody is attractive. Mod

ARIZAGA, RODOLFO (Arg), 1926- .

Prize-winning composer of cantatas, symphonies and chamber music.

Toccata, Op 5 (1952). Brief but brilliant and effective study in dissonant style, with climactic ending. Mod Dif

ARNE, THOMAS (GB), 1710-1778.

Famous English amateur composer, noted for his settings of Shakespeare, Fielding and Addison. Written at the time when J. C. Bach was just introducing the new fortepiano in London, the music of TA is effective on either the harpsichord or piano. There are also six concertos, which have been recorded (with organ).

Eight Sonatas. Suites of two to four movements, alternating ariosos and dances, deriving more from Purcell than Handel, with an occasional English lilt. Though only a few separate movements have musical merit, they are easy and effective, and "save wear and tear on the masterpieces" (Lockwood). Mod E

ARRIAGA Y BALZOLA, JUAN CRISOSTOMO DE (Sp), 1806-1826.

Short-lived composer who might have represented Spain in the Romantic Movement, had he lived longer.

Estudios de Caracter. Three of the type popularized later by German composers, contrasting tempi, mood, harmony. Melodious. Mod

ASIOLI, BONIFAZIO (It), 1769-1832.

Though Italians claim to have beat the Germans to the piano (Cristofori, 1709; Silbermann 1730), they have produced few important composers devoted to the new instrument. D. Scarlatti, the greatest, never gave up the harpsichord. Asioli, a contemporary of Beethoven, devoted himself to opera, like a true Italian, but also performed on the harpsichord and wrote a treatise on it. Two of his sonatas have recently been recorded, saddled with the vulgar title "Switched-on Piano: the Electrifying Sounds of the 1795 Broadwood Concert Grand, and the unique swinging music of Bonifazio Asioli." No evidence is brought forward that BA ever played the instrument.

Three Sonatas, Op 8. These are all three-movement works, F-S-F, the opening movement marked allegro brillante, presto, etc., and setting forth a series of flashy scale-arp-chordal keyboard figures, with little development, and no recapitulation. Middle movements are "soulful" minor adagios, with bits of operatic melodies over Alberti basses broken by agitato passages of rumbling triplets or hammered chords. Finales are ornamental variations on popular operatic airs, or on themes brazenly labelled "original," building excitement with speed and volume in the manner of a comic opera overture. Might be given to the man who has played everything. Mod

AURIC, GEORGES (Fr), 1899- .

One of the lesser of "Les Six"; still active but with little piano music.

Petite Suite (1927).   Six dances in a lucid, Gallic, linear style, with alternating expressive and lively movts. Mod

Sonata in F (1931).   Big sprawling neo-classic work, demanding drive and virtuosity.   Dif

BABBITT, MILTON (USA), 1916- .

Leader in the American avant-garde, MB has applied the serial principle to all phases of music, totally organizing his compositions in rows based on pitches, note-values, intervals, timbres of instruments.   His highly cerebral music has little of interest for the mere pianist, the mere listener, or the mere musician.

Three Compositions (1947).   Both pitch intervals and four different note values are organized in these pieces, described as "straight-forward middle-of-the-road serial style" by S. Bradshaw.   Dif

Semi-Simple Variations (1956); Partitions (1957); Post-Partitions (1966).   Virtuoso draughtsmanship.   Should be framed and hung in the Museum of Modern Art.

BABIN, VICTOR (Rus-USA), 1908- .

Fantasia, Aria and Capriccio (1932).   Solo works by the male half of the famous duo-piano team, Vronsky and Babin, these are eminently pianistic in a late romantic keyboard style.   In the manner of Bach's ternary organ works, this begins with a free improvisory section, followed by a quiet cantabile chorale, ending with an ebullient caprice. Mod Dif

Variations on a Theme by Beethoven (1960).   Using the familiar Turkish March for a theme, these ten variations are imaginative, brilliant and effective.   Dif

BACEVICIUS, VYTAUTAS (Lith), 1905 .

Poème contemplation, Op 5; Poème mystique, Op 6;
Poème astral, Op 7; Sixième mot, Op. 72. Four pieces,
of which the latest is by far the best, are obviously by a
pianist rather than a composer. Early works are derivative, with short, eager phrases meant to evoke mystic con-
cepts, à la Scriabin. Ranging from fragile figures to massive virtuoso cadenzas, they are pianistic, but dated and
passé. The last (what is the "sixteenth word"?) is more
original and better structured, with four contrasting sections
in one movt, ranging from lyrical to dramatic, with much
fragmentary and improvisory writing still retained. Mod
Dif

BACH, CARL PHILIPP EMANUEL (Ger), 1714-1788.

A rather uninspired careful workman, CPE was never-
theless an inspiration to Haydn and Mozart, both of whom
quickly surpassed him. A prolific composer, many of his
over 400 solo keyboard works are still unpublished, as are
many of the 52 concertos. Interested parties should be careful to select either an ur-text edition (Kalmus, Breitkopf,
Peters) which is faithful to CPE's own meticulous editing;
or some of the recent scholarly editions, which strive for
authenticity; and shun the 19th-century virtuoso-editors, like
von Bülow.

Solfeggietto in c. This popular favorite is one of
many studies. This appears to be for the lute, with its
single-line melody, and sounds well on guitar. Mod E

Characterstücke. Modelled after Couperin, these are
named after girl friends or cousins or pupils (La Stahl, La
Bach), or rococo gallantries (Les Langeurs Tendres--Fred-
erick the Great, his Prussian employer, always spoke
French).

18 Probeststücken Vols I, II (1753). These early pre-
cursors of the Etude contain some attractive music. The
Allegro Siciliano in f$\sharp$; Allegro molto in f, a fine cross-hand
study; Fantasia in c, a bold improvisatory work almost worthy
of the old man (all are in Vol II). Mod

Für Kenner und Liebhaber Vols I, II (1779-87). The
name, "For Connoisseurs and Amateurs," aptly describes
the chamber character of these works, few of which sound
well in the concert hall. Among the sonatas those from Vol
I in a, G, and A are best; in Vol II, the Sonata in f, and
some of the rondos. Mod

12 Variations auf die Folie d'Espagne. This is one
of the most original of CPE's works, on the famous Sarabande in d, so brilliantly varied by Corelli for violin, and
by Rachmaninoff for piano. Mod Dif

The numberous concertos of CPE sound best with
harpsichord. There are two (or more) double concertos,
calling for both pianoforte and harpsichord, but they are disappointing, as the two instruments simply alternate parts
throughout.

BACH, J. C. (Ger), 1735-82.

The youngest son, only 15 when J. S. Bach died, JCB
led an interesting life, accepting Catholicism (in order to
play the cathedral organ at Milan?) and introducing the first
piano recitals in London. He was also one of the first composers to identify his works with opus numbers, for which
we must be grateful.

Sonatas, Op 5; Sonatas, Op 17. The 10 sonatas in
these two books were all written for the early fortepiano,
and all explore the new two/three-movt form, with allegro
(lengthy), expressive slow middle movt, and presto or rondo
close. Good fingering and scale-playing required. Musical
content meagre, but some good listening and playing fun.
From Op 5, the Sonata No 5 in D is recommended; No 2 in
c, from the second book, a big, dramatic work. Mod

BACH, JOHANN SEBASTIAN (Ger), 1685-1750.

Bach's preeminent place in keyboard music is acknowledged by all. Though regarded in his day as an organ
virtuoso, Bach wrote works for string-keyboard instruments
that equal or surpass the organ works in both quantity and
quality. He owned both a harpsichord and a clavichord (and

spurned Silbermann's early piano).   Anybody possessing modern counterparts of these instruments may enjoy the thrill of
authentic performances.   For the mere pianists, the delights
to be found in the music are still enough to last a lifetime.

Bach's keyboard music falls into three general types:
fugal or contrapuntal writing, glorified dance tunes in a variety of rhythms, and free, rhapsodic passages, when he
"takes off on a trip."   These latter are usually found in preludes, toccatas and fantasias, though often interspersed with
knotty fugal passages.   The dances are collected in the
suites.   The best approach to Bach is through the Notebooks
and dance suites, followed by the Two-Part Inventions; the
the Well-Tempered Clavier (hereafter known as WTC), then
the Three-part Inventions, which are more difficult than many
of the preludes and fugues (P&F) of WTC.   More advanced
pianists may tackle the bigger suites, the toccatas and concertos.   At the peak stands the Goldberg Variations, a whole
concert in itself.

Sonata in D.   The earliest surviving keyboard work
seems to be a Fugue in e minor.   Its unavailability seems
to be no great loss as Geiringer says it appears to have
been "written against, rather than for, the clavier."   A
youthful Sonata is modelled on Kuhnau's Biblical Sonatas, and
substitutes for "the stamping and rage of Goliath," the picturesque element of a "Theme in imitation of cock and cuckoo."   Also negligible.

Capriccio "On the Departure of a Beloved Brother":
This work separates the men from the boys, and marks
JSB a genius.   Quaint Kuhnau captions mark each movt.

Arioso; Andante; Adagio assai; Andante, Aria; Fugue.
Arioso uses French ornaments to depict "the blandishments
of his friend."   Andante portrays the "kinds of accidents
that can happen in strange lands" in daring modulations and
leaping intervals.   Adagio assai, "Lament of friends," is an
expressive passacaglia on a chromatic bass anticipating many
great latter works.   A brief chordal andante leads to the
Aria of the Postillion, which needs harpsichord registration
for echo and trumpet effects.   Though Bach never resorted
again to subtitles, many of these effects became staples.
Mod to Dif

Little Notebook of Anna Magdalena.   Containing the
easy minuets, marches, polonaises written for AM and WF.

The Kalmus ur-text has also numerous songs and early versions of suites, so is confusing. Many separate editions of little P&F and easy Bach for beginners exist.

15 Two-Part Inventions. Standard teaching, but a little off-putting for students not first acquainted with dances and simple preludes. None goes beyond four ♯'s or ♭'s. Essential studies in fingering, staccato-legato, voice balancing, ornamentations.

15 Sinfonia, or Three-Part Inventions. Musical and intellectual problems intensify here. These might well follow some of the easier P&F in WTC, or suites. (The hand-crossing problems disappear on the two-manual harpsichord.) All are fine, many concert calibre, but none is easy. No 6 is a good starter, in steady 8th notes for all three voices. Nos 3 and 4 are without ornaments, though all three overlapping voices keep busy. No 2 is a good recital piece, with its trilled pedal points. No 5 is basically a simple two-voice canon in RH with an arpeggiated chord in the left, but it is made formidable by the plethora of ornaments. No 9 is a masterpiece, sometimes called "The Little Passion." Played largo espressivo, its sighing motifs over a chromatic cantus firmus are deeply moving. No 15 is a virtuoso piece; and the others, all challenging. Mature.

Six French Suites. All Bach's suites follow the same pattern: ACSOG (allemande, courante, sarabande, optional group, gigue). The penultimate dance (the "option" is the composer's, not the performer's) varies from one to four dances, with French minuets (usually two), gavottes and bourées (called Galanterien) predominating. The allemandes are all in steadily flowing 4/4 16ths. Sarabandes are all slow and expressive, triple with dotted second beats. Bach distinguished two types of courante: the Italian (correctly labelled "corrente") is a simple fast triple meter dance, not unlike the menuetto; the French one, called courante, is a compound triple, usually 3/2, with a shift to 6/4 (two big beats to the bar) at cadences, and is much more elaborate and contrapuntal.

Suite No 1 in d. Three-voice allemande, requiring good voicing. Three-four voice courante of the French type, light and fast. Sarabande 4-v, harmonic. Two 3-v minuets form the optional group. The gigue is, exceptionally, in 4/4, and requires precise division of dotted beats and careful distinction between 16ths and 32nds. Mod Dif

No 2 in c.   Somewhat easier.   Allemande is a duet
with plucked bass.   Italian corrente.   Easy, attractive air
and minuet (2-v); gigue also 2-v.   Mod E

No 3 in b.   Least inspired; two-three voice throughout.   Mod E.

No 4 in E.   As so often in this key, the pastoral
mood prevails.   Flowing 3-v allemande.   Graceful 3-v
courante (the Baroque tradition was that in triplet writing a
dotted figure was also played like a triplet).   Attractive
gavotte, minuet, gigue.   Mod

No 5 in G.   Bach at his best.   All movements worthy
of loving study.   Unusual additional dances: gavotte, bourée,
loure.   A sparkling gigue which (like many others) is also a
3-v fugue.   Often performed.   Dif

No 6 in E.   A trifle pedestrian, although a snappy
tempo for courante, bourée, and gigue, helps to ignite it.
Mod Dif

Six English Suites.   A more proper title for those
would be "Suites with Prelude."   They follow the ACSOG
form, but each has a prelude, some very extended.   The
suites themselves are only slightly more difficult than the
French, but demand more endurance!   Some of the preludes
are fine enough to be played alone.

Suite No 1 in a.   The prelude is a flowing 3-v movt,
without the binary division of almost all dances, and pleas-
ingly short.   There are two courante, and the second has
two "doubles" or sets of variations.   The courantes alone
make a nice group, but prolong the suite unduly, as it also
has two bourées.   All movements are attractive, including
the expressive sarabande and vivacious 2-v gigue.   Mod Dif

No 2 in a.   The prelude is 3/4 (lively), mostly 2-v.
It is seven pages long, but attractive enough for a solo.
The Sarabande "agreements," or ornaments, are written out
in a separate version.   The Baroque custom was to play the
ornaments only on the repeat of each section, the performer
improvising them when not written.   The two bourées add to
the length, and the gigue has a da capo!   Mod Dif

No 3 in g.   Another seven-page 3-v prelude (good
for a solo) introduces one of the best of the suites.   The

second gavotte is a musette or bagpipe imitation, with G
drone throughout, and should be played pp, di lontano, on
the repeat.   The charming gigue is a 2-v fugue, inverting
the theme for part two.   Mod Dif

No 4 in C.   Prelude begins like a two-part invention,
but runs endlessly on with devices much better used elsewhere.   The same comment applies to most of the dances.

No 5 in e.   For the prelude, a well-made 3-v fugue
(seven pages), and another fugue for the gigue make this one
of the duller of the suites.   Mod

No 6 in d.   Beginning with preludizing broken chords,
this breaks into another 3-v fughetta that runs on for 10
pages, which for a monothematic movement is about eight
too many.   There are two sarabandes and two gavottes.   The
closing gigue is stunning enough to be a Goldsberg variation,
for those who get that far.   Dif

The Well-Tempered Clavier, Book I.   Written in
1722 at the Ducal Court of Anhalt-Cöthen, these 24 preludes
and fugues (P&F) in all major and minor keys championed
the new tempered tuning which made possible for the first
time free modulation and the use of such complex keys as
7♯ and 7♭.   Using a didactic and rigid form (like Chopin in
the etudes), Bach wrote some of his most inspired music.
Very few of the 24 are "fillers" and the second book repeats
little, and carries inspiration even higher.   The major and
minor P&F may effectively be performed in pairs, like the
Scarlatti sonatas.

P&F No 1, C.   Both of the first two preludes illustrate the imaginative treatment of modulating chords in brok-
en figures.   This possibly grew out of the transfer of the
more sustained organ "preludizing" before the service, to
the short-lived string-sound.   Bach here proved that melody
can be dispensed with (though Gounod tried to disprove it
with his saccharine Ave Maria).   Other preludes of the purely chordal figure type are Nos 5, 6, 11, 15 and 21.   Fugue
No 1 is a fine example of fugue writing with no episodes
(passages where the complete fugue theme is absent).   The
second fugue has four of these episodes, where fragments
of the theme are developed.

P&F No 3, C♯.   A dazzling prelude, with all seven
scale-tones sharped, introduces a graceful dance-like fugue.

P&F No 4, c♯. One of the loveliest, this prelude is
a duet between soprano and tenor, with alto and bass adding
to the soulful harmonies. Here one glimpses the genius of
Bach for infinite variation on a single figure. The fugue
(5-v) is a triple fugue, with three distinct themes developed
separately and together. It is to be played only by virtuosi
or ardent aficionados (Bachantes?) of the Bach fugues.

P&F No 5, D. A charming prelude, like a lute or
guitar solo with plucked bass. Keep it leisurely. The fugue
is a grand orchestral work, not difficult, but requiring the
strictest subdivision of beats.

P&F No 6, d. The d minor prelude is most effective if torn off at lightning speed, pianissimo throughout.
The fugue is a simple andante, in three voices.

P&F No 7 E♭. Prelude in pastoral vein is longer
than most (four pages) in steady flowing 16ths, broken once
by a fugato passage. Fugue (3-v) maintains the mood; requires good phrasing and staccato.

P&F No 8 e♭. One of the grandest of all, this pair
has a solemn chordal prelude in sarabande rhythm. The
fugue (originally d♯) uses all contrapuntal devices, but is
slow and eloquent. Its theme is a Gregorian chant setting
of "Behold the Lamb of God."

P&F No 9, E. A fresh three-part invention of the
accompanied duet type for prelude. Cheerful, busy 3-v fugue.

P&F No 10, e. Flowing duet-prelude with chordal
punctuation (much ornamentation). Begin moderato so that
the presto second page will contrast. A two-voice fugue,
the easiest in the book.

P&F No 11, F. A dashing, brief prelude; attractive
3-v fugue.

P&F No 12, f. A simple, fine prelude; 4-v fugue,
expressive and not excessively difficult at a slow tempo.

P&F No 13, F♯. A gigue-like prelude, with attractive singable fugue. Piacevole.

P&F No 14, f♯. The prelude seems a little dreary,
but builds to one of Bach's ineffable endings. The 4-v fugue

is complex, but lovely and satisfying.

P&F No 15, G. This and the minor pair make a
fine group. The G prelude must be played "in a single
breath." The 3-v fugue is long but full of charm.

P&F No 16, g. The minor prelude is for the broken-
hearted; but the fugue has Beethovenesque affirmation.

P&F No 17, A♭. This prelude is a graceful dance
with sarabande rhythm, but lighter. A 4-v fugue, rather
cerebral.

P&F No 18, g♯. A lesser work, with a rather
crabbed fugue.

P&F No 19, A. Short three-part invention, 3-v
fugue, of no great distinction.

P&F No 20, a. Prelude, a bold, effective piece.
Fugue, long, extremely complex, and hard to play well.
Good for analysis.

P&F No 21, B♭; P&F No 22, b♭. Another matchless
pair, the one in major, a brilliant toccata, followed by a
playful fugue. The minor prelude is unsurpassed for poignancy, with a slow, steady, relentless dropping bass under
a duet that rises to a fermata on the rolled dim 7th chord
which Bach reserves for the expression of utmost grief.
The 5-v fugue is also lento espressivo, and not excessively
long or complex.

P&F No 23, B. A joyous youthful-sounding work.
Mod Dif

P&F No 24, b. The andante is pleasant to play, a
2-v canon with slow scale accompaniment. The fugue theme
is too chromatic and tortuous to be expressive, and though
the working out (6 pages) is scholarly, it is not "ear music."

The Well-Tempered Clavier, Book II. Written at
Leipzig, 22 years after Book I, these follow the same format, and are obviously meant as a continuation. The greater maturity of the composer is often evident, though his
good-humor remains.

P&F No 1, C.   The charm and fluency of the prelude are not quite matched by the fugue.

P&F No 2, in c.   This prelude uses a form found on-ly once in Book I, but several times here: binary form, with repeated first part, anticipating the sonata allegro devel-oped in the next generation.   The fugue is attractive at a slow tempo.

P&F No 3, in C♯.   An early prelude re-written for this set, this has the unusual feature of a time change from 4/4 to 3/8.   A lesser work.

P&F No 4, c♯.   This prelude bristles with problemat-ic ornaments; and the fugue is a virtuoso tour de force. Dif

P&F No 5, D.   Four splendid movements in D, major and minor.   The "Trumpet Prelude" must have Baroque splendor, with the 2-against-3 strongly stressed.   The fugue, expressive but restrained, is full of exquisite harmonic de-lights.

P&F No 6, d.   Both prelude and fugue are dazzling, the latter made iridescent with chromaticism.

P&F No 7, E♭.   Lyrical prelude, and quiet, simple 4-v fugue.

P&F No 8, d♯.   Six sharps, instead of flats (as in Book I).   A quiet binary prelude, suddenly comes to life with a florid new theme half-way through, and ends, in the words of Roselyn Tureck, "with a flourish and a sigh."   An almost religious fugue, recalling Netherlands polyphony, a joy for performer and hearer.

P&F No 9, E.   Considered by Hutcheson "the crown-ing glory of the 48" for its "ineffable serenity."   The fugue, another religioso, is noble and stately.

P&F No 10, e.   A playful prelude, with a real virtu-oso fugue.

P&F No 11, F.   Another expressive prelude, 3/2, molto sostenuto, sempre legato.   The fugue is good-humored and rollicking.   Eminently playable.

P&F No 12, f.   An embryonic sonata allegro, simple

but deeply expressive; the fugue is also expressive.

P&F No 13, F♯. Rather austere prelude. Both Hutcheson and Tureck agree that the opening dotted figure in the right hand should be an 8th note tied to a 32nd, instead of dotted. The unusual fugue theme begins with a trill, seemingly on the leading tone; but in the Baroque tradition, beginning on the upper partial (the tonic), as does the answer, in the dominant.

P&F No 14, f♯. The prelude (not to be rushed) is Bach at his most imaginative. The 3-v fugue is not difficult, in spite of its complex use of three separate themes (a true triple-figure).

P&F No 15, G. A delightful pair, the prelude to be played vivacissimo, the fugue delicatissimo, sempre staccato.

P&F No 16, g. A largo prelude in 4-v, with the square rhythms of a French or Handelian overture.

P&F No 17, A♭. Beginning quietly, with alternate measures of rocking chords and linking scales, the long prelude builds to an impressive close, as does also the lento fugue.

P&F No 18, g♯. Almost a sonata allegro, this reverses the two-measure pattern of the last, scales leading to chords. Long complex 3-v fugue.

P&F No 19, A. Not perhaps Bach's favorite key; rather dull.

P&F No 20, a. Perhaps the absence of ♯'s and ♭'s in these white-key preludes is what suggests chromaticism to Bach, downward in the first half, up in the second. Could be effective either molto espressivo, or allegrissimo. The fugue is bold and grand. A good work, but not easy.

P&F No 21, B♭. The fast, cheerful prelude anticipates the style of C.P.E. Bach. The fugue theme is rather uninteresting.

P&F No 22, b♭. Bach in the pathetic vein. Scholarly fugue introducing all contrapuntal devices. Grand; not up to its mate in Book I.

P&F No 23, B.   Beginning like a two-part invention, the prelude breaks into lute-figures.   The fugues grow more cerebral, building toward the great abstract "Art of the Fugue."

P&F No 24, b.   Returning to simplicity, Bach closes with a delightful 2-v dance for prelude, and a charming fugue, with amusing octave skips in the theme.

Six Partitas.   Bach was partial to sets of six.   These are later and more mature than the suites (the name means the same thing).   All use the same program with the addition of an opening number, this movt bearing a different title and character for each partita.   They are among Bach's finest, most musical keyboard works.

No 1 in B♭.   The short praeludium (4/4 adagio) is Bach at his best; one flowing part, full of Baroque arabesques, accompanied by two, moving steadily in 8ths or quarters, augmented with a fourth and fifth voice for the rich close.   Each section of the binary allemande begins with a single line, like a lute arpeggio, later accompanied by plucked eighths in rising sequences.   The simple Italian 2-v corrente can be either a graceful pastorale, or a dazzling whirl (are you a Tureck or a Gould?).   In the sarabande the melodic line becomes so richly Baroque that a firm (though very slow) LH beat is essential to keep the shape.   The two minuets can also be effective at break-neck speed; but spoil the climax of the stunning gigue, which looks like two simple voices, but is actually three, the LH crossing to supply both bass and obbligato.   A tour de force.   Mature.   Mod Dif

No 2 in c.   Another masterpiece.   The opening sinfonia begins grave adagio, with dramatic declamatory phrases; but after seven measures shifts to andante for a charming 2-v duet, and a third section in triple time.   Not difficult and immensely satisfying.   The 2-v allemande, built on a series of descending imitations, should not be rushed. The distinction between Italian corrente and French courante is evident if this elaborate one is compared with the simple one in Partita I.   The sarabande here, however, is simpler; and a delightful 2-v rondeau is the single optional dance. This is the only suite without a closing gigue; its place is taken by a capriccio, enormously effective if hammered out unflaggingly.   Dif

No 3 in a.   The simplicity of the opening fantasia

(3/8, 2-v, andante) is offset by an elaborate allemande.
The corrente is again simple, the sarabande rather grand
and austere.   A most original burlesca is followed by a
scherzo (Bach's only?).   The gigue is of the 3-v fughetta
type, with inverted second theme, difficult to bring off.
Mod

   No 4 in D.   The grandest of all (unless you prefer
No 1, 2, 5 or 6!).   The opener is called an overture, and
moves from dramatic orchestral opening to a spirited (and
long) fughetta in 9/8.   The allemande is long and elaborate
but full of such felicities, rhythmic, melodic and harmonic,
that one wishes it would never stop.   After it, the courante
must be played very fast.   The two extra dances are a
simple unhurried 2-v air, and a short minuet.   One, however, is played before the sarabande, and one in the usual
place before the gigue, perhaps because the sarabande is
another un-simple piece.   It is Baroque at its finest.   After
establishing the sarabande rhythm in two measures, the RH
proceeds to describe delicate calligraphic swirls, while the
LH paces steadily forward, six to the bar.   Dif

   No 5 in G.   Simpler in texture, yet very imaginative.   The preamble is a rondo, with rhythmic chord introduction that recurs, between lute-like arpeggios, and sequences of 2-v passages.   One of the most complex of all
the allemandes is followed by the simplest of correntes.
The sarabande should be treated as an instrumental trio,
with appoggiatura receiving half the value of the major note,
in the Baroque manner.   The minuet may be played fast, but
the 3/4 beat must never be lost in the steady 8th note writing.
The passepied is another trio with tricky ornaments.   The
gigue is a very original one.   Mod to Dif

   No 6 in e.   Written in the Leipzig years, these late
partitas experiment.   This follows the formula of No 5, with
a simple air before a sarabande, which is even more elaborate than No V.   The gavotte is charming, and the gigue has
a curious time signature, signifying eight quarter notes to
the bar, and uses the daring dim 7th.   The opening toccata
is fine enough to stand alone.   Dif

   French Overture.   There is a seventh partita, not so
named by JSB, perhaps because he had a "thing" about sixes.
The opening French overture which gives the name, is
rounded off with a return of the majestic opening, after a
gigue.

This suite is the only one to omit the allemande. A series of well-structured and contrasting dances follow: a courante, two gavottes, two passepieds, a sarabande, two bourées, and, to close, an "echo." A minor masterpiece. Mod to Dif

Seven Toccatas. There are also seven (one keeps hoping some budding musicologist will prove one of them spurious, so that we can keep the Bachian six). Most are early, and rather immature, though the rhapsodic and chordal parts are fine. The formula is much freer than the suites. All are continuous, but alternate thorny contrapuntal sections (too many, too often) with free fantasias: expressive arioso, chordal, arpeggiated or dance-sections (too short and few). They follow the Italian organ "touch-piece" style (Bach's organ toccatas are better).

Toccata in d. Youthful exuberance (and endurance) evident in the direction "adagiosissimo," and in the interminable closing fugue. Mod Dif

Toccata in e. Effective 12-measure fantasy-like opening; expressive allegro and adagio; a five-page, 3-v fugue. Mod E

Toccata in g. Many attractive short sections, spoiled by a seven-page fugue in a jigging rhythm, with an effective lute-like flourish at the end. (Does one dare make a cut in a fugue?) Mod

Toccata in D. Starts well, brilliant scale-chord passages; dance-like allegro; adagio, almost theatrical in its excessive freedom, with fermati in many measures and marked con discrezione (freely); again a fine work ending with an interminable and dull fugue (effective at a Gould-en tempo, prestissimo possibile?)

Toccata in c. This is placed by Geiringer in the Weimar period. Considered by Friskin and Freundlich as one of the best. Mod Dif

Toccata in f♯. Also highly rated, with real passion expressed in both opening and fugue themes. The first fugue is marked presto e staccato, but the closing one must be more leisurely, to bring out the pathos.

Toccata in G. More a three-movt concerto, in

Italian style, than a toccata, flawed only by a rather in-
consequential fugue. The opening movement is true toccata style, effective on either piano or large cembalo;
and the adagio was a favorite of Schweitzer. Mod

Chromatic Fantasy and Fugue. This is more
properly a "Fantasy and Chromatic Fugue." It is a masterpiece related to the great organ toccati and fantasias.
After an opening flourish, toccata-like triplets give way to
great undulating arpeggios, and a dramatic recitative, in
which a single declamatory line is punctuated with chords,
recitative secco-style. Musical maturity is needed to
bring out the hidden beauty of the fugue. Dif

Fantasy in c. This, in striking contrast to the
improvized style, is a highly organized sonata allegro,
lacking only return to the finely contrasted second theme,
to make a balanced exposition, development and recapitulation. Mod

Concerto in the Italian Manner. Another big independent piece, in three movements, with concertante effects in the opening allegro. Though written for the large
harpsichord (on which it sounds magnificent) the singing
cantabile of the second movement brings out the finest in
the piano, and would no doubt have won over the old man,
if he had lived another ten years. Brilliant and difficult,
requiring drive and control. Dif

Variations in the Italian Manner. This early work,
though seldom played, is full of delightful surprises (and
no fugues), and if the "just" tempo for each variation is
found, is very effective. The stately binary theme is repeated at the end.

Aria with Thirty Variations (or Transformations).
This masterpiece, known as "Goldberg Variations," was
written for a pupil of Bach's to lull to sleep the Count
(who may remain nameless). They seemed at one time
in danger of becoming the "Gould-berg Variations" when
an unknown pianist woke up a lot of somnolent critics
with a dazzling recording. Even at the more leisurely
tempo of "the high priestess," Miss Tureck, they remain

exciting music, delightful for all to hear; but not for all
to play, many being fantastically difficult.   Fun to explore, and the Aria in itself (found in Anna Magdalena's
notebook) is a big assignment.   Every third variation is
a canon, running from 2nds and 3rds through 9ths.   It
is not compulsory, Miss Tureck, to play all repeats and
the amateur may browse with pleasure among them taking his own sweet time (and tempo).   Performance time
à la Gould, 36 min 30 sec; à la Tureck, 1 hour, 12
min.

BACH, WILHELM FRIEDMANN (Ger), 1710-1784.

The sons of J. S. Bach, all thoroughly grounded in
their father's style, came to maturity in the "Age of Enlight-
enment," that era which rejected the complex and abstract
(and with it all the music of Bach père) and proposed to sub-
stitute simplicity, intimacy, and comfort.   Three of the
Bach boys contributed to the rise of the new three movt sonata, written to be enjoyed in the comfort and intimacy of
the home, rather than at court, and simple enough "not to
tax a ladies minde."   This is also the period when three
keyboard instruments vied for popularity.   WFB seems to
have remained loyal to the small, portable clavichord, though
requiring the larger cembalo (harpsichord) for his concertos;
but the younger sons all adopted the new pianoforte.   The
experimental nature of this music makes it of more interest
to the historian than to the modern pianist, and most of it
can be passed over.

Six Sonatas.   Three early Sonatas, in G, D, and E♭,
are all in three movts with embryonic allegros.   A late one
in D is almost Mozartian.

Twelve Polonaises.   This dance form from Germany's
northern border, Poland, with its triple meter, highly sub-
divided boat in a variety of rhythmic motifs, was a favorite
of WFB.   Though the characteristics we have come to asso-
ciate with this dance through Chopin's music are mostly lacking, the Polonaises by WFB are very playable.   The slow
ones in minor are the best, often recalling the eloquent sarabandes of JSB.   Specially recommended are Nos 2 in c,
4 in d, 5 in E♭, 6 in e♭, 8 in e and 10 in f.

Though this book discusses only solo literature, one must mention the very fine Concerto in c minor for Cembalo and Strings, by this composer.

BACON, ERNST (USA), 1898- .

Pianist and composer of vocal, choral, symphonic works has these for piano.

Sombrero (1946).   Latin dance in 5/8, easy-going, short.   Mod E

Flight (1949).   A character piece in virtuoso toccata style, with Caribbean rhythms.   Effective.   Mod Dif

BADINGS, HENK (Neth), 1907- .

Sonata (1934).   Dutch composer of symphonic, and more recently, electronic works (including ballets for magnetic tape and optical siren) has an early keyboard sonata, four-movts, taut, well-constructed in dissonant counterpoint, with lyric second movt, scherzo third, and propulsive finale. Dif

BALAKIREW, MILI (Rus), 1837-1910.

A disciple of Ginka, this ardent nationalist spurred "The Five" (The Mighty Heap) to use Russian material in their work, and his own best piano music is based on folkloric material, though profiting from his German and Lisztian background.

Islamey.   One of the masterpieces of the repertoire, this virtuoso concert etude takes its name from the religion of Caucasian Russia, where the tunes for its themes were collected.   A Khabardian dance tune, in harmonic minor, is first hammered out in single-notes, divided between the hands in the manner of the "santur." It is then doubled in 3rds, harmonized, ornamented with chromatic scales, again doubled in octaves with leaping chords, building to a Lisztian whirlwind climax.   The central andante (an Armenian love lyric)

receives the same treatment, starting as a gently undulating
barcarolle in 6/8, and gathering speed and acretions of
scales and ornaments till it merges into the opening dance,
more exuberant than ever. V Dif

Sonata in B♭. After Islamey anything would be anti-
climactic. The attempt to forge folk material into classic
form is less than inspired, and ends up being more of a
suite than a Sonata. The use of counterpoint and development are unconvincing. The second-movt mazurka has vitality, and is often played alone. The finale is another wild
dance, with a quiet intermezzo. Dif

Berceuse. A genial work in cantabile style, graceful
and pianistic. Mod

Two Scherzos in b, b♭. Shorter works, well-structured but brilliant and dashing. Dif

The Lark. A song by Glinka transformed into a lyrical piano solo, with avian cadenzas, that deserves an occasional hearing. Mod

BARBER, SAMUEL (USA), 1910- .

The few piano works from this meticulous composer
are of such fine calibre that one wishes for more. Though
traditional in form and basically tonal, all make free use of
dissonance. Complex rhythms and unique piano figuration require technical mastery. (GSch pub)

Four Excursions, Op 20 (1945). Folk and popular
sources for this set of intricate and brilliant pieces include
the blues, boogie, cowboy song, square-dance fiddling, harmonica, accordion and banjo effects. Strikingly original yet
delightfully musical. Dif

Nocturne, Op 33 (1959). Subtitled "Homage to John
Field," this is understandably derivative, yet manages at the
same time to sound like SB. Very pianistic, this is that
rare program item, a slow single piece. Mod Dif

Sonata, Op 26 (1950). Acclaimed one of the best
sonatas of the 20th century, this has become a standard repertoire number. Allegro energico: The first movt, while

classical in form, and anchored in B♭ minor harmony, co-
ruscates with unique melodic motifs, harmonies, figuration,
moving from the allegro energico opening to misterioso and
espressivo before the powerful amplified recapitulation.
Allegro vivace e leggero: The whispered scherzo has the
bewitching quality of Chopin's B♭ Sonata finale, but is teasing and tantalizing, with wisps of waltz tunes and scurrying,
vanishing figures. Adagio mesto: This grand movt uses a
12-tone row in the LH throughout, over which an unrelated
melody, richly chromatic and cantabile, builds to an enormous climax. Fuga; Allegro con spirito: This 3-v fugue
is a modern masterpiece of contrapuntal writing, with acmes
built on augmentation (doubled in octaves and 6ths) and a
countersubject which turns into a very American jazz tune.
So dazzling it makes a brilliant encore, for those who can
cut it. Dif

BARGIEL, WOLDEMAR (Ger), 1828-1897.

One of the many 19th-century "also-rans," much admired in his day by fellow musicians and relatives (a half
or step-brother of Clara Wieck Schumann). Some of his
numerous piano compositions may be turning up most any day
now. They are a faint echo of Schumann, whose style, as
well as form and titles, he borrowed.

Nachtstücke, Op 3; Fantasiestücke, Op 9, 27; Drei
Fantasias, Op 5, 12, 19; Suite in g, Op 31. Short character pieces in lyrical, romantic, mildly polyphonic Schumann-
esque style. The suite is similar to Carnival or Fassching-
schwank. There are also three Sonatas, which, like the Drei
Fantasias, suffer from the 19th-century failure to master
the larger forms. Mod

BARRAUD, HENRI (Fr), 1900- .

Six Impromptus (1944). Highly regarded in France,
but little known elsewhere, this composer of chamber music
and opera has also written children's pieces and this set of
Impromptus. Tonal-polytonal, with much pungent dissonance,
the six are finely contrasted and pianistic. (EV pub) Mod
Dif

BARTÓK, BÉLA (Hun-USA), 1881-1945.

One of the great innovators of the 20th century,
grounded in the classics but using central European folk music as the basis for a rich and highly original collection of
piano works from teaching pieces to chamber and concert
numbers. BB is assured a niche in the hall of fame by his
great orchestral concerto, his Third Piano Concerto, his six
string quartets and other chamber works. But his piano music remains problematic for many. It is seldom immediate-
ly appealing to either student or audience, but has solid
worth that rewards study and performance. Like Picasso,
who never paints abstracts but always retains vestiges of
imagery, BB treats harmony with extreme freedom verging
on non-tonality, but never totally relinquishes a key center.
The early opus numbers are in general diffuse, difficult and
idiomatically traditional; those of the middle years are sometimes ideal music, enormously difficult, percussive and dissonant. The later ones tend to be shorter and more pianistic. The Sz numbers from the Andras Szöllösy catalog have
become standard. There is a recording of the complete piano music by György Sandor, and many recordings of various works.

Rhapsody, Op 1. The true Hungarian vein, purely
Lisztian in its virtuoso keyboard texture. It has been transcribed as a concerto. Dif

Fourteen Bagatelles, Op 6 Sz38. These shocked the
musical world at their premiere, and established BB as an
innovator. Brief sketches in piano sonorities, folkloric but
highly dissonant. The best are Nos 2 to 7, 12 and 14. A
good place for the Bartók explorer to begin. Mod

Ten Easy Pieces, Sz39. Though most of these are
teaching material, using folk-themes and rhythms freely harmonized, three are small gems not to be overlooked: Evening in Transylvania, Aurora, and Bear Dance. There are
also two volumes "For Children," containing 79 pieces (Sz
42). Mod E

Two Roumanian Dances, Op 8a, Sz43. Not to be confused with the more popular set of six, these two are in the
early rhapsodic style, long, brilliant, high-spirited and driving. Mod Dif

Six Roumanian Folk Dances, Sz56. This later set is

lighter, more taut and appealing in harmony, vividly contrasted in mood and tempo. Good program material, though
the violin transcription by Szekaly is even better. Mod

Three Rondos on Folk Tunes, Sz84. An attractive
concert set, though 10 years and a change of style separate
the first from Nos 2 and 3. The first is naive, wistful and
simple; the latter two more propulsive and brilliant. Mod

Roumanian Christmas Carols, Sz57. There are two
sets of 10 each, with the original short carols printed in
full (UE). The first set is simple and full of winsome charm,
alternating gay and grave, major and minor. The second
set is more suitable for performance, and BB himself provided expanded versions in an Anhang. Both the normal and
the double Hungarian minor are found, with the irregular
meters and phrase lengths that add such an element of surprise. The short ones are repeated as many as seven times
with BB's inimitable changing harmonies. Mod E

Fifteen Hungarian Peasant Songs, Sz71. A good suite
of short contrasting pieces for study or performance (15
min). Mod

Three Burlesques, Sz47. Non-folk character sketches.
High spirited scherzos, brilliant and entertaining, especially
The Quarrel, and Slightly Tipsy. Mod Dif

Allegro Barbaro, Sz41. BB was in Paris when Picasso was discovering African primitive masks and cubism,
and Stravinsky was staging the atavistic Rites of Spring.
This uses the piano as a larger drum, with pounding triadic
chords in a tribal dance. Sensational when new, and still
fun. Mod Dif

Sonatina (1915), Sz55. Actually a suite of three short
picturesque movements in folk style, light and effective.
Good for recital. Mod

Suite, Op 14, Sz62. BB's most popular work, more
traditional and accessible in idiom and harmony. Its three
short fast movements, followed by a slow one, are pianistic
and pleasing. Mod

Three Etudes, Op 18, Sz72. Large-scale virtuoso
studies in BB's most acerbic style, with little of the folk
element. The first is violently rhythmic and percussive; the

andante sostenuto has an eerie surrealistic quality; and the
last is in a rubato parlando style. Dif

Petite Suite, Sz105. Though transcribed from violin
duos, this set of five pieces is good piano music, with a
slow melody, three contrasting Slavic dances, an arpeggio
study called "quasi pizzicato," another dance and a closing
"bagpipe." Mod

Improvisations on Hungarian Peasant Songs, Op. 20,
Sz 74. Written at the peak of BB's experimental period,
these use eight actual folk-tunes (some attractive, some banal) in a wide variety of keyboard styles and a free-wheeling
harmonization. The first has a wistful air, heightened by
the unexpected harmony; the second is brisk and bright,
though the step-wise theme is a bit intransigent; No 3 is
moody, evanescent and fragmentary (and dedicated to the
memory of Debussy who had just died). The fifth has a commonplace rhythm, repeated too often, and No 6 is a rather
inane tune. Intended for concert use, the set takes from 15
to 18 min. Mod

Sonata (1926) Sz80. BB was never a neo-classicist,
though his Third Piano Concerto is a fine example of the
form. This is percussive, driving, dissonant, lacking in
contrast, and overblown. The folk pieces are, after all,
better. Mod

Out of Doors (1926) Sz81. It is understandable that
after writing more than 180 piano pieces in folk-style (count
them), BB should have been in a bit of a bind. The tunes
do begin to sound alike, and the effort to avoid conventional
harmony produces rather predictable "wrong-note" chords.
But when he abandons the style, the music sounds like two
kids let loose at the piano, when Momma is out of the house.
In the first, big brother beats out a drum in the bass, while
sister tries to find the right keys for the piccolo tune. In
No 2, both are lost, hunting for a tune and a beat in two
scrawny lines, which, for some reason, is called a barcarolle. A bagpipe figure is then tried out, in as many different positions as possible. Night's Music turns out better,
with a scary tune (soft pedal down) played unison, with properly tuneless bird-calls at the top of the keyboard (BB used
the same effect beautifully in the middle movement of Concerto III). In the last, it sounds as if Momma suddenly
came home, and the kids quickly shift to Hanon. 15 min, if
you hurry. Mod

Mikrokosmos, Vol I to VI.   This work with the
unique title began as BB's "Notenbücher" for family teaching,
and grew into six volumes containing 153 pieces, graded in
difficulty from beginners' exercises and easy sight-reading
material in Vol I and II, to attractive student pieces in III,
IV (In a Mist, From Bali).   Some in VI are of Concert calibre: Ostinato, From the Diary of a Fly.   Finest of all are
the Six Pieces in Bulgarian Rhythm.   (Possibly the best of
BB?)   Here, out of a life-time of living with folk-music, BB
takes the authentic rhythms, 8/8 (divided into 3+2+3, 3+3+2),
9/8 (4+2+3), 5/8, the ethnic modal scales and creates a set
of fresh, vivid and charming pieces.   Mod Dif

BATE, STANLEY (GB), 1912-1959.

Pianist and composer of symphonic chamber music
and film scores.

Seven Pieces (1942).   The pieces in this set are contrasting in character and meter (a polka and valse to close),
with superimposed dissonances for "flavor."   Pianistic.
Mod

BAUER, MARION (USA), 1887-1955.

Better known as an author, educator and promoter of
contemporary music, MB was one of the first women composers to write serious, professional piano music.   Though
her broad studies in contemporary styles led to an eclectic,
derivative type of composition, much of it now dated, all her
music is finely wrought and boldly pianistic, and some has a
vigorous originality.

From the New Hampshire Wood, Op 12.   Raised on
the Pacific coast, MB was intrigued by New England, and
borrowed MacDowell's type of genre piece for these three
sketches: White Birches, Indian Pipes, and Pine Trees.
Mod

Six Preludes, Op 15 (1922).   These are more original (with echos of Scriabin).   No 1 is a quiet threnody for
LH solo.   No 3 ("very fast") uses the unison style of some
of Chopin's sonata and concerto movts (and Prelude No 14)

with much chromatic dissonance building to a robust climax. Vigoroso, 5/4, 7/4, are the markings of No 4, another bold one (with echos of both MacDowell and Scriabin). No 6 is in ternary form, "exuberantly, passionately," and is of the best of the set. Mod Dif

Turbulence, Op 17:2. Well named, this expresses its agitation in the sweeping keyboard style of a rhapsody. Dif

Four Piano Pieces, Op 24. Moving with the times, MB explores quartal and atonal writing in four pieces in her vigorous and driving manner: Chromaticon, Ostinato, Toccata, and Syncope. Mod to Dif

Dance Sonata, Op 24. A three-movt neo-classic work, foregoing the bombastic for a more winsome cantabile style. Mod Dif

Patterns, Op 41 (1946). Having written so lucidly about dodecaphony in her book on 20th-century music (see Bibliography), MB tries her hand at tone-rows in five pieces that alternate simple linear counterpoint with dance rhythms and her favorite "fast and ferocious" style. Mod Dif

BAX, SIR ARNOLD (GB), 1883-1953.

Great keyboard fluency can be both a blessing and a curse to a composer, and is so in the case of this prolific English pianist-composer, pupil of Tobias Matthay and prize graduate of the Royal Academy of Music. His piano music reflects an intense interest in the revival of Celtic art, literature, and influences from Russia, which he visited in 1910. His music is unabashedly romantic and lavish in harmonic richness.

Two Russian Tone Pictures: Nocturne, Gopak. A lyric and poetical piece, and a driving staccato moto perpetuo, pianistic and well written. Mod

Sonata No 1; Sonata No 2. The Russian visit is also reflected in the rather folksy themes of the second sonata. Both Nos 1 and 2 use Liszt's one-movt form, but the themes of AB do not lend themselves well to sonata development. Mod Dif

Sonata No 3. The third sonata is more extended,
with a second movement suggesting an Irish folk-song; the
pianist gets the upper hand, and writes some rather wild
keyboard passages, experimenting with chromatic dissonances.
Dif

Sonata No 4. Simpler in texture, with a Slavic cantabile allegro. Mod

Moy Mell, for two pianos. Bax is perhaps best represented by his exuberant two-piano piece, Moy Mell. Mod

BECK, CONRAD (Swi), 1901- .

Sonatina (1928). Still active, this successful composer of larger forms, has two for piano. The three-movt
sonatina is actually a full-scale sonata, experimenting with
atonal polytonal harmonization and tone-rows, in a classical form. Musically and technically demanding. (BSS pub)
Dif

Piano Pieces: Books I and II (1930). Pianistic and
well-crafted, the contrasting moods of the 11 pieces explore
the same tonal organization as the sonatina (still experimental
at the time). (BSS pub) Mod Dif

BECKWITH, JOHN (Can), 1927- .

Four Conceits (1945-48). Established Canadian pianist-composer has collected four pieces from his early
years as a piano student, before taking up composition under
the modest and intriguing title "Conceits." They are indeed
well "conceived," though obviously composed at the keyboard.
JB seems to be a right-handed piano player, as all four
works, though contrasting in tempo and texture, initiate all
themes and motives in the top, with the LH entering for harmonic and melo-rhythmic contrast. The four are designated:
(I) With an easy Lilt; (II) Moderately fast, airily; (III) Fast;
and (IV) Singingly, but strongly rhythmical. Six min, 30 sec.
Mod

BEETHOVEN, LUDWIG VAN (Ger), 1770-1827.

Every pianist must come to grips with this giant; and for some, playing his works will be an exalted musical experience. Others may be driven to water, but refuse to drink, finding not the elixir of life, but a flat, bitter dose. The former will wish to explore the less familiar works, though few may care to emulate Schnabel or sundry Japanese pianists by playing all 32 sonatas bumper-to-bumper, or all the five concertos on successive evenings. For audience appeal, the player must have fine sensitivity to melodic and harmonic devices, an intellectual, analytical approach, infallible finger control, and restrained emotional drive. Since Beethoven has a uniquely personal keyboard style, an intense emotional content, and since he introduced significant changes in form through his 40 years of writing, a knowledge of his life cycle is also essential. So pitch in!

Easy pieces. After the student has gotten past Gertrude's Dream, Für Elise, and the Farewell to the Piano, he may proceed to the Variations in G, the Ecossaises, and the two early Sonatas, in F and G (without opus numbers). Of the 32 sonatas, the easiest is Op 49, No 2 in G.

Sonata No 1 in f, Op 2:1. Since Beethoven players will start at the beginning it is fortunate that No 1 is typical, well-rounded and not too difficult. One is plunged at once into the intricacies of allegro form, with its scraps of melody, bound together with strings of passages, its photomontage development with the same subjects superimposed and shot at odd angles. The second movt is naive and youthful (written when Ludwig was 16), but calls for intensity of feeling. A courtly menuetto has a trio similar to the famous Minuet in G. Still further Beethoven devices appear in the furious prestissimo, which must never flag in tempo. It is another allegro, with a new theme substituted for the development. Mod

No 2 in A, Op 2:2. In the second (not for the beginner), Beethoven moves out of the shadow of Haydn and Mozart. The first and last movts are brilliant and difficult, the second requires great poise, and the third, the light quick staccato that gives the humor to LvB's "unbuttoned" scherzos. Dif

No 3 in G, Op 2:3. Another concert work, to be attempted only by those able to discover and convey the musi-

cal message clothed in what can sound like clichés; chains
of octave scales, arpeggios rattling up and down the tonic
chord.   The adagio can be deeply moving, the closing allegro, scintillating.   Dif

No 4 in Eb, Op 7.   More Beethoven idioms are introduced in this big work, in fast 6/8, like the six-note bridge
motif, which sounds like the final filip of a cadence, but is
instead an introduction.   (Inverted, it introduces the coda.)
The largo is to be played "con grande espressione."   A
rather naive folksy allegro provides a third movt.   The rondo has a graceful rococo theme, with the busy LH leaping
up to share in the melody.   Mature.

No 5 in c, Op 10:1.   The next two sonatas are somewhat easier and shorter (three movts only) though LvB's
mastery of the form increases steadily.   The fine Allegro
has a somewhat labored second movt.   All is forgiven when
the finale is reached, a stunning sonata allegro.   It is as if
a superb clown were tripping, flipping, pirouetting, strutting
in mock solemnity.   There is even a miniature development,
a "dying fall," and a cadenza, all within three pages played
prestissimo.   Mod

No 6 in F, Op 10:2.   Another sonata that begins with
a cadence for an introduction.   A gracious allegro, songful
allegretto with a chorale in Db.   The presto again is the unbuttoned genius, pretending to write a fugue and ending by
jigging up and down on the tonic and dominant.   Mod

No 7 in D, Op 10:3.   A larger work (four movts) and
requiring mature musicianship.   Here the first movt is
presto, and must race along if its banalities are not to show.
Sheer keyboard wizardry takes the place of substance.   But
the largo is one of the most eloquent of all the slow movements.   A folksy minuet.   A rondo using again the "final
filip" for an introduction, this three-note motif assuming
much importance in the elaborate working out.   Mature.

No 8 in c, Op 13.   Here in the "Pathétique," LvB
uses for the first time all the keyboard and compositional
devices which he has been perfecting, to express powerful
drama.   To convey this, the performer must have similar
mastery over his art.   The grave passages may be almost
histrionic in their dynamic contrasts, if a steady relentless
16th-note pulse is maintained.   In the allegro as in the closing rondo a strong rein must be held on tempo and dynamics

to convey the latent, suppressed agitation.   There is no
tempo change in the moving adagio, though a judicious use
of rubato can underline the melodic nuances.   The last movement, though slighter, need not be anti-climatic.   Dif

No 9 in E, Op 14:1.   A joyous work in three movts,
not excessively difficult.

No 10 in G, Op 14:2.   Another cheerful well-knit
work, with a Neapolitan duet for the second theme; variations
on a chorale for second movt; and a scherzo (in rondo form)
to finish.   Mod

No 11 in Bb, Op 22.   Technically more difficult, and
longer (four movts).   A tune worthy of Schubert leads off the
long rondo.   Dif

No 12 in Ab, Op 26.   This turnip had better be left
to the specialists, who may squeeze a little juice from the
jejune variations.   They may even fool us into believing in
the dead hero, and his pompous empty march.   The joke of
the scherzo is wearing thin by now (a final cadence for an
opener); and the busy-ness of the closing allegro fails to redeem the overblown work.   Mod

No 13 in Eb, Op 27:1.   This sonata, subtitled "fantasia," is pretty quasi.   LvB had little gift for free fantasy
and this turns out to be a series of variations on the tonic
dominant of Eb worthy of Weber.   The shift from alla breve
to 6/8 in c (V-I, yet) hardly makes it a "fantasia."   Shall
we take the harmonic dreariness, like the occasional dissonance of No 9, as an example of LvB's "disdain for the mere
amenities of sound"? (Schnabel).   An eight-page perpetual
motion (à la Weber) delivers the coup de grace to this moribund work.   Mod

No 14 in c#, Op 27:2.   A comparison of the two
"quasi fantasia" sonatas leaves no doubt as to why the second
remains a perennial favorite, with or without moonlight.   The
ear and the heart will not be cheated, no matter what is giv-
en to the head and the hand.   Though the adagio can be
played by a sentimental teenager, it is incomplete without the
presto agitato which demands maturity for its leashed fury.
Mod Dif

No 15 in D, Op 28; and No 16 in G, Op 31:1.   No 15
is a good standard four-movt, pastoral in mood, moderately

difficult.   No 16 is a less inspired (though longer) work.
Mod

        No 17 in d, Op 31:2.   One of the great Romantic
works.   With its alternating slow arpeggios, declamations,
and urgent agitatos, it is a true fantasia.   The stately adagio
requires poise, and the breathless onrushing allegretto, sustained drive.   Mature.

        No 18 in E♭, Op 31:3.   This seems to be a return to
the classical style, but at its finest.   "Lov-ing-ly," Tobias
Matthay wrote over the opening three-note motif, to get the
rhythm, and the gentle touch.   The staccato scherzo is not
easy.   The con fuoco of the last movt refers to speed, not
mood, which is playful, with two bars of coda for an introduction!   Mod Dif

        No 19 in g, Op 49:1; and No 20 in G, Op 49:2.   Two-
movt works, rather uninteresting, and guaranteed to turn
most any student off LvB for life.   Mod E

        No 21 in C, Op 53.   The "Waldstein," in the white key
of C, ranks among the great sonatas.   It is almost Mozartian
in its clarity and the chordal second theme can pass as a
melody; but the tissue of piano figures, in themselves rather
ordinary, modulates with great subtlety, advances and recedes in delicate dynamic nuances.   The tempo can be quite
strict and still sound free.   The very slow adagio gives the
melody the sonority of a bell.   The rondo, one of LvB's
finest, demands utmost control.   Mature.   Dif

        No 22 in F, Op 54.   Musicians not concerned with
mere duration will welcome the two-movt sonatas of LvB's
middle period.   This one, in spite of its unconventional
"Tempo d'un Menuetto" for a first movt, is not easy.   After
the naive opening section, it plunges into a page of fast octaves, sempre f e staccato.   And the allegretto rondo must
be played like a brilliant toccata, unflagging in tempo.   Mod
Dif

        No 23 in f, Op 57.   Long arcs of unison melody are
answered by short breathless trill phrases.   One of LvB's
few fine melodies is the second theme in A♭.   First and last
movts are among the most difficult for sheer articulation,
and require, along with this, intense emotional drive.   "Appassionata."   Dif

No 24 in F♯, Op 78.   Another pleasing, intimate two-
movt work with a leisurely lyrical first followed by a scherzo-
like vivace.   Mod Dif

No 25 in G, Op 79.   A fast German dance that must
keep a lilt is followed by an andante that suggests a Neapolitan barcarolle.   The short vivace is again a fun movement.
Mod Dif

No 26 in E♭, Op 81a.   Is LvB's one "sonata charac-
teristique" inspired by Bach's "Departure Capriccio"?   After
telling us, in French, that the program is "Farewell, Absence and Return," LvB kindly labels the opening three-note
theme with the three-syllable German "Goodbye" (Le-be-
wohl).   (Any child will identify the theme at once as "Three
Blind Mice.")   This seems to be a sort of Picasso joke,
and one must not take the program seriously, nor play the
work pompously.   When tossed off as a brilliant trifle (over-
blown), the allegro is dazzling.   The middle movement is only andante, and must not be lugubriously slow.   The vivacis-
samente has even less musical substance than the first movt,
and therefore requires all the more musical aplomb of the
performer.   Dif

No 27 in e, Op 90.   Another two-movt work, simple,
clear and melodious in content, but involving problems of
legato, timing, hand-span that assign it to the more mature
pianist.   Dif

No 28 in A, Op 101.   The first of the "last period"
sonatas is a curious work, with a quiet reverie ("lively, but
with inmost feeling"), followed by a jagged march in the dotted rhythm that obsessed Schumann.   Here the giant shows
disdain for the mere limitations of the human hand.   An interlude "full of longing" quotes again the opening reverie, then
plunges into a rather trivial allegro, marked "not too fast,
and very resolutely."

No 29 in B♭, Op 106.   "The Hammerklavier," longest
and most difficult of the 32, is still tackled by brash young
debutants and lovingly belabored by the aged after a lifetime
of study, while audiences sit through its 50 minutes in silent
tribute to their efforts, and to the mighty deaf genius.   A
brilliant analysis by Schnabel as well as many fine records
are available for those planning to study, hear or perform it.
V Dif

No 30 in E, Op 109. The last three, sometimes considered a trilogy, can be a joy to hear and to play, though
thorny with problems. The opening movt of No 30 is agitated, fluttering, and quickly over. The prestissimo second
movt is even shorter (2 min), but full of urgency and rest-
lessness. A magnificent set of variations closes the work.
The spacious theme is chorale-like, andante molto cantabile
ed espressivo, and each of the six variations offers new delights (one is inevitably a fugue, an obsession of LvB's late
years). Non-purists might even dare to program these glorious variations alone, without the two lesser movts.   Dif

No 31 in A♭, Op 110. Easiest of the last three, this
also closes with a fugue. The first movt is amiable and
songful throughout. A humorous, brusque allegro molto, re-
vives the "unbuttoned scherzos" of early years. A lovely
free recitative leads into an arioso dolente that can be heart-
breakingly beautiful, and enables Bach-lovers to forgive and
endure the ensuing fugue. (Schnabel tries to disarm us by
saying, "Beethoven's fugues do not make a point of being
beautiful.") This is interrupted by a restatement of the arioso, half a step lower, marked "exhausted and broken."
Then LvB, a little like Anna Russel announcing a cadenza,
informs us that "the fugue theme is now inverted," but adds,
surprisingly, "little by little reviving." (Some may wish,
with Job, that it had never been born.)

No 32 in c, Op 111. The tragic c minor is chosen
for the ultimate sonata, which opens with a bold flourish of
octaves on a dim 7th chord, hinting at new harmonies, never,
alas, realized. A rather Rossinian allegro is compensated
for by a deeply moving arietta, "simple and songful" in C
major, the key in which the mighty sonata cycle fades to an
end.

32 Variations in c. Some of the many sets of variations deserve attention. The 32 in c minor, without opus
number, is one of the finest examples of the form. Each
variation (there are actually 35) follows closely the simple
eight-meas sarabande of the theme to its poignant penultimate
chord and cadence. Basic for all serious students and an
excellent program number. (12 to 15 min) Mod Dif

Variations in F, Op 34. Two sets from the end of
LvB's first period were highly prized by the composer,
though they differ widely. Op 34 is misleadingly named "in
F," since only the theme and the last variation are in this

key. Each of the other four moves down a 3rd (D, B♭, G,
E♭, c). The theme is gentle and classic in its simplicity,
and the set is of more value for study than for performance.
Mod

Eroica Variation, Op 35. LvB meant these to be
called "Variations on a Theme from Prometheus," but the
symphony whose variation finale grew out of these is much
more famous than the ballet; hence the name. It is a unique
masterpiece, combining elements of suite, sonata and fugue
in one continuous movement. The introduction is a set of
variations on the bass of the theme; the main body of the
work comprises 15 sparkling and euphonious variations with a
kaleidoscopic display of keyboard figures. The light-hearted
fugue which closes is a far cry from the late lucubrations,
and, in fact, soon gives up counterpoint for more variations.
The absence of a climactic ending weakens the fine set for
public performance. (About 20 min.) Mod Dif

Rondo in G, Op 51; and Rondo Capriccioso in G, Op
119. Two rondos, both probably middle period, are attractive study and performance works. The first has a suave
andante cantabile theme, floridly elaborated and contrasted
with a lively E major mid-theme. The second is subtitled
"The Fury over a Lost Penny," and can be both brilliant and
characteristic of the temperamental, fun-loving genius. Mod

Andante "Favori" in F. Another large-scale movement (originally intended for a sonata) similar to Op 51, with
a brilliant octave finale. Mod

Variations on a Theme by Diabelli, Op 120. This is
our "dark horse" entry for the also-rans race, a work by
the acknowledged winner who left the others all far behind;
but one seldom heard in concert today. His last major piano
solo, written a year after Sonata Op 111, (and two years
late for Diabelli's dead-line), it is delightfully fresh and
youthful, and, though seldom profound, always absorbing.
The inane tune, (Diabelli made a good thing out of it by publishing variations by 50 of the also-rans), offers LvB a field-
day, free from the schoolroom of allegro-form, and he is
like an old pro playing with amateurs and winning all the
tricks with such masterly ease that it is euphoric to hear.
After turning the silly waltz into a pompous march, in Variation 1 he follows with four variations that build excitement
with sheer speed, and spill over into a canon with trills.
Variation 9 is pesante e risoluto in minor, 4/4, but 10 re-

turns gleefully to the waltz beat over bass trills.   No 20 is
an eloquent chorale in quartet style, followed by a breezy
swing across the keyboard, alternating 3/4 and 4/4 passages.   Variation 22 is a spoof of Leporello's opening aria
in Mozart's Don Giovanni; 24 is a pensive fughetta.   No 29
is only 12 meas long, but another elegy in minor key.   The
last four variations are in the late sonata style: a highly
ornamented but expressive arioso (31), followed by a double
fugue (32) superior to any in the sonatas, using both tune and
harmony from Diabelli for its two themes.   LvB chooses to
close with a graceful Viennese minuetto, putting in his place
such hacks as Diabelli, and paying homage to his distinguished forebears, Mozart and Haydn.   Not excessively difficult, this takes only 25 min, without repeats (and who wants
repeats nowadays, with ears that can retain the subtleties of
serialism?)   Recommended for any young eager beavers con-
sidering yet another Hammerklavier, or any of the forgotten
three R's, three H's, or (heaven help us!) more junk from
CHVM (see p 3).   Dif

Bagatelles, Op 33, 119, 126.   These sets of short
pieces deserve the name of "trifles" for they were pot-boilers,
lacking the inspiration of the sonatas.   They range from easy
to moderate.   Mod E

BENDEL, FRANZ (Ger), 1833-74.

Pastorale Variée avec Cadenza; Romanza.   This German contemporary of Brahms has left three romantic pieces,
attractive, if not profound.   Both the Romanza and the Pastorale Variée were attributed to Mozart for years, a token of
their quality.   The variations, though over-extended, are well
developed and worthy of an occasional performance.

German Fairy Tales, Op 135.   Six of Grimm's familiar tales treated in a humorous and pianistically fresh manner
Good program items.   The best are Frau Holle, Red Riding-
hood, and Bremen Town Band.   Mod

BEN-HAIM, PAUL (Ger-Isr), 1897- .

One of the many musicians who migrated to Israel,
PBH is esteemed as an educator and composer.   His music

derives from his German romantic background, which has
been enriched by the folk-music of Palestine, though at times
in his piano music the two do not blend, and a dichotomy en-
sues.

Nocturne, Op 20b (Leeds).   Brief lyric piece with
plaintive folk-song quality.

Five Pieces, Op 34.   Pastorale in the manner of
Eastern cantilation.   The piano seems inadequate for the melisma and nuance, and the chords become cliches.   Intermezzo in compound rhythms.   Capriccio agitato is an arpeggio
study ending with a chordal melody.   The quiet canzonetta,
molto dolce e cantando is attractive.   Closing toccata uses
pianistic device of repeated notes in alternating hands to
build a powerful climax, with quiet close.   Mod

Sonatina, Op 38 (1950).   Attempt to write a classic
work on ethnic sources.   Three movts; second freely rhapsodic; third a frenetic dance.   There is also a sonata.   Mod

Melody and Variations (1953).   A single child's piece,
using only white keys and five-notes, is expanded to a large-
scale concert work (10 min).   A more successful blend of
traditional and folk, using free rubato, rich ornamentation,
broad octave melodies.   Mod Dif

Music for Piano, Vols I, II (1957) (1967).   A return to
traditional piano figuration, for educational purposes.   Mod E

BENTZON, NIELS VIGGO (Den) 1919- .

Fantasy (1939); Toccata (1941); Passacaglia, Op 31
(1945); Partita, Op 38 (1945); Three Concert Etudes, Op 48
(1950); Five Sonatas (1946-56); Kaleidoscope, Op 86 (1954).
This prolific and disciplined Danish composer who premiered
an operatic trilogy on Faust in Germany in 1964, has numerous works for the piano.   His music is formally classic but
freely dissonant, often based on a harmony of 3rd and octave-
doublings, in a thickly woven texture whose density becomes
turgid at times, and requires virtuoso technical equipment
for performance.   A driving energy finds expression in moto
perpetuo and ostinato figures.   His works are published by
Wilhelm Hansen, available through G. Schirmer.   Mod

BERG, ALBAN (Aus), 1885-1935.

Sonata, Op 1 (1909). The only piano work by this
brilliant composer was written during the experimental student years with Schönberg, before the 12-tone row evolved.
It is still a viable work, though demanding of both performer
and audience. It is in a single movement (a large sonata
allegro) 3/4 moderato throughout. This lack of metric variation, along with the continuous unresolved chromaticism,
and the absence of a contrasting section, make it heavy going, in spite of some very attractive melodic and harmonic
passages, and a development that rises to ffff. (AMP pub)
Dif

BERGMAN, ERIK (Fin), 1911- .

Composer and educator (Sibelius Academy, Helsinki)
has written numerous choral and instrumental works, recently employing a modified serial technic.

Intervalles, Op 34 (1967). Seven pieces each based
on a different interval--2nds, 3rds, etc.--ending with unison
and octaves. Moods and keyboard idiom are contrasting but
pianistic. In spite of dissonant intervals, often sounds tonal.
Mod Dif

BERGSMA, WILLIAM (USA), 1921- .

Tangents, Vol I (1956); Fanfare; Prophecies; The Animal World. Tangents, Vol II: Masques; Pieces for Nicky;
Fanfare. The one piano work by this busy composer and
educator is so original and pianistic that one wishes for
more. Though WB disarmingly compares the 12 pieces to
an old vaudeville show in which high tragedy is followed by
slap-stick, the pieces are so heterogeneous that they might
better be programmed in groups of two or three. The two-
page Fanfare, mostly on white-keys, hints at the attractions to come, and sums them up at the end, with a brilliant toccata coda.

The two prophecies, the first on one of the "woes" of
Zephaniah and the second, Micah's "swords to ploughshares,"
are suitably contrasted, with declamatory, dissonant chords,

alternating with linear and chordal lyric passages, not evidently serial, but very free in tonality.   Passage work throughout is pianistic and expressive.   In "The Animal World," Unicorns is fast, brilliant; the weeping Fishes, simple and moving in its three-part dissonant harmony.   Mr. Darwin's trumpet serenade to the vines, with its diatonic waltzes, marches, two-steps, all harmonized with wrong-note triads, is a comic ending.   Vol II seems less attractive; an idea carried too far, perhaps.   Dif

BERIO, LUCIANO (It), 1925- .

Avant-garde multi-media composer who combines magnetic quadra-sonic tape with human voices for operas, and has a work for electronic piano and electronic harpsichord.   His set of Sequenza are for various solo instruments or voices.

Variations (1952): Sequenza IV.   An eclectic work, in which the composer tries out various types of avant-garde writing in a series of seven variations, fragmentary and incoherent, forming a theme only at the end.   Dif

BERKELEY, LENNOX (GB), 1903- .

That very English gift of understatement characterizes much of the music of this talented composer, whose Third Symphony and an opera have had recent premieres (J& W Chester pub).

Five Short Pieces (1937).   Simple but distinctive and appealing pieces, in varied rhythms and moods.   Mod E

Sonata (1941).   Three-movt neo-classic work showing influences of Stravinsky and Fauré.   The dissonances and even virtuoso drive are all "understated" but present.   Mod

Six Preludes (1945).   These fine works alternate flowing and singing textures, the first built on an ostinato figure, Nos 2, 4 and 6 spicing the cantilena with tasteful dissonances. Most attractive is No 5, using an irregular surging figure in 7/8 time.   Mod

Scherzo (1950). Technically more demanding in a moto perpetuo style with a variety of staccato-legato, repeated-note figures effectively used. Dif

Four Concert Studies (1940). More difficult, exploring contemporary harmonies and keyboard figures, in a clear musical style. (BSS pub) Dif

BERNSTEIN, LEONARD (USA), 1918- .

Anniversaries--Four Sets. These pieces would probably never have found their way into print if it were not for the distinguished name of the composer. It is a nice gesture for such a busy man to write a birthday-piece for all his family and composer friends, but they might more tastefully have been presented to the celebrants in manuscript form (or left on the graves of the dead) rather than inflicted on pianists, who have a right to expect something better than this one from the composer of Mass, Westside Story, Chichester Psalms, etc. A comparison of these with the far superior set of elegies and rondos for dead and living dogs (for brass and piano) would lead to the conclusion that LB likes animals better than people (at least than pianists).

BETTINELLI, BRUNO (It), 1913- .

Sonatina (1969) (CFP). Distinguished Italian pianist-composer of chamber, instrumental and choral music, has a new Sonatina--three movts, F-S-F, and basically tonal, though written without key signature; overall it is pianistic and melodious though piquantly dissonant. Mod

BINKERD, GORDON (USA), 1916- .

Well known for his choral and sacred works, Binkerd has also added to the piano repertoire.

Piano Miscellany. Five short pieces, good for teaching. Mod E

Entertainments for Piano. In seven sections, contemporary in idiom   Mod E

Sonata (1955).   Large four-movt work in traditional
form and tonality.   Fine original material, well-developed in
sonata allegro, alternating linear and chordal-clusters.   The
second movement is superlative in its build-up and harmonies; a rhythmic swinging scherzo is followed by a burlesque
finale.   About 20 minutes.   Fine repertoire number.   Mature technique needed.   Dif

Concert Set (1969).   Four pieces of moderate difficulty, pianistic and appealing.   Witch Doctor is non-tonal,
free-wheeling.   Legend is pastorale, more tonal and organized over ostinati.   The Etude deploys the hands in scarry
skips, fast, tricky.   Mice scurries and scampers, with darting motives.   Original.   Mod Dif

BLACHER, BORIS (Ger), 1903- .

Ornaments, Op 37 (1950).   Studies in variable meter.
These seven pleasant pieces try to organize rhythm much on
the manner of a tone row (or an Indian raga) with a formula
followed throughout.   Some of them begin with a measure of
2/8, and add one eighth note per measure till they reach 9
or 12, after which they reduce in mirror form.   Harmony
is mildly atonal, chords of 7ths, 9ths, alternating with scale
or melodic figures.   (Hovhanness uses a similar device.)
An orchestra work bears the same name.

Sonata, Op 39 (1951).   Employs same variable meter.
Thin texture, linear with chordal punctuation.   Allegro, andante (andante reversed), vivace.   Not long.   Mod Dif

BLACKWOOD, EASLEY (USA), 1930- .

Three Short Fantasies, Op 16 (1967).   Avant-garde
serial pieces of extreme technical and musical complexity.
F-S-F, with percussive wide-ranging first piece, lugubrious
second, and intense dynamic and rhythmic contrasts in the
last.   (GS pub)   V

BLOCH, ERNEST (Swis-USA), 1880-1959.

The haunting Hebraic melancholy that imbues so much
of the string and instrumental music of EB is largely absent
from the piano works, which are mystic, modal, sometimes
declamatory, or infectiously gay. Keyboard writing is original, individual, basically tonal but fresh and free of harmonic
cliches.

Poems of the Sea (1923).   Three pieces with an epigraph by Whitman.   Waves has a steady rolling triplet figure,
under a bardic modal theme which gathers intensity, sings
briefly above sustained chords, then subsides. Chanty,
marked andante misterioso, evokes the loneliness of the sail-
or, in irregular phrases of song in Dorian mode, shifting
briefly to A major for a bright snatch of folk-song with a
Scottish snap.   At Sea is a rollicking boisterous hornpipe,
unflagging in its exuberant drive. (GSch pub).   Mod Dif

Five Sketches in Sepia (1923).   A five-part suite,
sensitive, impressionistic and monochromatic: Prélude,
Fumées sur la ville, Lucioles, Incertitude, Epilogue.   Unity
is established by combining earlier themes in the final movement.   (GSch pub)

Sonata (1935).   Three-movt, 26-page work, probably
never to be played until unearthed in the year A.D. 2075.
Its chronic chromaticism, tonally anchored but built of unresolved altered triads offers little satisfaction either to the
traditionalist or to the adventurous.   Basically unpianistic,
in spite of bold octave and chordal melodies, in the outer
movements, and unique ornamentation in the quiet Pastorale.
Bloch seems to have been most at home with the more flexible string family or the human voice.   Dif

Visions and Prophecies (1936).   Set of five pieces,
declamatory and meditative.   The subject seems to cry out
for that middle Eastern wailing melisma, but little comes
through on the piano.   Mod

BOSMANS, ARTURO (Bel-Bra), 1908- .

Belgian-born educator, conductor and composer who
immigrated to Brazil, via Portugal.   His numerous piano
pieces reflect both the Portuguese and the Brazilian experience.

Sonatina Lusitana. Three-movt, neo-classic work using Portuguese folk tunes in each movt, much quartal harmony. Two songs provide themes for the light first movt.
The second is sustained with pedal effects in an austere
chordal style; vivacious, genial third, building from double-
note figures to chords and octaves. Mod Dif

Sonata en colores: Rojo, Cris, Verde. Three-movt
work (Scriabin inspired?) relating three styles to colors:
agitato toccata-style for red; and atmospheric, static chordal grey; and then a fluent, rhythmic closing green. Mod

BOULEZ, PIERRE (Fr), 1925- .

The conducting activities of this brilliant musician,
once in the vanguard of experimental composing, seem to
have halted his creative productivity. Each of his three sonatas has explored a different style, and the third has never
been completed, though two parts have been published. Something of the rhythmic theory of Messiaen is evident in the
early work, as well as Impressionist color. Added to this
is a brilliant keyboard virtuosity, thematic material highly
compressed, constantly developing, and rarely repeating.
Though the pages are often deceptively simple, the music is
enormously difficult to perform, and the sound is rich and
highly involved.

Sonata No 1 (1946). The only relation to the traditional sonata form is a division into two movts. The first
movt also contrasts and combines two ideas, the first polyphonic and linear (mostly 2-v) and chordal, and marked
"very fast"; the second more rhythmic (4/4) and chordal,
and marked "still faster." Words cannot convey the dense
resulting sound. The effect of the first movt is evidently
intended to be improvisatory and ecstatic, while the second is
more propulsive and extroverted (if possible). Since the
once "impossible" Brahms Variations and Ives' sonatas are
now standard repertoire items, perhaps there will one day
be pianists and audiences for this. Vir

Sonata No 2 (1948). This expands the form to four
movts, and attempts to add to the total serial organization
of material the florid keyboard figuration of the "grand manner." The two styles, each formidably difficult, are incom-
patible, and the result is an impossible amalgam. Vir

Sonata No 3 (1958): Trope, Constellation. The confusion of modern music is well illustrated in this five-movt
work, reportedly completed in 1958. The composer has released only two movts, or "formants," being still dissatis-
fied with the others, as well he might be, to judge by these
two. This ideal music, which, like late Bach and Beethoven,
disdains the limitations of the human hand and ear, and of
the piano keyboard, attempts the impossible feat of totalitar-
ian organization with anarchistic freedom, in a blend of the
serial and the aleatory (once excoriated by PB as an irre-
sponsible refusal of the composer to face the duty of decision). The freedom of choice here consists on the rather
infantile liberty of rearranging the four sections of the
"trope" (a Mediaeval term totally meaningless in this context). There is also the startlingly new use of ossia passages of slightly less density (first used by Carissimi, or
Peri in the 16th century?). Yet another "innovation" of PB
is the use of two colors to clarify the text (Guido used it in
1100, and Baroque opera gave us "coloratura" or colored cadenzas). Boulez is one of the three contestants for the title
"most difficult contemporary piano composer," along with
Xenakis and Stockhausen.

BOWLES, PAUL (USA), 1911- .

Most of the piano music of this ex-patriate American
is in a popular vein, inferior to his published fiction.

El Indio; El Bejuco (1943); Huapango, 1, 2. The
Latin American music is authentic in rhythm, but popular in
style, and better heard in some of his ballet orchestrations.
Mod E

Six Preludes. These well written pieces have more
viability, variety, musicality. A tantalizing dissonant chromaticism usually resolves to a familiar chord; jazz rhythms
are effectively used. The quiet closing prelude has the serenity of a peasant song. Mod

Sonatina (1947). This neo-classic, light-hearted work
has some good piano writing, if you can get past the inane
first theme. The andante cantabile is quite fruity. The
angular, rhythmic third is brilliant and difficult. Mod to
Dif

BRAHMS, JOHANNES (Ger), 1833-1897.

One of the all-time greats, this composer's complete works for piano fill only three volumes (Kalmus), but range from 4-min lyrical intermezzi to brilliant award-winner variations, and mammoth concerti. Some, like G. B. Shaw, may be repelled by this music, and choose to use the fire escape, which, he said, was "in case of Brahms." For mature pianists with more than basic technic and musicianship. Even the simpler works require a special Brahms style.

Sonata in C, Op 1. Written at the precocious age of 20 (the second movt at 14) this dazzled Schumann and catapulted the composer to instant fame. It is immature and full of angularities, but already very Brahmsian. Best enjoyed after acquaintance with later works. The allegro uses classical form (and an opening theme recalling Beethoven's Hammerklavier). Requires driving energy and great control, as well as intense concentration for the mildly lyrical second theme.

In the andante (Variations on an old German Minnelied) the student is not yet the master of his good ideas. The scherzo introduces JB's favorite con fuoco style, alternating fast 6/8 and 3/4 and linking them with the hemiola shift that becomes a Brahms hallmark. In the furioso finale scampering passages of 3rds build to soaring octave-with-3rd climaxes. Dif

Sonata in f#, Op 2. Written before Op 1, this has the same four-movt structure and similar texture, but is inferior, and the closing movement is disappointing.

Sonata in f, Op 5. Best of the three. Like Schumann, Chopin and Mendelssohn, JB wrote only three piano sonatas, though he continued to use this form for his finest chamber and orchestral works (and even piano pieces called rhapsody or intermezzo.) The opening passage plunges from one end of the keyboard to the other, then alternates this theme with a five-meas tranquillo chordal passage over a timpani bass. The contrasting second theme fails to rise to the eloquence of the early songs, but is built into a fine development. The expressive andante alternates a delicate pizzicato passage (JB is already writing symphonies for piano) with a flowing theme in 3rds, ending with a triumphant coda. The scherzo ("after Chopin") is one of JB's best. A brief intermezzo leads to a large finale, full of a rich variety of

themes, skillfully developed.   Requires mature musicianship
and big technic.   Dif

Scherzo in e♭, Op 4.   This bumptious piece shows
the marks of immaturity and of its source of inspiration.
Like Chopin's four misnamed scherzi, this is also in a fast
3/4, which is actually 12/4, and has a chorale mid-section.
Though it has a heavy-handed humor, it lacks Chopin's joyous lyricism.   The sonata scherzi are all better.   Mod Dif

Four Ballades, Op 10.   The Nordic love of legendry
and the gruesome breathes an exciting chill into these works.
The first, in d, vividly evokes the grisly Scottish Ballad of
Edward with octave melodies in a ghostly march rhythm and
tapping triplet figures in the bass, which at the end become
a spine-tingling whisper.   Good program number.

The same devices are used in No 2, with a fine doppio movimento, and a new figure in which the LH rocks back
and forth on the afterbeat.   The third and fourth are in triplet meter, the third more of a scherzo, and the last a romanza.   The four make a fine group (20 min) or can be
played with other later works.   There is another fine Ballade
in Op 118.   Mod

Variations, Op 9.   These are a trial-run for the big
sets to come, and a tribute to JB's hero, Schumann, who
provides the theme.   Disappointing musically, due largely to
the monotony of the theme.   Mod

Variations, Op 21, No 1, No 2.   The first set is on
a theme by JB, the second on a Hungarian theme.   JB's
own theme is so impressive that the long and difficult variations fail to improve on it.   The Hungarian set is shorter
and easier; but not very attractive, in spite of the irregular
3/4-4/4 folk rhythm.   Mod Dif

Variations and Fugue on a theme by Handel, Op 24.
One of the mountain-peaks of the repertoire, the attractive
theme is used by Handel for a set of variations of his own.
JB's follow inflexibly the binary form of the theme, but offer
one after the other, a kaleidoscope of rhythmic, melodic,
coloristic and character transformations.   Though interspersed with dramatic and lyrical variations, the prevailing
style is the classical ornamental variation.   When it seems
impossible to wring anything further from the tune, JB creates a two-meas fugue theme, and in 4-v polyphony, using

all known contrapuntal devices, doubled in octaves and massive chords, builds a magnificent climax. Dif

Variations on a Theme by Paganini, Op 35, Bk I, II.
Once rejected as unplayable, these are now rated by many
as the acme of piano writing (along with the two concertos,
and Liszt's sonata). The violin caprice which has inspired
so many composers from Schumann and Liszt, down to Rachmaninoff, inspired JB to write 27 variations, 13 in Book I,
14 in Book II. They can be played separately or together
(about 25 min), or a selection made from both books. They
range from formidable technical studies to lilting lyrics, and
are an apotheosis of all Brahms pianistic devices. For virtuosi only. Dif

Variations on a Theme by Haydn, Op 56b, for two
pianos. Though not solo piano repertory, the set for two
pianos on Haydn's "St. Anthony Chorale" must be mentioned.
Here each variation is a separate movement, ranging from
a graceful siciliano and a brilliant toccata, to a powerful
passacaglia finale. Dif

Brahms lovers unable to cope with the large early
works will be pleased to discover that the late works,
grouped in sets of short pieces, are, on the whole, finer
and more playable, and get better as one proceeds from Op
76 to Op 119.

Eight pieces, Op 76. Variously titled intermezzo or
capriccio (there is little distinction) these have the intimate,
intensely personal character of Chopin's nocturnes, impromptus, and preludes. They range from two to six pages in
length, some binary, some with a contrasting middle section.
Best of this set are the first four. Mod

Two Rhapsodies, Op 79: No 1 in b, No 2 in g.
Though incorrigibly romantic, JB was so grounded in classic form that even a rhapsody turns out to be a well-rounded
allegro. These are big dramatic works, and have a Nordic
quality. Contrasts of dynamics must be broad and uninhibited, and rubato may be freely used, but no time changes,
unless indicated. No 2 was inspired by a Scots ballad,
"Archibald Douglas." Mod Dif

Fantasias, Op 116. Seven pieces, the livelier titled
capriccio, the quieter ones, intermezzo. All are good, and
the set might take the place of a sonata on a program.

There is remarkable variety among them, though Brahms'
unique mannerisms are everywhere apparent: rolled diminished 7th chords, melodies in parallel 3rds, bass octaves
thickened with a 3rd or 5th, inner voices framed in bell-like
chords, 6/8-3/4 hemiola shifts. Mod

Three Intermezzi, Op 117. Though all three are
andante, each is unique. The first is a lilting lullaby with
a Scots folk-poem for epigram, and a passionate minor section; the second, a sonata-allegro with the same theme serving for both principal and second subjects, first in minor,
then major, and for development section and return, in a
work of unsurpassed lyric loveliness. The third is less inspired.

Six Pieces, Op 118. Six more gems. A short appassionata is followed by an exquisite andante teneremente.
An energetic ballade has a five-meas phrase throughout the
1st part, and a gentle rocking una corda counter subject.
The quiet romanza in the rare key of F is superb, and a
fine pair for Schumann's F♯. Best of all is the great No 6
in e♭, based on the mournful Gregorian chant for the dead,
the "Dies Irae." Its whispered bass arpeggios are spectral;
its G♭ major section rises from sotto voce to fff, like a
choir of trombones, and the treble answer is a celestial
choir. There must be no tempo change, but a relentless
hammered march beat in the middle-section, and much rubato and nuance in the first and last. Mod Dif

Four Pieces, Op 119. A short adagio and a longer
andantino. The last two of the set are among JB's finest.
The grazioso e giocoso must not be too slow, to keep the
lilt of the alto solo, which is augmented from 6/8 to 6/4
for the bridge, and coda. The closing rhapsody is unsurpassed for structure and content, and its ringing confident
risoluto. Find the right tempo and hold it. Dif

For the insatiable Brahmin, there are several other
delights: two transcriptions of a Bach presto; a Weber
rondo with hands reversed; an etude after Chopin, which
turns out to be Op 25:3 doubled in 3rds and 6ths. There
are also 57 studies (virtuoso!) which are a far cry from
Hanon, and a good preparation for the bigger Brahms pieces.
Best of all is a LH arrangement of Bach's tremendous Chaconne in d for Violin, scrupulously faithful to the original,
and eminently playable.

BRIDGE, FRANK (GB), 1879-1941.

Composer, conductor and educator who, some British critics consider, might have been great, if born in another country at another time. His considerable ouvre of piano music is largely neglected today. He experimented with many styles without achieving much distinction in any of them.

Capriccio (1903). Remarkable for its early anticipation of later polytonal experiments. Mod Dif

Three Improvisations for the LH. Short atmospheric sketches, delicate, evanescent. Mod

The Hour Glass. Rather cryptic series of 3, titled: Dusk, The Dew Fairy, and The Midnight Tide. All are pianistic, the second swift and eerie, the last climactic and powerful. Mod

Sonata (1921-24). Virtuoso work in three-movt, employing a dissonant non-tonal scheme, expressive and varied, demanding imaginative musicianship to reify. Dif

BRITTEN, BENJAMIN (GB), 1913- .

For comments on Holiday Suite, read notes on Bernstein's Anniversaries.

Holiday Suite, Op 5 (1934). The splendid operas, choral works, art songs of this composer, would reprove one for discussing this youthful folly.

Night Piece (1963). Commissioned for a contest, this is a test of the player's musicality, with a long lyric melodic line, delicate figuration in the cadenza and fine pedalling. (B&H pub) Mod Dif

BURGMÜLLER, NORBERT (Ger), 1810-1836.

Born in the Wunderjahr that bore so many of the great Romantic piano composers, NB (not to be confused with his older brother, Johann, of the "25 Progressive and Easy Stud-

ies") wrote one major work for piano, before his early
death.

Rhapsody in b. Composed the year of Schumann's
Fantasy, it has the same grand sweep, and a distinctive
blend of Weltschmerz and Spiel-Freude. The impassioned
and agitated opening has a broad singing octave melody; the
dreamy ending in B, ppp, is quite magical. Mod Dif

BUSONI, FERRUCIO (It), 1866-1924.

FB was a pianist noted in his day for his remarkable
repertoire, orchestral power, depth of tone color and clarity
of delineation. Of his complex experimental compositions,
only occasional performances by specialists are heard today,
and he contributed almost nothing useful to the piano repertoire. His Bach transcriptions and editions, once admired,
are now considered unauthentic and lush.

Six Sonatinas. These have little appeal because of
their vague meandering tonality, shapeless undistinguished
melodic motifs, and commonplace rhythms. The one subtitled Christmas Day 1917 may intend to suggest the war with
its austerity. The date also reminds us that Bartók had already mastered his style in Allegro Barbaro; Schönberg written most of his unique works; Alban Berg, his superb Sonata,
and Charles Ives, his two. The sixth Sonatina is a fantasy
on themes from Carmen, a device which other composers,
lacking in melodic gift, have used.

Fantasia Contrapunctistica. This horrendous work is
meant to be another Art of the Fugue, alternating three turgid fugues with chorale preludes, toccatas, Lisztian cadenzas,
variations; and combining them all at the end, with the theme
from Bach's "Kunst." FB wrote four versions of it, one
"abridged," one for two pianos. All are moribund, though
the drawing of the Papal Palace at Avignon is nice.

Indian Diary, Op 47; Toccata (1920). Four somewhat more approachable pieces based on Indian airs. There
is also an Indian Fantasy for Orchestra, which has been recorded, as has the 80-min Concerto (with male chorus yet).

BUSSOTTI, SYLVANO (It), 1931- .

Mixed-media artist who combines painting, photography, illumination with music that ranges from strict serial writing to vague aleatoric verbalization. His largest work is "The Passion according to de Sade."

Five Pieces for David Tudor. The dedicatee has become famous for his memorization and performance of fantastically difficult contemporary piano music. Here chord-clusters, for which Ives (70 years ago) used a wooden-stick and Cowell (50 years ago) used the forearm, are produced by thick gloves, to prevent any clear melodic outline from emerging. Next?

CAGE, JOHN (USA), 1912- .

Experimental composer-philosopher and mushroom authority, highly regarded in both European and American avant-garde circles. JC has moved from the total organization of his teacher, Schönberg, through innovations in piano sound begun by his teachers, Cowell and Varèse, to Music of Chance and Change and finally to non-music and nullity of composition related to Zen and the I Ching. It seems probable that the importance of his innovations will exceed the significance of most of his compositions, the more recent ones (especially the silent ones) being evanescent "happenings" only intended to occur once.

Sonatas and Interludes for Prepared Piano (1948). The invention of the device of changing the pitch and timbre of piano strings by inserting screws, erasers etc. grew out of a need for percussion for a dance on a stage only large enough for a piano and dancer. The effect is exotic, Oriental, haunting and hypnotic. The diagram of "preparation" is reproduced in JC's unique calligraphy, as are the 16 sonatas (mostly one- or two-page) and four interludes. The process takes two or three hours to accomplish, and your piano will be incapacitated for all other music while you learn and perform the works; so better have a second piano handy. The sound is somewhat like the Javanese gamelan, heard at a distance. (Was JC an Asian in one of his previous incarnations?) The effect is heightened by the preponderance of duple rhythms (though there are irregular measures, only two are in triple meter, one in 7/4). The melodic and

rhythmic motifs are remarkably varied and imaginative (they
sound well on a harpsichord, without any gadgets). My favorites are Nos 2, 4, 5, 6, 10, 11, 12 and Interlude 14.
There are some remarks about them tucked away in JC's
book Silences, if you have the patience to hunt them out.
Requires more patience than technic or musicianship. Mod

    Music of Changes, Vol I to IV (1951); Music for Pi-
ano (1953). A discussion of these is really superfluous,
since it is highly improbable that anyone will ever wish to
play or hear them, a fact which will not trouble the composer since he points out that composition, performance, and
listening have nothing to do with each other. JC's prose ex-
planation of his composition methods--of the tossing of coins,
the consulting of the I Ching, etc.--is as turgid and obfus-
cating as the music notation. Two things seem clear: no
consideration of sound or keyboard execution deterred JC;
and his chief obsession was filling a predetermined period of
time. This was apparent in the "Theatre Piece" which JC
"conducted" in the Circle in the Square in 1960, when he
stood for an hour with a stop-watch in one hand, and an um-
pire's whistle in his mouth, signalling David Tudor, Merce
Cunningham and sundry others to select from a cue sheet another stunt, and do it. JC also seems to be to blame for
the minuscule calligraphy of the drawing board school of
composers, a form of inverted snobbery, which purports to
make the most outrageous demands of the player seem modest by writing them as tiny as possible, while actually mag-
nifying their difficulty. However the illegibility of a few
notes is of minor importance, as the player is generously invited to "use his own discretion, if the notation seems irra-
tional."

    4' 33". A "tacit" piece, for one or more instru-
ments, which would be welcome, with several repeats and
da capos, as an interlude in some contemporary quadrasonic
electronic music.

CAMPOS-PARSI, HEITOR (PR), 1922- .

    Distinguished music promoter, critic and composer,
writing both the popular native danza, and in neo-classic
forms.

    Sonata en Sol (1954). Prize-winning work in neo-classic three-movt form.   After an ejaculatory introduction, a traditional allegro follows.   Quiet mesto is tonal and pastoral; finale contrasts a hymn-like chordal passage with propulsive vivo.   (PIC pub)   Mod Dif

CARDEW, CORNELIUS (GB), 1936- .

Avant-garde composer and instigator of happenings, who has been distinguished by election to the Royal Academy of Music.   His published piano pieces, while odd enough, do not represent the recent imaginative verbalized group performances.

February Pieces (1959).   Miniature mood pieces with slow-moving non-metric lines, serial or polytonal, punctuated by ornamental figuration.   Dif

Three Winter Potatoes (1961-1965).   More extended set (15 min), attempting to fuse traditional keyboard figures, diatonic chords, trills, repeated motifs and octave doublings, with contemporary "prepared" string timbre and dissonant counterpoint.   A bleak winter and cold potatoes.   Dif

CARPENTER, JOHN ALDEN (USA), 1876-1951.

American composer who reversed Ives' procedure, and after a successful career in business, resumed composing to win honors and honorary degrees.   Of his voluminous out-put, only the ballet, Skyscrapers, and the song-cycle Gitanjali, to poetry of Tagore, remain in the recorded repertoire.   His Concertino for Piano and Orchestra has three original, attractive well-structured movts, and deserves an occasional hearing.   Jazz-beat, as well as the popular, the whimsical and the humorous are featured.

Diversions.   This suite of five pieces contrasts moods and rhythms, with much use of the 9th, chromatically altered melody notes, atmospheric pedal effects.   Mod

Danza.   Little melody, but driving rhythm in mildly dissonant chord patterns, demands control and endurance.   Mod

Little Dancer, Little Indian. Character pieces, the
first sprightly, the second introspective. Mod

Polonaise Americaine, Tango Americaine. There is
little that is American (or very original) about these two
rather elaborate settings of traditional dance forms. Mod

CARR, ARTHUR (USA), 1908- .

Five Pieces: Toccata, Aria I, Sonata, Aria II Finale. The pianist, accompanist, and composer has just published (in Italy, Ricordi, BM) a set of five pieces of moderate difficulty, based on a Schönbergian row and its permutations; three vigorous movts are linked and are contrasted
with two in lyrical, improvisatory style. Pianistic. Mod
Dif

CARTER, ELLIOT (USA), 1908- .

Esteemed award-winning composer, frequently performed and recorded, has a concerto for piano and orchestra and a double-concerto for piano and harpsichord and orchestra, which are very striking. His early sonata is highly
regarded by scholars, and deserves more attention from
serious pianists, though too arcane to appeal to audiences.

Sonata (1946). A two-movt, 20 min (44-page) work,
written before EC adopted serialism. The first movt moves
from b♭ to D♭; the second is basically D major. Much
original (and tricky) piano figuration alternates and underlies
big chordal themes, octave melodies, a quiet 2-v passage.
The first movt is more appealling musically than the rather
austere, fragmented and anti-climactic second. The opening
polyphonic chorale, later enhanced with bell-like treble pedal-
points, before disintegrating into disjunct scraps of sound,
leans heavily on Roy Harris for its harmonic scheme; and
the impressive fugal core of the movt paves the way for
Barber's even better one. But the many parts lack organic
cohesion, and wind down soporifically to a disappointing end.
Dif

CASADESUS, ROBERT (Fr), 1899- .

To be one of the world's greatest pianists, husband of another, and father of a 3rd, would satisfy most men; but not so for RC. (Two uncles and a cousin were famous string players.) He must also compose. His Concerto, Sonata No 2, and music for two pianos have been recorded.

24 Preludes (Books I-IV). Dedicated to Ravel, these have a Gallic lightness and brightness. One is Spanish; another a funeral march; two are in antique dance forms. Mod Dif

Eight Etudes (1941). If you do not wish to pay by the minute to learn the famous Casadesus technic, you can pay by the page. These are utility music for people who still believe in digital gymnastics, and do not care much about the sound (after all, anything sounds better than Czerny; and sound has long ceased to be a criterion among the avant-garde). Thirds, octaves, 4ths and 5ths, 2-against-3, chords, and lightness of touch are given a workout. The mildly modal quality of the music seems to be the fortuitous result of the conjunction of motor patterns. A very attractive unproblematic berceuse on the name Claude Pasquier has strayed among the etudes. Mod Dif

Toccata (1950). Large-scale virtuoso piece whose technical problems in octave playing, double notes, endurance, accuracy and drive far exceed the musical results. Dif

Sonata No 2 (1953). A three-movt work with propulsive first movt, cantabile adagietto in the style of a barcarolle; rhythmically unique percussive finale. Dif

CASELLA, ALFREDO (It), 1883-1947.

Composer, conductor and classical pianist, from the land of opera. His duties as editor, teacher and conductor affected his composition style, which is highly eclectic, and original only in the later works which explore polytonal and atonal harmony. One may by-pass the early pseudo-classical dances, the two volumes called "A la Manière de...." There is little point in playing imitations of Fauré, Debussy, Ravel, when one can play the real McCoy.

Pometti Lunari (1909). Not Schönberg's moon-struck
Pierrot, but Debussy and Ravel peep through these tiny
moon poems. Mod

Sonatina (1916): Allegro con spirito, Minuetto, Finale. Though this is a form perfected by German and Viennese composers, the influences here are AC's Italian ancestors', dance rhythms alternating with vocal lyricism, ending with a large brilliant movement effectively using keyboard figuration and chordal writing. Dif

A la notte (1917). Large atmospheric nocturne, employing impressionistic devices to build an effective lachrymose climax and a dolce far niente. Mod Dif

Due Ricercare sul nome B. A. C. H. : Funebre, Ostinato. Every composer is allowed to play with this unprom-
ising four-note theme; and the short introspective choral lament and accelerating ostinato march are a good try. Mod
Dif

Sinfonia, Arioso e Toccata, Op 59 (1936). Here AC
achieves a style of his own for the first time in a large-
scale neo-classic technically demanding work. Since the
Italians invented all three of these forms (as well as the
pianoforte) it is good to find them so successfully used by
an Italian pianist. Dif

6 Studies (1946). Written in his last year, these
Chopin-inspired keyboard etudes are a kind of summation of
AC's compositional explorations. Dif

CASTALDO, JOSEPH (USA), 1927- .

Sonatina. This music administrator (President of the
Philadelphia Music Academy) has found time for two significant piano works. In free tonality, with much dissonance,
the Sonatina has four brief contrasting movements. The rapid wide-ranging figuration of the first movt is studded with
7th chords; a quiet lyrical meandering theme is followed by
a bustling third movt, with moments of repose; and to close,
an exuberant and vigorous keyboard-spanning finale. (HE
pub) Dif

Toccata. Virtuoso work, brilliant and highly dissonant, non-metric, written in continuous 16th-note figures, allegro scorrevole [flowing or scurrying]; a contrasting chordal passage is ejaculatory and joyous, before the dashing close. (HE pub) Dif

CASTELNUOVO-TEDESCO, MARIO (It-USA), 1895-1968.

Remembered today chiefly for his fine guitar music, MCT was born in Florence, and settled in Hollywood, after the hegeira of 1939, adding film writing to opera, symphonic, song and piano composing. Most of his large piano output is neglected, being in a 19th-century romantic style, fluent, florid and uninhibited, but also un-original. There are two Hebraic Suites, an English Suite, a three-movt Viennese Rhapsody, a four-movt Neapolitan Rhapsody, an Alpine Suite, two Film Studies, and countless single large solo pieces.

Alt Wien (1923): Walzer; Nachtmusik, Memento Mori. Considered his best by Friskin and Freundlich, this contrasts a suave waltz with an impressionistic barcarolla. The curious but brilliant close is a "Fox-Trot Tragico" built on leaping chord and octave passages. Dif

Tre Corali su Mélodie ebraiche (1926). Large scale suite, following invocation in cantilation style with two vigorous primitive dances, one "rude," the other "stamping." Effective. There is also a "Dance of King David," based on Palestinian motifs. Dif

Candide (1944). Voltaire's novel illustrated with six lightweight genial pieces. Best is "The Young Girls and the Monkeys," a Latin samba. Mod

Two Film Studies (1931): Charlie, Mickey Mouse. Even before the Hollywood hegeira, MCT was a film-fan, and wrote these two humorous pieces on his two favorite stars. Mod

CASTRO, JOSE MARIA (Arg), 1892-1964.

Music has been a thriving art in Argentina ever since the days when the Jesuit Father Zipoli came from Rome to

teach and play the organ.   Three brothers named Castro have
been active, and have written extensively for piano.   They
often rise above the regionalism of many Latin American
composers with music that makes a universal appeal.

Sonata (1931).   A neo-classic three-movt work.   The
piano style is traditional and fluent, the mood gentle, the
texture light.   Six variations follow an allegro, closing with
a finale in fast tempo.   Mod

10 Short Pieces.   Experiments in polytonality and dissonance in a contrasting series, including an Etude, a Lament, a Lullaby, a Galop.   Mod

Sonata de Primavera (1939).   A larger, more complex work, basically tonal, and flowing in style.   Three
movts contrast tempi and idiom--the second, martial and
chordal, the third, running figuration.   Effective.   Mod

CASTRO, JUAN JOSE (Arg), 1895-1968.

This French-trained member of the family has adopted
a more international style, using polytonality and a rich polyphonic texture.   Has several successful symphonic works.

Toccata (1940).   A virtuoso work aspiring to the category of Ravel's and Prokofiev's, this is technically difficult,
but musically rather conservative.   Demands drive and endurance.   Dif

Sonata Espagnol (1956).   An experiment combining
serial and tonal writing, with first allegro theme using a row,
and the second, a diatonic cantabile melody.   The third movt
is bitonal, with the witty device of a black-theme scherzo
superimposed on Weber's famous C Major Moto Perpetuo.
Mod Dif

CASTRO, WASHINGTON (Arg), 1909-   .

The youngest of the family has devoted himself to
teaching and composing chamber and choral works.   Has
numerous pieces for children.

Four Pieces on Children's Themes (1942).   Like
Dohnanyi's famous Nursery Tune Concerto, this is not children's music.   The four pieces are fresh and pianistic, varying from toccata style, a haunting lullaby, to a racing rondo.
Mod

Rondo.   Brilliant and not excessively difficult, this
achieves its effect through bi-tonality and a series of episodes with sudden changes of mood.   Mod Dif

CATURLA, ALEJANDRO GARCIA (Cuba), 1906-1940.

Promising composer whose career was cut short by
murder.   One of the first to use Afro-Cuban motifs in his
contemporary writing.

Son en Fa minor.   Theme and variations exploring
melorhythmic motifs from primitive sources in a highly dissonant harmony.   Mod Dif

Doz Dansas Cubanas.   Virtuoso Caribbean bongo-
drum beats superimposed on jungle tom-toms, in a Danza
del Tambor, Danza Lucumi, etc.   Mod Dif

CHABRIER, EMMANUEL (Fr), 1841-1894.

Remembered today largely for his orchestral Rhapsodie España, and orchestra transcriptions of some piano
pieces, his best keyboard writing is the two-piano Trois
Valses romantiques.

Habanera.   A trip to Spain was the inspiration not only for the Rhapsodie, but also for this rather innocuous piano
dance.   Mod E

Pièces Pittoresques.   Ten sketches of varying merit,
of which four have become popular in orchestral arrangements.   Mod

Bourrée Fantasque.   The classical duple dance, with
up-beat, in a lush and brilliant style.   Mod Dif

CHAMBERS, STEPHEN A. (USA), 1940- .

One of the youngest composers represented here, SAC
deserves watching. Though his style is at present eclectic
and derivative, he may, with the rising tide of black culture,
enrich the repertoire with some distinctive music.

Sound-Gone (A Poetic-Philosophic Sketch). Five
linked sections, each with a Rod McKuen type epigram, cele-
brate the evanescent and ephemeral qualities of music in a
melange of styles. Best are the interior pieces, with hypnotic tom-tom bass, finger-nail glissandi and plucked melodies; worst is a movement lifted straight out of Cyril Scott.
Dif

CHAMINADE, CECILE (Fr), 1857-1944.

Probably the first woman to make a career of composing (she was also a concert pianist, performing her own
works). Earlier women composers of talent were outshone
by their kin (Mozart's sister, Mendelssohn's sister, Robert
Schumann's Clara). CC wrote more than 200 piano pieces,
a half dozen of which were standard student works for years,
and still have a faded charm.

La Lisonjera. Lyric work in G♭, with melody in RH
thumb. Requires a teasing rubato. Mod E

Scarf Dance. Most popular of all; fluttering and graceful. Mod E

Automne. Longer work, sombre and atmospheric.
All are pianistically deployed. Mod

Toccata. Well-written chord study. Mod

The Spinner. Effective moto perpetuo. Mod Dif

CHAVEZ, CARLOS (Mex), 1903- .

Mexico's leading composer-conductor has several
works for piano, rather dated-experimental in nature, un-
compromisingly dissonant and unpianistic (for some reason

the composer avoids the black-keys!).

Sonatina 1924. Single moderato movt in flowing linear style, 3 to 4 voices, freely chromatic. Mod

Seven Pieces (1923-30). Contrasting styles ranging
from blues and fox-trot to abstract and abstruse. Many are
percussive, driving; some quiet, linear. Mod

Etude (Homage to Chopin). Large virtuoso work,
highly dissonant. It is doubtful that Chopin would have been
honored by the tribute. Dif

10 Preludes. Might be called 'Studies in white-key
eighth-notes." In spite of the limitations, there is some
imaginative alternating of Latin dances, contrapuntal writing,
cross-rhythms, touch technics. R. Ganz recommends the
set for sight-reading. Once through is enough, already.
Mod

Sonata (1965). Neo-classic rococo-style work; simple
ornamental variations on a theme; a dance movement and finale eschewing the composer's usual dissonance for a simple
homophonic texture. Mod

CHOPIN, FREDERIC F. (Pol-Fr), 1810-1849.

Whether or not FC would still top the list of a public
popularity poll of favorite "classical" piano composers, as
he would have up to 1950, is not certain. He would undoubt-
edly remain very high. For pianists, several other composers have moved up beside him, and many younger players,
though dutifully learning and performing his works, prefer the
more acerbic moderns, the more austere early classics, or
the more florid Baroque masters. The 19th-century revivalists have yet to exhume any forgotten composer who can challenge him.

One of the remarkable things about FC is that in a
period of shameless keyboard exhibitionism and unabashed
sentimentality, he maintained his own unique character, giving us no Gallop Fantastique, no operatic transcriptions, no
Carnivals or Scenes from Childhood. Instead we have sets
of pieces, ranging from four to 50, in a single form, with
generic titles and only keys and numbers to identify them.
The other remarkable thing is that the pieces, with few ex-

ceptions, are all carefully crafted and at the same time inspired, original, intense expressions of a unique musical
personal style.

Though himself a meticulous copyist, FC has suffered
greatly at the hands of editors, students, and "friends"; and
even today an entirely satisfactory edition is not to be had.
The OxU ed, begun before World War II and based on a complete set of his manuscripts left with Miss Jane Stirling, was
probably the best.   It was withdrawn after the war, and is
now practically unavailable.   Even this generally excellent
edition contains an amusing example of what so often hap-
pened.   Prelude 14, now marked allegro ¢, and obviously
meant to be played very fast, was marked moderato in her
copy, probably because Jane could not play it any faster, and
poor FC wanted to be done with her, and bundle his tired
chest out of the Scottish fog and into bed.   The discontinued
OxU ed became the basis for the Italian Curci ed, the second best available (poor paper and bad binding).   Best at
present is the FC Institute ed (Warsaw), well edited and
printed.   Kalmus, so authentic in other cases, used question-
able sources, and is to be avoided.   Most other publications
are over-edited, though the French Durand edited by Debussy,
and Salabert edited by Cortot, offer interesting insights.

Etudes, Book I, Op 10.   The etudes, Op 10 and 25,
are unique in the repertoire for being both brilliant treat-
ments of 24 distinct technical problems, and at the same
time inspired music.   A Portuguese pianist who claimed to
have been a pupil of Alfred Cortot dropped in on me in my
village studio in China once when I was practicing.   With a
sigh, she said (in all seriousness), "I always found that
when I had finished the 24 etudes each day, I was too tired
to practice my music."   I have always been grateful to her
for the humor of putting Op 10 and 25 in a class with Czerny,
Op 499; and also for inspiring me to master all 24.   Though
I have never used them as a warm-up "before the music,"
a Japanese pupil of mine (after leaving my tutelage) played
all 24 as a group in a concert.   I do not recommend it.
Timewise, they are only about 15 min longer than the 24
preludes of Op 28, (45 to 50 min as against 30 to 35 min).
They lack, however, the cyclic key unity, the delightful contrasts of the preludes; and are all together too over-power-
ing for both audience and player.   Three or four make a
good recital group; or better, group them with a nocturne
and some of the neglected mazurkas.   One is forced to the
conclusion that FC considered the RH more important, as
only three are specifically LH studies (many have equal

rights), a conclusion contradicted by important bass parts in other works. All are difficult.

Etude No 1 in C. This arpeggio study in RH 10ths is easy for a Cliburn hand, hard for a della Rocha (though one would never guess it from her performance). A magnificent bass octave melody makes a grand chorale. Long pedals.

No 2 in a. Exercise in chromatic scales and trills with the weak outside fingers (who does not need it?) with triads by thumb and forefinger on every beat, to keep you from cheating. At the same time a purling, rippling, shimmering thing of beauty. Little or no pedal.

No 3 in E. This is so hardy that it survives the saccharine text of "No Other Love," a title, which, if applied to the piano, might well label FC's life. The section beginning with meas 38 (which earns it a place among the etudes), the chromatic augmented 4ths which are actually diminished, descending 7ths, must be carefully fingered; there seems to be only one possible fingering for the bravura passage in 6ths which follows. There is nothing to indicate that it should be played at torrential speed, like a cadenza, but do it if you can. It can be equally powerful, when hammered out relentlessly in tempo, but with enormous dynamic contrasts. Master this, before drooling over the nocturne-like first part; and remember, Chopin's rubato was always discrete, never abandoned.

No 4 in c♯. Extremely difficult, this has the virtue of combining and alternating a variety of technical problems for both hands, thus giving "breathing spells." Velocity is of the essence. It ends "con più fuoco possibile," and is a very exciting number.

No 5 in G♭. The "Black Key" is so familiar as to need no comment. Pedalling, nuance and rubato are of utmost importance if it is to come alive.

No 6 in e♭. One of the three with slow tempo marks, this andante is technically easier, but requires the highest degree of musicality to realize its poignant, restrained, emotional message.

No 7 in C. A brilliant toccata, difficult and effective (the RH has all the exercise).

No 8 in F. One of the greats, an arpeggio study for RH with a lilting bass melody; the LH has its share of practice in the middle and ending and the piece is capped with a shout of sheer joy.

No 9 in f. One for the LH, not excessively difficult (a good place to begin). The minor key, chromatic shifts, dynamic contrasts, and molto rubato give it the true Polish "zal."

No 10 in A♭. A difficult chord study in endurance, touch variation, and phrasing; somewhat less attractive musically.

No 11 in E♭. Like his prelude in the same key, a joyous piece, both hands rolling widespread chords, with hidden melodies. The bass note needs constantly a strong emphasis.

No 12 in c. The "Revolution" is not all in the "Left" and the powerful RH must dominate throughout with its alternating slogan-shouts and snatches of victory chant, demanding precise timing, great dynamic contrast, and a bravura sweep. The left rumbles menacingly away in the background, surging up, and hurtling down the keyboard, always under perfect control.

12 Etudes, Op 25: No 1 in A♭. A workout for both hands, the overt simplicity of this "Aeolean Harp" is deceiving for its melodic leaps are treacherous. The real problem, however, is development of an even touch, clear melodic line, and the phrasing, nuance and rubato to bring it alive.

No 2 in f. The rhythmic problem of a quarter-note triplet against a half note triplet must be mastered until the etude can purl and ripple. Sounds best by players with hands large enough to keep the LH legato, without excessive pedal.

No 3 in F. Another unique rhythm study (the two make a fine pair), also requiring the utmost lightness.

No 4 in a. This is a fine study for the LH in accurate leaping chords, and contrasting legato-staccato in the right. It is pp throughout, with a forte only before the lento ending.

No 5 in e. A study in a variety of ways of treating a passing tone. When these have been mastered, the first part must be playful and whimsical, the E major section (only slightly slower than the opening vivace), broad and singing. The E major ending is a masterpiece of original-ity.

No 6 in g#. For some the sustained trills and chro-matic scales in the RH will make this the most difficult of all. Somewhat longer, with a fine LH cantilena, it is an excellent program number, for those who can cope.

No 7 in c#. My own "all-time favorite" among Cho-pin's works, this is in reality not an etude, but a nocturne. Often called "The 'Cello," it is, after the opening " 'cello" recitative, a duet between treble and bass throughout its four sections, the steady pulse of the inner 8th notes--two-note chords of 2nds, 3rds, 4ths, 5ths--to be played with the ut-most gentleness, and only stressed when the changing inter-val gives the exquisite poignancy of the expression. Pedal-ling is difficult at several points. In the eloquent duet of the second page, it should be sparse and saved for the fff climax. The following B major section should use it only for the 16th-note bass chords, and requires una corda for the melting smorzando, as also at the end.

No 8 in D♭. If we must have a "Minute Waltz," here are two "Minute Etudes," not to be tackled by anybody who cannot finish in 60 sec or less. Only two crescendos, one at the half, the other at the end. If the next must be "The Butterfly," why not "The Moth" for this?

No 9 in G♭. Master of the use of the four- or five-note figure, Chopin here outdoes himself, weaving into the simple unbroken texture an unforgettable melody.

No 10 in b. Another of the greatest, the endurance and power needed for the torrent of octave scales (with sus-tained inner voices) is formidable. The unique cantabile is only slightly less taxing because of its constant legato, and requires total mastery of the arts of nuance, rubato, phras-ing. Andante con moto seems a better tempo indication than FC's lento, the dotted half being felt as a single slow beat, after the fast half note of the opening. This allows for a very flexible rubato, and makes possible the gradual accele-rando of the interesting 14-meas cam-like figure of the bridge.

No 11 in a.   The "Winter Wind" sobriquet, derived
from the hurricane velocity of the right-hand figures (24
notes to the measure but very pianistically laid-out), does
not do justice to the martellato chordal bass, which, like a
fanfare, opens and closes the work.   The LH has several
breezy passages to master too.

No 12 in c.   A favorite of mine ever since hearing
the 88-year-old Tobias Matthay totter to the piano, place the
music on the rack, pull it out to the limit, and proceed to
storm through it (without a glance at the book) at fantastic
speed, with impeccable accuracy, bringing out every booming bell tone in the bass, the great chorale B-A-C-H theme
of the RH thumb, and the little off-beat sighing interludes.
A glorious memory; and a glorious finale to the 24 "daily
exercises."

24 Preludes, Op 28.   This opus is one of FC's greatest, consisting of 24 miniature gems, each exquisitely crafted
and profoundly expressive.   Every serious pianist will wish
to try them all.   Because they are so short (eight of them
take less than one minute to play) for a program it is best
to play a group of from four to eight or a dozen.   The entire set takes only 30 to 35 min (I would like a showing of
hands from the audience on how many would prefer this to a
30-minute Sonata by Beethoven or Schubert?).   The great
cycle of keys, up through the sharps, down through the flats,
gives to the book a fine unity.
Three or four of the preludes are simple enough for
children, but unless the child is musical enough to love them,
and disciplined enough to wait and work several years before
tackling the others, they should be withheld.   Several are as
difficult as the etudes, and all require sensitive musicianship.   I shall always remember watching a Chinese student
thrill to the discovery of tempo rubato in "The Clock." (Its
long melodic lines, with their penultimate climaxes, are
ideal for the rushing-lingering type of rubato.)   Metronome
marks are largely editorial, and may be taken as suggestions.   The very fast tempo taken by Alfred Cortot in Nos
1, 3, 5, 8, 10, etc. enabled him to make great surging rubatos and ritardandos; but a more leisurely tempo can be
equally musical.   The fingering is seldom by Chopin; the
pedalling often is, but must often be amplified for our modern larger pianos.

Prelude No 1 in C.   Two arcs of melody, the second
rising to a great crest then subsiding in little ripples, all

over in 40 sec (and one of the most frustrating pieces to play, because one has no "second chance.") A comparison of No 1 in 2/8, with the similar No 8 in 4/4, where two measures equal eight of the first, will give an insight into phrasing.

No 2 in a. Bleak as a Polish winter snowscape, or a Majorcan mountain fog, this must not be too slow (though lento, it is ¢) and the three lines must always be distinct. Ask not for whom the bell tolls!

No 3 in G. The first eight preludes make a fine group, with their alternation of fast and slow, gay and grave. This vivace, leggierimento must sound radiantly joyful (after blood, sweat and tears over that LH part).

No 4 in e. Played at Chopin's funeral, this is as sad as the Marche Funebre, but grief recollected in tranquility. Molto rubato.

No 5 in D. Ebullient, evanescent, iridescent, and pure Chopin, as exciting for the intellectual analyst as for the emotional absorber. The major-minor slur on the 6th in the brief introduction and interlude (more a chuckle than a sigh) grows to four notes (and four beats) in the coda, and becomes a peal of joyous laughter.

No 6 in b. No matter how often belabored by students (who might better be playing "Raindrops Keep Falling on My Head"), this, in the hands of a musician, is a deeply moving miniature, with its final sob. The LH must play as freely as a 'cello, and the una corda and pedal marks are Chopin's.

No 7 in A. Also much abused, this should not sit and sigh, but have the lilt of a teasing mazurka: Zerlina saying to Don Giovanni, "I won't, I won't!--I will."

No 8 in f♯. Another masterpiece both for the sensualist and for the analyst. The shifting chromatics that produce such a sense of restrained passion, may possibly, Mr. Weinstock, be the "regulated accidents of trained hands straying on the keyboard," but the "accidents" can all be scientifically graphed in harmonic terms; and the music makes straight for the heart.

No 9 in E. The dramatic alternating of moods brings

here a work of Handelian grandeur, rising in its 12 meas
to two climaxes.   There are, as in many preludes, three
distinct figures throughout, a duet between bass and treble,
and the steadily rocking inner triplet.   It looks disarmingly
simple, but there are six distinct note values in the first
measure; and in the seventh still another is added, where
two equal 8ths appear above the triplet for the first and only time, and ease us down from the mighty A♭ chord (which
Cortot always used to roll) back to the basic key.

No 10 in c♯.   After the largo e grave, here is a
molto allegro--a fey, will-o-the-wisp thing of sheerest gossamer.   Thirty sec, no more, a closing sigh; then on to the
song and dance of No 11.   Brigadoon in miniature.

No 11 in B.   Nobody seems to have noted that the
hemiola shift of a 3 to a 2 (or vice versa) without changing
meters--a hallmark of Brahms--is anticipated by Chopin in
numerous places, and gives both a dance-like lilt, and a bewitching shift of shape to the music.   Molto rubato, please.

No 12 in g♯.   Four pages, but only a little over a
minute long, this presto toccata is technically one of the
more formidable of the preludes.   After the powerful hammered climax of the first half, the descent of the last page
is sheer wizardry, with one of those uniquely Chopin endings
that introduces a new motif for a coda, and makes it sound
inevitable.

No 13 F♯.   A beautiful slow chordal melody over an
eddying broken-chord bass is stated twice, with FC's device
of reiterating the chords in triplets to intensify the "con
grand' espressione"; and then repeated after the still slower
minor mid-section, with its new melody and glowing counter-
themes in tenor and bass.   At the close the chorale adds a
single high bell-tone over each chord--sheer delight.

No 14 in e♭.   Poor Miss Stirling!   How dreary this
must have sounded moderato.   The allegro in ¢ makes it
really a presto.   The pesante is surely a mistake.   Was it,
too, added in despair over poor bemused Jane Wilhemina's
playing?   Though it rises to a brief ff in its 19 meas (22
sec), it must be legerissimo and fleet as the flight of a bird,
but perhaps a shrike and not a swallow.   It is a trial-run
for that witching unison finale to the Sonata in b♭.

No 15 in D♭.   Another contender for the "Raindrop"

title, this can sound as dull as some of the Schubert Andantes; or may be a small drama. It is the longest of all
(almost six min) and the c♯ section is one of the most original and dramatic in all piano literature. The dynamic and
pedal marks are the composers, and essential to the drama.

No 16 b♭. This four-page one-minute presto con
fuoco is so technically difficult that it is often used as a contest "eliminator." Anyone who can cope with its leaping
bass chords and racing passage-work deserves to be heard
in the semi-finals. (As a test for musicality, as distinguished from sheer keyboard gymnastics, No 13 is recommended.)

No 17 A♭. Another delight for ear and mind. It
must be played quite fast to make the frequent chromatic
key-changes a surprise, and to allow for numerous (but discrete) rubatos; and especially for the largamente of the climax. FC marks the long dying coda "sotto voce, una corda"
and it must sink to a whisper, above the 11 deep bongs of
"The Clock."

No 18 in f. Another "tricky" one, its short agitated
sentences, punctuated by chords, grow longer and faster and
more agitated until they burst into leaping octave chords,
descend in a great rocket, sputter, and end with two shots.

No 19 in E♭. This graceful, undulating "pas de seul"
is in reality a most difficult etude, and can be brought off
with the proper élan only after disciplined practice as rigorous as that of a ballerina. There must be no ritard, for
Chopin has written it in (compare No 5). Beginning on the
second beat of meas 65, the 3/4 clearly changes to 6/8;
and the dancer vanishes in the wings, with a parting kiss.

No 20 in c. In the brief grand chorale, the player
must make clear the growth of the phrase from one measure,
to two, to four, with the last line starting like an echo featuring the alto (you can take or leave the final crescendo,
though it is Chopin's own mark). No large-handed child, or
stupid adult pupil must ever be allowed to make a triplet of
the third beat, which is dotted in every measure. Chopin's
two ritards are the only rubato needed.

No 21 in B♭. The cantabile song (a slow waltz) can
be spoiled by over pedalling the rather odd bass, so find a
viable legato fingering. The glorious 16-meas G♭ mid-sec-

tion, on the other hand, requires one single long pedal for
the eight meas of forte, and flutter-pedal (plus una corda)
for the eight-meas echo.

No 22 in g.   When we begin to think the composer
can't possibly have anything new to say, he brings out these
last three stunners.   This is a 40-sec bravura solo for LH,
octaves throughout.

No 23 in F.   This key seems to suggest purling arpeggios and sonorous bass melodies, with trills to give them
a lift, (see Etude No 8, Op 10).   Delicatissimo and una corda
(except for the middle eight measures).   The flatted 7th in
the penultimate measure gives it a fey touch.

No 24 in d.   A grand finale, this will evoke for older
players the film, A Song to Remember, where it rumbled
away (much too slow) as background music for the much-too-
handsome Chopin (Cornel Wilde) and the much-too-beautiful
George Sand (Merle Oberon).   This virtuoso piece has an almost angry defiant mood, with its series of hammered descending minor thirds, giving way only briefly to a dolce passage.   It ends with a dazzling descending chromatic scale in
3rds, and three great trajectories of arpeggio, the last sweep
ing from top to bottom of the keyboard, and ending with three
resounding D's, of unassailable finality.

Prelude in c#, Op 45.   Two other preludes exist,
which are well worth playing.   This one is somewhat larger
than many in Op 28, though it takes only 4 min to play, and
is built on a single motif and its accompaniment.   The RH
octave chime is reminiscent of the octave theme in Beethoven's "Moonlight" (and in the same key).   It recurs insistent
ly and urgently over an arabesque that swirls up through
three octaves, in a luxuriant series of modulations, pausing
for a chaste, quiet LH recitative, and a brilliant double-note
cadenza.   Comparable to the best in Op 28, but large enough
to stand on its own.   Mod Dif

Prelude in Ab.   This dashing little work, written for
a friend of Chopin's youth, is in the style of the "Butterfly"
etude, and flits by in 45 sec.   It has been published twice,
but is hard to secure.   (Rossignol, Paris; Henn, Geneva.)
Fou Tsong plays it with great brio.   Mod Dif

Polonaises.   How much of the inspiration for these
brilliant stately pieces was derived from actual national

dances, and how much from polacas by Weber and others, we do not know. The form had attracted composers as early as Bach and sons. Its walking tempo, suggesting a promenade through a great country estate or castle, lends itself to a great variety of rhythmic motifs, while keeping always within the slow three beats.

Polonaise Op 26, No 1 c#. A bold opening figure in the bass is answered by a short cantabile which breaks the angular beat with linked triplets, and serves as a "rondo-return" between other themes: a declamatory section rising, with arpeggiated graces from sotto voce to fff, and a very songful theme in D♭, with trickling chromatic slides, and its own a-b-a, elaborating the song's return, after a delicate duet, hovering over diminished chords. Not difficult, and Chopin at his best.

Op 26, 2, e♭. Marked maestoso, it begins misterioso with a five-note whispering ripple in the bass, answered by delicately tapping chords that build in power for the entrance of the 1st theme. The mood is agitated and tragic throughout. The material is not as original as in some others, and is repetitious; but the ending return of the opening whispering ripple is effective.

Op 40, No 1 A. The familiar "Military," played so often and so badly. A slower, unflagging tempo would help.

Op 40, No 2 c. Begins well, with bold bass octave melody, as does the contrasting A flat cantilena; but both peter out in commonplace modulations. Simpler.

Op 44, f#. Seldom heard, this is one of the best. It is much longer than the earlier ones, and contains a mazurka. All the material is fine, and well developed. Dif

Op 53, A♭. "The" polonaise, for most people, though Iturbi's fiery performance in the movie "A Song to Remember" is beginning to fade (one hopes). A slower more majestic tempo relentlessly carried out, with rubato saved for the wistful transition to the return, would redeem it.

Op 71, 1, d; 2, B♭; 3, f. Three early works, published posthumously can be played with pleasure, but are immature and unsatisfying in form.

Op 61 Polonaise Fantasy, A♭. The last big work by
Chopin, this seems to explore new forms, not quite realized.
The musical contents are of the highest, but the profusion of
themes and the loose organization make the piece difficult to
project. Mature.

Andante Spianato and Polonaise in E♭, Op 22. The
orchestra accompaniment is superfluous. The andante is
Chopin at his best; and the brilliant polonaise is effective and
not excessively difficult.

Berceuse, Op 57. This single lullaby by FFC would
seem to owe much to the pianist's erstwhile Paris neighbor,
V. Bellini. Through those paper-thin hotel walls they cannot have helped hearing each other compose; and the richness of the fioratura and the poverty of harmony in this long
melisma on the D♭ tonic-dominant sound much like Casta
Diva. Only pianists with a full mastery of melodic nuance,
delicate, rapid and intricate finger passage work, fine pedalling and strong sense of line should attempt to bring to life
this otherwise soporific work. Dif

Barcarolle, Op 60. A late single work on a scale
comparable in grandness to the ballades and scherzi. The
name is well chosen, as the richly varied music reverts re-
peatedly to an undulating theme in compound rhythm, suggestive of a Neapolitan or Venetian boat-song, but as far above
its naive origins as Bach's classic dances, in its encompass-
ing keyboard demands. One of the greatest. V.

Four Scherzos. These are among his greatest works,
boldly conceived and executed, each sui generis, though all
have similarities in form. Chopin's understanding of the
name scherzo was certainly not that of Haydn or Beethoven,
who substituted it for a minuet, and derived it from a rustic
dance, with humorous devices. The word means "joke," but
there is in Chopin's music no humor; and a better title for
these free fantastic pieces might have been rhapsody or caprice. Man's whimsy seems to confront the fate decreed by
gods here, like a Greek tragedy conflict. All are in one
movt with a slow passage at center. Though all four are in
fast 3/4 time, all would be better served with a compound
12/4 or 4/♩. meas; and it is helpful in understanding the
form, to add these bar-lines.

Scherzo (No 1) in b, Op 20. Written in Vienna, when
the 20-year-old composer had just heard the traumatic news

of Poland's invasion. This may be reflected in the clanging
opening chord, a VII^7 high on the keyboard, like a great
alarm bell. It ushers in a series of agitated, breathless,
surging themes broken by declamatory octave passages left
unresolved, all magnificently deployed. Though thoroughly
pianistic, the tempo of the opening presto con fuoco and of
the close, make it fiendishly difficult. One must protest the
excessively slow tempo taken by many performers for the
middle part. Molto più lento does not mean molto lento;
and "much slower" than presto con fuoco, at one beat to the
bar, 110-130 = dotted half,would be andante, or about 50-70 =
half note. Instead of this, it is played molto lento (50-60 =
quarter note) by many players. It thus loses the character
of suppressed agitation that all the mid-movements suggest.
Even as a Christmas carol (its origin), it could not be sung
at that tempo, and the melodic arch, the counter-theme and
the rotary-bass all languish. A comparison with the other
three, where the contrast is marked sostenuto (No 1), meno
mosso (No 3), and più lento (No 4), confirms Chopin's intention.

Scherzo (No 2) in b♭, Op 31. The most popular of
the four, it endures as a grand piece, in spite of the mur-
derous treatment often given it in the name of "Chopin rubato." A rigorous observance of the time, and strict attention to dynamic contrasts, ranging from sotto voce to ff within one phrase will restore it. The brilliant cascade of the
second theme in D♭ major is not marked più mosso, and
the con anima of the soaring song that follows does not re-
fer to tempo but to character. Only the avvivando and con
bravura of the endings call for acceleration. The sostenuto
is more free, with the effect of fermati at the ends of 16-
meas phrases, produced by Chopin's delicate ascending tremolos on 4ths and 5ths. A veritable sonata development follows, building from playfulness to fury, before the recapitulation. The ending has two più mossos that race to a grand
curtain-ringing ending. Dif

Scherzo (No 3) in c♯, Op 39. Somewhat more difficult, and less played, but equally fine. The short (five-note)
breathless, whispering motif so uniquely Chopin's, here appears again punctuated with chords and leading to a brilliant
descending octave scale passage, answered by a rapid staccato melody in inner voices (urgent and restless). A great
chordal chorale provides contrast--each phrase of the hymn
rounded off with a delicate fluttering figure, requiring fine
finger articulation.

Scherzo (No 4) in E, Op 54. The only scherzo in a
major key, it is also the most joyous of the four. Without
introduction, the opening three themes sound forth, one after
the other, then are expanded and extended. The cantabile
center section begins minor, but soon changes to major.
There is something of the lilt of the waltz about this scherzo,
though it is grand and triumphant. Dif

Ballade in g, Op 23. Again Chopin has created his
own unique form, carried out in four works, each different,
yet all related. All are in a compound duple meter, 6/4
or 6/8, which lends itself to poetic augmentation and diminu-
tion by shifting to 3/2 or 3/4 within the bar. The rhythm
is evocative of balladry and narration. Rich modulations,
sensuous harmonies and long sweeping melodic lines require
mature musicianship in the player. Dif

Ballade in F, Op 38. A simple folk-like melody,
rocking in and out of the tonic seems to come to an end in
a fading bell-tone, only to burst forth in great cascades of
sound. Requires great sensitivity, technical skill, endurance, and drive. Mod Dif

Ballade in Ab, Op 47. Melodies, harmonies and
rhythms all unique and enchanting. Almost a sonata, with
development section in c# minor. Somewhat easier. Mod
Dif

Ballade in f, Op 52. In all ballades a brief, tentative introduction suggests the bard's prologue. The many
slight variations and nuances in the simple theme require
great sensitivity; and the powerful singing climaxes, great
power and drive. The penultimate pages are perhaps the
most difficult, in all Chopin, both to play and to interpret.
For the masters. Dif

Nocturnes. All of Chopin's finest gifts find expression in the 19 nocturnes (plus two); his sensuous harmony,
expressive cantilena, exquisite fioratura, original chord figuration, and his use of forms which he made uniquely his
own. John Field, the Irish pianist who spent his life in Russia, would seem to have invented this form, specially for
Chopin's use. It differs from that other night piece, the
serenata, in that it is meant not as entertainment for other
ears, but as a solitary outpouring of personal feeling. The
introspective melancholy which, in other works provides only a wistful undertone, or a moment of contrast, here is

given full rein.   Yet the variety of the nocturnes is remarkable; no two are alike, yet all are akin in mood and all are
worth exploring.

Nocturne No 1 in B♭, Op 9:1.   The three nocturnes
of this early opus all experiment with devices perfected in
later Nocturnes.   No 1 uses a single LH rhythmic figure
throughout its five pages, and in the mid-section uses a
single chord for 16 meas (later an entire piece, the Berceuse, was written on practically the same chord).   The
piece is lifted to a high level, by the beauty of its two contrasting melodies, and the uses he puts them to: espressivo, appassionata, sotto voce, dolcissimo, smorzando.   The
learner will do well to start here, and grow along with Frederic.

No 2 in E♭, Op 9:2.   One of "Chopin's Greatest
Hits," from the day he first played it, even a Liberace cannot destroy it.   The mature musician will evoke its mood
with dynamics and delicate nuance, rather than with wild rubatos (and candelabras).

No 3 in B, Op 9:3.   The melodic and harmonic chromaticism that elsewhere seems so sensuously expressive,
here seems maundering.   Sprawled over nine pages, it is
unredeemed by time and key shifts, and vocal fioratura
(stolen from Bellini's studio, next door) and leaves one at
the end uncomfortable, rather than disconsolate.

No 4 in F, Op 15:1.   Part of the popularity of No 2
in E♭ may be its brevity (only three pages).   Nos 4 and 5
are only four pages each, and infinitely finer.   The fourth
in F moves from a tranquil cantilena through a turbulent exciting minor section back to a serene close.   Not to be
skipped.

No 5 in F♯, Op 15:2.   One of the greatest, this is
also one of the most difficult.   The opening major section
has two themes, the first as stately in its sadness as a pavane and the second (only six meas), almost heart-breaking
in its slowly sinking sorrow that leads to the agitated doppio
movimento (molto più mosso would be a better instruction).
Its restless rotations begin in a whisper that rises to a moan-
ing as the pedal point rises from c♯ to d.   The brief return
of the stately opening is enriched by too many uniquely Chopinesque devices to name; and the coda, with its muted fanfare and dying-fall, is matchless.

No 6 in g, Op 15:3. Subtitled, "after a performance of Hamlet" (perhaps with Berlioz' Miss Smithson as Ophelia?) the connection is obscure. This is lighter in substance, but, with imagination and a fine touch capable of sustaining a single melodic note for four slow measures above soft chords, it is a thing of beauty. The F major religioso passage sounds like a Christmas carol, remembered by a death-bed. Another unique coda.

No 7 in c♯, Op 27:1. This and the c minor nocturne, No 13, are often considered the greatest and with justice, as both are larger in scope, with boldly contrasting sections, and a profundity of feeling seldom plumbed even by the melancholy poet. Here the intensity is created at once by a wide-meshed bass in which the tonic is always unaccented, under a simple melody that rises on the harmonic minor scale, and descends on the melodic. The più mosso continues to gather speed and power to an exultant climax in A flat; then drops to an ominous muttering, before bursting into a lively mazurka theme. This too builds to an acme of fff chords, and a unique declamatory octave cadenza in the bass. The return holds the usual surprises.

No 8 in D♭, Op 27:2. More serene than the great minor nocturnes, this one is also fine, and though lacking a contrasting section, rings all the changes on its single bass figure, and its long sweeping melody. Full of Chopinesque fioratura, difficult to play and maintan the mood.

No 9 in B, Op 32:1. Shorter and somewhat easier but rather repetitious and square, this nocturne has a grand ending, that might well have been written "after a performance of Hamlet," with its ghostly tapping bass, its histrionic chordal gestures, and declamatory theme.

No 10 in A♭, Op 32:2. Also rather square and plodding, much of this might have been written by John Field or Weber, with its harmony limited to tonic-diminished-dominant. There is a 12/8 mid-section, agitated and restless, and some deft retouching of the melodic profile on its return.

No 11 in g, Op 37:1. Imagination and a fine touch can bring this to life. The chorale-like passage in E flat should be più mosso, to allow for rubato, phrasing, rolled chords, and the four fermati before the return.

No 12 in G, Op 37:2. It is a pity this one strayed

into the book of nocturnes (its place might well have been filled by a couple of the etudes). It is a lovely barcarolle, with a rocking undulating bass, gliding Neapolitan 3rds and 6ths for a melody; and a lilting gondolier's canzonna in the middle (più mosso, not meno mosso). The cruise may well be nocturnal, in shimmering moonlight; but this should certainly not sound like Liszt's "Gondola Lugubre e Funebre," and melancholy must give way to serene quiet joy.

No 13 in c, Op 48:1. Here one may vent all the pent up brimming sorrow. The opening tempo can hardly be too slow, and every LH chord and RH arabesque must be weighted with grief. Another unique mid-section, and the screwing up of the passions in the return by a doppio movimento (read più mosso, sempre agitato) make this perhaps the greatest of all.

No 14 in f#, Op 48:2. Nostalgia rather than grief seems to be the mood of this exquisite nocturne. The molto più lento in 3/4, Db, is as grand as a Bach sarabande, and quite similar, with its alternating chords and arabesques.

No 15 in f, Op 55:1. The next two nocturnes are dedicated to Miss Jane Stirling, and we can perhaps detect something of FC's feeling about this enigmatic nemesis and her austere northern island by the plodding, pedestrian nature of the pieces. But don't be put off too soon; FC's inspiration awakens on the third page and he rises to his old self with new devices that continue to amaze. For a not too advanced (but loving) pupil.

No 16 in Eb, Op 56:2. Lacking a contrasting movement this one becomes repetitious in spite of some very imaginative variations on the theme and the introduction of counter themes.

No 17 in B, Op 62:1. Nicknamed "Tuberoses," after Chopin's favorite flower, this has rather a forced hot-house air about it, as if the composer would not give up, in spite of his aching chest. All the same it is 'the real guy," though pale. It is to be played with drawn shades and lowered lights, wallowed-in and inhaled.

No 18 in E, Op 62:2. Grief in grandeur returns with this nocturne. It becomes intense and tortuous in the mid-section (and a bit over-extended) but its Chopinisms are not to be missed by any devout Chopinese. Incredible though it seems, FC devises still another unique coda, meltingly melodious.

No 19 in e, Op 72:1 (post). Composed in the same year as that "hit," No 2, this has all Chopin's finest qualities, before the inflation of fame or the attrition of illness affected him.

Nocturne in c♯. A Nocturne in a♭, recently published but written when FC was 17, is not worth bothering about. The lento con gran espressione in c♯, also recently published, was probably intended as a sketch (two pages only). Though it is rather disjunct, it has qualities that make it worth revival.

Mazurkas. The simple peasant dance which FC heard and watched and danced, from childhood, and began making up at the keyboard as soon as he could play, became the form in which he cast more than 50 of his piano pieces, thus leading the way for Bartók and many ethnic-oriented 20th-century composers. Fortunately the mazurka is a richly varied dance. A vivid description of the impression it made on Franz Liszt on his visit to Poland is found in his early biography of Chopin.

Though never merely transcriptions or arrangements, Chopin's 52 mazurkas are very authentic, rhythmically and melodically. His own unique chromatic harmony, so calculated to express intense emotion, raises these dances to the level of an art form by intensifying the native "zal," that capacity for being both sad and glad at the same time.

They span FC's life, from age 15 to his death. Two are only one page in length; one is only half a page, and has a D.S. senza fine, as if, like the peasant dance, it could break off at any point, when dancers or fiddlers grew tired. There were often drums and bagpipes, and a drone bass is common in the trio (Haydn got his from Hungarian peasants). Many are five pages in length, and as richly varied as a chain of Viennese waltzes. Only two or three descend to the level of the "salon waltz" for the titilation of bored Parisians. Most of them have a wistful intensity that demands a fine empathy on the part of the player, for communication. FC had a genius for original introductions, transitions and codas, and these, sometimes framing rather banal themes, lift the music to an inspired level.

In the collected edition of 52, the last ten were published posthumously. No 49 is the last piece he ever wrote, but most of other 10 are early, therefore fresher and closer to the soil. A good place to begin is with these (No 47 in a is my favorite among them). The pianist must play all the infinite variety of dotted figures with the utmost crispness, distinguishing sharply between 8ths and 16ths. A constant shading of tempo and dynamics, following the contour of the melody, is also essential. Above all remember that they are rural, out-door dances, but the uninhibited expression of a highly emotional people. Technically they are, with two or three exceptions, all moderate or easy, but all require mature, imaginative musicianship.

Mazurka No 3 in E, Op 6:3. Among so many, one can only suggest a few that seem outstanding. No 3 is characteristic of one type of vigorous mazurka, opening with drums and drone, and a bass theme.

No 5 in F, Op 7:1. This has always been popular (also has bagpipe trio). It makes a good pair with No 7 in f, as the minor ones have more of the wistful "zal."

No 10 in B♭, Op 17:1; and No 11 in e, Op 17:2. Another fine contrasting pair of mazurkas, the B♭ joyously zestful, with a mid-section that plays off a 2/4 bass against a triple theme. The e minor has sobs beneath the singing, and requires great sensitivity for the numerous subtly varied repeats.

No 13 in e, Op 17:4. This one, in the Lydian mode (F major without a flat) has a hauntingly beautiful Middle-Eastern wail that has earned it the nickname "The Little Jew."

No 20 in D♭, Op 30:3. Another boisterous one in major key, followed by a gem in C♯ (a good group). The second must be as restrained as the first is uninhibited, and the wide rolled bass chords must be as light as a guitar (or balalaika).

No 36 in a, Op 59:1. This was included in the Van Cliburn contest numbers in 1964. A good test of rhythmic precision, ornament playing, and imaginative melodic nuance.

No 39 in B, Op 63:1. A favorite of the author, this begins in bold and bumptious manner, but soon shifts to a

teasing, clinging theme that leads to a change of key, and a
game-like question-answer section. The coda introduces an
exquisite chromatic melisma (in 6/8) smorzando, with two
shouts at the end, to remind us it's all in fun.

No 49 in f, Op 68:4. A welcome new edition of this
mazurka, written during FC's last months, has just appeared,
edited by Jan Ekler who has added an entire new section, giving it a small rondo form. Worth having. (EBM pub)

Impromptu in A♭, Op 29. Four works bear the name impromptu; all are good for teaching and recital use. The first and
last are similar in texture and form (a-b-a), though the Fantasie-Impromptu is more popular. Op 29 is a good study in
finger dexterity, and sustained melody; not difficult.

Impromptu in F♯, Op 36. A larger work, this impromptu requires maturity for the building up of the introductory andantino, the broad but somewhat square D major section, and dexterity for the passage in 64th notes.

Impromptu in G♭, Op 51. Similar compound triplet
figuration, but lacking a contrasting slow section. Less often played, though the equal of the others.

Fantasie-Impromptu in c♯, Op 66. In spite of the
"Chasing Rainbows" song (the theme is repeated a little too
often even in the original!), this remains a good piece, with
its effective coda, combining both principal and second
themes.

Fantasia in f, Op 49. This is considered one of FC's
finest works by pianists and music "analysts," but has never
been very popular with audiences, lacking a big melodic line.
When the player brings to it a deep empathy, and complete
technical mastery, it is a powerful work. The opening marcia should begin misterioso, like a rumination; but the march
that follows must not be square and military; rather a bold
bardic hymn. For the "analysts," this is a very fine free
sonata allegro, and the march is by way of introduction. The
real allegro begins with the ₵, returning to the mysterious
opening mood, beginning slowly in the depths gradually rising and doubling the tempo. The agitato must be repressed
and anguished, but leads into a second theme in major key,
that is light lyric and lilting. This song is never given a
chance to finish, but each time it recurs breaks into a sequence of arabesques. Still a third theme, a chromatic oc-

tave melody wailing down the scale, ends in a bold affirma-
tive E♭ major bridge, then bursts into another hymn of epic
grandeur, with a striding martial bass.   The development
which follows breaks off for a contrasting lento sostenuto.
Though only one page in length, it is one of the finest and
most poignant pages ever penned by FC.   All of the material is recapitulated, with a lingering adagio cadenza, like the
minstrel, reluctant to end the tragic tale.   The ending is
quiet, all passion spent (one pedal throughout) till the final
bold sweeps of the lyre.

Valses.   When FC became the lion of Paris society,
the waltz was the popular dance of the day having replaced
the more stately minuet.   Chopin wrote more than a dozen
for his pupils and their salons.   Some are easy-going and
as pensive as the mazurka; some quite brilliant and fast, perhaps played by the master.   They do not show him at his
best, because he is deprived of those unique broken-chord
basses, with their very chromatic harmonies.   They are
still very usable.

Op 18 in E♭; Op 34: No 1 in A♭, No 2 in a.   Op
18 is an effective brilliant waltz, as is the first of Op 34.
The second of Op 34 is a popular favorite of the expressive
type, with opening theme in the tenor.

Op 42 in A♭.   Perhaps the finest, featuring a trill introduction, hemiola between the hands, a chain of contrasting
waltzes and a brilliant close.   (A "four-minute waltz.")

Op 46: No 1 in D♭, No 2 in c♯, No 3 in A♭.   The
famous "Minute Waltz" needs no comment; and the second in
c♯ of the slow lingering type, is almost equally popular.
The third in the set is another bold and brilliant one, with a
bass solo for middle section.

Op 69: No 1 in A♭, No 2 in b.   Easier waltzes,
early-period Chopin, quite chromatic and attractive.

Op 70: Nos 1, 2, 3.   Three more early works, all
fluent and pianistic.   The 1st in G♭ combines the brilliant
and the sad, and is quite effective.

Early works.   For the "complete Chopinzee," who
must know the worst as well as the best, there are three
rondos, Op 1, 5, 6; a set of variations, Op 12; a bolero,
Op 19; a tarantelle, Op 43 and three eccossaises.   If they

had been written by some of Chopin's contemporaries, the musical archeologists would probably be featuring them on their programs now. Since Chopin himself so far surpassed them in his many other works, they may be disregarded by pianists who are also musicians.

Sonatas. The sonata, which reached its peak, both in quantity (43 by Haydn, 32 by Beethoven) and in quality at the hands of the four Viennese masters, languished after the 19th century and though some 20th-century neo-classic writers have gotten up to 10, a single sonata is about all we can expect from contemporary composers. FC wrote three, two of which are still popular repertory items.

Sonata No 1 in c, Op 4. No 1, written while FC was still a student in Warsaw, is unattractive, and Chopin himself later suppressed its publication. The 5/4 Larghetto is rewarding to play, as it anticipates so many later works.

Sonata No 2 in bb, Op 35. Highly regarded by pianists and popular with audiences each of the four movts is a masterpiece. Full musicianship is required both for the technical problems, and for the restrained, tragic mood of the opening and the famous "Funeral March." Between them is a brilliant and difficult movement, misnamed scherzo by this intense, humorless composer. The beautiful Db major threnody of the marche Funebre's trio must be kept light and singing. The finale, pp and unison throughout, is unique, and can be a fitting close, if kept eerie and ghostly.

Sonata No 3 in b, Op 58. Full of beautiful passages, this work is difficult to bring off. The discursive, sprawling development sections of the first and fourth movts can be played quite fast.

CHOU, WEN CHUNG (China-USA), 1923- .

The Willows Are New (1958). An oriental composer who has achieved a viable synthesis of Eastern and Western styles, at its best in small ensembles featuring coloristic timbre contrasts. His one published piano piece uses a classical Chinese "Ch'ia" (the original "Koto") melody, and takes its title from a T'ang poem. It ranges over the entire keyboard, with wisps of the tune punctuated by augmented octaves, which must be brushed with the utmost lightness to

suggest "an out-of tune ch'in," while the curious treatment
of the theme suggests the gradations of the calligraphic line.
Exotic and effective. Requires musicianship. Dif

CLEMENTI, MUZIO (It-GB), 1752-1832.

Noted in his youth as a pianist, and in later life in
England as teacher, publisher and piano manufacturer, MC
is known today mostly for his technical studies, "Gradus ad
Parnassum," and for his student sonatinas. Overshadowed
by Beethoven, he wrote twice as many sonatas (64 in all),
several of which are worthy of survival. His texture is
similar to that of Beethoven, though he experimented with
cyclic form, leit-motifs, and program content.

Sonata in f#, Op 25:3. Brilliant three-movt work,
revived by Horowitz. Mod Dif

Sonata in b, Op 40:2. Large two-movt work, both
movements combining an adagio with a fast section. The
Beethoven texture and development technic are apparent, and
only the melodic and harmonic systems lack distinction.
Mod

Sonata in Bb, Op 47:2. This brilliant two-movt work
was played by the composer for the Emperor Franz Josef.
Mozart was present, and borrowed the opening theme for his
"Magic Flute." MC, who outlived Mozart by 40 years, was
in turn influenced by him. Mod Dif

COPLAND, AARON (USA), 1900- .

A composer whose influence is much larger than his
output. His blend of folk, jazz and classical elements has
produced popular ballets and orchestra suites. A unique triadic harmony, lucid but artful, is a hallmark of his style:
but his piano works often sound contrived and lacking in spontaneity.

Scherzo Humoristique (1920). 'The Cat and the
Mouse." Fragmentary in form, but pianistic, and great fun
to play. Mod

Passacaglia (1922).   Dedicated to his teacher, Mlle. Boulanger, this is a beautiful large-scale solo, basically tonal, but with haunting, ambiguous unresolved harmony, and highly diversified variations.   Dif

Variations (1930).   Highly original piece, austere and acerbic, but exciting for audience and player.   Its tightly coiled four-note motto (B-A-C-H inverted?) is the thematic material for the entire 10-min work.   Analyses are found in Eschmann, J. Smith, and there are numerous recordings. Dif

Sonata (1941).   This 29-page work reverses the usual order and frames a fast movt with two slow ones, which proves somewhat anti-climactic.   Spare chords of 3rds and 9ths in wide slow skips alternate with a scurrying tremolando figure that starts on a single trill, and widens with each repetition, till it covers an octave.   Uningratiating to play or hear.   Mod Dif

Fantasia (1957).   The concept of a fantasy is carried out by AC in a single continuous movt, 30 min in length, with a rondo-like structure.   A wide-spaced ringing 10-note tone-row answered by quartal chords, using all 12 tones, provides the material for the opening and following episodes. The tightly coiled four-note motto of the Variations, and the scurrying tremolando again appear.   An episode in moderato 3/4, marked "delicate, uncertain--poetic, drifting," leads to a climactic passage of trills and incremental scales over chords, followed by a lengthy 2-v scherzando in irregular meters.   The tone-row chime occurs again above glissandi; and for coda the row and its inversion begin at the extremes of the keyboard and meet in the center.   All the elements of a great work seem to be here, but the player senses the lack of a viable keyboard style, and the ear misses the big melodic line and the urgent, progressing, stirring harmony of great music.   Dif

Four Piano Blues.   Light-hearted movts in contrasting jazz styles: Freely poetic, Soft and languid, Muted and sensuous, With bounce.   Mod

COWELL, HENRY (USA), 1897- .

Once admired for their novelty, these works are now

of more interest historically than musically.   HC, who may
be remembered by future generations for his orchestral
pieces, is credited with inventing several tonal devices for
the piano which actually antedated him.   Tone-clusters appear in Ives' Concord Sonata, and F.W. Rust was already
reaching inside the piano for effects, back in Beethoven's
day.   In Cowell these become an end in themselves, and his
musical ideas seldom match the novelties.   He has a widespread influence as an editor and champion of new music,
in the USA, Latin America, and in Europe.

The Tides of Manaunaun (1912).   Already experimenting at the age of 15, HC calls for one-octave and two-octave
clusters, played with palm of hand, or the forearm, on the
white keys of the bass, while the RH plays a broad arc of
melody in D♭, to suggest the ebb and flow of tides.   Mod

Tiger (1928).   Cowell's European tours were sensational, and this was first published in Russia.   This ferocious allegro uses dissonant chords in percussive primitive
patterns, building to tone-clusters using both arms.   Out of
this roar of sound, a chord (played silently) is floated (in a
manner discovered by Schumann a hundred years ago).   Dif

Aeolian Harp (1923).   A one-page pedal study, with
one hand depressing chords in a rather commonplace progres-
sion, silently, while the other sweeps the strings inside, or
plucks arpeggios, in the manner of a harp.   Demure ances-
tor of many later and more imaginative works.   Mod E

The Banshee (1925).   This requires an assistant to
hold down the damper pedal (a wooden wedge does as well)
while the "player" stands at the curve and produces single,
double and triple glissandi in 12 different ways, emitting a
wild wailing sound.   Rather ho-hum.   It at least reveals
where to place the credit (or blame?) for much of what
passes for "keyboard" music today.

CRAWFORD (SEEGER), RUTH (USA), 1901-1953.

Composer interested in contemporary trends, folk-
music, socio-political developments, who would no doubt
have joined Women's Liberation, had she lived longer.
Chamber music was her specialty before her marriage to
the folksinger, Pete Seeger, and her untimely death of can-
cer.

Study in Mixed Accents (1929). Brilliant 1-min work
in a single wide-ranging line of rapid equal notes (with a
tone-row sound), well-deployed between the hands and given
shape and distinction by the surprising accents. Mod Dif

Nine Preludes. These are so finely wrought and original that they should be made available to pianists (Nos 6 to
9 pub by NME). Mostly slow, introspective, atmospheric,
they have surprise climaxes and codas, and a remarkable variety of keyboard devices in a freely-tonal texture. Only No
8 is fast, a toccata, but many build to powerful acme with
pedal-points, cumulative ostinato figures, transferred from
high treble to deep bass. Best is No 5, with throbbing hypnotic chord beats, surrounded by melismatic filigree. Mod
Dif

CRESTON, PAUL (USA), 1906- .

Important composer of symphonic works and chamber
music for rare instruments, PC carries over into his few
piano works the big melodic line, a fruity modern harmony,
sprightly rhythms, and some virtuoso display.

Five Two-Part Inventions, Op 14, (1937). Studies experimenting with freely chromatic writing in two voices.
Rather over-extended. Mod

Prelude and Dance No 1, 2, Op 29. Improvisory opening, freely modulating with opulent chords, gathering momentum for the rhythmic dances that follow. Mod

Six Preludes, Op 38. Diversified set of pieces contrasting meters, rhythms, piano figuration. No 2 in D♭ is
attractive. Mod

CRUMB, GEORGE (USA), 1929- .

Five Pieces (1962). This highly imaginative musical
innovator, derives all five of these pieces from a single
three-note cell. The entire set is played inside the piano on
the strings, with pizzicato and glissando effects. Mod

CUMMING, RICHARD (USA), 1928- .

Music for theatre has occupied this Shanghai-born, Manila reared, California-trained composer.

24 Preludes (1969). Written for John Browning, who stipulated that they should be "hard," these are very easy to take, and do not sound difficult under Browning's fingers. They follow the Chopin key cycle, and are tonally oriented, and closer to that composer than to some of the later sets. One is based on a 12-tone row, and No 12 is for RH alone, No 15 for LH. All are pianistic and fluent, but few are original and many so derivative that one could pin a name on them. Perhaps it is that Shanghai background, as originality was never a virtue in Chinese art, and landscape paintings are usually "after--" some great master. Mod Dif

CZERNY, CARL (Aus), 1791-1857.

Variations on "La Ricordanza" by Rode, Op 33; Variations on a Haydn Theme, Op 73; Toccata in C, Op 92. Members of the KAA (Keyboard Athletes Association) are trying to convince us that there is music among these dumbbells and calisthenics, left behind by the greatest coach of all time. Young body-builders may wish to try heaving some of them off the ground, but it takes a Horowitz to do so; and even then, what we admire is not the music, but the strength, endurance and training of Mr. Universe, and his audacity in attempting it. Non-members may safely stash the lot in the waste-basket, along with Op 299, 399, 740 (Schools of Velocity, Dexterity, Finger-finishing, et cetera).

D'ALBERT, EUGEN (GB-Ger), 1864-1932.

Not yet discovered by the grave-diggers, this phenomenal pianist left two concertos (the second is best), and numerous suites that may one day be heard again, then again interred.

Suite Op 1. Though Baroque titles adorn five pieces, the music is elegantly late romantic. Mod

Four Pieces, Op 16.   Similar to above: titled Waltz,
Scherzo, Intermezzo, Ballade.

DALLAPICCOLA, LUIGI (It), 1904- .

This distinguished composer of choral, operatic and
instrumental works has added little to the piano repertoire
that is significant.

Sonata canonica sui Capricci di Paganini in Bb (1942).
This provides tricky reading matter on three staves and a
few odd hand-crossings, mostly anticipated by Liszt and
Schumann in their superior variations on the same themes.
Mod

Quaderno musicale di Annalibera (1952).   Such a fine
(if not very original) idea, the "Notebook of Annalibera"
(LD's daughter); and such clever titles: Simbolo: Accenti--
Contrapunctus primus; Linee--Contrapunctus secundus; Fregi
[Friezes]--Andante amoroso e Contrapunctus tertius; Ritmi--
Colore--Ombre; Quartina.   The names are worthy of Satie;
and a good idea would be to print them on a program, and,
in tiny print below, put (in Dada fashion) "not to be played."
For the sound emerging from these serial compositions is
so anemic, drab and banal as to be bathetic.   The other joke
is better.   Mod E

DEBUSSY, CLAUDE (Fr), 1862-1915.

This composer was a one-man revolution, creating
single-handedly a music with a new aim, content, texture,
which we often call Impressionist after the contemporary art
movement.   Few innovators have maintained such a high
quality level, and left so many fine works.   Almost everything he wrote is still played and still gives pleasure today.
CD, like Franck, Fauré and many other composers, requires a special mystique--cool, objective, atmospheric
mood-evoking--and unless the player has it, he had better
stick to the three B's.   Now that the original copyrights have
expired, many new editions are appearing, not as handsome
as the out-size folded sheets of Durand & Cie, but far more
durable.

Two Arabesques (1888): No 1 in A, No 2 in G.
Early but mature and pianistic in a late-romantic style. The
name is suggestive, as No 1 describes great arcs in RH and
LH, which break up into undulating, descending whorls. No
2 is more square and dance-like, the small curlicues falling
like a series of drop-shaped motifs in an "Arab-esque" pais-
ley pattern. Good recital pieces. Mod

Reverie. Already CD is blurring the edges of melody
and rhythm and building chords on the 9th. Popular. Mod E

Valse Romantique; Valse: Le Plus que Lent. An
early and a late work, similar in their graceful treatment of
the salon valse. The second title would seem to lampoon the
popular valse lent ("slower than slow") though the piece is
not humorous. Both are long. Mod

Suite Bergamasque (1890). Like many of his contemporaries, CD was fascinated with Italian commedia del arte
(from Bergamo). The prelude is brilliant but easy; the menuet and passepied are archaic and evocative. Clair de Lune
has taken its place as an all-time hit, beside another famous
Moonlight piece. Mod

Pour le Piano (1901). Ten years separate this suite
from that above. The 1901, though not typical CD, is a brilliant concert work, pianistic and effective in the prelude;
stately and ethereal in the sarabande (here the real CD begins to appear); scintillating in the neo-classic 2-v toccata.
Mod-Dif

Masques. Another brilliant (and lengthy) period piece.
To understand this and the next, one should become acquainted with CD's stunning song-setting of Verlaine's poem "Mando-
line." Mod Dif

L'Isle Joyeuse. Rococo aristocracy at play (inspired
by Watteau's painting, "Embarkation for Cythere"). Mando-
lins, dances, love-making. Virtuoso piece demanding both
musical and technical maturity. V Dif

Estampes [Prints] (1903). Now fully master of his
new blurred floating harmony, free-wheeling-rhythms and
tiered structure, CD abandons generic titles and makes each
piece a picturesque evocation of a scene, mood, time, place,
scent.

Pagodes. This memory of the Javanese gamelan at
the Paris Expo 1890 (13 years before), captures the booming
gongs in a big duple beat, and the tinkling tiny metalophones
playing the pentatonic "flower-parts." CD adds his own exotic piano "washes" derived from these same figures. His
new three-tiered texture (requiring three staves) also illustrates the structures of the title. Exotic and effective.
Mod Dif

La Soirée dans Grenade. Time and place vividly
evoked in a long difficult habanera, rich in melodic and
rhythmic variations, including guitar chords, flamenco wailing, castanet clicking and stomping. Dif

Jardins sous la Pluie. What Manet, Monet and Japanese prints did with color, CD here does with piano sound,
in a light staccato, toccata style, building to a radiant sun-
burst climax. Mature. Mod Dif

Images, Set I (1905): Reflets dans l'Eau. An
uneven suite, the first piece is one of CD's most original
and successful; the other two, of lesser interest. "Reflections on the Water" requires superior technic for its cascad-
ing arpeggios, delicate control for dynamics ranging from
ppp to ff, and sensitive imagination. All tempo changes in
CD are carefully indicated, and he abhorred wild rubatos.
Dif

Hommage à Rameau. One of the many homage
pieces the French are so fond of, this has little to do with
Rameau or the Baroque clavecin. It is a slow complex and
long sarabande, less attractive than the one in Pour le Piano. The short one to Haydn is also better. Dif

Mouvement. Though CD later played down the
Impressionist inspiration for his music, his finest pieces
are those with picturesque titles. This is a rather inconse-
quential Etude. Mod Dif

Images, Set II (1907): Cloches à travers les
feuilles. Seldom played, No 1 in this suite is one of the
finest examples of Debussy's unique tiered style, with three
levels of whole-tone scales going at the same time in different tempi. Unique bell effects, "through the leaves," with
intricate fluttering figures. Dif

Et la lune descend sur la temple qui fut. Intriguing title--"and the moon sets on the ruined temple"--
for a disappointing piece, difficult to project. Named by
Louis Laloy after hearing it; one wonders how many other
titles are mere appendages. Mod Dif

Poissons d'or. Here the title came first, and
it is CD at his most inventive, with overlapping tremolo figures under floating melodies in 3rds, darting, pouncing
chords, liquid arpeggios, and a superb coda. Inspired by a
Japanese print, (CD collected them), it can sound more like
the Loch Ness monster than a goldfish, unless the player
has a flawless technic and utmost control of dynamics.
V Dif

Children's Corner (1908.) A set of six exquisite miniatures written for CD's five-year old, Claude-Emma, called
in the dedication, "Little Cabbage Head." The titles are in
English (supplied by the Governess?). Though not for children to play, they are technically undemanding (except for
No 4), and worthy of devoted attention.

Dr. Gradus ad Parnassum. Spoofing a child's
struggles with Clementi, this builds a glorious toccata finish.
Mod Dif

Jimbo's Lullaby. "Sweet, and a little awk-
ward," are the directions for the lullaby for the toy elephant
(Jumbo?). A lumbering pentatonic theme punctuated with an
irregular beat using CD's favorite mashed 2nds. Later a
counter-theme must be brought out and contrasts of staccato
and legato strictly observed. Little pedal. Tongue-in-cheek
humor. Mod

Serenade for the Doll. Another of CD's genial
mandolin pieces, to be played una corda throughout, but with
very little sostenuto pedal, so as not to spoil the plectrum
effect. Tempo changes are clearly indicated. Mod Dif

The Snow Is Dancing. An exquisite atmospher-
ic etude with a haunting melody, requiring good technic, utmost control and imagination. Dif

The Little Shepherd. A doll this may have
been, but CD's two-page gem evokes a whole landscape.
Again con sordino and never rising above p, but with an infinite variety of nuance and rubato. Rests must be counted,

as well as notes, and CD warns "conserve the rhythm."
Mod Dif

The Golliwog's Cakewalk. So popular that it
is murdered on hundreds of recitals each year. All necessary indications for a scintillating and humorous performance
are on the pages. The jibe at Wagner, with the love-theme
from Tristan "avec une grande emotion," followed by muted
giggles, adds to the comedy. Mod

Preludes, Book I. Following in the footsteps of Bach,
and Chopin (who eliminated the fugues), CD wrote 24 preludes.
No arbitrary key system is followed, however, and the real
titles appear at the end of each Prelude, in parentheses, as
if to suggest that the impression grows from the music and
not the reverse. Since, however, the character of each prelude is epitomized in the title, the performer should be thoroughly familiar with the connotations and sources.

No 1: Danseuses de Delphes. A slow hypnotic dance,
like a sculptured frieze of Grecian dancers. The chromatic
chord progressions suggest a dancer's glissade. A firm 8th-
note pulse must be felt throughout, freedom resulting from
CD's irregular measures. Mod Dif

No 2: Voiles. This title may mean either "snails"
or "veils" (the former seems more suggestive). Written in
whole-tone scale throughout except for six meas of black-key
pentatonic, it requires both delicacy and boldness, and much
rubato (all scrupulously indicated). Mod Dif

No 3: Le vent dans le plaine. "The Wind on the
Plains" must be "as light as possible," with rapid whispering susurrus of minor 2nds and octaves, and an alto melody,
broken by sudden leaping chords and trills. Mod Dif

No 4: Les sons et les parfums tournent dans l'air
du soir. The Beaudelaire line (from "Fleurs du Mal"),
"Sounds and perfumes mingle on the evening air," labels a
rather voluptuous, decadent chordal prelude. Subtle pedalling required, as in all of CD (none of which is indicated).
Mod Dif

No 5: Les collines d'Anacapri. Shepherds' pipes,
tinkling goat-bells, laughter, pursuit, echoes of song from
nearby Naples, a lively tarantelle, make this impression of
the back-side of the isle of Capri one of the most brilliant

of the Preludes.   Mature musicianship.   Mod Dif

No 6: Des pas sur la neige.   "Footsteps in the
Snow," one of CD's few sad pieces, has a stumbling mesmer-
ic beat under a haunting tune.   Sotto voce and pp throughout.
Simple but profound.   Mod Dif

No 7: Ce qu'a vu le vent d'Ouest.   This is a Debussy
piece for those who dislike Debussy.   Uncharacteristic 7ths
and triadic arpeggios in a virtuosic typhoon off the Atlantic.
(What did the West wind see?)   In spite of the directions:
"plaintive and distant, strident, anxious, furious," it ends
up as a brilliant show piece.   Technically the most difficult
of all the preludes, (except No 24?).   Dif

No 8: La Fille au cheveux de lin.   This most popular of all preludes has a Scots lilt, and the sweetness of the
pre-Raphaelite "Blessed Damosel."   Extreme care is needed
for timing and a great delicacy of nuance.   Not for children.
Mod

No 9: La Sérénade interrompré.   One of CD's many
effective Spanish numbers, the staccato must be secco to
contrast with the pedalled song phrases.   The humor of the
slammed shutter, or the night-watchman, need not be exaggerated.   Mod

No 10: La Cathédrale engloutie.   Another perennial
favorite, which vividly evokes, with its parallel organum,
bell-tones, rolling waves, the sunken island that emerges
once a year at midnight, dripping in the moonlight.   Why two
climaxes?   Seven min.   Mature but technically simple.   Mod

No 11: La Danse du Puck.   A most imaginative and
spritely piece.   (Read "A Midsummer Night's Dream" for the
character.)   Not 2/4 but 4/8, with a steady rapid 8th-note
pulse.   Puck is teasing, never bumptious.   Mod Dif

No 12: Minstrels.   Not the Mediaeval juggler, but
the black-face music hall clown, this must never be heavy-
handed, though the mock-sentimental snatch of song can be
drawn out.   Mod

Preludes, Book II.   No 1: Brouillards.   The title,
"Mists," allows CD to carry even further his blurring of
melody, harmony and rhythm.   Swirling and muted throughout.   Much pedal.   Mod

No 2: <u>Feuilles mortes</u>. Marked lent et melancholique, "Dead leaves" resembles No 4, Book I in its loose chordal harmony over wisps of melody. Mod

No 3: <u>Puerto del vino</u>. Another superb Spanish piece from a Frenchman. Meticulous attention to CD's dynamic and rhythmic markings, which call for "extreme violence, sweet passion, distant, graceful," plus free rubato and restrained fire, for a curtain-ringer. Mod Dif

No 4: <u>"Les fées sont d'exquises danseuses."</u> This must be as sheer as gossamer, yet volatile, iridescent and lilting, to convince that "Fairies are exquisite dancers." Mod Dif

No 5: <u>Bruyéres.</u> Another idyllic landscape ("The Heath"), demure, yet teasing and playful. CD eschews MM marks in Book II, except here (66 seems too slow). Mod

No 6: <u>"General Lavine--eccentric."</u> As antidote to Wagner's Ring Cycle, CD watched "the celebrated American juggler," and hit him off in a comic portrait. Mocking throughout. Imaginative. Mod

No 7: <u>La terrasse des audiences du clair de lune.</u> "Terrace for Moonlight Audiences," is in a class with the great Images and Estampes. Tiers of chords, cascades of moonlight, pulsing bass gongs, one above the other. Requires mature musicianship. Mod Dif

No 8: <u>Ondine.</u> Like the painters, CD was fascinated by water. The legendary water-sprite is a scherzo, music for a ballerina, full of witchery, insouciance, grace. Fine pair for Ravel's shimmering showpiece of the same name. Mod Dif

No 9: <u>Hommage à S. Pickwick, Esq., P.P.M.P.C.</u> Another comic portrait, which has great fun with a pompous cantus firmus on "God Save the King," a jaunty walking tune, a little whistled air, soft and far away. Mod

No 10: <u>Canope.</u> Canope was an ancient Egyptian city which gave its name to burial jars. This is admired by Debussy specialists; but for most it is rather ho-hum; slow chords with two haunting wisps of melody. Mod

No 11: <u>Les Tierce alternée.</u> Properly an etude (and

better than many of the 12), this is a brilliant study in alternate 3rds, which might well have borne a more poetic title. Mod Dif

No 12: Feux d'artifice. A dazzling virtuoso finale in which arcs of jet-propelled arpeggios, sputtering trills in mashed 2nds, explosive chords, glittering glissandi evoke a gorgeous illumination over Paris, dying out with a wisp of the Marseillaise. Dif

Twelve Etudes, Books I, II. Three years before he died, CD published these, dedicated to the memory of Chopin. A summation of his considerable contribution to piano technic, they contain much of worth, though the didactic form and generic titles seem to have inhibited his imagination. "Find your own fingering," CD wisely advises, but some pedal marks by him would have been welcome.

Book I, No 1: Pour les "cinq doits" d'après M. Czerny. The same idea as Dr. Gradus (Children's Corner) but rather labored and long. Brilliant finish. Dif

No 2: Pour les tierces. Good practice, but Prelude No 11, Book II is more musical. Dif

No 3: Pour les quartes. Both white and black-key passages imaginatively explored. Dif

No 4: Pour les six. Begins and ends lento with rapid rubato passages; elegant. Mod

No 5: Pour les octaves. "Joyous and freely rhythmic," a stylized valse with some rather pedestrian passage work (directions for use of pedals here). Dif

No 6: Pour les huit doigts. The thumbless scales of the clavecinists (CD's footnote says that to use the thumb would be acrobatic). Amusing. Mod

Book II, No 7: Pour les dégres chromatique. Little musical value, but a good exercise.

No 8: Pour les agréments. CD considered dedicating the series to his other hero, Couperin; and here pays tribute with Baroque ornaments. A barcarolle, but requiring precise division of beats.

No 9: <u>Pour les notes répétées</u>. Another tribute to
the clavecin in a toccata-like scherzo.

No 10: <u>Pour les sonorités opposées</u>. The contrasts
of dynamics, legato-staccato, layers of sound so basic to
all CD, restated.

No. 11: <u>Pour les arpèges composés</u>. Perhaps the
most musical, with touches of humor, a "luminous" middle
section, and soft ending.

No 12: <u>Pour les accords</u>. Brilliant, anticipating
Bartók and Stravinsky.

<u>Six Epigraphs Antiques</u>. The titles of these are so
quaint, it is a pity the music does not live up to them. One
might print them all, but play only the first and last, which
are the best. They were arranged by CD for four-hands,
well done. 1, To invoke Pan, god of the summer wind;
2, For a nameless tomb; 3, That the night be propitious;
4, For Croatian dancers; 5, For the Egyptian; and 6, Giving thanks for the morning rain.

<u>Hommage à Haydn</u>. Written in the centennial year,
this little known work is attractive, moderately difficult.
The arbitrary anagram of Haydn's name--ti, la, re, re,
sol--is developed in four pages of spirited and idiosyncratic
writing. Mod

DELIUS, FREDERICK (GB), 1863-1934.

This English contemporary of Debussy wrote little
for piano, though his rhapsodic concerto is worth revival.

<u>Three Preludes</u>. Simple, lyrical, demure short, they
sound very dated and tepid in their timid harmonic experiments. Mod E

<u>Five Piano Pieces</u>. Derivations from Grieg and De-
bussy are apparent, and the short simple works are a rather insignificant contribution to the repertoire. Mod E

DELLO JOIO, NORMAN (USA), 1913- .

Prolific composer of operas, symphonies, choruses, ballets and chamber music has the following pieces for piano.

Suite for Piano (1940). Four short contrasting movts, the second in jazz rhythm; the opening a quiet cantabile; the third, impressionistic; the close, bravura. Mod

Prelude for a Young Musician (1944). Pianistic accompanied melody, varied rhythms, tonal but wayward. Mod

Prelude for a Young Dancer (1947). Longer, more brilliant, all the ingredients for a fine recital piece are here, but they somehow fail to live up to the attractive names. Mod

Sonata No 1 (1943). Basically tonal but chromatic, chordal chorale prelude over sustained bass; 4-v canon, expressive; the boisterous capriccio requires a mature technic. Mod Dif

Sonata No 2 (1943). Percussive, dissonant, à la early Bartók, three movts, each building to an acme. Dif

Sonata No 3 (1948). Lighter-textured, linear, key-anchored. First movt, five variations on Gregorian chant; sparkling presto e leggiero; adagio, expressive and tuneful; exuberant finale, vivo e ritmico. Mod

Nocturne in E; Nocturne in f♯. Welcome additions to the small number of slow, lyric separate pieces, each is A-B-A form. The first contrasts homophonic middle with elaborate four-part opening and close; the second alternates lyric chordal parts with staccato, dance-like middle. Mod

Capriccio on the Interval of a 2nd (1970). Commissioned as a contestant-eliminating number, this bristles with difficulties, but seems to be a durable work, with rich variations on a theme, driving, martellato. (Marks pub) Dif

DEL TREDICI, DAVID (USA), 1937- .

Fantasy Pieces (1962). It is heartening to find serial
compositions for piano in which beauty of sound is still the
ideal. These four pieces, played as a cycle, are contrasting in moods, yet unified by their material and texture. The
first, beginning with slow single tones in the lower registers,
demure and meditative, weaves a sensuous pattern, making
interesting use of a tremolo on the interval of a 3rd. The
more agitated second piece develops this same figure, interspersed with clumps of sound in a restless and fractious
manner. In No 3 the same material is used in an ominous,
threatening mood. The final piece sounds like a Rachmaninoff cadenza on a row, with a great arc of meaningful melody moving throughout, against a shimmering background of
glowing threads, with parallel lines of melody chiming in the
treble and booming in the bass. A quiet coda adds a bene-
diction to the ecstatic celebration. (B&H pub) Dif

DETT, R. NATHANIEL (Can-USA), 1882-1943.

First Negro composer to win recognition in the field
of serious music, he wrote numerous piano suites, from
which several numbers deserve to survive.

In the Bottoms (Suite) (1913). The popular Juba dance
is the last number of this Suite. The Prelude and His Song
are also attractive. Mod

Eight Bible Vignettes. An uneven set, unique in the
concept of a scriptural interpretation in music. Some of the
pieces (Martha Complained; Other Sheep) derive their rhythmic motifs from quotations; others interpret the mood. Best
are Father Abraham, based on a Spiritual, but with Hebrew
overtones; As His Own Soul (David and Jonathan) and Barcarolle of Tears. Mod

DEVRIES, KLASS (Neth),

Chain of Changes (1971). The title and the elegant
calligraphy would please John Cage. For avant garde pianists there is little that is new; completely non-tonal, alternating big chord passages with widespread lines. Rhythmi-

cally undistinguished, though touches of jazz, marked
"Swingin'," add humor. (Donemus pub) Dif

DIAMOND, DAVID (USA), 1915- .

Esteemed award-winning composer of five symphonies
and numerous concerti (one for piano and orchestra, and one
for two pianos) has three solo works.

Sonatina (1939). Simple neo-classic three-movt work,
basically tonal but so freely chromatic as to sound polytonal.
Opening largo begins in E♭ and ends in E. A neat 3-v invention in C with modal alterations is the second movt; a
gay vivace on irregular rhythmic motifs, the close. Mod E

The Tomb of Herman Melville (1949). In his desire
to honor the author of Moby Dick, DD had produced more of
a white elephant, than a white whale. The lengthy single
slow movement rises from a misterioso una corda to a fff
pronunziato climax, freely chromatic, chordal and polyhphon-
ic, but amorphous and mammalion. Mod

Sonata (1947). Large-scale three-movt work combining elements of neo-classic, post-romantic style with an
idiosyncratic and introspective personal style. Both first
and last movts end with well-wrought fugues (the last a
double-fugue). In the first, the tempo labels andante molto
espressivo and allegro molto appassionato indicate the highly-charged emotional content, culminating in the fugue. An
effect of four movts is achieved by inserting a lively scherzando in the lugubrious central Adagio. The intensity light-
ens at the end of the finale-fugue with a boisterous coda.
Dif

DITTERSDORF, KARL DITTERS VON (Aus), 1739-1799.

Genial companion of Gluck, Haydn, Padre Martini,
social-climber and autobiographer, KDvD is currently having
a revival, with more than 12 of his symphonies and operas
available of records. He also wrote 72 piano preludes, 14
sonatas for four hands, and two solo sonatas, only one of
which seems to be in print.

Sonata No 2 in A. A three-movt work with a Minuetto and "Alternativo" da capo, framed by two full-fledged
allegro movts. The writing is fluent and pianistic, the
themes contrasting if not of great distinction, and full of surprise modulations. Good for an occasional relief from his
more exalted contemporaries. (UNC pub) Mod

DOHNANYI, ERNST VON (Hun), 1877-1960.

This contemporary of Kodaly and Bartók was only
lightly touched by the Hungarian folk renaissance and wrote
consistently in a 19th-century romantic style. His works
are all very pianistic and effective, but seldom very original.

Four Rhapsodies, Op 11. These large scale works
derive their form from Liszt's pseudo-Hungarian rhapsodies.

No 2 in f♯. Perhaps the best of EvD, this has an
imposing adagio, with cross-hand tremolo, a lilting, lyric
second theme, and an effective agitato development that rises
to a crashing climax, before a delicately ornamented close
on the lyric second theme. Mod

No 3 in C. More uneven in musical inspiration, this
can be brilliant in performance, with a broad bardic second
theme, toccata chordal passages. Mod

No 4 in e♭. Less brilliant than the other rhapsodies,
this somber work uses "that granitic old tune Dies Irae" in
an imposing manner.

Capriccio in f, Op 28:6. The only one of six concert
etudes to keep its place in the repertoire, this is enormously effective, if played, as marked, vivace and more vivace
to the end. A series of variations on a Paganini-like theme,
it is bristling with technical problems, but worth mastering.
Dif

Ruralis Hungarica, Op 32a. These might well be
called concert etudes for only the title gives them any national identity. The simple folk-tunes have all those distinctive Magyar rhythmic and melodic angularities ironed out,
and the simplicity soon gives way to opulent romantic harmonies, elaborated with marvelously pianistic arpeggiated ac-

companiments.   The odd-numbered ones are the best--1, 3,
5, 7.   The third is somewhat less of a concert study, and
more lyric, andante poco moto, rubato.   The fifth is a brilliant toccata etude, and the last a dazzling closing clincher.
Mod Dif

DUKAS, PAUL (Fr), 1865-1935.

Distinguished French composer and professor chiefly
remembered today for the 'Sorcerer's Apprentice." His two
large piano works are currently available on records.

Sonata in e♭.   Massive monumental work owing more
to Liszt and Franck than to PD's national heritage.   Formally well structured, both the opening modérément vif, with its
turbulent minor theme that clarifies to a major, and the second movt, calme, un peu lent, are in allegro form.   The
Puckish PD of the "Sorcerer's Apprentice" brightens the
scherzo, which has a 3-v contrasting trio, da capo.   The
last movement is interminable, ponderous and devoid of surprise.   Dif

Variations, Interlude and Finale on a Theme by Rameau.   Like most French composers, PD is better when
following in the footsteps of his French forebears than when
writing in a borrowed Teutonic style.   These are fresh,
resonant, intriguing in their variety.   The theme is Rameau's
Minuet, La Lardon ("The Interlarding" qv), and PD moves
from quiet harmonic writing to free improvisation, in the interlude, to a brilliant close which ranges through a dozen
(rather predictable) keys.   The trio of the minuet is the
theme of this movement, but the "interlarding theme" is
brought in for contrast.   The movement accelerates to an
eight-meas passage in whole-tone scale (vif, pp) whose sound
is so foreign in the diatonic context that it can only be a
humorous spoof of Debussy.   Dif

Plainte au loin du Faun.   Debussy's Faun again, but
rather flat-footed and pedantic.   PD is better with the scherzo mood of the "Sorcerer's Apprentice" (and with orchestra).
There is also a Prélude Elégiaque.

DUKE, VERNON [pen-name of Vladimir Dukelsky] (Rus-USA), 1903-1969.

Russian ex-patriate composer (California via Paris, Turkey, and New York) who had more lasting success with popular songs (April in Paris) than with serious music. Some of his chamber music and two-piano works have been recorded. For an excruciating excoriation of "V. D.", see I. Stravinsky's (craft-y) Themes and Episodes.

Three Caprices (1944). Light-weight entertainment music, in three tempi with some pleasing rhythmic and harmonic effects. Mod

Souvenir de Venise (Sonata 2) (1948). One-movt neo-classic piece in ternary form, repeating the opening grave, after a lively Venetian salterello-type passage. Mod

Parisian Suite. Set of 10 genial genre pieces with humorous titles. Mod

DURKO, ZSOLT (Hun), 1934- .

Psicogramma. Dedicated to Petrassi, this Hungarian work, like much Italian avant-garde writing, looks fascinating on the page, and sounds simple-minded and soporific. Added to the linear-serial technic is a repeated-note effect (possibly meant to suggest the Hungarian cimbalom, or a psychotic obsession?) the Psicogramma relates its jittery effects to nervous states, labelled in nine sections, including a "motto" (Dallapiccola calls his "symbols"), first, second and third psicogramma, "Un Enfant Terrible," "Anti-Evidence" and an epilogo. The effect of the totally unpianistic work is nugatory; and the quaint titles only add to the disappointment. Dif

DUSSEK, JOHANN LUDWIG (Czech), 1760-1812.

Touring keyboard virtuoso whose travels took him from his native Bohemia (where he was Jan Ladislav) to Berlin, where he studied with C.P.E. Bach; to London where he went broke in business; to Paris, where he played for the doomed queen, Marie Antoinette. He found time to write 12 concertos, 40 sonatas and numerous program pieces. Though never rising to the inspiration of his great Viennese contemporaries, he anticipates Weber and Schubert in his use of modulation and the sonata form. His early works seem to have been written for the harpsichord, later ones for the piano. He was admired for his singing tone, and for sitting with his profile to the audience. Currently being revived.

La Chasse. The hunting horn is suggested in a simple fanfare figure, developed into a graceful allegro movt. Mod

Sonatas: In B♭, Op 9:1. A two-movt rococo work, with well-structured allegro and rondo, pianistic but harmonically dull. Mod

In G, Op 35:2. Similar to the B♭ above. One can imagine the brilliant effect JLD produced with the passage work in the fast allegro and racing rondo episodes. Mod

In A♭, Op 70. Larger more mature late work in four movts. There is good writing in the long Allegro, which has seven changes of key signature. The adagio moves to E, and the tempo de menuetto begins in f♯. The closing rondo is brilliant, but harmonically impoverished. Mod

Elégie harmonique (1806). One of several programmatic works, this is a tribute to JLD's patron, Prince Louis Ferdinand of Prussia, who died in battle. The music contrasts elements of conflict, nobility and lamentation.

Sufferings of the Queen. The composer played the harpsichord at Versailles for Marie Antoinette shortly before her execution, and later worked the experience into a keyboard piece similar to the soap opera for the Prussian prince, above. Mod

DVOŘÁK, ANTONIN (Czech), 1841-1904.

Little of the Czech-folk finds its way into this composer, who spent part of his career in America. His piano music is similar to Grieg's short lyric pieces, with rather commonplace harmonies, lacking the piquancy of Grieg. (Artia [B&H] and Bärenreiter pub)

Silhouettes, Op 8.   Two of these are very attractive
recital pieces.   No 2 is only one page in length, andantino,
but harmonically intriguing, with a delicate cadenza in 6ths,
and a charming perdendosi ending.   No 4 is more difficult
and brilliant, with a bold f♯ octave theme in LH alternating
with a grazioso and a meno mosso, and an allargando finale
giving great variety of its three pages.   Mod

Dumka à Furiant, Op 12.   Dumka means meditation
or reverie, and this slow lyric movement is followed by a
fast Czech dance.   There is another Dumka, Op 35, more
extended.   Mod Dif

Humoresque in G♭, Op 101.   This survives the bar-
rage of a century of young pianists, and is still fresh and
humorous, if played with precise division of beat, yet great
abandon of rhythm, and a delicate touch.   Mod E

Slavonic Dances, Op 46, 72.   More varied than Smetana's polkas, these must be given a romantic treatment,
like a gypsy violinist, rushing the spirited parts, lingering
over the langorous ones.   The one in e, from Op 72 is very
representative, but others are attractive.   Mod

Poetic Tone Pictures, Op 85.   No 3, "In the Old
Castle," is quiet, hymn-like, rhythmically varied, but harmonically prosaic.   No 8 is a Goblin Dance, with attractive
staccato figures and a quiet songful middle.   No 13 is
called "On the Holy Mount," and begins with a Parsifal
Grail theme (the familiar "Amen").   Unfortunately its many
repetitions add up to very little, though varied with arpeggios and delicate cembalo tappings.   Mod

ECKART-GRAMATTE, SONIA (Rus-Can), 1902- .

Suite No 6 (Drei Klavierstücke).   This unique virtuoso piece is in three-movts (15 min), the first a brilliant
LH etude, prestissimo e molto preciso, basically tonal, but
free-ranging and chromatic.   Challenged to pair it with a
RH piece, the composer did so (24 years later) with a moderato, based on a simple three-note theme freely varied,
expanded into chord patterns and arpeggios.   Still later the
idea of playing both movements simultaneously occurred, and
the tour de force produced a finale, driving, exuberant and
coruscating.   Dif

EGGE, KLAUS (Nor), 1906- .

This distinguished music critic, music ambassador and composer is a worthy successor to Grieg, and his fine piano works should be better known. Besides five symphonies, he has two concertos and numerous chamber works.

Sonata No 2, Op 27 (1934). Three-movt neo-classic work, well-structured and pianistic, basically tonal, but freely chromatic. The first movt has a motto based on the composer's name, e-g-e, and this rising-falling minor 3rd figure (often harmonized in augmented intervals or quartal chords) turns up in all movts. The middle movt is haunting and moody, with two slow linear patterns alternating with unisons, pedal-points, ornamental curlicues, and "the motto" approached with an appogiatura slide. The last movt is a national dance in a driving 16th-note motion that breaks off for an echo of the motto. Superior work. Mod Dif

Fantasy in Halling-Rhythm; Fantasy in Springar Rhythm, Op 12: a, c. These national dances, first used by Grieg in his orchestral suites and piano dance sets (Op 34, 72) are here treated with a contemporary tonal freedom. Similar to the sonata finale, they are in duple rhythm, with much 2-v part writing. The rhythmic and harmonic surprises are pleasantly euphoric. Mod Dif

EL-DABH, HALIM (Egy), 1921- .

Mekta' in the Art of Kita', Vols I, II, III, IV (1961). True to form, this edition tells us everything about this first Egyptian composer to win international fame for his ballets, operas, symphonic works, (even tracing his ancestry back to the Pharaohs) but not a word about the music in hand, or even a translation of the title of the book, or the pieces (Basseet, Samai, Nawakht, Sayera, etc.). They seem to be studies in rhythms (one has the exciting pattern of four 16ths followed by two 8ths, in 2/4 throughout!). Melodic patterns are limited to three- or four-note motifs, with a scale which often includes two flats and a sharp, though why B and E should be written with flats, and A with a sharp (rather than B♭) is not clear, unless the piano is incapable of reproducing the sounds intended. This, in fact, seems to be the case, and the piano music of El-Dabh turns out to be very drab. What "blazes forth from his pen in

fiery music" is obviously not the piano music.   (CFP pub)
Mod

ELWELL, HERBERT (USA), 1898- .

Critic and educator, has several large choral and instrumental works, and a Sonata for Piano, somewhat dated.

Sonata (1933). Neo-classic, three-movt work, basically tonal, with modal themes and free chromatic harmonization in a contrapuntal texture. Well-structured allegro in
flowing 3/4-v writing, with clear-cut rhythmic motifs. Expressive andante is florid but stately, with soft timpani effects. A propulsive third movt, basically E, but written in
5♯'s, the raised 4th of the scale giving a modal atmosphere.
Could be revived. Mod Dif

FALLA, MANUEL DE (Sp), 1876-1946.

One of the most authentic Spanish voices of the 20th-
century national revival, MdF's finest keyboard works are
concertos: the Impressionist "Nights in the Gardens of
Spain" and the highly dissonant harpsichord concerto. The
smaller works are pianistic and full of character.

Homenaje. Tribute to Debussy at the time of his
death, this was transcribed from a guitar solo, and loses
some of its muted, sombre passion on the keyboard instrument. Mod

Ritual Fire Dance. Another transcription (from a
ballet score) this is effective and popular, in spite of its
unpianistic writing. Mod Dif

Quatre pièces espagnoles: Aragonesa. A richly
textured, but unified and straightforward dance movement.
Mod. Cubana: Built on a hemiola triple-duple shift, this
is both lyrical and sensuous. Mod. Montañesa: This "landscape" is evoked by a cantabile melody, with chiming cow-
bells, and an urgently ambiguous harmony. Andaluza: Popular and brilliant number, marked "very rhythmic, with sav-
age energy," this blends the fiery and the melancholy in a
modal melody with melismatic cadences, played at half-

tempo for the contrasting middle, before returning to the
barbaric dance. Mod

   Fantasia Baetica. Written for Arthur Rubinstein,
who first championed Spanish music, this is a large, rather
amorphous work (15 min) with some brilliant keyboard writing, but is over-extended and repetitious. Dif

FAURE, GABRIEL (Fr), 1845-1924.

   Often considered one of the most French of all French
composers, GF (like Debussy, with his English Melisandes)
has found some of his finest exponents outside that country.
In the 1940's the American, Frank Mannheimer, played the
complete nocturnes for BBC Third Program; and another
American, Grant Johannesen, made the first complete recording of Fauré's piano music (there is another by Crochet).
The music is all eminently fluent and pianistic, with something of the exciting German "Spiel-Freude" about it.   There
is a fondness for compound rhythms using long fronds of arpeggio, often with a hemiola shift from triple to duple.
Themes are of two types; a tight coil (like the haunting soprano aria Pie Jesu in the Requiem); or a broad stair-step-
ping phrase in that pianist's delight, slow-paced octave melodies.   On the debit side, the music is sometimes undistinguished, repetitious and over-extended.   GF had a French
reticence about showing emotion, and abhorred "expressive"
playing.   Though a contemporary of Debussy, there is nothing of the imagist or impressionist here, and titles are generic types, as with Chopin.   There are 13 nocturnes and 13
barcarolles, five impromptus, and nine preludes.   (The opus
numbers are in most cases confusing and superfluous.)

   Three Songs Without Words. These early works have
the keyboard fluency of the master with folk-like themes.
They are simpler and easier than later ones. Mod E

   Impromptu No 1 in E♭. A brilliant, showy number
with the finest of GF's qualities listed above. Mod Dif

   Impromptu No 2 in f. A long but superb work, keyboard-spanning arpeggios and scales giving way to a lyric F
major song featuring hemiola rhythmic variations and a
broad octave melody.   Both themes return, and an enchanting coda, sempre pp, grows from a long trill.   Mod Dif

Impromptu No 3 in A♭. GF's fondness for a boat-rocking theme and rhythm is featured here. (The impromptus are often indistinguishable from the barcarolles.) Mod

Impromptu No 5 in f♯. Shorter and somewhat angular in rhythm (4/4 in quarters and 16ths) this builds an imposing octave climax. Mod

Barcarolle No 3 in G♭. The Boat Song, with its gentle undulation and fluid melodic line appealed to GF. (Only Mendelssohn's simple Venetian gondola songs, and Chopin's one barcarolle provided models.) The first and second barcarolles are rather experimental and of less importance. No 3 features GF's unique harmonic devices to create an evanescent, vaporous effect, with purling scales, above a swaying beat. Mod

Barcarolle No 4 in A♭. Beginning and ending in the soothing key of A♭, this modulates freely and rapidly, varying the 6/8 long-short boat-roll with a 3/4 beat. Mod

Barcarolle No 5 in f♯. The most brilliant and longest in 9/8. An effective Fauréian device of a single-note melody phrase, which supplies the beat, answered by a harmonic bass, on the after-beat. Builds to a climax. Mod Dif

Barcarolle No 6 in E♭. Very representative of the genre, this begins with a lyric four-meas theme in 8ths over flowing 16ths, allegreto vivo, then doubles the theme in octaves, quickening the pulse with triplet 16ths. The mid-section, dolce, is in B, with the ornamental accompaniment moving to the treble at the close, for a quiet ending, the boat anchored at last on a firm pedalpoint.

Barcarolle No 9 in a. The large sets of barcarolles and nocturnes span a long life, and later works become simpler, more austere. Melody here is more important than figured accompaniment, and is of a wistful, nostalgic character. Mod

Nocturne No 1 in e♭. Since GF eschewed rubato and emotional expression, the player must make full use of dynamic nuance, pedal, accents. No 1 is mature GF, master of subtle modulation under a long lyric line. Mod

Nocturne No 3 in A♭. Like Chopin, GF often uses

ternary form, with contrasting middle section, often agitato, as here, returning to the serene opening for finale. Mod

Nocturne No 4 in E♭. The deceptively naive opening theme is repeated in octaves, then subtly slides into the minor in six flats, and simplicity gives way to complexity, with both hands playing rocking note figures, under a bell chime, all dolce tranquillamente. After the return, the coda is Chopinesque in its surprises: a cadenza, the bells again, and a fadeout on the rocking theme. Mod

Nocturne No 6 in D♭. Brilliant and difficult, this is rated first by Friskin and Freudlich. Dif

Nocturne No 7 in c♯. Considered by Frank Mannheimer the finest in the set, this is a subtle work, modulating from 6♯'s to 6♭'s, full of suspended resolutions, with three layers of melody woven into a rich tissue of sound. Dif

Nocturne No 13 in b. One of the finest products of the late years, this begins with a grave chaconne in 3/2 with a dotted second beat; this is gradually enriched with layers of voices lingering over chromatic suspensions. A middle section in 2/2 g♯ introduces an agitated triplet accompaniment under a counter-theme, which, like the first, moves step-wise and coils around the first three scale-tones. A joyous return of the chaconne above scales soars to an acme, then ends quietly, like the great b minor Chaconne of Couperin, of which it is a direct and beautiful descendent. Dif

Theme and Variations, Op 73. This work might almost qualify as great also, but there is very little of Fauré in it. Written for a competition at the Paris Conservatory, of which he was director, it is his only venture in variation form. The model is obviously Schumann, and each of the 11 variations has a parallel in the Etudes Symphonique. The theme is unmistakably Fauré, but rather undistinguished. The variations are pianistic, very diversified. Only in the last variation (which might have served better as the penultimate one with No 10 for a brilliant finale) does the real Fauré stand out in two pages which might have crowned the 13 nocturnes. These deserve to be heard. Dif

Preludes, Op 103; No 1 in D♭. These nine pieces

are uneven in quality, and only a few are attractive to hear.
The first has Fauré's best rhythmic and melodic qualities
and unique harmonies in a quiet lyric mood.   Mod

   No 2 in c♯.   This curious work is in 5/4, each
measure one staff in length, a three-fingered typist figure,
corkscrewing up and down in five great arcs, with a sudden
lift to the harmonic major for a chordal coda.   Quite stunning.   Dif

   No 4 in F.   A folksy, pastoral piece.   Mod E

   No 5 in d.   A lively opening in the manner of the
barcarolles, with a quiet modal ending.   Mod E

FELDMAN, MORTON (USA), 1926- .

   Avant-garde composer inspired by abstract paintings
of de Kooning, Franz Kline, Philip Guston, after whom
some of his pieces are named.   His own abstract graphed
notation (a reaction to serialism) leaves the choice of actual notes to the performer, indicating only general area of
the scale or instrument, approximate duration, etc.   (sometimes transcribed into traditional notation by the composer,
for the illiterate).   Most of the music requires the contrast
of more than one instrument ("Two Instruments" is the title
of one piece.)

   Intersection Three for Piano; Last Pieces for Piano.
A far cry from the frenetic busy-ness of the serial and
mathematical scores, these open-ended leisurely non-struc-
tures have a certain hypnotic aural appeal, with their long
silences, irregular clumps of chord patterns, surprise dynamics, though it soon becomes soporific.   Since they are
sheer improvisation, with only the sketchiest guides, no two
performances will be alike.   Played by a master of contemporary idiom like David Tudor, they are attractive,
though one suspects Tudor could do quite as well on his
own, without the help of MF.

FERGUSON, HOWARD (GB), 1908- .

   Influential teacher of many contemporary British

composers, HF has two published works.

Sonata in f (1940). An expansive three-movt work
in neo-romantic style, very pianistic, much chromatic ambiguity. Bold, declamatory lente, introduces allegro inquieto using minor 2nds and 7ths for an urgent, restless
quality. Adagio uses same motifs to achieve a serene tranquility. Propulsive finale drops to a mysterious whisper,
then builds to a powerful and triumphant restatement of opening lento. (B&H pub) Dif

Five Bagatelles. These deserve a better title, for
they are anything but trivial. Five finely-wrought imaginative and pianistic pieces dedicated to a fellow musician,
Arnold Van Wyck from South Africa, "who kindly contributed
twenty-five notes." At the end of each piece is a motif,
from three to six notes in length, written out like Schumann's Sphynx. These brief tone-rows serve as motivic
material for each of the highly contrasting sketches: allegro con fuoco; andantino amabile; allegro scherzando;
molto moderato; allegretto non troppo. Mod Dif

FIALA, GEORGE (Rus, Can), 1922- .

This important Russian-born Canadian composer has
passed from late Romantic to dodecaphonic style with numerous successes in large forms.

Sonatine, Op 1. Lightweight three-movt work, undemanding: andantino melancholico, linear and homophonic;
larghetto espressivo in quartal harmony; driving tarantella,
in free tonality.

10 Postludes, Op 7 (1970). The page-long sketches
are in free tonality, pianistic and in a variety of contrasting idioms and styles. Mod

FINE, IRVING (USA), 1914-62.

Music for Piano (1949). This successful composer
and influential teacher has left a pleasant four-movt suite,
called Music for Piano. Tonal with a few surprises harmonically, it is pianistic and euphonious. Prelude is 2-v

with sudden dynamic shifts. Waltz-Gavotte introduces deviations in a triple rhythm, 2/4, 4/4, 5/8, 6/8. The four Variations of the third movt are the most attractive, linear, lyric and expressive, with No. II sempre staccato for contrast. The closing Interlude-Finale unifies the work with quotations from the Prelude, first lento, then gathering speed for a fast, jazzy ending. (MCA pub) Mod Dif

FOSS, LUCAS (Ger-USA), 1922- .

Prize-winning composer who has moved from a conservative neo-classic style to experimentation with electronics, amplification, etc. Both early and late styles are still represented in concerts and recordings. There are two piano concertos, and piano pieces mostly in the early style.

Four Two-Voiced Inventions (1938). These works of the 16-year old student so impressed G. Schirmer that they were published with a special introduction. Their imaginative rhythmic and melodic motifs anticipate many of the quirks of the mature LF, and are still playable. Mod

Grotesque Dance (1938). Large-scale virtuoso piece, displaying LF's solid grounding in keyboard classics. The highly original piece inserts a mock-solemn Andante, Baroque in ornamentation, in the lively asymetrical dance of the opening and close. Mod Dif

Fantasy Rondo (1946). Bold extended solo, sonorous and pianistic, basically e minor, but with much quartal harmony and polytonality; unisons, canons, broken-chord figures. There is a similarity of texture to Copland's early Sonata and Variations; and Copland's own Fantasy (1957) seems in turn to grow out of this. Dif

Passacaglia. Large-scale set of 22 linked variations on a four-meas cantus firmus, exploring problems similar to the above. Dif

FRANCK, CESAR (Bel), 1822-1890.

Born in Belgium, CF spent his quiet life teaching and playing the organ in Paris, where his fond pupils called

him "Pater Seraphicus." The sostenuto of organ tone, and
a mystic spirituality pervade his three great piano works.

Prelude, Chorale and Fugue. Possibly one of the
half dozen greatest piano works ever written, this derives
its magnificent three-part form from Bach organ works, and
its rich chromaticism from Wagner. The bold, but restrained opening is like arpeggiated improvised "preludizing"
with an inner theme suggesting B-A-C-H. This alternates
with bold chordal declamations and mystic, meditative passages, building through a series of modulations to a climax. The Chorale, introduced by an almost voluptuously
sensual theme, is itself a great chime-like hymn that spans
three octaves with each chord, and grows grander with each
repetition. Franck followed Liszt in unifying his work with
transferred themes, and the 4-v fugue is built on a phrase
borrowed from the Prelude. A free-wheeling cadenza brings
back the arpeggios of the Prelude, combines them with the
Chorale, and rises to exaltation combining all themes in a
glorious B major ending. Dif

Prelude, Aria and Finale. Less grandly structured
than the great cathedral of the P-C-F, this sprawls, with
too many fine side chapels, transepts and crypts to lose
one's way in. There is a detailed analysis of it in Lockwood, and it deserves occasional performance, perhaps with
some judicious pruning. Dif

Prelude, Fugue and Variations. For those too lazy to
tackle the great one, this organ work is simpler, and available in transcriptions for either two or four hands. It has
most of the fine Franck qualities on a smaller scale. The
greatest of all, of course, is the Variations Symphoniques,
with orchestra. Mod Dif

FRICKER, PETER RACINE (GB), 1920- .

That rara avis among modern composers, one who
seems to write at the keyboard, not the drawing board, producing music to be played on the piano, and enjoyed for its
sound.

Four Impromptus, Op 17. The graceful, lyric linear
quality of early 20th-century French music marks the early
impromptus. Mod

14 Bagatelles. The bagatelles are kaleidoscopic miniatures, freely diatonic. Mod

Four Sonnets. Also brief sketches, experimenting in
serial style.

Variations, Op 31. For the tightly-knit contemporary
variations six separate motifs are introduced in the theme,
then developed in the six contrasting but continuous variations. Dif

12 Studies. A return to the more pianistic early
style; conventional, but fresh, exuberant and original. Demanding. Dif

FUGA, SANDRO (It), 1906- .

The two works by this Italian are neo-classical, clear,
light-textured and pianistic.

Sonatina (1937). The Sonatina has an allegro vivo
with two attractive themes, well developed. The largo is a
two-page sarabande, unornamented, but with some surprise
harmonization, doubled in octaves on the return. The third
movt is not a fuga, but a 4-v fughetta, imaginatively worked
out. Mod E

Toccata (1947). Large-scale work in C, using steady
triplets, 12 to the measure, against chords and melodies in
varied metric patterns. Tonal but spiced with dissonance.
Brilliant and not difficult. Mod

FULEIHAN, ANIS (Gr-USA), 1900-1970.

Colorful pianist-composer-educator, whose career
took him from his native Cyprus to the U.S. and back to the
Middle East.

Cypriana. Suite of six pieces evoking Cyprus with
folk-like rhythms, scales instrumental effects. Original,
fresh. Mod

Sonatina 1, 2. Short two- or three-movt works in

free adaptation of traditional form, simple to complex, tonal modal or mildly dissonant.   Mod-Dif

Harvest Chant.   Short solo evoking regional festival with folk-like tune, chime effects.   Mod E

15 Short Pieces.   Original suite, with picturesque titles, contrasting irregular meter, touch and tone effects. Free tonality.   Mod Dif

Sonata 12 (1969).   Traditional fast-slow-fast form, but freely dissonant in harmony.   Forward driving first movt broken by moments of repose.   After the quiet but climactic second, a toccata and fugue, with snatches of a tarantella rhythm finish this pianistic work.   Mature.   (B&H pub) Dif

GADE, NIELS (Den), 1817-1890.

Aquarellen, Op 19, Op 57.   Denmark's proximity to Germany has always brought it strongly under Teutonic influence, and at the same time made it strongly nationalistic. NG is an example, his piano music being strongly Mendelssohnian (of whom he was an ardent admirer), while his eight symphonies attempted to be Danish.

Mendelssohn in fact invited him to conduct the famous Leipzig Gewandhaus orchestra.   NG wrote short pieces like the Songs Without Words, which might be called "Watercolors without color."   Neat and uninspired, their simplicity is that of the commonplace, rather than that of genius. There is also a negligible Sonata, Op 28, dedicated to Liszt. Mod E

GALUPPI, BALDASSARRE (It), 1706-1985.

Venetian known as "The father of opera buffa," court-composer to the Russian Czar, and harpsichord virtuoso. His sonatas range from Baroque four-movt works to the lighter three-movt transitional style.

Sonata in D.   An early Baroque work often anthologized.   The four movts are S-F-S-F.   The brief opening

adagio is expressive, elegant and melodious. The third
movt is a stately, orchestral largo, with awkward but dramatic leaps. The faster second and fourth are more effective on the harpsichord, with contrasting registration for the
brilliant repeated passages. Mod Dif

    12 Sonatas. Venice was one of the first cities to pub-
lish music, and this volume appeared during the composers
lifetime. (Now reprinted by Bongiovanni, available through
BM.) These three-movt works are in nine different keys,
with a slow introductory movt followed by two fast ones.

    No 2 in c. A brilliant and difficult work, with virtu-
oso display, dramatic fire, and sprightly dance figures.
Mod Dif

    No 8 in Bb. The andantino has the amiable charm
of Haydn and the rich ornamentation. A graceful 3/4 allegro might be a minuet. The closing Giga is a 2-v trumpet
fanfare, con spirito. Mod

    Many of his other sonatas are equally attractive.

GERSHWIN, GEORGE (USA), 1898-1937.

    America's greatest composer of popular music is an
example of man's eternal dissatisfaction with his lot, for he
always wanted to be known as a composer of serious music.
His Rhapsody in Blue has become a classic, and even his
piano concerto, though less inspired, is a staple of the repertoire; so GG should be satisfied.

    Three Preludes. The composer refrained from call-
ing them "jazz preludes," but they are fine examples of both
genres. The first and last are 2/4, molto ritmico, with the
steady 8th-note beat of jazz, a veritable vade mecum of syncopation. The slow middle prelude is Blues, and worthy of
Chopin in its nocturnal rumination, and its fine keyboard lay-
out. A large hand is essential to all of these. Mod Dif

GIANNINI, VITTORIO (US), 1903-1966.

    Music educator and composer of symphonies and

operas (brother of the soprano, Dusolina), has left two
large piano works.

Variations on a Cantus Firmus (Four sets). An enormous work in traditional idiom and harmony. The 24 variations can be played entire, or in sets: moderato (1-10);
aria (11-12); toccata (13-22); interlude (23-24). Dif

Sonata (1967). Large scale neo-classic work, with
romantic melodic lines but experimental harmony. Lively
allegro, moving cantabile adagio, and brilliant finale, built
on hammered ostinati. 24 pages. Dif

GINASTERA, ALBERTO (Arg), 1916- .

Latin American contemporary, who has won kudos for
recent opera and concerto premieres, has several piano
works. AG's music is basically tonal and neo-classic though
the concertos for piano and violin experiment with tone-rows.
Early piano suites use Latin rhythms and folkloric themes.
Though somewhat eclectic and derivative in style, the music
is very pianistic and appealing.

Danzas Argentinas. Three-movt suite, the first dance
pitting black keys against white in polytonality; the second,
euphoric and swinging; the third, propulsive and vivacious.
Mod

Tres Piezas. More extended, these three also use
Latin color; the first a wistful, bucolic song over broken
chords; the second and third, characteristic dance motifs.
Mod

Suite de Danzas Criollas. Similar to the above.
Mod

12 American Preludes (1944). Short vivid sketches
in a variety of styles from jazz to calypso and primitive
ritual dance. Some have the character of etudes; some pay
homage to other composers. Very effective. Mod

Sonata para Piano (1952). Large four-movt neo-classic work whose brilliant effect in performance surpasses its
technical demands. (The debt to Copland and Barber is in-
escapable.) Allegro marcato: The traditional first movt

begins with a simple martellato theme in 3rds that accumulates power with added beats and expanded chords; a delicate, wistful tune in 5/8 is the second theme; the two are worked into an exciting development, and return for a flashy close. Presto misterioso: A wiry, scampering theme, played ppp at the extremes of the keyboard. Adagio appassionata: The third begins with another cumulative motif, a slow harp roll that rises from ppp to fff with hammered chords in a free rhythm. Sounds like a row, but isn't, until the last measure. Ruvido et Ostinato: "Rough and Obstinate," but enormously effective, this alternates triple and duple measures, brilliantly deployed across the board. 20 min. Mod Dif

GLAZUNOFF, ALEXANDER (Russ), 1865-1936.

Prolific composer once highly regarded, AG is represented today largely by his ballet Raymonda. His piano music is a blend of romantic and academic with little originality.

Gavotte in D, Op 29:3. Genial and melodious, it requires a large hand span, but is otherwise not difficult. Mod

Etudes, Op 31. The first of these three is most attractive (C), brilliant and technically demanding, in a repeated-note toccata style. Dif

Sonatas 1, 2. Complex and academically correct, there is little musical content. Dif

Prelude and Fugue in e. Large-scale maestoso prelude; scholarly fugue. Dif

Variations in f#, Op 72. His best, 14 attractive and brilliant variations requiring musical maturity. Mod Dif

GODARD, BENJAMIN (Fr), 1849-1895.

A 19th-century salon composer most of whose superficial entertainment music is forgotten today. His first love was violin (his second, opera), but the piano music lies well under the hand.

Valse II, in B♭.   Favorite salon piece (along with many mazurkas), it flows under the fingers.   Mod E

Valse Chromatique (No 5 in G).   Showy scale study, four contrasting passages all build on the chromatic scale, with much dynamic nuance, and a smashing ending.   Mod

Jonglerie.   Toccata type study, with melody divided between the thumbs.   Effective.   Several other works exploit this technic, including En Route, and Le Chevaleresque.

Le Cavalier Fantastique, Op 66.   Brilliant octave study, rising from d to D for the coda.   Effective encore; requires endurance.   Mod Dif

Chopin; Alfred de Musset.   A delicate valse is appropriately named Chopin; and the tribute to the poet is lyric and melancholy.   Mod

GODOWSKY, LEOPOLD (Rus-USA), 1870-1938.

Noted pianist and teacher who wrote his own formidable studies for teaching.   He is sometimes recalled today with his Viennese Pieces, or his Asian travel music.

Alt-Wien.   One of 30 "Moods and Scenes in Triple Measure" (Triakontameron), this is the pianists' counterpart to Kreisler's Caprice Viennoise, for it is the Old Vienna of Strauss and Kreisler that is evoked in this chromatically sinuous waltz--molto rubato.   Mod

Phonoramas (Java Suite) (in four parts).   Here the composer tries to capture sights and sounds of Indonesia. The first number, Gamelan, is the most interesting, using the strictly duple-beat of so much Asian music, pentatonic scale (with "ti" instead of "do") clanging chords of 2nds and 9ths.   A difficult task, at which Colin McPhee's two-piano suite, and Debussy's Pagodas, succeed better.   The other numbers in Java Suite are programmatic, and less attractive.

GOEHR, ALEXANDER (GB), 1932- .

Prolific second-generation composer, writing in atonal and serial style for chamber groups, symphony, stage.

Sonata, Op 2 (1952). One-movt experimental work, wide-ranging but pianistic, thick-textured, verbose, intense, and elegiac (tribute to Prokofief). Dif

Capriccio, Op 6. A brief sketch, transitory in style; complex rhythmic figures in an unpianistic web of polyphony.

Three Pieces, Op 18. AG seems to have arrived at a viable style of his own. Free in tonality, but clearly defined harmonically, well conceived as three short varied and imaginative pieces. No 3 is an expressive Passacaglia, contrapuntal but terse and expressive. Dif

GOTTSCHALK, LOUIS MOREAU (USA), 1829-1869.

America's first international musical figure, this pianist-composer was a typical product of the melting pot: German-Jewish-French-Creole. His colorful career barnstorming from Paris and Madrid to California and Latin America, with two nine-foot concert grands, is vividly recorded in his journals. It is also reflected in his compositions; for, though he himself preferred to play Bach and Chopin, he met the demands of his audiences with program music, "occasional pieces, sentimental salon poems," and some of the first music to use authentic American folk material. None is very original or distinguished; but the music is of historical importance, and some of the pieces have a superficial charm.

A March in the Night, Op 17. Inspired by an incident in a Venezuelan revolution, the music suggests the ominous approach and passing of an army in a steady Tempo di Marcia, varied with glittering ornamental effects depicting revelry viewed from afar. "Arrant trash" (see below). Mod

L'Union, Op 48 (1862). Though from New Orleans, LMG's sympathies were with the Union, and he raised the roof with performances of this thundering number, incorporating The Star Spangled Banner, Hail Columbia and Yankee

Doodle. The style is Lisztian, with cadenzas, octave passages, a sotto voce dead march.   Still rather hair-raising.
Mod Dif

The Banjo. The pieces using authentic ethnic material are all more simple, fresh and attractive, suffering only
from padding and repetitiousness. This plectrum imitation
in F♯ is one of the best. Mod

La Bananier. Lively folk-song transcription, weak-
ened by a monotonous bass and an excess of chromatic
scales and arpeggios. At its premiere in Paris, police had
to be summoned to quell the ovation. Mod

Bamboula. A brilliant rondo on "Sweet Potatoes,"
with plaintive contrasting minor themes, dance rhythms and
showy keyboard passages. Deserves an occasional hearing.
Mod Dif

Tremolo. As a youth I was presented by our piano-
tuner with a brand new copy of this, which I promptly hid at
the bottom of a drawer in shame. (On his return I had to
dig it out and pretend to sight-read it.) In 1890 in London,
G. B. Shaw, reviewing a concert by the brilliant Venezuelan
pianist and pupil of LMG, howled at her substituting this for
a Mendelssohn prelude and fugue: "...a thumping scamper
through arrant school-girl trash. Certainly she is a superb
executant, and her bow is Junonian; but Gottschalk--Good
Gracious!"

GRAINGER, PERCY (Aus-USA), 1882-1961.

This pianist shares picturesque qualities with America's pioneer, Louis Moreau Gottschalk. Both men played
with dazzling panache; both loved massed-piano performances.
Neither was a very original composer, but both used folk-
material well, PG making numerous arrangements of English
folk-songs for choral and instrumental groups, as well as
these piano solos.

Country Gardens. Popular transcription of a Morris
dance tune that keeps the boisterous exuberance of a May
Day festival. Requires drive, verve and a large hand. Mod

Shepherd's Hey. Another Morris Dance, similarly

arranged, but handicapped by a rather monotonous tune.
Mod

Londonderry Air.   This beautiful song is tastefully
set, with imaginative harmonic and keyboard devices.   Mod

GRAMATGES, HAROLD (Cuba), 1918- .

Dos Danzas Cubanas (1953).   Local place names for
dances (following Albeniz example) give to much Latin American music a provincialism that restricts it.   "Montuna" and
"Sonera" are the titles of these two dances.   Rhythm is basic, but rather undistinguished (calypso to most of us).   The
first is in G, the second in A♭, but the composer uses many
7ths and chromatic alterations.   Both are Allegro Moderato.
(Peer pub)   Mod Dif

Tres Preludios.   Allegro experiments with harmony
based on various intervals, and constant shifts of time and
meter; the second prelude is slow and lyric, with long melodic line; toccata-like percussive allegro finale.   (Peer pub)
Mod

GRANADOS, ENRIQUE (Sp), 1867-1916.

Third member of the troika reviving Spanish music,
EG was killed in World War I.   His piano style is florid and
discursive, less ethnic than the others.   But there are choice
items.

Spanish Dances, IV Books.   Alicia della Rocha has re-
vealed to the world many unknown and attractive dances in
these books.   Two have always been favorites: No 4 Villa-
nesca: A quiet, hypnotic piece with a bagpipe bass, and a
cross-hand chime over a simple lyric.   A moody minor passage with contrapuntal and canonic writing leads to a DC.
Mod E.   No 5 Playera: José Iturbi first dazzled audiences
with this dance, with its throbbing primitive drum bass, its
sudden major cadence; and its exquisite slow sarabande in
treble chords.   Molto rubato, and with much dynamic contrast.   Mod

Los Requiebos.   One of a suite called Goyescas of

six tributes to the painter Goya (later expanded into an
opera), "Flattery" is a brilliant, shallow salon-music piece,
fluent, but over-blown. A "Love-Duet" in similar style follows. Dif

El Fandango de Candil. Lighter, more distinctive
dance, with castanet and guitar effects accompanying the
lengthy cantilena. Mod

Quejas o la Maja y el Ruisenor. A favorite of Myra
Hess, this haunting poem is richly sensuous and complex
but a true lament. The nightingale consoles the lovers with
trills (in double-stops) throughout the piece, and has a plaintive cadenza at the end. (6-7 min) Mod Dif

GRAZIOLI, GIOVANNI B. (It), 1755-1820.

Sonata in G. One of the many famous organists at
St. Mark's cathedral in Venice, with its three organs. This
contemporary of Mozart wrote 18 keyboard sonatas, which,
though lightweight and thin, have pleasing qualities. The
one in G major included in the IMC Italian Masters of the
XVII-XVIII Century is attractive enough in its three well-developed movts to make us wish for more. Mod E

GRIEG, EDVARD (Nor), 1843-1907.

Lyric Pieces, Vols I to X. EG's popular and imposing piano concerto leads one to expect other large works
from him, a hope which he did not fulfil. The small works,
the Lyric Pieces, however, are very attractive and should be
familiar to every pianist. They are collected in 10 volumes
of from three to eight short pieces each. Of these, the
best are Vol: I, III and V. The first is on the level of in-
termediate students. Vol III contains four of the most popular pieces, including Butterfly, and Little Bird; the fourth,
To Spring, is a miniature masterpiece.

From Vol V, The March of the Dwarfs is a brilliant
uninhibited scherzo, the Notturno, an exquisite aftermath of
Chopin, and Bell-Ringing a fine pedal study.

Wedding Day at Troldhagen (Vol VIII) blends folk-dance, program elements, and some virtuoso keyboard effects. At the Cradle, from Vol IX, and Puck from X, also deserve to be played. Mod E

Ballade, Op 24. Two larger works are flawed, but viable. The long Ballade, Op 24, is a set of variations on a folk-theme, fine but over-extended and suffering from a rather monotonous theme. Mod Dif

Sonata in e, Op 8. Well constructed, and pianistic, this four-movt work lacks the distinctive Nordic character of the later pieces. Mod

Norwegian Peasant Dances, Op 72 (1902). Late in life EG, who had always loved and freely imitated the folk music of Norway, turned ethnomusicologist, and notated the Slatter or folk-dances of a Hardinger fiddler. He worked them into a set for piano solo which have a verve and freshness often lacking in the sentimental lyrical pieces. (An earlier, more stylized set is for four hands, Op 35.) The strong rhythm is usually duple with dotted and 16th-note groups predominant, but a lyric melody often appears, frequently in Lydian mode (with raised 4th). The wide leaps require good control. Mod Dif

GRIFFES, CHARLES T. (USA), 1884-1920.

The early death of this gifted, devoted and developing composer was a blow to American music. The few works which he left all have the breath of inspiration and are well-crafted, and the late ones show potential for a new style. Though German-trained, CG most often employed a French impressionistic keyboard approach, painting scenes, moods, atmospheres in washes of sound, diffused rhythms, expanded and altered chords (9ths, 11ths), often in foreign keys and unresolved, giving a floating iridescent color.

Three Tone Poems, Op 5 (1915):   The Lake at Even. The "lapping of lake water" of the Yeats "Innisfree" epigraph (added after composing the music) is vividly evoked in the insistent, off-beat pedal-point that gives concinnity to this brief Whistlerian landscape. Mod

The Vale of Dreams. Similar in its use of a hypnotic trance-like beat, but varying the rhythm for a climax in its brief four pages.   Mod

   The Night Wind.   Best of the three, this produces its eerie effect with fleeting arpeggios of 2nds and
9ths, under a sighing chromatic motif in 3rds.   Strident
chords, hammered high in the treble, are the acme, after
which the wind abates misterioso, quasi da lontano with broken
echos of the sigh.   Mod

   Fantasy Pieces, Op 6: Barcarolle, Nocturne,
Scherzo.   More Teutonic than French, these post-romantic
pieces were once favorite concert items.   They are on a
larger scale than the Three Tone Poems, with opulent harmonies.   The scherzo is vivacious and bravura.   Mod Dif

   Four Roman Sketches, Op 7.   The White Pea-
cock.   Most popular of CG's piano works, the White Pea-
cock has been orchestrated, and has provided the music for
many a dancer.   No orchestra is needed, however, the writing is so fluent for the fingers.   Perfectly structured, it is
a sonata allegro with a mirror recapitulation; and though including four distinct themes, illustrates Busoni's concept of
concinnity by relating all material, either rhythmically, melodically or harmonically.   Deserves its popularity.   Dif

   Night Fall.   Each of Griffes suites has a night
or twilight piece.   There are two in Op 5, the first calm,
the second alarming.   The one in Op 6 is more subjective.
This (Op 7) is a virtuoso piece suggestive of a glori-
ole over the Eternal city, with the multifaceted lights of day
and night reflected from dome and river.   Mod Dif

   Fountain of the Aqua Paola.   Liszt, Debussy,
Ravel all come to mind, but the music is original, marvelously pianistic, rising in a great splashing cascade, and
worthy of at least three coins.   Mod Dif

   Sonata (1917-1918).   This magnificent Sonata is one
of the first modern American works to use classical sonata
form, and it remains one of the best.   In and out of New
York City, where he struggled for a hearing and a living,
CG was aware of new trends, and here explores new scale
figurations and tone rows (two flats plus $C\sharp$ and $G\sharp$) with
dissonant and non-traditional harmonies.   The three movts
are continuous.   Feroce-allegretto con moto combines highly original material, contrasting a restless motif and a bold
declamatory one, linked by brilliant passages and built into

a fine frenzied development.   The unique scale, clearly
stated in the bold up-rushing introduction, is molded into a
chord for the coda.   A chant-like theme, espressive tranquillo stands at the center, gathering excitement at its close.
The final Allegro vivace is a masterpiece worthy of Prokofief (and written the year of his No III).   An excellent analysis of the sonata is found in Maizel's frank biography.   Dif

     Three Preludes (1920).   Published in 1967, these are
three of the "Five Pieces for Piano" on which CG was working at the time of his death.   They continue the exploration
of new scales and harmonies begun in the Sonata, and are
perfectly realized, highly musical miniatures, an important
addition to the repertoire.   As in the sonata allegro the basic row is usually summarized in the penultimate measures
of each piece.   It is not clear why the publisher had to pay
and credit an "editor," since nothing whatever has been added to help the player.   The author suggests playing them in
the order: I, III, II; the first, Allegro agitato, MM, quarter
note = 80-90, col ped with two crescendi molti and a closing
dim.   For the second, No III, Lento, quarter note = 56-60
(the night-piece of the set).   The seemingly abstruse chordal
passage at the end of each page is a canon between LH-RH,
using only two chords, e♭ and c♯ aug.   To close, No II
could be played agitato e leggerio, MM, quarter note = 120,
with a final crescendo to ff.   Mod

HALFTTER, CRISTOBAL (Sp), 1930-   .

     A second-generation composer (nephew of the ex-patri-
ates, Ernesto and Rodolfo Halftter) who teaches in the Madrid
Conservatory.   Like younger Spanish painters who have produced an impressive number of abstract works largely collected in the unique gallery at Cuenco, CH has adopted totali-
tarian organization of all elements of music in a series of
chamber and instrumental works, some including electronic
tape.

     Sonata para Piano (1951).   Early one-movt work, pay-
ing tribute to Soler in a classic, linear style.   Mod

     Introducción, Fuga y Final, Op 15 (1957).   Serial com-
position, in classic forms, strict, taut and correct.   Cerebral and bleak.   Dif

HALFTTER, ERNESTO (Sp-Por), 1905- .

Member of a prominent Spanish musical family, who,
after the artistic exodus, (Casals, Picasso), settled in Portugal. His piano works are early, more recent ones being in
larger forms.

Dos Bocetos. These two delicate mood sketches,
subtle yet impassioned miniatures, were later instrumented.
The piano version is still best. Mod

Sonata (1931). Succinct one-movt work combining neo-
classic form, a linear calligraphic clarity with piano sonority. Tonal-bi-tonal, in a flowing 8th and 16th note figuration. Pianistic and meritorious. Mod

Two Dances: Dance of the Gypsy, Dance of the
Shepherdess. Traditional keyboard writing with a few original rhythmic, harmonic ideas. Effective. Mod

ER's Portuguese Rhapsody for Piano and Orchestra
has been recorded.

HALFTTER, RODOLFO (Sp-Mex), 1900- .

Dos Sonatas. Spanish composer and editor who has
found freedom for his work in Mexico. Besides concertos
and symphonies, he has written two sonatas and other piano
works. (EMdM pub)

11 Bagatelles (1940). Brief lighthearted works, contrasting Latin and standard rhythmic motifs, in a flowing
keyboard style, experimenting with dissonance and bitonality. Mod

Tres Hoyas de Album, Op 26 (1961). Well written
study pieces combining tonal and polytonal writing in a variety of idioms. Mod

HAMILTON, IAN (GB), 1922- .

British professor at City College of New York, a
prolific composer of successful chamber music, has several

piano pieces.

Sonata (1951).   Large-scale work, tonal-bitonal, with dissonance effectively used for color; well-deployed over the keyboard, but rather unpianistic.   Dif

Three Pieces, Op 30.   Three atonal works, with harmonic pedal-points, fragmentary, motivic figures.   Dif

Nocturnes with Cadenzas (1966).   LH here borrows an old name for a very original idea, linking four elegiac night-pieces with free passages, fast, furious, and demanding fearless fingers.   The widely dispersed melodic line of the serial style nocturnes is blended with pedal.   Not for the timid.   Dif

HANDEL, GEORGE FREDERICK (Ger-Eng), 1685-1759.

Though a virtuoso on the harpsichord in his youth, GFH's compositions for the instrument are the least attractive of his output, surpassed not only by the choral works but also by the violin-harpsichord sonatas and organ concertos.   The spare, austere quality of the music is due partly to the fact that, in performance, GFH himself provided rich ornamentation and expected others to do likewise.   Eight suites published during his lifetime contain the best of his music, and are found in Vol I of most publications.   The second volume usually contains an assortment of unpublished early works (he wrote nothing for harpsichord in his later years), among which are a few choice items.

Scholars will wish to acquire the definitive, critical (German only) edition of his keyboard works by HHA (only vols II and III have appeared to date).   The eight suites contain usually four or five pieces, not limited to Bach's ACSOG formula (allemande-courante-sarabande-optional group-gigue) of dances, but including variations, gigues, and adagios.

Suite II in d.   Here two highly-ornamented adagios alternate with an allegro and a fuga, entirely unornamented. Very attractive, if tempos are strongly contrasted, ornaments neatly executed, and voices clearly delineated. Though nuance is limited on the harpsichord, there is no reason why the pianist should not use to the full this capacity of the piano.   Mod

Suite No 5 in E. This opens with two of those typically Baroque movements with a pattern of continuous flowing 16th notes, moving from one voice to another, reposeful
and placid. The chords of the first movt break into a free,
rolling cadenza at the end. The Courante must be much
lighter and faster; and the closing variations on the hymn-
like "Harmonious Blacksmith" theme, can end with dashing
bravura. Mod Dif

Suite No 7 in g. The longest of all, with six movts,
this begins well with a bold orchestral overture. The Sarabande should be played with the freedom of an improvisation, with harpsichord "doublings" and additional ornaments
on repeats. The other movements are less attractive,
though contrast of andante, allegro and vivo tempos will help.
The once admired Passacaglia seems dull, with its simple
four-meas theme, by comparison with the grand one by
Couperin in b, or Bach's for organ in c.

HARRIS, ROY (USA), 1898- .

Revered and prolific composer who has had the integrity to maintain his own style in the face of changing
trends. He has shaped a distinctive idiom out of tonal harmony, with frequent quartal chords, modal scales and folk-
like rhythms.

Sonata, Op 1 (1928). A four-movt work, experimenting with devices perfected in later suites. Harris' fondness
for massive slow-moving chords appears in the Prelude and
Coda, with an Andante Ostinato and a bustling Scherzo between. Mod

Suite (1942): Occupation, Contemplation, Recreation.
Three contrasting movements, all idiosyncratic and pianistic.
Occupation has a broad octave theme with a steady beat but
cross-meters. Contemplation shows Harris at his best, improvising on a folk-tune (The Irish hymn, "Be Thou My Vision") with surprising harmonization and resolutions. Recreation is a dancey piece, as vigorous and bumptious as a
tarantelle. Mod

American Ballades. Intended as solo pieces inspired
by folk-song, these turn out to be little more than rather
pedestrian arrangements of Laredo (cf. Barber's inspired Ex-

cursion No 3), Wayfaring Stranger, The Bird, Black Is the
Color of My True Love's Hair, Cod Liver Ile. Mod

Toccata (1949). The best work by Harris, this bravura piece is modelled on Bach, and might have been called
Toccata, Chorale and Fugue, after its three linked parts.
Bright unison figures in highly diversified rhythmic and touch
patterns come to rest in quiet chordal cadences. A gigue-
like passage breaks into a cadenza bridge to the sonorous
chorale, in 9/4 time. A 3-v fugue is neatly developed from
toccata motifs, and ends with flashy coda. Good concert
piece. Mod Dif

HARRISON, LOU (USA), 1917- .

Six Sonatas (1943). A maverick composer of odd but
highly musical works, his one-movt sonatas are better for
harpsichord, with their intimate linear 2-v writing, in modern harmony. Mod E

Suite (1964).   LH here adopts the serial idiom,
with a free-wheeling Prelude marked by wild dynamic shifts.
The lyric Aria is also free in tempo. A Mediaeval conductus
is the surprising third, using a cantus firmus overlaid with
keyboard acrobatics. A breezy Rondo closes. Dif

HAUFRECHT, HERBERT (USA), 1909- .

Folk-song collector, editor, arranger, and composer
has written numerous works for band, and some useful piano
pieces.

Sicilian Suite. The three movts, a Prelude, Sicili-
ana, and Tarantella, capture the atmosphere of the colorful
island. Require drive and control. Mod Dif

Passacaglia and Fugue. Sixteen variations on a
ground bass form a solid sizable work and mount to a powerful coda. Mature musicianship demanded. Mod Dif

Toccata on Familiar Tunes (1970). Lively, imaginative recital piece for advanced students. Tonal-bitonal;
scintillating. Mod

Five Etudes in Blues (1951). Well-conceived and contrasting within the context of early "soul-music" and jazz, the five are a toccata, ostinato, dialogue, nocturne, and capriccio. Mod

Three Nocturnes. Mood-pieces, contrasting, with passages in tonally anchored chromaticism. Mod

Sonata (1958) A three-movt full-scale work, somewhat more dissonant than the Passacaglia, but conventional in harmony and piano idiom. Mod

HAYDN, JOSEF (Aus), 1732-1809.

Born three years before Bach's youngest son, Haydn saw the meteoric arc of Mozart's brief career, watched Beethoven become "the grand Mogul" of Vienna, and died the year before Chopin was born. He thus not only linked the Baroque Era with the Romantic, but also lived through the Rococo Age, and brought its finest product, the sonata, to flower, with his 104 symphonies and 52 piano sonatas.

There is much confusion about the numbering of the sonatas. Haydn scholars will welcome the new three-volume critical edition just released by the Joseph Haydn Institute of Cologne. The serious piano student is urged to acquire the four volumes of the Lea Pocket Scores, which contain the Breitkopf-Härtel edition, chronologically arranged, with a complete thematic index in Vol I (the numbering used here) and some helpful notes. Unlike Minerva (and Brahms), Haydn did not spring full-blown from the head of Jove, and his progress from simple early works, to mature (but still experimental) late ones is fascinating.

Sonatas in G, Nos 6 and 11. Vol I (LPS pub). No 6 is an embryo of the later, large-scale, four-movt work, No 11. The latter has a dashing presto in 3/8, an andante in the rare key of g minor, and a closing Minuet. E

Sonata in E, No 13. The E Major (Moderato 2/4) though somewhat dry and angular, is a neat, taut, example of Allegro form in the outer movements, with a major-minor menuetto da capo. E

Sonata in D, No 14. More winsome and expansive,

with a fuller treatment of the development, is No 14. The
Presto shows Haydn already experimenting with odd phrase
lengths, using a five-meas period instead of the usual four.

Sonata in D, No 19. Full maturity is reached here
with a bold dramatic Allegro, a lyric Andante (really adagio),
and a fine Finale that combines the qualities of a light-
hearted scherzo with variation form, and a brilliant ending.
Mod

Sonata in c, No 20. Only five of the 52 Sonatas are
in minor keys (Mozart has only two) but all are good. This
(moderato 4/4) is Haydn's "Sturm und Drang" period (when
he married the wrong wife); and is full of agitation, yearn-
ing, resignation, carried out on a Beethovenian scale. One
of the best. Mod Dif

Sonata in A, No 30. As Haydn develops, his allegros lengthen with a series of contrasting themes. This unusual one (allegro 2/4) has only two movts, but at the end
of the first JH introduces an adagio, a slow 3/4 cantilena
ending in E that serves as an Intermezzo. The other movement is a Menuetto with variations, a form which JH handles
well. Mod

Sonata in b, No 32. Vol III contains three of the
minor key sonatas. This bold one is full of surprising and
satisfying sounds, and ends with one of those characteristic
presto scherzos that require sure-footed finger work. Mod
Dif

Sonata in e, No 34. This has an attractive presto
6/8 first movt, but the slow middle movt is one of many with
a highly elaborated melodic line, difficult to sustain. One
is tempted to call in a flautist, to help out. Mod

Sonata in C, No 35. The popularity of this is probably due to the catchy first theme, which suggests the "Clock
Symphony," the "Surprise Symphony," etc. It is not, however, a children's piece, and played allegro con brio C, is
a brilliant recital number, with another elaborate andante,
and a very eupeptic finale. The Esterhazy Princes dined
well, and enjoyed cheerful background music. Mod Dif

Sonata in D, No 37. Another all-time favorite, this
has lured many a careless student to his downfall, with its
jolly introduction. It is also a virtuoso piece requiring a

polished technic.   The four-line Largo e sostenuto is moving-ly eloquent; and the Finale is the boisterous, folksy Haydn at his best.   Mod Dif

Sonata in F, No 47.   A favorite of the author, and one of only three in F major (Moderato 3/4), the first movt is a suave, flowing duet between the hands, full of surprise modulations, and doubling in 3rds and octaves for the coda. The Larghetto in f minor is as fine as an aria from a Mozart opera, and needs the same vocal legato and nuance, and careful ornamentation.   It ends on an unresolved dominant chord.   While the closing allegro does not quite rise to the inspiration of the other movements, it is effective, if played non troppo allegro.   Mod

Sonata in E♭, No 49.   Haydn's second youth (at the age of 70) produced some of his greatest symphonic and choral works, but the last four piano sonatas are mostly of interest to the historian.   No 49 was dedicated to Frau Mari-anne von Gensinger whose friendship gladdened these years (with the unsatisfactory wife ensconced in her own house). Another friend, Mozart, who as a youth had imitated Haydn, now, after his death, influences him (compare the cross-hand passage of the adagio with Mozart's great Fantasy in c). Mod

Sonata in E♭, No 52.   For some curious reason, this, the last and one of the least attractive of Haydn's sonatas, appears as No 1 in most collections, where its formidable complexity must have frightened many a student away from the finer things to follow.   Dif

Andante with Variations in f.   JH was fond of varia-tion form, and wrote several sets, often using variations as a sonata movement.   The first movt of Sonata 42 in D is similar to this set, with an andante for the theme.   In the f minor variations the theme is a full-fledged two-part piece in itself, following the minor section with one in F major. Only three variations and a grand coda and reprise follow, but they are among the finest things written by Haydn, ex-pressive, original and brilliant.   Mod Dif

Adagio in F.   Three separate solo movts of value are to be found, along with the variations, in a Kalmus volume of pieces.   The Adagio promises much, and employs all FH's keyboard devices in an over-elaborated manner, but the basic melodic and harmonic materials are not sufficiently attractive to sustain interest. Mod

Capriccio in G. Highly regarded by the composer, this is a good solo piece. A minuet-like folk tune in uneven phrases of 5 and 3 meas is treated as a rondo theme, with many related episodes and excursions. Though marked moderato, it is more effective at an allegro tempo. Mod

Fantasia in C. This should be played presto possibile, and is a delightful example of Haydn's keyboard mastery employed to evoke a whole orchestra, and create a jolly outdoor mood of merriment. Fine solo number (5 min). Mod Dif

HEIDER, WERNER (Ger), 1930- .

Landschaftspartitur (1970). Successful composer of small ensemble works (including jazz combo) this Stockhausen disciple has produced a "Landscape Score," which, like some of the paintings exhibited nowadays, gives one a feeling of déjà vu. The ten separate sheets (at one dollar a sheet) might be worth the price, if they were more colorful, and one could paper a room, or frame them. As music, they resemble so closely Stockhausen's Klavierstücke (he wrote 11) that little new seems added to the totally organized yet hermetic writing. If this sort of thing is to continue (it is on the wane), we can only hope that Moog, Muzak & Co. will invent a machine into which such sheets can be fed, in the manner of the old player-piano rolls, and one can sit back and hear the sounds intended, without the blood-sweat-and-tears of trying to read it. While at it, Mr. Moog could produce an audience of robots wound-up to clap at the right time, and leave musicians, pianists, and listeners free for their legitimate activities. (CFP pub) V Dif

HEININEN, PAAVO (Fin),

Sonatina (1957). Traditional short F-S-F in highly contemporary idiom. Fine finger-passage work required in wide-ranging 1st; crepuscular 2nd, building to expressive climax. Rapid unison figures alternate with clashing chords for finale. For those who like intransigent dissonance. (Westerlund pub) Dif

HELLER, STEPHEN (Hun-Fr), 1813-1888.

Rival of Chopin, as a piano virtuoso, SH wrote quantities of salon pieces, dances, studies, of which only the latter are known today. They still provide good material for the student not yet ready for the big time. Some of the pieces deserve revival.

The Art of Phrasing, Op 16. Though the musical content of these is pale and faded, it is several cuts above Czerny, and gives the student some purpose in wiggling his fingers. Mod E

Studies, Op 45, 46, 47, 138. Similar to the above. The late set is somewhat more difficult. Mod

Tarantelles, Op 85. Though easy, these are attractive and effective. No 2 in A♭ is best known. Mod E

Nocturne in c♯. Not likely to replace Chopin's in the same key, but more musical than Field's. Mod

Promenades d'un Solitaire. Many other sets bear picturesque titles: White Nights, Trips Outside My Room, In the Woods. There are also four sonatas and three sonatinas probably not thumping enough for the "revivalists."

HELPS, ROBERT (USA), 1928- .

Pianist and award-winning composer, Helps continues to write only for 10 fingers, 88 piano keys, and a good piano. The latter is mentioned advisedly, as the composer's predilection for the extremes of the keyboard and for a rich string sonority demand a good instrument but no gadgets.

Recollections (1959). It is permitted, when reminiscing, to be discursive, and this extended work in large A-B-A form lasts eight minutes. The opening "recalls" Griffes' Lake and night music, with its insistent syncopated 2/4 triad accompaniment in the middle of the keyboard. A wide-spaced slow melody rings in the treble, with an occasional deep bass chime. When the recollections threatened to become "long-winded" with their mesmeric beat, double-note trills break in with a new train of thought, returning only briefly at the end to the "memory" rhythm. Mod Dif

Three Etudes. The first of these brief brilliant
sketches is a bright moto perpetuo in double notes, with an
unflagging rhythm that says it all in one min. In the second
a delicious fruity piano sound emerges from a sequence of
arpeggiated figures which provide a wash for a slow silvery
chiming melody, based on the same notes. Ternary form
again introduces contrast in the 3-min piece. The third
etude is a busy toccata, non-symmetrical, but persistently
propulsive, with both melody and counter-themes hammered
out in 2nds. All are demanding. Dif

Portrait (1960). This attractive mood-piece might be
a Self Portrait of the Dual Nature of the Artist, like Schumann's Florestan-Eusebius music. Brash metallic chords
clang out an introduction, but soon give way to a gentle songful style in 3- and 4-v, often at the outer reaches of the
keyboard. Though the noisy extrovert bashes in occasionally, the introspection wins out and ends in a sanguine mood.
Mod Dif

Quartet. This 15-min piano solo derives its title
from the four movts, each of which is said to use "only 22
notes of the keyboard." Like good serial music, this conceals the device on which it is built; but four distinct movts,
all in Helps' highly personal style, emerge. Here are no
subito fff, followed by subito ppp, three sec later. Instead
large arcs of slow melody, often in 2-v, swell and diminish,
enhanced with a rich variety of repeated secondary figures,
sonorous and hypnotic in their impact. Dif

HENSELT, ADOLPH VON (Ger), 1814-1889.

Virtuoso performer, composer, friend of Liszt and
for 40 years a teacher of young Russian girls, AvH is emerging again today with two recordings and occasional performances of his concerto, and books of etudes.

Etudes, Op 2, Books I, II. In those days (as now)
the clever pianist specialized. AvH became noted for his
smooth execution of widely extended chords and arpeggios.
Many of the etudes provide such stretching exercises, along
with staccato repeated notes, hammered octaves, scale passages. No 6 was once ubiquitous under the title Si j'étais
Oiseau. Mod to Dif

HENZE, HANS WERNER (Ger), 1926- .

Outstanding in Europe for his operas and instrumental works, frequently recorded, HWH has, like so many others nowadays, written little for piano alone (he has two concertos for piano and orchestra). His vocal writing is more traditional than his piano music, but all are non-tonal, highly dissonant, frequently dodecaphonic.

Variations (1948). More scholarly than musical, the set is effective, but angular and unpianistic. Dif

Sonata (1959). Large-scale three-movt work in free tonality, concerned with rhythmic and contrapuntal contrasts, indifferent to limitations of keyboard and hands, and hence technically and musically formidable. Dif

HERNANDEZ MONCADA, EDUARDO (Mex), 1899- .

Costena (1964). Brilliant etude on rhythmic problems and sonorities. Passages in bi-tonality give piquancy; no key signature, but 6/8, allegro giusto. (SMP pub) Mod

HERZ, HENRI (Aus), 1803-1888.

Variations on the March from Bellini's "I Puritani"; Etude in A♭, Op 153:2 "Au bord du Lac"; etc. Piano-manufacturer, teacher and virtuoso performer who, while barnstorming in the U.S., was offered a contract by P. T. Barnum, along with Adelina Patti, who was to be billed as an actual angel in captivity. A record of selections has recently been released. It is not likely to cause a stampede on music stores for copies of the music, though the record is good for a laugh, the first time through. "Truly crunchy knuckle-breakers"; and "...you hear one, you've heard 'em all" (New York Times).

HILLER, FERDINAND (Ger), 1811-1899.

This contemporary and friend of Chopin, Liszt, Berlioz and Mendelssohn was an active composer and conductor and his concertos are now having a brief revival. His name rounds out the litany of rehabilitated 19th century "H's"--Hummel, Heller, Herz, Hünten, Henselt.

His many collections, Schumann-like, are mostly inferior, but a few stand out. Op 54, 81 and 130 each contain a piece called Ghaselen, from an ancient Persian verse form which FH converts into an attractive lyric rondo alternating a ritornello with disparate episodes.

HINDEMITH, PAUL (Ger-USA) 1895-1963.

Highly esteemed as a teacher and theorist, PH seems
not to be very popular with pianists. Though he has written
three piano sonatas, two dance suites, a large contrapuntal work
and a concerto, none of these is, at the time of writing, available on records. The blame for this must rest with pianists,
since there are records of 23 chamber sonatas, for combinations ranging from tuba and piano to viola d'amore and piano.
The lack of appeal in the piano music is due to its severely intellectual structure, to an absence of keyboard exhibitionism
(though the writing is always pianistic), and to a harmonic schem
devoid of sensuous appeal--dry and arcane.

PH early found his personal style in the revival of Baroque counterpoint, and of the classical sonata allegro. He also developed a very personal harmonic scheme, based on the
cycle of overtones, variously described as "expended diatonic-
ism," "chromaticized tonality," "polytonality." Tonally anchored, and full of recognizable cadences and resolutions, the
sounds between these nodal points shift so swiftly and unpredict-
ably that the hearer is bewildered; and ears that accept both traditional harmony and the unresolved dissonance of contemporary
writing reject this, as people reject semi-abstract art (Picasso's Chicago monstrosity: dog, woman, free form?). The finest writing for piano is the large concerto, called "The Four
Temperaments." Careful study and sympathetic performance
of the other works might well win over an audience.

Suite "1922," Op 26: Marsch, Schimmy, Nachtstuck,
Boston, Ragtime. The attraction to classical forms that was to
dominate his life is here coupled with an interest in popular music; and instead of the traditional minuets and gigues are five
contrasting movts using jazz rhythms from the frenetic post-
World War I years. The slow aria is replaced by a lyrical nocturne, fine enough to stand alone. Though the fourth piece is
called Boston, the scene evoked is the brilliant pre-Hitler Berlin of Weill, Brecht and Isherwood.

Sonata No 1 (1936). Already master of his idiom,
PH is still experimenting with form in this massive five-
movt work. Inspired by Holderlin's poem, "The Sea," the
composer's obsession with form rather than program is apparent. The short two-page first movt is actually only an
exposition, with two themes in A and E. The slow march,
marked II, and the "Lively" III, take the place of a sonata
development, while IV is the allegro return, with the B and
A themes reversed. The finale has the unusual time signature
of 3 dotted half-notes, again marked in English, "Lively, but
building a mighty climax with very idiosyncratic figuration and

chordal writing.   Dif

Sonata No 2, 1936.   Shortest and most accessible of
the sonatas, this three-movt, 10-min work has attractive
melodic and rhythmic figures, finely organized.   Though no
key-signatures are ever used, the essence of sonata writing
is key contrast and modulation, and every sonata movement
written by PH ends with as firm a tonic chord as a Handel
aria.   Though the key is often unpredictable, the alert player
may work back from the final tonic, and find that all the
elements of sonata allegro are there and clearly defined.
What PH lacks (as does much of Prokofief) is an emotional
impact; and only in the brief "ruhig," bridging to the rondo
finale, and serving as coda, is the music truly expressive.
Mod

Sonata No 3, 1936.   This large-scale work (four-
movts, 20 min) has all the features and faults of PH.   Built
on imaginative motifs in faultless structure, it has a gray-
ness and monotony of texture that soon palls.   The opening
theme has an English folk-song mode, but lacks a suitable
contrast.   The melodic material of II is too slight for such
extended treatment, even with the brief unison running passage for contrast.   The closing fugue is finely crafted, and
adds a broad coda, settling firmly on B♭.

Ludus Tonalis (1943).   Driven from Nazi Germany,
PH wrote the sonatas in Turkey, and this work at Yale University; but wherever he was, his world was one of classical forms.   This is subtitled "Studies in Counterpoint, Tonal
Organizations and Piano Playing."   Obviously meant as a
contemporary Well-Tempered Clavier, it succeeds very well,
consisting of 12 fugues in different keys, (each key is named
though no signatures are written out), linked by 12 Interludes, each beginning in the key of the previous fugue and
ending in the key of the ensuing one, framed by a Praeludium and Postludium, in Bach's free fantasy manner, with arpeggiated broken-chord sequences alternating with quiet arioso sections.   The Postludium is an exact retrograd inversion of the Praeludium, a device employed on a smaller
scale many times throughout the work, along with all the other standard contrapuntal conceits.   The inspiration is remarkably high throughout, with lilting dances, cool pastorales, boisterous marches, scurrying scherzos, flying toccatas, and one poignant lyric, for Intermezzos.   Though separate pieces might be lifted out for performance, the whole
80-min work is so organically unified that it should be played

as a whole. When pianists have grown tired of tricks inside
the piano and climbed out, this solid work should again find
its place on programs, perhaps paired with the Diabelli or
Goldberg variations. Dif

HODDINOTT, ALUN (GB), 1929- .

This Welsh-born composer has the fluent musicality
of his people and a pianistic style that resists the urge to
be contemporary. He has six sonatas and many small
pieces.

Sonata No 3, Op 40. A one-movt work--taut, brilliant
and original. Expressive free rhapsodic adagio leads to vigorous, propulsive allegro with wavering bass figures under
ringing chords in declamatory phrases. Mod Dif

Sonata No 5 (1969). Traditional-modern four-movt
15 min work. Fast outer movts frame two slow arias--
rhapsodic, coloristic and dynamically contrasted. Tone-
clusters, free rhythms and original motifs add to the interest. Closes with driving Toccata. Difficult to read, but not
to play. Mod

Sonatina for Clavichord, Op 18. Though intended for
the small but expressive clavichord, these can be effective
on piano. Four brief movts, prelude, scherzo, solemn
elegy, and presto finale. Thin-textured, ornamented, imaginatively modern. Mod E

Second Nocturne, Op 16:1. Delicate adagio (without
key), introspective, lyric, building to an impassioned turbulent climax. Effective and affective. Mod Dif

HOFFMANN, E. T. A. (Ger), 1776-1822.

This contemporary of Beethoven is important as one
of the first romantic fiction writers (his "Tales of Hoffmann" inspired not only Offenbach's operetta, but also many
works by Schumann). He was both an amateur composer and
an established music critic, whose writings on Mozart (the
"A." in his name is for Amadeus) are still admired. His

four piano sonatas rank with those of the many epigone who
tried their hand at this form.

Sonata No 1 in f: Adagio e con gravita; Allegro,
Larghetto; Allegro. The bold romantic novelist was neither
a keyboard virtuoso nor a fugalist, and here reverts to an
early classical form, homophonic, harmonically unadventur-
ous. The derivations from Mozart and C. P. E. Bach are obvious, but need not deter one from enjoying an obscure work.
Mod

HOFFMANN, RICHARD (Aus-USA), 1925- .

Variations: Piano Pieces (1947). This colorful composer, born in Austria, educated in New Zealand, amánuensis
to Schönberg, writes in an original serial technic (not neces-
sarily 12-tone) highly organized as to intervals, rhythms,
meters, timbres and dynamics. Preceding the variations
are a Fantasy-Grave, a Scherzo and Trio--Presto. Dif

Three Small Pieces (1947). These three serial miniatures take a unique form; the first is for LH; the second
uses mutations of the row for RH alone; and the third combines the two. Dif

HOFMANN, JOSEPH (Pol-USA), 1876-1957.

Three Impressions: L'Orient, L'Occident, Penguins;
Four Old Dutch Songs; Tone Pictures, Op 88. One of the
all-time great virtuosi of the keyboard (another Pole), JH
shared with other greats (Schnabel, Casadesus) the desire to
leave a more permanent legacy than his playing, in the form
of compositions. These appeared both under his own name
and under the pseudonym of Michael Dvorsky. They are
florid, fluent, Romantic-Impressionist and of minor importance. Mod Dif

HOLZMAN, RUDOLPH, (Ger-Peru), 1910- .

German music educator and composer living in Peru
has two piano suites.

Première Petite Suite (1941). Six-movt, neo-classic work, conventional, academic and correct, but offering nothing new. Mod

Pequeña Suite (1944). Similar to the above, but based on Peruvian song and dance melo-rhythms, which gives it some freshness. Also six-movts. Mod

HONEGGER, ARTHUR (Swi-Fr), 1892-1955.

A blend of Swiss Protestant phlegm and "gaiety Parisienne" met in this member of the Les Six. His best works are big religious dramas or small chamber sonatas. The piano music is less important and suffers from the dichotomy. Always basically tonal, his writing uses a free chromaticism that adds an attractive astringency.

Trois Pièces (1910-1915). The Prelude is introspective, harmonically acerbic but climactic. Best is the moving Cantabile Hommage à Ravel (can be played separately). Fast closing dance requires endurance and control. Mod Dif

Toccata and Variations. Large scale work, pianistic and basically tonal but with pungent dissonances. Toccata is vif alla breve, with a rapid three-note figuration over a bold tune, alternating with chordal passages, and a brief lento version of the tune. A chorale in e♭ provides the theme for six well-developed characteristic variations, with changes of rhythmic motif, key and tempo building to a serene close in the major. Demanding musically. Dif

Sept Pièces Brève (1919-1920): Souplement, Vif, Très lent, Legerement, Lent, Rhythmique, Violent. French brevity is an important factor in this charming suite (all one-page except the last). Nos 1, 2 and 4 call for a very feathery touch, a fast tempo and discreet pedal. Unique rhythmic motifs over shifting chromatic chords build a climax in No 3. No 5 is a flamenco dance, alternating an almost torpid habanera with wailing Moorish melisma and the rattle of castanets. No 6 suggests the circus, so recurrent in French art of this period. No 7 is a brilliant, explosive toccata. Dif

Le Cahier Romand (1921-1923). This "Swiss Sketch Book" contains five short pieces, mostly quiet, bucolic, though No 4 suggests a rural dance. Requires imaginative interpretation. Mod

Hommage à Albert Roussel (1928). Another of the many French "hommages," which, like portraits of unknown individuals, often fail to communicate. This brief sketch is homophonic, varying the martial rhythm with a syncopated theme. Mod

Prélude, Arioso et Fughetta (1932). "On the name of Bach," all three parts of this work use the familiar tight four-note theme, with its harmonic ambiguity (both B and B♭). The form also derives from Bach's Fantasias, with an arpeggiated improvisory opening, free arioso over a cantus firmus, and a 3-v fughetta, non legato. Not excessively long or difficult; effective. Mod

Deux Esquisse (1943). The first sketch is in free wide-ranging improvised style; the second, quiet and elegiac. Mod

HOVHANESS, ALAN SCOTT (USA), 1911- .

AH should be picketed with placards reading UNFAIR TO PIANISTS; for though he has vastly expanded the quantity of piano literature, his music is completely without editorial marks, and information which would greatly enhance the performance of his exotic and enigmatic works is completely absent. The pieces, which include numerous large-scale sonatas labelled "Madras" or "Lake of Van," as well as many suites and small pieces, have now passed the Opus 300 mark, and the composer has started using dates. AH seems never to use the wastebasket, and the failure to select, re-write and edit has resulted in the burying of the few gems he wrote in a mass of mediocrity. His finest work to date using piano, is a Concerto for Piano, Four Trumpets and Percussion, named "Khaldis" (why?). The blend of Oriental instrumental effects and Renaissance polyphony is unique and exhilarating.

Sonatina, Op 120 (1964). This simple and effective 3-movt work is an example of the need for information. The entire work is based on Japanese pentatonic (sans tonic or dominant). Mod E

Jhala, Op 103 (1952).   This exotic program number bears an Indian name, but begins with a three-phrase Japanese "haiku" (5-notes, 7-notes, 5-notes) and continues throughout with "samisen" figures, punctuated with deep temple-bell tones, played with a timpani mallet on the bass strings.   Mod

Fantasy on an Ossetin Tune, Op 85:6.   This place name, not to be found in an atlas, is kindly identified for us by William Masselos, to whom the piece is dedicated (a district in the Armenia of AH's ancestors).   A fine work in two parts, combining the plaintive Middle Eastern wail and cimbalom tremolos with a spirited dervish dance.   Mod

Pastorale, Op 111:2.   Space music, this has more helpful directions for the interior effects of thumb-nail glassandi and timpani beats.   Like many of AH's works, it ends with a charming passage of polyphony.   Mod

Shalimar, Op 177.   This suite suggests Indian ragas, with its Jhala of the Fountains, of the Rain, of the Waterfall.   The irregular repeated-note figures imitate plectrum and percussion; but the alternating contrapuntal interludes are rather commonplace.   Simpler; good for students.   Mod E

Achtamar: Adagio (imitating the Tmpoong), Allegro (imitating the Kanoon and Oud).   Again we are indebted to Masselos for the news that the "Tmpoong" is a clay drum; the "Kanoon" [also, "canun"], a zither; and the "oud" a lute. This exotic yet pianistic work also has a programmatic basis in the Biblical legend of Tamar.   Mod

HUMMEL, JOHAN NEPOMUK (Aus), 1778-1837.

A good example of how false our judgments of contemporaries can be, JNH was "discovered" by Mozart, taken into his home and trained for two years.   Both his playing and his music were considered the equal of Beethoven's in his day.   Today a few of the concertos are occasionally taken out for an airing, but the many piano sonatas and solos are largely forgotten.   The four-hand music is better.

Rondo in E♭, Op 11.   Fluent and innocuous.   Mod

Variations on a Gavotte by Gluck, Op 57. Naive and amusing, they anticipate Chopin in their use of a vocal fioritura and decorative filigree figures. These are also the characteristics of his harmonically and formally banal concertos. Mod

HÜNTEN, FRANZ (Ger), 1793-1878.

Etude in C, Op 81:1; Galop in A; Grand valse brillante, Op 120; Variations on the March from Bellini's "Norma." Like his pupil, Herz, FH dazzled Paris with his keyboard wizardry, made a small fortune teaching jeunes filles and published over 200 pieces (actually the same piece with 200 titles.) For comments, see Herz.

HUZELLA, ELEK (Hun), 1915- .

Cambiate (1968). Brief contemporary suite in three-movts, 4 min 3 sec, pianistic, clear-textured and appealing. Invocazione is a free canon in inversion, each hand playing a theme of two-note chords in small intervals, atmospheric. Esclamazione alternates rapid ostinatos of massive chords for the "exclamatory" effect with expressive thin-textured chromatic lines. Closing Nenia is another canon (strict) using the same device of two-note chords in both hands, but wider-spaced, for an introspective effect. Mod Dif

IBERT, JACQUES (Fr), 1890-1962.

Petit maître whose music is marked by Gallic wit, clarity and brevity.

Histoires: The Little White Donkey, A Giddy Girl. Mood and program music of moderate difficulty, with impressionistic harmony, jazz syncopation. Best known are the sparkling staccato study The Little White Donkey and the sentimental Giddy Girl. Others are: The Crystal Cage, Abandoned Palace, and Cortege of Balkis. Mod E

INDY, VINCENT D' (Fr), 1851-1931.

Noted French pedagogue whose ventures into piano writing were rare and not highly successful. The strongest influences, which he passed on to his many pupils, were Bach, Beethoven and Wagner (via Franck) and the Gregorian chant, for the revival of which he founded the famous Schola Cantorum. The cyclic form of Liszt and Franck and the Wagnerian leitmotiv become an obsession with Vd'I.

Poème des Montagnes, Op 15. Large symphonic poem for piano, whose three connected movts contain 10 tableaux inspired by the composer's courtship, marriage, and honeymoon with a "theme of the beloved" leitmotiv unifying them. In spite of all the brouhaha, it ends up as rather plodding sentimental salon music. Mod

Helvetia Waltzes, Op 17. Named after three Swiss villages, these lengthy works are pianistic but boringly unimaginative. Mod

Sonata in E Major, Op 63. Currently being revived, this triptych exemplifies the best and worst in d'Indy. Its bold structure is its finest feature, framing a scherzo (with contrasting trio in 5/4) with two sets of variations, all parts derived from the same motifs. But pious mysticism and academic scholarship suffuse the work and it fails to take wings. Dif

Fantasia on an Old French Air, Op 99. Here VDI is at his best, retaining the charm of folk-music expressed in exuberant ebullience. Folk songs also inspired the fine "Symphony on French Mountain Airs," which is actually a piano concerto. Mod

IRELAND, JOHN (GB), 1879-1962.

The many fine piano works of this composer, though seldom heard today, will probably survive, when all the brouhaha over forgotten 19th-century hacks and the 1960's "glossolalia" have died down. His finest music was for the piano, and an original recognizable voice can be heard throughout.

Decorations (1912-1913): The Island Spell, Moonglade, The Scarlet Ceremonies. Three contrasting pieces

(about 5 min each)--pianistic, evocative, not easy but with
a brilliance of effect surpassing their difficulty. The first,
inspired by the Channel Isles, uses a bell-tone melody above
unique undulating piano figures that build to a great storm
crest, then subside. Moon-glade is hypnotic and lyric. The
Scarlet Ceremonies is both mystic and brilliant, with virtuoso
keyboard writing that requires mature technic. (Aug pub)
Mod Dif

    London Pieces (1920). The mystic and pastoral here
give way to the bustle of city life. Three pieces: Chelsea
Reach, Ragamuffin, and Soho Forenoons. The second is
best, with its quirky humorous scampering figures, harmonic surprises and jaunty rhythm. (Aug pub) Mod

    Four Preludes. These also have evocative titles, and
begin to explore dissonances and rhythmic freedoms not
found in earlier works. The Undertow, Obsession, The Holy
Boy, and Fire of Spring. (B/H pub)

    Rhapsody (1915). A 14-page, neo-Brahmsian, thick-
textured, intense work that contrasts rugged chordal writing
with lyrical linear passages building to a fine frenetic climax. Dif

    Sonata (1920). Well-structured, pianistic three-movt
(31-page) work in late-romantic style, with original harmonic texture, the brilliant octave passages and double-note figures always serving musical ends. Requires mature musicianship. (Aug pub) Mod Dif

    Sonatina. Shorter and lighter, but taut, terse and
fully-realized. Atmospheric floating second movt, between
a flowing moderato and a moto perpetuo rondo in a gigue
rhythm. (OxU pub) Mod

    Sarnia (1941). A later work, again inspired by is-
lands; this time Guernsey, whose ancient Roman name the
three-piece suite bears. JI fled from the island just before
World War II occupation. Mod

    There is also a piano concerto that deserves revival
and survival.

IVES, CHARLES (USA), 1874-1954.

This American maverick, so much admired today, so snubbed in his writing years, has left a quartet of piano pieces that are the admiration and despair of pianists. The two Sonatas are sui generis masterpieces surpassing any such works written at their time in Europe or America. They are likely to stand as representative of the best American music of the century; and the centennial year will no doubt bring many opportunities to hear them.

They are not so unplayable as considered in Ives' day. Even as late as 1952, Friskin and Freundlich speak of them as "impossible to play," and do not even list No 1, which has now been played in public, and recorded by three pianists (No 2 has four recordings). Ten years after the historic first performance of No 2 (the "Concord") by Ralph Kirkpatrick, William Masselos premiered the first. Back in pre-recording days, people became acquainted with symphonies, operas and other large-scale works through four-hand arrangements. Someone might do a great service to music lovers by arranging Ives' two Sonatas in the same way, or for two pianos. CI would have loved it and probably suggested using four!

A good approach to Ives is to begin with the violin sonatas, for while the pianist sweats it out, he can enjoy the lyric line of the violin, and chuckle at the wry, illusive, winsome quotes from familiar tunes. Perhaps only those who grew up singing "Watchman Tell Us of the Night," "Bringing in the Sheaves," "The Old Oaken Bucket," "Work for the Night Is Coming," can enjoy these to the full. No 3, of the four for violin and piano, is perhaps easiest.

Some South-Paw Pitching (1908). Next tackle this, which is only five pages in length. The humorous name is misleading, since the RH has as much work as the LH, as well as several glorious chordal passages, based on "Down in the Cornfield." After the first page, the music uses barlines, but few time signatures. It is within the scope of any serious pianist, and very rewarding. Dif

Three-Page Sonata (1905). CI must have had mammoth manuscript paper, for the printed version runs to 12 pages, and takes over 7 min to play. It is a true sonata in being a grand "sonal" work for keyboard in several related (and continuous) movements. They are labelled allegro moderato, andante, adagio, and allegro-march time, with two più mosso sections (pure rag-time, and better labelled prestissimo) separated by a return of the march. Ives was very contemporary in his desire for all to have a part. In the fine Cambridge recording (which includes a detailed analysis by H. Farbermann) the soloist is joined by a second person playing a slow independent melody on the celeste. The concept (though not the sound) of the fantastically complex lines of independent rhythms in CI is not unlike the Indonesian gamelan.

Sonata No 1 (1902-1909). Though this waited 40 years for its premiere, it is now accorded the highest praise. Lou Harrison, who so painstakingly reconstructed the lost work from surviving sketches, states: "In the tradition of the Hammerklavier and Liszt's b Minor, this is probably the penultimate romantic sonata, the ... Concord, probably the last, for it is almost unthinkable that a work of this kind might be written now or in the near future...." The flowing, sumptuous character of the Sonata, its range of contemplative and heroic, as well as fantastic, expressions, indicate the "grand manner." In 1952, Friskin and Freundlich cautiously warned that such judgments were premature. In 1973, with the quantities of drawing board obfuscation and keyboard glossolalia that have poured forth in the 50s and 60s, we may affirm this with more confidence. The English writer, Wilfred Mellers, pays high tribute to CI in his book; and the composer is greatly admired on the Continent. The Peer edition includes Harrison's detailed analysis of the five-movt, 45-min work. V Dif

Second Pianoforte Sonata, "Concord, Mass., 1840-1860": I Emerson, II Hawthorne, III the Alcotts, IV Thoreau (1902-1909). This programmatic sonata is as formidable as No 1, though the third movt is only 7 min in length and well within the scope of the advanced pianist. Ives was verbose as well as prolix, and his "Essays Before a Sonata" are of more interest to the metaphysician than to the musician. But the brief quote about the Alcott family, before movt No III, will help the performer to identify the thematic material: Beethoven's fate motif, a gospel hymn, a Scots tune, the opening bars of the Lohengrin Wedding March; and thus recreate the homely, whimsical, yet often frenzied and frustrated mood that prevailed under the roof where Little Women and Jo's Boys were written. Lou Harrison points out that the interval of the major 3rd dominates this entire work and gives it its sanguine character. The first Sonata, on the other hand, "is concerned with the minor 2nd and minor 3rd, a motive born of the Baroque pathetic affection, subject of all compositions on the name of BACH, and (14 years later) the subject of the first piece in Schönberg's historical 5 Piano Pieces, Op 23." The movements on the other three Concord "transcendentalists" are formidably difficult (including chord-clusters played with a stick 14 inches long). Any eager beavers wishing to tackle them will find suggestions in Gillespie, Mellers, and a fine analysis in Cowell's biography.   V Dif

JANÁČEK, LEOS (Czech), 1854-1928.

A late-flowering Czech composer with a unique style derived from speech patterns, modal scales, and irregular folk rhythms of Moravia, wrote some striking chamber music using piano.

From an Overgrown Path (1902-1908). Experimental pieces, the first ten simple enough for students, the five in series II, more advanced. The titles of Book I indicate the composer's obsession with short speech motifs (and the mistranslations add to the poetic charm!) "They Chattered like Swallows"; "A Blown-away leave"; "Good Night"; "My word stop" (Tongue-tied?); "So Unutterably Anxious." The music though bewildering in its constant metric shifts and key-changes, is intriguing and fresh.   Mod

Sonata 1, October 1, 1905, "In the Street." This programmatic work was a tribute to a one-man protest staged by a working man in favor of establishing a free University in Brno (where LJ taught in early years). The man was bayonetted, and the three movts were titled Foreboding, Death, and Dead March. The last movt was burned by the highly critical composer, and the manuscript of the first two was thrown in the river, after the premiere. A copy survived, however, and is now published and recorded. One is inclined to agree with LJ's opinion of the sonata, which might have made a good opera, or song cycle (like "One Who Vanished") but is too morbid and intense for the varied moods of a piano sonata. Though somewhat inchoate, much of the remaining music has poignant beauty. The opening theme is modal, quietly intense and unresolved. The contrasting episode is more sanguine, in chorale style; and the development is both pianistic and emotionally powerful. The second frag-

ment suffers from too much use of a unison theme strongly
resembling the "Goin' Home" tune in Dvořák's New World
Symphony but is also expressive. Dif

JARNACH, PHILIP (Sp-Fr), 1892- .

Jarnach was born in France of Spanish and German
parents and lives in Spain; his music however is fundamen-
tally Teutonic. He has numerous piano works, freely chromatic and dissonant; pianistic but demanding.

Sonatina, Op 18. Subtitled "Romancero I," this challenging three-part work requires full musicianship and technic for its dense texture and introspective moods. Dif

Three Pieces. Contrasting dances, grotesque, rhythmic, vivacious. Ballabille, Sarabande, Burlesca. Dif

Kleine Klavierstücke. Brief but not simple, these 10
sketches are mostly in a sinewy, linear two- and three-part
writing. A cycle. Mod

Das Amrumer Tagebuch. Curious but effective "diary" in three-movts: organ-like hymnus, ethereal elegie that
rises to an acme of power; "Sturm Reigen" (Storm Dance),
a wild dashing finale, and a quiet ending. Mod Dif

Sonata No 2 (1952). Large-scale traditional form,
freely chromatic with tonal and unison passages. Demure,
linear first movt; intense, dramatic second. The closing
scherzo is broken by an elegiac passage, but ends with a
flourish. Dif

JELINEK, HANNS (Aus), 1901- .

12-Tone Work, Op 15, Books I, II, III, IV. This
pupil of Schönberg takes the student of serial music from
where Křenek left off, with the row printed in its four permutations. The four two-part inventions of Book I are light
and transparent. More difficult are the six character
sketches of Book II. Three dances make up the third book.
The four Toccatas of Book IV are concert level. Mod to
Dif

JELOBINSKY, VALERY (USSR), 1912-1946.

Six Short Etudes, Op 19.   The early death of this
Soviet composer deprived the world of some fine piano music, to judge by this set.   All are pianistic, original, melodic, quirky and gay, finely organized, tonal, but spiked
with dashes of dissonance.   They are titled :   Toccata,
Nocturne, Valse, Reminiscence, Danse, Recitatif.   An excellent set (about 15 min) or separately.   (Leeds pub)   Mod

JENSEN, ADOLF (Ger), 1837-79.

One of many 19th-century German romantic composers
whose works are so uniform in form and style as to be largely neglected today.   The Romantic movement produced, between Schubert and Brahms, so many successful composers,
that the many less successful ones, who might have shone in
a more arid era, are forgotten.   There is a freshness about
AJ's music that makes it worthy of a hearing.   The Sonata
has recently been recorded.

Wanderbilder, Op 17.   The Romantic fusion of music
with painting, poetry, nature, are evident in the many small
character pieces.   The Mill and Will o' the Wisp are the
best known of this set.   Mod E

Lieder und Tänze, Op 33.   The discovery of "das
Volk" was another enrichment of 19th-century music: Elfin
Dance and Barcarolle are recommended.   Mod

Sonata in f♯, Op 25 (Sehr lebhaft; Nicht zu langsam,
sehr ausdrucksvoll; Scherzo: Unheimlich bewegt mit präg-
nantem Rhythmen; So schnell als möglich, in leidenschaft-
licher Bewegung).   This bold pianistic work has such a
plethora of ideas that the composer could have given us at
least two Sonatas, and still thrown the second movt in the
wastebasket.   The writing reveals both an accomplished pianist and a songwriter, with its bold keyboard figuration and
flourishes, its strong chordal patterns and its long cantabile
lines.   Though there is an exuberant "Spiel-Freude," there
is remarkably little of the keyboard noodling that mere pianists give us.   The impossible second movt uses the song-
writers cheap device of accompanying a banal melody (heard
four times, in soprano, alto, etc.) with after-beat chords.
The Dies Irae is said to be lurking in the background of the

lush, fruity harmony. The third movt, after a bold fanfare,
breaks into a delightful 3-v fugue, with episodes enough for
at least two scherzos. Some of the first movt motifs might
well have been saved for the finale (all movts are in or per-
ilously near to f♯) which is not quite up to the first and
third. Deserves to be heard--33 min (if you must play the
second movt!). Mod Dif

JOHNSON, ROBERT SHERLAW (USA),

Sonata No 2 (1969).   Large three-movt (17-page)
avant-garde virtuoso work, deriving from Messiaen and
Boulez.   Features contrasting piano sonorities produced
both from the keyboard, and inside the piano with finger,
fingernail, soft mallet, etc. Metrical organization in pseudo-
Oriental "ragas," and manipulated thematic intervals are intellectual problems whose aural effect is minimal. (OxU
pub) Dif

Seven Short Pieces (1970). Like the Sonata this is
the sound-for-sound-sake type of avant-garde writing, devis-
ing new ways of making the piano sound like something else.
Directions for these extra-curricular activities, inside the
piano, are explicitly given, and if followed, along with the
legitimate keyboard notes, carefully timed and controlled,
should produce a variety of delicate effects. As Richard
Swift points out (Notes, 28:4:775) exactly this sort of thing
was being done to the piano back in the 1940s in the movies
by Chico Marx and Jimmy Durante, for laughs. Now we
know better; and only smile and applaud. (OxU pub) Dif

JOLIVET, ANDRE (Fr), 1905- .

Established French composer who reacted against the
"laughter of Les Six" (Gibbs), with dense, intense works,
has left two Sonatas almost as formidable as those of Charles
Ives.

Sonata (1951). The first, a tribute to Bartók, is appropriately aggressive, percussive, driving, chordal in style
(like Bach's Op 1, this seems to be written against the piano, rather than for it). Extreme dissonance, complexity
and much obfuscation are present. For those who dare.
(TP pub) V

Sonata II.   Similar to No 1, but using serial technic
in part.   The second theme has a chromatic lyricism that
relieves the unmitigated dissonance of the rest.   The last
movement is fearfully difficult.   (TP pub)   Dif

Five Ritual Dances (1947).   An earlier suite, inspired by the neo-primitive Parisian movement, suggests
Stravinsky's "Sacre" by its titles: Danse initiatique; Danse
du Héros; Danse nuptiale; Danse du rapt; Danse funéraire.
Evidently a piano transcription of an orchestra suite premiered in Paris in 1942.   The piano is inadequate, and the
work is demanding.   Dif

JOPLIN, SCOTT (USA), 1869-1917.

This early American black rag-time pianist and composer rates a place here as the finest exponent of a uniquely American type of music, without which the sonatas of
Ives, the concertos of Gershwin, much of the piano music
of Barber, Copland, Ravel and others would have been impossible.   He is currently being rediscovered and honored
with recordings, a 2 vol ed of his music (pub by New York
Public Library) and a revival of his rag-time opera, Tree-
monisha, a prototype of the folk and rock opera of today.
SJ added to the native musicality and finger-fluency of his
people an education in European classics from a German
teacher in Texas, before devoting himself exclusively to rag-
time, a distinctive type of music which antedated blues and
jazz by some 30 years.   (352p pb version of NYPL hardcover
ed pub by Belwin Mills.)

Maple Leaf Rag; The Entertainer; Wall Street Rag.
SJ's most famous piece is the Maple Leaf Rag, though there is
much fun and excitement in the 30 some others.   They are considered the classics of rag-time, and are characterized by a
hammered, relentless I-V bass, a frenetic drive, rippling arpeggios and ebullient, sparkling RH figures.   Mod to Dif

JOUBERT, JOHN (S Af), 1927- .

Distinguished South African composer of operas, symphonic and chamber music, has a piano concerto and a suite
for piano.

Dance Suite, Op 21 (1958).   Five movements in traditional style, spiced with dissonance, melodic, varied in
rhythms and tempos.   (HWG pub)   Mod

KABALEVSKY, DMITRI (USSR), 1904- .

Children's Pieces, Op 14, 27, 39, 40, 51.   Outstanding Soviet pianist, composer and teacher, DK's educational
work is of first rank.   Master classes in China and Japan,
as well as throughout Soviet Europe are highly successful,
and his many children's pieces are very popular.   Since this
book does not discuss teaching material, these works will
only be listed.

Two Sonatinas, Op 13: No 1 in C, No 2 in G.   The
first sonatina, while easy enough for moderately advanced
students, is so finely wrought in neo-classic style, and so
full of verve and élan that it is concert material.   No 2 is
less attractive.   Mod E

Sonata No 2, E♭, Op 45.   This long three-movt work,
traditional in harmony and classical in form, contains many
of the devices more successfully used in No 3.   The festivamente opening movt has pompous square rhythmic motifs;
the second movt is conventionally romantic; the finale is
lively and sparkling.   Mod

Sonata No 3, F, Op 46.   Neo-classicism at its best,
belonging beside Prokofief's Classic Symphony.   The entire
work is built around a four-note re-do-ti-do motif: sparkling allegro with imaginative bridge passage; rather thin second theme; wistful closing theme, all built into a fine frenzy
in the development, with surprises in the return.   Sentimental 19th-century cantabile; scintillating third.   Firmly tonal
throughout, with occasional bitonality, augmented 9ths,
sprinkled like the soupçon of spice used in a French dish
for piquancy.   Like Liszt, it "sounds better than it is, " but
since sound is the ultimate criterion, Bravo!   Mod Dif

Preludes and Fugues, Op 61.   Six original, but rather overextended works, simple and good for the anti-Bach
student.   Mod E

24 Preludes, Op 38.   The pianist can never have too
many preludes, to balance the big sonatas, suites, variations.

Here are 24 more, attractive, varied, short (two or three pages each--without fugues) arranged in Chopin's key-cycle. They range from moderately easy to moderately difficult, and a set of six or more makes a good program group.

Prelude No 1 in C; No 2 in a. The same chromatic trill-motif introduces both the lyric andantino and the sprightly scherzando.

No 3 in G. A fleet and effective moto perpetuo with a LH cantando theme and staccato patterns under the RH motor.

No 5 in D. Broad sostenuto in triple meter, building to a powerful octave ending.

No 6 in b. Very fast tempos in the quick ones; this is unison throughout, broken chords giving way briefly to solid chords and octaves.

No 7 in A. Opening with a duet contrasting two striking themes, this doubles into 6ths and octaves, using DK's favorite chromatic gruppettos to link melody notes.

No 8 in E. Genial and fetching dance tune, staccato-legato.

No 10 in c♯; No 12 in g♯. Two highly original slow pieces in minor, harmony, rhythm and melody all uniquely developed.

No 13 in F♯. Similar to No 5, on a larger scale.

No 14 in e♭. Scurrying prestissimo possibile, sotto voce, secco. Numerous key/time changes and an added melody make it one of the best.

No 15 in D♭, 16 in b♭. Short amiable scherzo, unison; longer tenebroso, agitated, and brilliant.

No 17 in A♭; No 18 in f. 2-v andantino tranquillo, each voice doubled two octaves higher; dramatic largamente, with wide-span chords.

No 19 in E, No 20 in c. In the style of Prelude No 8, but original; the minor is a waltz melancolique alla Russe.

No 21 in B♭; No 22 in g. Joyous festivamente chordal study in 5/4; and yet another dancey staccato scherzando.

No 23 in F. A tiny masterpiece, unison cantando, with surprise chordal punctuation.

No 24 in d. Bold toccata introducing a Russian folk theme. Large enough to stand alone.

KADOSA, PAUL (Hun), 1903- .

Distinguished composer, pianist and educator who has remained in Budapest through the many changes some of which are reflected in his music, which includes three concertos for piano and orchestra, four sonatas, numerous piano suites, and music for children. His style is harmonically advanced, but introduces national elements.

Four Capriccios, Op 57. Short contrasting pieces with very pianistic keyboard devices, tremolos of octaves and 9ths, undulating arpeggios, distinctive rhythmic motifs. There is little regard for sound, and the form is capriciously free. No key signature, and the sharps and flats sound as if flung on the page as an afterthought. Mod

Sonata No 4, Op 54. Large scale four-movt work with irregular meters boldly treated in first; narrative quality giving way to complex agitato passage; third replaces the minuet with a jazz movt, and a free cadenza leads to closing allegro barbaro. Freely dissonant. Dif

Suite No 2. Four-piece set of moderate difficulty, contrasting a free recitative, unison study, LH study, and closing dance movt. Mod

KASILAG, LUCRETIA P. (Phil), 1918- .

This prominent music educator and promoter has, besides numerous choral and ensemble works experimenting with a synthesis of eastern and western intruments, several piano pieces using folkloric music rhythms.

Burlesque. Sprightly genial 2/4 dance tune in simple

linear style with quartal drum-bass, a triple central andantino sostenuto on the same theme building to an effective
climax, before a return and octave coda.   Mod

Theme and Variations Based on a Filipino Folk Tune
"Walay Angay."   The plaintive eight-meas folk-song in g
has the ideal thematic qualities of Beethoven's c minor Variation theme, with a built-in harmonic scheme leading to a
climactic chord in the penultimate measure.   A harmonized
chordal setting is the first of the 11 variations with running
triplets in alto and tenor gathering momentum in nos 2 and
3.   New rhythmic and melodic variants are developed in the
next group: No 9 moves to c and is boldly chordal with arpeggiated bass.   After a spirited lilting 12/8 dance variation, a modulation to d introduces majestic Russian chime
effects.   A vigorous finale caps the climax.   (Peer Pub)
Mod Dif

KAY, ULYSSES (USA), 1917- .

This successful black choral and symphonic composer seems to have been brought up on Bach's two- and
three-part inventions; and has added two sets of his own,
which are true to Bach's use of the term, though UK's emphasis seems to be more on compositional invention rather
than on keyboard skill.

Eight Inventions (1946).   Pieces in the earlier set
are more difficult and diffuse, ranging from a 3-v allegro,
to a 4-v larghetto, a dramatic improvisory grave, and a
sparkling, rambunctious presto finale.   Mod

Four Inventions (1964).   Lighter, more refined writing.   No 1 in g (without key signature) develops an attractive four-meas idea in three voices, andante moderato; No
2 is 5/8 Scherzando, 2-v, alternating staccato-legato, with
chordal ending.   No 3 is sempre legato, larghetto, four-
part harmonic writing (basically A♭) with a short cadenza-
like bridge, and rolled-chords for coda.   No 4 would make
a good number for the "Swingle Singers," with its bouncing
figures and scales in 2-v.   Mod

KHACHATURIAN, ARAM (USSR), 1903- .

Ranking Soviet composer whose popular works often feature a Middle-Eastern Orientalism (he is of Armenian extraction). A late-starter in composition, his works, while spontaneous and emotional, often suffer from awkward, amateurish writing.

Two Characteristic Pieces (1942-1947). Studies in two-part counterpoint, with programmatic subjects; the first lyric and sombre, the second, introspective and dense. Mod

Two Pieces: Valse Caprice, Danse. Capriciousness is achieved through tempo rubato; the more strongly rhythmic dance is also free. Mod E

Toccata. Musically shallow, but brilliantly effective, with original rhythms in the dashing opening and close; and a fruity contrasting mid-section. Much easier than it sounds. The Poem and Hymn in the original set of three are negligible. Mod

Sonatina (1959). Long educational work, making attractive use of traditional scales and harmony; three movts. Mod E

KIRCHNER, LEON (USA), 1919- .

Better known for chamber and orchestral works, this 1967 Pulitzer prize-winner has written two piano concertos. The keyboard writing compensates for lack of fluent pianism with complexity of texture and intensity of expression.

Sonata (1948). A virtuoso work of formidable technical difficulty. The first three movts are connected, moving from a lento introduction to a doppio movimento section, requiring great power and control; this is linked with a ruminative slow movement. The closing "Allegro Barbaro" takes not only its title but also many of its percussive chordal effects from Bartók. V Dif

KODALY, ZOLTAN (Hun), 1885-1967.

This influential educator, compatriot of Bartók, wrote several children's pieces and two early suites which deserve to be heard.

Nine Pieces, Op 3 (1910). Opens with a lento, simple, original, grave and expressive. No 2 introduces a new voice, later heard in orchestral works: melismatic and free passages alternating with bold proclamatory chords. No 4 is a vigorous Scherzoso, No 5 a Bartókian chordal Furioso, 6 is slow and achieves tristesse with a modal scale; 7 and 8 are sprightly moto perpetuo studies, and the closing one a burlesco--pianistically awkward, but as bold and promising as early Bartók. Mod

Seven Pieces, Op 9 (1910-1918). An uneven set, confirming that piano was not ZK's métier, this contains some choice items. After an experimental opening lento, comes a Szekely Lament (with the words of the plaintive theme written in). In his efforts to "express" at all costs, the composer doubles the theme first in 3rds, then in octaves, and double-octaves; and ends with a ringing bass G, unfortunately below the range of the piano. The early Impressionist poem (No 3) after Verlaine ("It rains in my heart, like the rain on the roofs") is exquisite. Mod

KOHN, KARL (Aug-USA), 1926- .

Pianist and composer of choral and chamber music for exotic combinations, has two works for piano and orchestra and the following:

Rhapsody (1967). Large-scale serial work, wide-ranging and intense, requiring full contemporary technic, including use of middle sostenuto ped. Dif

Five Bagatelles (1967). Fine contrast in five not-so-trifling "trifles" all in the same idiom as above. There are also two sonatinas and a partita among Kohn's works.

KOKAI, REZSO   see   REZSO KOKAI

KŘENEK, ERNST (Aus-USA), 1900- .

      Noted educator and prolific composer who continues to win prizes, if not audiences, with his hard-core serialism. Though converted to dodecaphony only in 1936, EK uses in earlier works a free tonality often unmitigated in its acerbity. There are five piano concertos, six sonatas, two large sets of variations, named "Hurricane" and "George Washington." None of the piano music, though published, is presently available on records.

      Toccata & Chaconne, Op 13 (1922). Written in Vienna, this early virtuoso work is based on a German chorale, combining romantic emotionalism, traditional piano idiom, and free tonality. Dif

      Little Suite, Op 13a. Genial tongue-in-cheek set on the same chorale tune, this includes, besides three Baroque dances, a waltz, fugue, and fox-trot. Perhaps his most useful work. Mod

      Sonata II, Op 59 (1928). One of EK's few tonally anchored works, this is spirited and driving. Mod Dif

      Sonata III (1943). Three-movt serial work. Since an Allegro-form is impossible in this style, the long opening movt uses canons and variations. After a scherzo on the same row, the close is adagio, ending quietly. Mod Dif

      Sonata IV (1948). Large four-movt work. In spite of distinctive melodic motifs, dance rhythms, changing tempo and varied keyboard idioms, the work is plodding and pedestrian. Mod Dif

      Twelve Short Pieces, Op 83; Eight Short Pieces (1946). Good introduction to the serial technic for the young, as the row and all its transformations are clearly set forth; then used in a series of attractive programmatic pieces. Perhaps another generation will develop ears able to retain the aural shape of a row, and pursue its plotted permutations. Mod E

KUBIK, GAIL (USA), 1914- .

      This winner of the Pulitzer Prize, British and Amer-

ican film   awards, and composer of numerous successful instrumental works has ignored most of the "isms" of our day,
and found his own style, basically tonal, clear-structured,
lean and aurally oriented.

Sonatina (1941).   A fine lightweight neo-classic 7-min
work in four brief movts.   The opening 9th chord, spelled
out and descending to a sharped 4th was nice when Gustav
Holst first used it in "The Perfect Fool"; and here effectively links the graceful moderato with the other movts: a
pawky second, a modal 2-v pastorale third, and a dashing
fourth.   Mod

Sonata (1950).   Large serious four-movt solo, imposing and brilliant.   Well-structured allegro flows to a climactic coda.   A spirited second is followed by a cantabile that
rises from introspection to exultation.   GK likes a smashing
ending, and both these works end "fast, hard and brittle"
("bright and mechanical," here).   Dif

Celebrations and Epilogue (1938-1954).   A collection
of pieces written for friends over a period of 15 years, and
offered to unsuspecting pianists in the guise of a serious
composition.   Anent this practice, see L. Bernstein.   GK
missed a good thing by not writing variations on "Happy
Birthday," along with the "Lohengrin," so subtly sneaked into "Wedded Bliss."   A tape-recording, gift-wrapped, would
spare pianists more of this sort of thing.   Mod

KURTAG, GYORGY (Hun), 1926- .

Composer who has moved from complexity to simplicity adopting a neo-classic idiom and form for later works,
which occasionally introduce the native cimbalom.

Eight Piano Pieces, Op 3.   Early works, so brief and
complex that the enormous difficulties of notation and execution surpass their musical value.   V Dif

Sonatina, Op 11b.   Short three-movt neo-classic work,
with a driving passionato first movt, and an elegiac close
with widespread chords.   Mod

LADERMAN, EZRA (USA), 1924- .

Successful composer of operas, chamber music, TV
and film scores, EL has two Sonatas.

Sonata No 1 (1967).   Four-movt contemporary
work in free tonality.   Allegro experiments with sonorities and shifting meters; light playful scherzetto; rhapsodic
arioso; fast climactic rondo.   (OxU pub) Dif

Sonata No 2 (1960).   The second piano sonata is a
large-scale four-movt work, of considerable difficulty.   The
first movt begins and ends quietly, with a complex and dashing fast section.   Romanza uses sonorous chime-like chords;
a precipitate scherzo follows, built on repeated short figures.
A cyclic form is achieved by repetition of early material in
the closing movement, along with a new lyric theme, and a
tumultous climax.   (OxU pub) Dif

LA MONTAINE, JOHN (USA), 1920- .

Composer-pianist whose first Concerto for Piano and
Orchestra won the Pulitzer Prize (1959).   The second is
called "Birds of Paradise."   Music is freely chromatic but
basically tonal, neo-classic in structure, keyboard-oriented.

Toccata, Op 1, (1957).   Brief showy keyboard work,
pianistic and effective.   2 min.   Mod Dif

Six Dance Preludes, Op 18.   Concert set of contrasting movts, ranging from an amiable Preamble, enigmatic
Aria, sprightly Burlesque, slow, introspective 4th, 5th, ending with bold panache.   10 min.   Mod Dif

Fuguing Set, Op 14.   Unique suite of three large
fugues, surrounded by a majestic prologue, bucolic pastorale,
free-wheeling cadenza and recapitulation in the form of an
epilogue.   Fugues are well-structured, combining strict contrapuntal devices and free meters.   Dif

Sonata (1970).   Large-scale three-movt (19-page)
work in traditional form but original and well deployed.   Good
octave playing required for brilliant first, which alternates
agitato and lyric themes.   Tranquillo expressive second movt
with bursts of passion.   A sustained introduction to the finale

leads to a brilliant close.   Dif

LEE, DAI-KEONG (Hawaii), 1915- .

In the two piano works from this Hawaiian-born Chinese the influence of his teacher, Copland, is more apparent than that of the Orient.

Sonatina (1948). The three-movt Sonatina opens with bold unison fanfare figures with an anacrusis and answer in parallel triadic chords; a quiet rambling linear andante follows; a bumptious good-humored Scherzo again alternates unison and chords, building to a martellato climax. Mod

Three Preludes (1941). Three short pieces, the first a folksy theme harmonized in 7ths, and doubled in octaves with quartal chords for a finish. No 2 is a four-line Andante espressivo. No 3 is a rondo with vivace con spirito theme in 5/4 alternating with two contrasting themes. Mod

LEES, BENJAMIN (USA), 1924- .

This California composer (born of Russian parents in China) has 2 concertos and numerous chamber works using piano, classic in form and polyphonic in texture in a contemporary style. Also for solo piano:

Three Preludes (1968). Traditional keyboard style but original and fresh. Maestoso produces dramatic quality through rhythmic motifs and recitando. Moderato is atmospheric, in ternary form, with middle declamatory section. Tumultoso provides a brilliant ending. (B&H pub) Mod Dif

Toccata (1953). Six-page allegro con spirito in 4/4, with steady running triplets, freely chromatic but gravitating around f♯ with explosive octave punctuation; contrasting giocoso builds to bruscamante, with accel to brilliant close. (A Tem pub) Mod   •

LIADOV, ANATOL K. (Rus), 1855-1914.

Distinguished teacher, promoter and composer, AKL came of a musical family, and gathered music lovers at his home in St. Petersburg each Saturday. Several orchestra works are available on records but his piano compositions are largely forgotten. His influence was enormous.

Tabatière à musique (1893). Still fresh and attractive, "The Music Box" represents AKL in most anthologies. Mod

Birulki (1876). An early cycle of miniatures based on folk-legends and national motifs. Mod

Preludes, Op 24. Chiefly of interest for their similarity to Scriabin's finer set (Alex attended the Saturday musicals at AL's home). Mod

Variations on a theme of Glinka, Op 35. Scholarly yet bravura set, lacking originality. Mod Dif

LIAPUNOFF, SERGEI (Rus), 1859-1924.

One of the many pianists turned out by Moscow Conservatory; later a director at St. Petersburg and a minor composer, though Russians still play his concerto.

Etudes d'execution transcendent, Op 11. All 12 of these are listed and discussed by Friskin and Freundlich but it seems unlikely that anybody will wish to play more than one or two nowadays. Liszt, to whom they are dedicated, did this sort of thing so much better, and these have little that is new. Leszhinka is probably best, a bravura piece based on folk-material, and modelled on Balakirew's Islamey, but inferior in inspiration. Carillon is sonorous and atmospheric in a 19th-century style. Dif

LISZT, FRANZ (Hun), 1811-1886.

Of the many-splendored art of FL, the most dazzling facet, his own piano playing--is lost to us. He was the first pianist to appear in solo recitals, without "intermis-

sion numbers" or "supporting cast." That the charisma of
his personality was a salient factor in his spell-binding is
evident from the superficial glitter of his transcriptions as
revived today by lesser artists. Italian cantilena and operatic recitative, Magyar ecstasy, Parisian gaiety and religious mysticsm all find a place in this most cosmopolitan
of artists. There is almost a disdain for mere piano sound,
and a desire to imitate the organ, the harp, the Hungarian
cimbalom, the brass, percussion, strings of the symphony.
Unfortunately these elements were not always compatible,
and his harmonic ingenuity and structural sense seldom
matched either his ideas or his digital facility. Consequent-
ly only a handful of his many works has found a permanent
place in the repertoire, though the current 19th-century revival is giving others an occasional hearing. Almost all are
technically difficult.

Années de Pèlerinage: Book I, Switzerland--Au Bord
d'une source (1842). An inveterate traveller (he has a Paris Period, a Weimar Period, a Roman Period) some of the
items in his musical diary which encompasses his long life,
are fresh, original and less superficial than the virtuoso
studies. "At the Spring" is the best of Book I, ebullient
and nostalgic; though others may be enjoyed by players with
moderate technic.

Book II, Italy (1856)--No 1 Spozalizio. Poetry and
painting inspired most of these which include some of the
finest of FL. The spacious stately gravity of Raphael is
captured in No 1.

No 2 Il Penseroso. Milton's melancholy Italianate
poem may have inspired this harmonically daring work.

No 3 Canzonetta del' Salvator Rosa. The gay verse
of this "Renaissance man" (painter, poet, composer) calls
forth a vivacious song in martial rhythm.

Nos 4, 5, 6 Sonnets of Petrarch. Less technically
demanding, these are also more lyrical and melodious. Mod

No 7 Après une lecture de Dante. Subtitled "Fantasia Quasi Sonata," this is known as the "Dante Sonata" and
is one of the most strikingly original works, developing its
3 contrasting, yet related themes in a brilliant allegro structure. The texture is dense and chordal, eschewing scales
for brilliant martellato writing, evocative of the Inferno and

Purgatorio, with shimmering treble tremolandi for Paradiso.

Book III, Venice & Naples (1883). A Gondoleria, a Canzona and a Tarantella make up this rather inferior book.

BOOK IV, Rome: Jeux d'eau à la Villa d'Esta. The best of these is the fountain piece, though the closing Sursum Corda attempts an apotheosis of the entire set, with a mighty climax over a ringing bass pedal point.

Harmonies poetique et Religeuse (1849). The frustrated philosopher-priest in FL was constantly seeking musical expression. Most successful of these is Funerailles, written the year of Chopin's death, and possibly a tribute to him, as were also the Ballades and Polonaises (and a flowery biography). The sombre piece is epic in its grandeur, with a bardic theme, followed by a lyric meditation, over tolling pedal-points, telescoped into a recapitulation. Dif

Two Legends: St. Francis Preaching to the Birds; St. Francis Walking on the Waves. The same narrative, epic quality was attempted in these. Once popular, they now seem rather tawdry in their striving for effects. Dif

Three Concert Etudes: No 2 La Legerizza, No 3 Un Sospiro. Most popular is No 3 in D♭ ("Un sospiro") with its broad pentatonic theme, shared between the hands, over rolling arpeggios, with two very Lisztian cadenzas. No 2 in f minor ("La Legerizza") is also popular.

Two Concert Etudes: Waldesrauschen, Gnomenreigen. German titles, but the same style, in two of his most brilliant and imaginative works. "Forest Murmurs" is properly susurrant; "The Gnomes' Dance" alternates a puckish staccato theme with a wild unfettered whirl, tip-toeing to a close.

Six Studies after Paganini. "La Campanella" with its fine chiming chord effects, survives from this set, written to prove that FL could be as diabolically dazzling at the keyboard as Paganini on his fiddle. Chopin's etudes proved this and far more; that he could also be completely original and constantly musical.

Twelve Transcendental Etudes (1839). These grand pieces transcend the etude form so far that they might better have been named ballades, or poems, since each has a program.

Etude No 4, Mazeppa's Ride. This brilliant study in
rapid toccata chord playing and endurance suggested the legend of the Cossack who, captured by his enemies, was
stripped and strapped to a wild horse's back.

Etude No 5, Feux follets. Once a standard concert
number, this difficult work requires great technical skill and
control to make it light and swift enough to suggest Fire-
Flies. A similar technic is called for in Etude No 8 (Wild
Chase), and No 12 (Sleigh Ride).

Sonata in b. The finest single work of FL, and one
of the mountain-peaks of keyboard literature, this one-movt
(25-min) piece is magnificently structured from five bold
themes, and skillfully uses for purely musical ends, a tremendous variety of technical keyboard devices, which elsewhere are merely ornamental or exhibitionist. For an analysis, see Hutcheson, or Lockwood (who devotes 13 pages
to Liszt and one to Chopin!).

Liebestraum, No 3. This hardy perennial continues
to fascinate--with its blend of soulful song-line, surging climax, purling cadenzas--both audiences and embryonic virtu-
osoi. Mod

19 Hungarian Rhapsodies. Bartók's authentic Hungarian music has dealt the coup de grace to these brilliant but
erratic works, and only a few desperate or unresourceful
pianists and teachers continue to employ them. Friskin and
Freundlich, writing in 1952, continued to recommend, besides
the inevitable No 2, Nos 6, 8, 11, 12 and 13. Hutcheson
also defends and discusses them at length.

Fantasy and Fugue on B-A-C-H (1871); Praeludium
on "Weinen, Klagen, Sorgen, Zagen"; Variations on a Theme
by Bach. Late in life Liszt paid tribute to Bach in three
works, one using the familiar B-A-C-H for theme in a
Bachian Fantasy and Fugue; two others using in the manner
of a passacaglia, the ground bass used by Bach in both the
Mass in b (Crucifixus), and in the Cantata, "Weinen, Klagen,
Sorgen, Zagen." These works eschew all ornament and display, and employ an opulent chromatic chordal style. The
four-page Praeludium is well conceived, not unlike the Lament in Bach's early "Farewell," doleful and expressive, yet
pianistic. The Variations on the same theme are on a much
broader scale (23 pages), with much more of the familiar

Liszt, combining the brilliant and the expressive, with a cadenza, a page-long recitativo-lagrimoso, and closing with a
chorale, as a tribute to JSB, in the manner of Mendelssohn's
Prelude in e (the variations resemble Mendelssohn's set also).
Worth revival.

Valse Oubliée in a. The Valse seems not to have appealed greatly to FL; but late in life he wrote four "waltz
remembrances," of which the one in a minor is best, with
bittersweet nostalgic strains. Mod

Mephisto Valses. Like so many 19th-century Romantics, FL was so fascinated by the Faust Legend, that he
wrote four different versions of the Kermesse scene, in
which Mephisto seizes the fiddle and plays such a diabolical
dance (shades of Paganini?) that Faust and Marguerite are
able to slip into the woods and make love among the nightin-
gales. Of these brilliant virtuoso program works, Ashkenazy
prefers No 1, (as do most others); John Ogdon, No 3.

Transcriptions: Schubert--Earl-König, Ave Maria;
Schumann--Widmung. The old stunt of making-up variations
on a well-known tune, dating back to early organ and clavier
music, and featured in public concerts by Mozart and Beethoven, was a sure-fire winner when helped by the spontaneity
of the occasion and the charisma of the player. Liszt gave
it a new twist; and his transcriptions, variously labelled
Paraphrase, Reminiscence, Fantasy, supplied his deficiency
in melodic invention with borrowed tunes (sometimes three or
four in the case of operas) on which to elaborate his own
brand of keyboard calligraphy, of unsurpassed complexity and
brilliance. For those who like this sort of thing, this is the
sort of thing they will like! The best of the art song settings are Schubert's Erl-König (actually easier than the song-
accompaniment), and his Ave Maria; and Schumann's Wid-
mung.

Verdi: Miserere from Il Trovatore, Rigoletto; Doni-
zetti: Lucia di Lammermoor; Mozart: Don Giovanni, Fantasy. My favorites among the operatic transcriptions are
the portenteous tolling Miserere, from Verdi's Il Trovatore;
the Rigoletto, where Liszt carefully takes apart what Verdi
has so carefully put together in the quartet, and, after showing off with each tune, puts them back together in his own
unique way; and the Lucia Reminiscences, which has an incredible introduction inevitably followed by a moment of mirth
when the wild chords resolve into the familiar sextette bolero

introduction.   The Don Giovanni is admired by many for its
symphonic organization and keyboard virtuosity.   For a complete (?) listing see Lockwood, who has six pages of double
columns.   (TP has an album of 20 transcriptions.)   There
are numerous recordings, some for piano duet.

Three Late Piano Pieces (B-V 1969).   The three late
works, discovered by Robert V. Lee, though of no great importance, are a genial addition to Lisztiana.   Less experimental than other late works, they yet have a tentative embryonic character, as though intended for a study, a scherzo,
or a song--never written (because not worth writing).

LOPATNIKOFF, NIKOLAI (Est-USA), 1903- .

Pianist-teacher whose works are basically neo-classical and traditionally formal; tonal though exploring new
harmonies, and often highly dissonant.

Five Contrasts, Op 16.   Mood pieces contrasted by
a variety of keyboard devices and unusual harmony; ranging
from the tender and impassioned to the vigorous and agitated.   Mod Dif

Dialogues, Op 18.   Five two-part inventions in a
modern idiom.   Mod

Sonata, Op 29.   This composer's "duty sonata," correct, difficult, long, and dull.   Dif

Intervals, Op 37.   A set of seven etudes built on various intervals, harmonized in a freely chromatic manner,
for developing technic and musicianship.   Mod

LUMSDAINE, DAVID (Ausl), 19-- .

Kelly Ground (1967).   Avant-garde serial composition
of enormous length (26 pages) in three cycles, the first containing five "strophes" all based on a complex transforma-
tion of a ground-bass.   Opens in hymn-like style, with both
chords and melodic intervals limited to 4ths and 5ths.   Chromatic grace-notes relieve the unmitigated monotony of this
type of harmony.   Cantabile passages and experimental ped-

alling resonances appear. Imaginative and well-structured; but formidable to study, play, or attend to. V Dif

McCABE, JOHN see page 195.

MacDOWELL, EDWARD (USA), 1861-1908.

Born only one year before Debussy, America's first internationally known composer looked to the past, rather than to the future and was more imitative than innovative. Programmatic in theme, his subjects ranged from his Scotch-Celtic-Norse ancestry to his New England home, and American folk-legendry; but his piano style derived from Grieg, Schumann and Mendelssohn. Yet MacDowell developed in his extensive piano ouvre a distinctly personal style. It is time to rediscover EM, now that the search for a uniquely American music is not so obsessive (with Ives and Gershwin comfortably occupying the chairs), and Americans are looking nostalgically at their not-so-distant past in paintings of the Wyeths, and poems of Frost. Pianists seeking an alternative for the arid cryptograms of our day, and the crunchy knuckle-busting acrobatics of the 19th-century Germans may well explore these, always a favorite with teachers and pupils.

Praeludium, Op 10. Of the two "modern" suites by EM, this is the most viable item, with a declamatory chordal opening, a distinctive arpeggiated accompaniment to a plaintive lyric melody, that ranges from ppp to fff. Mod Dif

Witches Dance, Op 17. Good imaginative etude, moderately difficult. Mod

Scotch Poem, Op 31. Best of a set of Poems after Heine, a wistful minstrel song with harp-chords is the core of this tone-poem, which opens and closes with rumbling, crashing wave figures that ebb at the end for an echo of the idyl. Mod

Four Little Poems, Op 43. All four of these are good, and make a fine group, with the bold experimental chords and rhythms of Eagle, through the more conventional Brook, and Moonshine, to the bleak eerie Winter. Mod

12 Studies, I, II, Op 39. For teachers and students who still distinguish between "technic" and "pieces," these are recommended as a compromise. Moderately difficult, each has a suggestive title, and a technical problem, and all are attractive. Mod E

12 Virtuoso Studies, Op 44. More difficult, and somewhat less imaginative than Op 39, the Moto Perpetuo, Wild Chase, and Polonaise require a maturing technic and a bold style. Mod-Dif

Air and Rigaudon, Op 49. Delightfully pawky dance tune, exploiting the entire keyboard, in delicate staccato, preceded by a quiet aria. Mod

Sonatas: Tragica, Op 45, Eroica, Op 50, Norse, Op 57, Keltic, Op 59. Like Chopin and Schumann, MacDowell was best in the smaller forms, and these are sprawling, repetitive, lacking in contrast. The program element is not of much help, but there are moments of beauty and of a distinctive personal style; and few of the many 19th-century Brobdingnagian Teutonic sonatas of this dreary era surpass them. The second, Eroica, has an Arthurian legend for theme, with movts for Guenivere, Merlin, and a furious battle with Modred, for finale. The last is the most taut and consistently good. Dif

Woodland Sketches, Op 51. It is the short tales and nature sketches of this perpetual adolescent that are most enduring. Besides the immortal To a Wild Rose, the hypnotic Water-Lily, this has three others of the same calibre: Uncle Remus, Will o' the Wisp, and Autumn. Mod

Sea Pieces, Op 55. These six short majestic pieces all have admirers; but are perhaps too much in the same "stern and rock-bound" mood to be played together (liven them up with Bloch's Hornpipe). My favorite is the picture of the Mayflower--A.D. 1620--like a Winslow Homer painting. Mod

Fireside Tales, Op 61. Br'er Rabbit is a catchy scherzo (not easy) good for an encore, or light number. Mod-Dif

New England Idyls, Op 62. The White Pine is stately, and demands wide dynamic scope, within its two pages. Joy of Autumn must race along with utmost insouciance (and utmost control). Dif

Concert-Etude, Op 36. This one-time sure-fire cur-tain ringer has regretably dropped out of the repertoire. It is perhaps EMacD's finest single work, a brilliant 10-page 7-min piece built on a broad arc of melody worthy of Tchai-kovsky. Developed in a series of pianistic and idiosyncratic statements, the theme is also the subject for misterioso bridge-passages, an ethereal a piacere, a grand peroration in octave cross-rhythms, and a dashing introduction and coda. Dif

The Second Piano Concerto in d has remained a rep-ertory favorite.

MALEČ, IVO (Yugo), 1925- .

Dialogs (1969). The experimental notation of this avant-garde work is perhaps its most successful feature, the use of large and small notes to suggest loud-soft dynamics. It is not clear who the two opponents are in this dialogue, which is written without bars or meter. The composer suggests piano or harpsichord, though how he proposes to make the crescendos and diminuendos that his notation calls for on that "terraced" instrument, is also unexplained. (MCA pub) Dif

MALIPIERO, GIAN FRANCESCO (It), 1882- .

One of a dynasty of musicians (his grandfather wrote operas, and his nephew Riccardo composes in serial style) GFM wrote extensively for piano in a romantic-impression-istic style, whose fragmentary formlessness weakens it for performance.

Preludi Autunali (1914). Four movts, the first three slow, alternately nocturnal, narrative, funereal, ending with a brisk, sparkling scherzo. Mod

Barlumi (1917). Five-piece set, similar to the Preludi Autunali, ending with a lively country dance. Mod

Hortus Conclusus (1947). Later work, similar in
texture; suite of eight contrasting tempos, styles, moods.
Mod

Five Studies for Tomorrow (1959). These are for the
tomorrow of yesterday, making only slight advances on
GFM's early style in exploration of dissonant harmony. For
studies for the tomorrow of today, try the Inventions of
nephew, Riccardo, in 12-tone technic. Mod

MALIPIERO, RICCARDO (It), 1914- .

Author and composer of operas and symphonic works,
RM destroyed all his early music after adopting dodecaphony.

Inventions (1954). A didactic set of nine pieces, of
more interest to the composition student than the pianist,
they make strict Schönbergian use of the row in inventions
of 1, 2 and 3-v. Mod

MARTIN, FRANK (Swi), 1890- .

The dean of Swiss composers, esteemed for his concertos and chamber music, wrote a set of eight preludes for
Dinu Lipatti. His best known work is a unique concerto for
piano, harp, harpsichord and two string orchestras, called
Petite Symphonic Concertante. His harpsichord concerto is
also fine. A recent piano Concerto uses serial technic in a
very aurally satisfying way.

Eight Preludes (1948). Highly musical, but not always pianistic, these short pieces are tonally oriented, though
no key signatures are used. Most pieces begin with decep-
tive simplicity, building to technically demanding climaxes.
Both the early and the late Scriabin styles find echoes here:
unison melodies sustained through staccato chords; fragmentary rhythmically-odd motifs shaped into four-meas phrases;
chronic chromaticism for expressive ends; hammered chords
at the acme of a climax. Good material for the serious advanced pianist. Dif

MARTINU, BOHUSLAV (Czech-USA), 1890-1959.

Prolific composer who settled in NY after the Nazi expulsion, writing numerous stage works which are occasionally revived, orchestral and chamber works some of which are recorded. Piano was not his forte, and the best are the short folkloric pieces.

Three Czech Dances. Brilliant and vivacious use of folk rhythms in chordal, octave and double-note writing. Mod Dif

Etudes and Polkas (Books I, II, III). Virtuoso technical studies alternating with lighter, graceful dances in the syncopated duple polka rhythm. Attractive but demanding. Mod to Dif

Fantasie et Toccata. Bravura work-out, exhausting and, in the end, unrewarding. Dif

Esquisses de Dance. Five dance "sketches," varied, sprightly and imaginative. Mod

Les Bouquinestes du Quais Malaquais. Program item depicting the bookstalls of Paris, fresh and original. Mod

MATHIAS, WILLIAM (GB) 1934- .

Sonata, Op 26 (1966). Large-scale two-movt work in free tonality. Wide-ranging 1st movt alternates passages of fervor and urgency; chordal and linear cantabile; uninhibited, scintillating finale. Demands mature technic and musicianship. Dif

MATRIANO, SALVATORE (USA), 1927- .

Cocktail Music (1962). Piece described by Nicolas Slonimsky, pastmaster of gobbledy-gook, as "quaquaversal vigesimosecular radical in the ambience of total musical action." Other works by this ultra avant-garde activist include one for a gas-masked politico with helium bomb and three 16mm projectors.

MATSUSHITA, SHIN-ICHI (Japan), 1923- .

Festival prize winner and recognized leader in avant-garde music used original devices in piano works, before turning to other gadgets.

Temps Mensurable et Temps Topologique (1959). Minutely detailed rhythms within larger fixed forms, and experiments with distinctive piano timbre, related to Messiaen and Boulez. Dif

Spektra 1-4 (1964-67). A series of experimental works (No 2 is pub by UE) using cluster-chords, interior-playing, aleatoric arrangement improvisation. There is also a Canzona da Sonare for piano and percussion. Dif

MAXWELL DAVIES, PETER (GB), 1934- .

Five Pieces, Op 2 (1955). This bearer of a double-barreled name (sans hyphen like Ralph Vaughan Williams) has moved from an intense, sometimes turgid dissonant counterpoint, in the first set, to a light lucid linear style in the second set. Op 2 is wide-ranging and attractive in score, but difficult to follow, and basically unpianistic. Mod Dif

Five Little Pieces (1960-1964). Brief sketches, each a complete ABA piece, though wispy, muted, fragmentary, non-metric. Little appeal for the ear or fingers. Mod

MAYER, WILLIAM (USA), 1925- .

Sonata (1960). Prolific composer of operas and pieces for children, and of chamber music, has a concerto for piano and orchestra called Octagon, and this sonata, a three-movt, 18-min composition which is musical and effective without being very original or profound. Though using tone-rows for the slow introspective opening and for bridges and occasional themes, the Sonata is basically tonal. The brief opening movt expands the simple calligraphic curve by widening its range, doubling into octaves, punctuating with rolled chords, to a climax of a brief unison flurry over a bass trill, then recedes to the opening mist. The second movt sounds like an expanded version of the first, with little new added--a banal rhythmic motto in 5ths and 2nds, and a quiet chorale over a throbbing bass. The jig-rondo finale is the best movt, spanning the keyboard in lively leaps; then attempting to assimilate nodes from other movts in a climactic coda, ending on a V^9 in C major! Dif

MAYUZUMI, TOSHIRO (Jap), 1929- .

The piano music of this internationally famous avant-garde composer is early works tracing his progress, but now dated.

12 Preludes (1946). These reflect French influences ranging from Franck and Saint-Saëns to Debussy and Ravel.

Hors-d'oeuvres (1947). More original, this dance number features popular rhythms of the rhumba and boogie-woogie.

TM's piece for Prepared Piano and Strings (1957) is recorded. Recent orchestral works have experimented with sonorities to evoke ancient Asian ritual.

McCABE, JOHN (GB), 1939- .

A former child prodigy turned critic and composer has written numerous chamber works using piano, as well as piano solos. Though often in classical forms (quartet, concerto, sonata) the works are highly original, rhythmically and tonally free.

Variations, Op 22. A 10-min virtuoso work, highly complex, in its 18 variations on a theme, which, in itself, is freely improvisory, and has an Oriental flavor. Dif

MEDTNER, NICOLAS (Russ-GB), 1879-1971.

Ex-patriate Russian (of German descent), friend of Rachmaninoff and Scriabin, this composer has now been re-instated in USSR and is having a popular revival. His conservative 19th-century Romantic style, stemming from Schu-

mann-Mendelssohn and the Russians, has less appeal elsewhere, though there are attractive numbers in his large
oeuvre. His writing is always pianistic, sometimes brilliant and difficult.

Idyl, Op 7:1. Fluent Allegro tranquillo e dolce in
16th notes, 6/8 with melodies and counter-melodies attrac-
tively woven into the texture. Mod

Two Fairy Tales, Op 8. NM was fond of this title,
but the works are seldom programmatic (only in a few cases
is there a clue to the story) and might equally well have
been called Preludes or Intermezzi. Most are short ternary
forms, like this pair of contrasting Andante and Allegrissimo. Mod

Two Fairy Tales, Op 14: Song of Ophelia, March of
the Knights. A mournful cantabile in 4-voice chordal writing,
that builds to a loud plaint, before the quiet close. Moderately easy. The second, a martial rhythm is one of NM's frequent narrative devices. A larger piece, developing a variety
of rhythmic and melodic motifs, in a complex and effective
manner. Dif

Two Fairy Tales, Op 20: No 1 in bb; No 2 in f.
The first is a flowing triplet Allegro con espressione,
marked pleno voce, and building to a big climax with LH arpeggios and repeated chords, à la Rachmaninoff. Moderately difficult. The second, subtitled "Campanella," is a
tale told by a bell, a ponderous descending ostinato bass
suggesting the tale tolled. Mod

Four Fairy Tales, Op 26. No 3 in f from this set
is a pleasant song in narrative style with interesting figures
around the melody, and a subtle cross-hand coda, veloce pp.
Mod

Four Fairy Tales, Op 34: No 1 "Magic Fiddle." A
large-scale brilliant and difficult work, combining waltz and
march themes. (Mephisto, or Paganini?) Dif

No 2 in e. The author's favorite, a ballad-like theme
that adds to each repetition incrementally, over a purling,
swirling bass, rises to a bardic triumph with the lift from
minor to major; then vanishes in the melting mist. Dif

No 4 in d. The martial rhythm, richly elaborated, with a contrasting pietoso cantabile, and a gorgeous three-page coda in D major. Dif

12 Sonatas. With the 19th-century keyboard revival, it seems likely that several of these finely-wrought, imaginative and pianistic works will find their way to the concert hall. Most are large one-movt works, some with suggestive titles: Sonate romantique, Sonata-Ballade, Sonate orageuse, Sonata minnaciosa.

Sonata in g, Op 22. A grand work, (in 15/8 time!) linking a series of imaginative and discrete themes, in NM's highly idiosyncratic but fluently pianistic style (suggestive of the best of Schumann), with declamatory and simple folk-song themes blended with florid passages, eschewing mere display and exalting song. A cyclic return reviews the subjects in fresh simplicity. (27 min) Dif

Sonata in F♯, Op 27. Less bold than Op 27, this has grace and charm, with a naive narrante opening theme, followed by a joyous chiming octave passage in C♯, broadly developed in a single movt. (25 min) Mod Dif

MENASCE, JACQUES (Aus-USA), 1905-1960.

Pianist born and trained in Austria, of Egyptian-French-German parentage, came to the U.S. in the hegira of 1940. His piano works, though of no great profundity, are genial, entertaining and playable.

Perpetuum Mobile. Brilliant virtuoso study, exciting for its sheer velocity. Flowing broken chords against a melody of 3rds, 6ths, 7ths ending with a flourish. Mod Dif

Five Finger-Prints. One-page sketches, varied and witty. LH parts often have an ostinato character, with RH doing sleight-of-hand tricks below and above. Mod

Sonatinas 2, 3. Two neo-classic works, contrasting the lyric, grotesque, graceful and brilliant. Mod

Romantic Suite. Amiable pieces in five contrasting moods: Rondino, Berceuse, Moment Musical, Romanza, Toccatina. Mod

MENDELSSOHN, FELIX (Ger), 1809-1847.

With the fad for Victorian decor, the Queen's favorite composer should be revived. While there is nothing in the piano repertoire to match the great violin concerto, there are several pieces with which every pianist should be familiar. Start with the 48 Songs without Words. It is hard to imagine today the sensation which this title caused in its day. "What can they be, 'Songs without Words'?" The simplicity of the accompanied melody, played on the piano alone, now so commonplace, was once refreshingly new, after the complexities of Baroque and the formality of Rococo. Jaded though our ears are by The Spring Song and The Spinning Song, there may yet be those who, finding them for the first time, are titillated.

Songs without Words. No 1 and No 15 in E are similar studies in accompanied melody, and both good; No 20 in Eb, 3/4, has a cantabile melody in 8ths against triplets. The Folk-Song variations in a minor (No 23), "The Flight" in A (No 24) and The Funeral March in e (No 27) are all worth exploring. Mod E

Andante and Rondo Capriciosso, Op 14. Though worn thin by countless generations of pianists, this remains a fine lyric slow movement, and a characteristic and brilliant Mendelssohn scherzo. Mod

The fairy world of the Midsummer Night's Dream, so vividly evoked by the 16-year old boy peeps through all the many scherzos and caprices which FM wrote throughout his lifetime. They must all be played with a crisp, delicate staccato touch, sometimes whispering, sometimes tinkling like far-off laughter. Phlegmatic, heavy-handed pianists "in the grand manner," stay away. (They may wish to tackle Rachmaninoff's transcription of the Midsummer Night's Dream Scherzo which must be played Presto Impossibile.) Dif

Scherzo in e, Op 16, No 2. FM considered calling this "The Little Trumpet" for the fanfare theme that recurs. A tiny masterpiece. Mod E

Scherzo in b. Without opus number, this two-page work is also true to form. Mod

Capriccioso in f#, Op 5. Written the same year as the Shakespeare fairy music, this is not as inspired, but

good, though over-extended and technically difficult.   Mod
Dif

Scherzo a capriccioso in f#.   Without opus, this
large-scale work carries this style to virtuoso proportions.
Dif

Variations, Serieuse, Op 54 in d.   The only major
concert work of FM, these are blessed with a fine, expressive theme, by the composer, rich in chromatic modulations
under a memorably simple tune.   (As many variations have
failed because of poor themes, as operas, because of poor
libretti.)   From a simple staccato 2-v variation, they ac-
cumulate power, in sets of three, separated by quiet, lyric
ones, including a serene fugue, and a noble D major chorale.   An exciting coda is built on Mendelssohn's favorite device of LH-RH clapped chord and octave passages, sweeping
up and down the keyboard to a final simple chord.   Dif

Six Preludes and Fugues, Op 35.   The first of these,
in e, is the best with a rolling prelude in 32nd notes
through which a bold melody sings.   The 5-v fugue is very
fine and introduces a hymn-tune above the fugue theme, at
the end.   Though excessively long (and difficult) the unorthodox and romantic use of the più mosso and accelerando keeps
the interest to the end.   Dif

Three Etudes, Op 104, Book II, Nos 1, 2, 3.   Set of
three attractive velocity studies, good enough for performance.   The RH works out arpeggio patterns above a shared
thumb-melody in No 1.   The second is a joyous triplet study,
hands taking turns.   In No 3 fast staccato chords in 7ths
over a flowing bass produce dissonance rare in FM.   All
have a genuine German Spiel-Freude.   Dif

MENNIN, PETER (USA), 1923- .

Busy music administrator (Peabody, Juilliard) has
found time for a piano and orchestra concerto and these solo
works.   Not easy, musically or technically.

Five Pieces (1951).   Complex metric plan requires
sustained drive as well as musicality.   Dif

Prelude & Aria.   Prelude is a light lively moto per-

petuo, short. Aria is reposeful but builds to a finish. Mod
Dif

      <u>Variation Canzona.</u> The song is in 5/8, varied with
rhythmic, melodic, harmonic transformations. Mod Dif

      <u>Canto & Toccata.</u> Another moto perpetuo (long) pre-
ceded by a long andante, lyric and sustained. Power, drive;
dissonant. Dif

      <u>Sonata</u> (1967). The composer's 'disdain for the mere
amenities of sound," here coupled with an indifference to the
limitations of the human hand produces a work of diabolic
musical complexity and technical difficulty. The dissonance
is unmitigated, though the adagio is expressive and powerful.
The presto possibile of the finale requires a più presto for
the closing canon. V Dif

MENOTTI, GIAN CARLO (It), 1911- .

      Though GCM reversed the usual procedure by coming
to America from Italy for his music education, he has remained true to the Italian ideal of opera as the greatest form
of music, and made a place at the top of the opera ladder
with a list of all-time hits (and many misses). He has (as
well as a triple concerto) a piano concerto that is at the
same time operatic, pianistic and very attractive.

      <u>Pometti.</u> These little-known children's pieces are so
charming that they deserve to be plugged. The 12 open with
a giga straight out of Amahl, include several miniature character pieces, modal, unpredictable and fresh, and close with
a bold octave War Song. E to Mod

      <u>Ricercare and Toccata.</u> On a theme from "The Old
Maid and the Thief" GCM writes a virtuoso work in the manner of early Italian organ masters, before the fugue became
so formal. Five short linked sections make up the Ricercare, moving from a free 2-v introduction, through a chorale, a cadenza, an octave passage and a keyboard sweeping
Baroque arabesque to the Toccata. This is in steady 16th
notes throughout, but with great variety of meter, touch,
dynamics. Dif

MERILAINEN, USKO (Fin), 1930- .

     Sonata No II (1970). Big three-movt work in serial
technic. Misterioso opening accumulates power to a bar-
less climax, followed by ethereal chime effects. Rhapsodic
second movt, uninhibited. Third movt based on original figuration divided between the hands, mounting to a tumultuous
climax. Dated avant-garde. (Weinberger pub) Dif

MESSIAEN, OLIVIER (Fr), 1908- .

     Strong influence in 20th-century French music, along
with Boulanger and Boulez, this composer-organist-teacher
has, unlike the other two, written numerous works for piano.
They remain relatively unknown because of their technical
complexity and an arcane, almost hermetic mystique with
little audience appeal. Both a scholar and a mystic, OM's
researches range from Indian ragas and Mediaeval church
modes through such antipodal fields as bird-song and mathe-
matics. Side by side in his notes are Biblical text, lyrical
epigraphs and analyses of "retrograde-aggrandizement, poly-
modal rhythmic canons," evoking "bird-song, carillons, sta-
lactites, galaxies, photons." Though this obfuscation is off-
putting for the pianist, most of it can, as with the Scriabin
and Satie gobbledy-gook, be safely ignored. What remains,
sheer piano sound, is often immensely attractive (OM sought
to emulate the orchestra and organ), but often poorly organized formally, over-extended and forced into rigid four-bar
phrases. The organ works are more satisfying, with their
wide color scale and dynamic range. There is also a two-
piano cycle, called Visions de l'Amen. Bird-song is an obsession with OM, and the infinite variety of keyboard figures
he devises to convey it, while tedious and difficult to master, have a refreshing appeal. Almost all are technically
difficult.

     Huit Préludes (1929). Most approachable is the set
of early preludes. Post-romantic and impressionistic in
flavor, they begin to experiment with harmonies and melodies based on modes and made-up scales, a favorite being
an eight-tone scale alternating whole and half steps, used in
preludes 1, 2, 3, 5; they display OM's sheer delight in
finger-play and piano sound, especially the chiming upper
reaches of the keyboard.

No 1 La Colombe.   No 1 suggests bird flight with arcs
of scales in 3rds, a tenor melody and fluttering chord sequences.   Short.

No 2 Chant d'extase dans un paysage triste.   The contrast of themes suggesting Sadness and Ecstasy excuses the
loose-jointed structure, and a rich tissue of sound with avian
ornaments results.   Mod Dif

No 3 Le Nombre Légor; No 4 Instants défunts.   No 3 is
a brilliant light toccata in 3rds (2 min 30 sec).

No 5 Les sons impalpable du rêve.   "The impalpable
sounds of a dream" are properly amorphous and repetitious;
but the work is richly florid and piquantly dissonant.   Mod
Dif

No 6 Cloches d'angoisse et larmes d'adieu.   Only the
bells of the extravagant title come through, rather monotonously, in No 6 (8 min).

No 7 Plainte calme.   A linear fragmented piece, alternating unison passages with chordal punctuation.
Mod

No 8 Un reflets dans le vent.   A large, brilliant piece
combining a busy Impressionistic rippling background with a
rhythmic cantabile line.   Best of the set.   Dif

No 20 Regards sur l'Enfant--Jésus (1944).   This mid-
dle-period work is the composer's magnum opus sustaining
through its enormous length (one hour and 20 min) a high
level of inspiration, blending all multifarious interests.   It
has been recorded in its entirety by John Ogdon, and though
too massive, intense and arcane for concert use as a whole,
separate numbers might well enrich a pianistic repertoire.
Once available only in a single volume of 177 pages (Durand
& Cie, at $20, which worked out at one dollar a "view").
Now separate editions of Nos 6, 10, 11, 15 and 17 are available.   The cycle is unified by leitmotifs signifying the "Star
and Cross," a close-coiled eight-note melodic theme, similar to B-A-C-H; a chordal theme in F♯ for "God the Father";
and a "Thème d'Accords," combining elements of both the
others, and suggesting incarnation.

No 2 Regards de l'étoile.   A good start can be made
with No 2, which introduces in two pages all the thematic ma-

terial, unison passages, with the hands three octaves apart, alternating with shimmering chordal and arpeggio passages, with dynamics ranging from ppp to ff. Mod

No 3 L'echange. OM's scientific theory of asymetrical aggrandizement here serves both a musical and mystical end, implying unity of the unchangeable with the mutable finite, by alternating the same tremolando figure with 12 passages in which a RH figure expands chromatically with each repetition, over a LH figure which contracts. Contrived, but dramatic. Dif

No 7 Regard de la Croix. Slow, majestic chordal movement with poignant harmonic progressions. Dif

No 8 Regard de hauteur. The avian obsession of the composer here finds delightful expression (the bird calls are identified) in a pianistic and entertaining 5-page movement. Dif

No 10 Regard de l'Esprit. Long, brilliant difficult "dance of joy," begins with running unison passage, adds chains of trills, a chordal passage suggesting hunting horns, ending in a "grand transport of joy." V Dif

No 13 Noël. Perhaps the most exciting number, crashing carillon chords of augmented 9ths at the extremes of the keyboard with pauses for meditation in passages of exquisite delicacy in F#. Fine program number. Dif

No 16 Regard des prophètes, des bergers et des Mages. Picturesque processional, advancing and receding, with tom-tom and oboe passages framing a bold rhythmic canonic march. Mathematical aggrandizements, a nuisance for the performer, and hardly evident to the hearer, add to the difficulty, but the colorful number is worth the sweat. Dif

No 19 Je dors, mais mon coeur veille. "I sleep, but my heart watches"; one of several intense meditations, muted and irridescent; good for self communion, but too subtly monochromatic for performance. Mod

Mode de valeurs et d'intensité (1949); Neumes rhythmiques (1949); Ile de feu, I, II (1950); Canteyodjaya (1953); Le rousselot effarvat (1958); Catalogue d'oiseau (1959). Perhaps the atavistic Franco-Germanic rivalry, which spurred Debussy and Ravel to some of their experiments, also led to OM's later explorations; total organization of all three elements of music, as an answer to Schönberg's melodic dodecaphony. Both take a lofty view of the capacity of the human ear to retain and assimilate and of the human hand to encompass keyboard patterns. Regarded as abstract, ideal scientific synthesis, the works, (and their spawn in Boulez, Stockhausen, Babbitt, etc.) are possibly laudable. As viable piano music, they are nugatory. In the last four works color is derived from nature sounds and Indian ragas; but the abstruse mathematical devices, inaudible to the ear, and recalcitrant for the hands, fail to mitigate the monomorphous, monochromatic mass. V

MIHALY, ANDRAS (Hun), 1917- .

Two Piano Pieces in Antique Style. Neo-classic composer; these freely chromatic pieces are pianistic but contemporary, though called antique. The allegro moderato pays tribute to olden times with a contrapuntal texture; the second piece is an uninhibited giga, ranging over the keyboard in rhythmic staccato figures. Dif

MILHAUD, DARIUS (Fr), 1892- .

Last survivor of Les Six, Milhaud has been a prolific composer. Though it seems doubtful if many of his works will endure, he has been an inspiring teacher and presence. The solo piano music is not his best; chamber works have the contrast of timbre. Exotic and ethnic elements give interest in the Brazilian, Caribbean works. Perhaps the finest thing he has written for the keyboard is the two-piano suite "Scaramouche," with its brilliant closing samba, Brazileira.

Printemps. Two early sets of pieces (three each), easy-going salon music. Mod

Sonata No 1 (1916). Milhaud begins to find himself here, with a French clarity, freedom, and popular song quality. Bitonality and splashes of dissonance in basically tonal chordal writing. Three movements: decide, pastoral, rhythme. Mod

Saudades do Brazil (1920), Vols I, II.   These "Nostalgic Recollections of Brazil," where DM spent the years of World War I are a lightweight "Iberia," with two books of six pieces each, named after districts in Rio de Janeiro. The orchestrated version is better.   Mod

L'Automne (1932).   Three piece set, flowing, lively, lyric.   Written with a meandering ambiguous chromatic harmony that mars much of the late piano music.   Mod

Four Sketches (1941).   Pastorale, Madrigal, and two Spanish dances (the best of the set).

Sonata No 2 (1949).   Neo-classic popular entertainment music in a thin linear style, with propulsive finale. Mod

The Seven-Branched Candelabrum (1951).   Commissioned by the New Israeli Publishing Co., the work does not live up to the promise of its picturesque titles (7 Hebrew feasts).   Intransigent dissonance, with vague hints of tonality; pedestrian rhythmic motifs.   New works by middle Eastern composers using their own tonal and rhythmic heritage are far superior.   Mod

Hymn of Glorification (1954).   Long, uninspired single-movement, without key-signature and afflicted by chronic chromaticism.   Though there are dynamic shifts and metrical changes, the moderato tempo remains unchanged and monotony sets in on page three (five more to go!)   (MEs pub)   Dif

MOERAN, ERNEST J. (GB), 1894-1951.

What might be called a regional composer, academically trained, but using folkloric material, of which he was a collector, as a basis for a quiet melodic traditional type of piano music.

Stalham River.   Like its subject, it flows gently, making slight demands of the player for a chromatic nostalgic nature poem.   Mod

Toccata.   A more brilliant keyboard work, which uses for a contrasting core a folk-song cantabile theme. Effective.   Mod Dif

Summer Valley. Moeran was a pupil of John Ireland; this has overtones of both Ireland and Delius, to whom it is dedicated. Mod

MOMPOU, FREDERICO (Sp), 1893- .

French-trained Spanish master of the miniature who blends something of Debussy and Satie with a Catalonianflavor in an individual manner.

Scènes d'Enfants (1915). Five brief simple sketches, varied and descriptive. Contains the encore so bewitchingly played by Gina Bachauer: Jeunes filles au Jardin. Mod E

Suburbis (1916-1917). Genre scenes featuring street songs, popular airs and dances, as well as sound effects. Mod

Canco y Dansa. Naive and genial, yet pianistic and polished; four-piece dance set. Mod

Dialogues. Extended work contrasting and combining two wide-spaced pianistic figuration, amiable, yet sonorous and brilliant. Mod Dif

Tres Variationes. Brief and simple yet contrasting, muted, nostalgic and poignant. Mod

Charmes. Six miniature moods, static, hypnotic, "like a primitive incantation." Mod

MONCAYO, JOSE PABLO (Mex), 1912-1958.

Three Pieces (1964). Three effective short sketches, basically tonal but with free use of dissonance, pianistic. No 1 is in upper and middle register, fast with metric irregularity. More euphonious cantabile middle piece has a wistful theme. Boisterous propulsive close. (SMP pub) Mod

MOORE, DOUGLAS (USA), 1893-1969.

One of the few successful composers of opera based on American material, has one bit of Americana for piano.

Suite (1951). Pianistic, genial well-made set of six. Prelude features staccato patterns in non-symmetrical measure. Reel, Dancing School, Barn Dance are authentic and fresh. Quiet lyrical linear-chordal Air; bold closing Procession. Mod Dif

MOREL, FRANÇOIS (Can), 1926- .

Deux Etudes de Sonorité (1967). Better known for ensemble works, many with a jazz beat. These two explore piano sonorities: the first, Impressionism, with chord-clusters; the second, asperity through rhythmic martellato, but with a free lyric mid-section. (BMI pub) Mod

MOROI, MOKOTO (Jap), 1930- .

Second generation Japanese composer who has moved from the traditional style of his father's pre-war works, to a serial technic.

Suite 1 (1941); Sonata 1, 2 (1950-52); Alpha and Beta (1954). MM's first work entirely on rows was groundbreaking (learning the new alphabet). The massive 15-min piece is strict and correct, and shows some versatility and imagination in its rigorous Schönbergian serialism. More significant historically than musically. Dif

Klavierstücke, Op 14; Sonatine (1966). Classical forms help give the following works a useful framework for the rows. Mod Dif

Eight Parables. Brief contrasting serial sketches, with detachable pages and a "superfluous cadenza" of eight separate passages to be inserted among the parables, at the player's whim. They exploit accelerandi (with innovative notation), tremolandi, echoi, etc. Handsome Japanese publication (ONT through TP), titles and parables in Japanese calligraphy, and a page of quaint, naive translations and com-

ments. The visual impact surpasses the aural which is
thin, muted, and tentative, and no Japanese atmosphere is
evident. Mod

        MM has also applied the serial technic to music for
native instruments. In 1969 at Osaka a player of the "sha-
kuhachi" (end-blown flute) astonished the audience by appearing in formal attire (kimono and hakama) and instead of
modestly squatting on the floor after his profound bow, stood
and swayed like Benny Goodman, while playing a highly original work using tone-rows, bits of ancient Buddhist flute-tunes,
and all the resources of this instrument, with its wide dynamics, wailing portamento, microtones. Coldly received
in Osaka, it would have been a sensation in Town Hall (or
the Fillmore East).

MOSCHELES, IGNATZ (Boh), 1794-1870.

        One of the first of the new breed of 19th-century tour-
ing virtuosi, IM was hailed in London, Paris, Vienna, Berlin; taught Mendelssohn, and later attracted pupils from far
and wide to Mendelssohn's new Leipzig Conservatory. Mostly
remembered today for his exercises, he was a conservative
unable to understand or to accept 19th-century changes in
music. He wrote several works for two pianos, four and
eight hands; eight concertos, some of which are now being
revived; many studies, and two sonatas.

        24 Etudes de Concert, Op 70. These were studied
and taught by Chopin, whose own genius lifted the form far
above the purely gymnastic in his Op 10 and 25. Brilliantly boring. Dif

        Sonata Melancholique in f♯. Attempting to be ro-
mantic, IM called his one solo sonata Melancholique, and
wrote it in the one-movt cyclic form popularized by Liszt.
The key of f♯ (later popular with Rheinberger, Jensen, etc.)
was considered suitably sad, but the dreary broken chords,
scales, tonic-dominant-diminished harmony leave us un-
moved. The chief function of a performance of such a work
today is to confirm the judgment of time, that Chopin, Schumann and even Liszt and Mendelssohn, were indeed geniuses
of quite a higher order. Mod

MOSZKOWSKI, MORITZ (Ger), 1854-1925.

Once famous pianist, teacher and prolific composer of salon pieces, now all-but-forgotten. His Concerto, a selection of pieces, and the Virtuoso Etudes have been exhumed for recording. His facile but shallow talent ground out volumes of pleasant dances, character pieces, studies, all fluent, pianistic, well-knit, and dull. The Spanish Dances for four-hands remain his most successful work.

Caprice espagnole, Op 37. Once a popular curtainringer, difficult and brilliant, but now faded and jaded. Dif

Etincelles, Op 36, No 6. Somewhat shorter than the above. Mod Dif

La Jongleuse, Op 52:4. One of six fantasy pieces, this staccato study is perhaps the best of MM's limited genius, at its best in a short, well-structured work. Mod

Concert Etude in G♭, Op 24:1. A good LH study to master before tackling Rachmaninoff, or Chopin. Dif

15 Virtuoso Etudes, Op 72. For those who like this sort of thing. V Dif

MOTTE, DIETHER DE LA (Ger), 1928- .

10 Fantasias for Piano (1968). A welcome revival of the improvisation or fantasy piece, composed at the keyboard and eminently pianistic. The old Bach-Schumann-Liszt conceit of musical anagrams is worked out in the opening "Toccata C-H," (dedicated to Conrad Hansen) with the C-B (or H) 7th providing an introduction, proceeding with gradually decreasing intervals. Eckart Besch has provided a motif, for No 5, B-E-S-C-H. Can be played as a set (35 min) or separately. Requires advanced technic. Dif

MOUSSORGSKY, MODESTE P. (Rus), 1839-1881.

This Russian "Bear," the most gifted and most misunderstood of "The Five" who roused Russia to national awareness in music, has left one operatic masterpiece, and

one great piano work, both of which have suffered at the
hands of editors and transcribers. Two orchestral transcriptions of the piano suite, complete with Cathedral chimes,
have become so familiar that many music lovers think the
original piano version is a "transcription." Horowitz, not
content with the notes written by MM, makes his own electrifying transcription, doubling everything he can for climaxes.
Harold Bauer published a "revised and edited" version (Schirmer), simplifying and eliminating to make it more "playable."
International has published a handsome edition with reproduc-
tions of some of the Victor Hartmann drawings in the mem-
orial exhibit of 1874, and excellent notes by the art critic
Alfred Frankenstein; and with the original Moussorgsky score.
The music is occasionally unpianistic, and somewhat repetitious, and Bauer's emendations are helpful.   It is a magnificent suite of contrasting numbers when played as a whole
(30 min plus); and separate numbers could be lifted out for
a Russian group.

Pictures at an Exhibition: Promenade. The "walking theme," which serves as introduction and transition, is
marked by Moussorgsky "in Russian mode, without hurry,
rather sustained." Alternating 5/4 and 6/4, and using a
pentatonic theme, it is to be played forte throughout, with
climax produced by the octave and chordal accretions.

Gnomus.   For a design for a nut-cracker with a
gnome's face, MM writes a humorous Disney seven-dwarfs
type of pompous march, with chuckles of laughter, and a
vanishing act at the end.   The Promenade to the next picture must be very quiet and legato.

Il Vecchio Castello.   Hartmann was an architect,
and his "Old Castle" drawing has a human figure in fore-
ground to indicate size, which suggested this melancholy
troubadour song, a fine work.   Some judicious cuts are in
order here.   The next Promenade begins boldly, but slows
down, as one would upon approaching another interesting
picture.

Tuileries [Children Quarreling After Play]. A dazzling little caprice, requiring fine sensitivity and technic for
its legato-staccato, rapid passage work, phrasing, melodic
line, so evocative of the title.

Bydlo.   The word means "cattle," but the drawing
has been identified as an ox-cart.   The piece has the plod-

ding inexorable mood of figures moving along the skyline of a Russian steppe. MM marks it ff and pesante, with an allargando and a final dim e perdendosi. The following Promenade must begin at the same dynamic level, rise to a forte, then hesitate, chuckle, and "attacca" the next picture.

Ballet of the Chicks in their Shells. A little gem, worthy companion to Rameau's "La Poule." MM's dynamic marks are quite adequate, and the ppp trill so suggestive of tiny chicks is quite possible, though difficult.

Two Polish Jews, One Rich, the Other Poor. For TV performance, with its rigid rules about ethnic jokes, one might have to change this title (as Bauer actually does), but it would be a pity. It is "Fiddler on the Roof," in miniature, and a jewel. The transitional promenade can be shortened; but retain the closing sustained B♭ link with:

Limoges, the Market Place. Chattering market women. MM wrote some suggested dialog in the margin, but scratched it. It reads for all the world like the quarrel over a horse-mule in "Tradition"! Vivo e sempre scherzando, this musical joke, with little rushing crescendos and shouted sfz marks, but una corda till the end where the dazzling toccata coda leads into the next piece ff. (Bauer's suggestions for deploying this difficult piece between LH-RH are helpful.)

Catacombas, Sepulcrum, Romanum. This brief chordal passage, with its strong dynamic contrasts leads to a lament for MM's friend, the dead painter, which uses the promenade theme under tremolo figures, rather unpianistic but essential contrast for the following.

The Hut on Fowl's Legs (Baba Yaga). Brilliant virtuoso piece using the flight of the witch of Russian folk-lore for a program. Leads with a great bravura octave passage to:

The Great Gate of Kiev. This grand climactic movement, magnificent though it is with Ravel's orchestra bells, can be very powerful on the piano, with its strains of chordal chant, sleigh-bells, cathedral chimes, and the Promenade theme again emerging, sempre maestoto.

Gopak. A popular toccata-style piece (not on Exhibition) based on the lively "hop-squat" dance of the Cossacks. Mod

MOZART, WOLFGANG AMADEUS (Aus), 1756-1791.

Students familiar with the Wunderkind stories of Mozart's childhood sometimes forget that none of the important
music was composed before he was 19 or 20, unlike Mendelssohn, two of whose greatest works were written at 16.
WAM was still living at the family home in Salzburg when
he wrote the first six sonatas, and the next seven date from
the visit to Paris with his mother in 1778.   Lovers of the
great operas, symphonies, chamber music and piano concertos often give the piano music an unduly low rating.
Much of it is equal to the best of WAM, but its performance requires a special sensitivity, a devotion to form and
detail and "tastefulness," that many pianists lack, especially the young.   Fine Mozart playing, in fact, requires a special mystique.   Fortunately the Köchel listing numbers have
become standard, and many good editions exist, though some
are incomplete, and a separate volume is required for the
pieces other than the Sonatas.   They are all only moderately difficult, some technically easy.

Sonata in C, K 279.   The very first sonata is so
full of typical Mozartean devices that it is a good place to
begin; bold orchestral chords, Alberti basses, chains of
trills and scales for modulation, and neatly rounded closing
themes.   The pianist who is too indolent to analyze and master the intricacies of Allegro form: exposition-development-
recapitulation, had better stop before he begins, for he will
be unable to convey much of the charm of the music, which
lies precisely in these subtle relationships.   Mozart's second movts are mostly quite slow, no matter what the mark-
ing; and closing movements quite fast.   Mod

Sonata in F, K 280.   WAM was fond of this key, and
three of his best sonatas are in F.   A bold allegro assai
(moderate) is followed by a deeply expressive adagio, which
owes much to Haydn.   Presto (possibile) for the closing
movt, which is another allegro, so find those transitions.
Even Artur Schnabel was heard to break down in a Mozart
allegro, because he forgot to make that second modulation!
Mod

Sonata in B♭, K 281.   The opening movt should be
marked 4/8, and played quite deliberately, to bring out its
beauties.   The second movt is quite dull, in spite of the
label amoroso.   But the last introduces us to one of WAM's
favorite games, hide-and-seek.   The rondo, carried to per-

fection in the concertos, always has a gay, fetching theme
(hereafter known as Ron) which ends with a polite bow. The
other themes (sometimes as many as six) always enter with
bold panache, like the doffing of a hat or the swirl of a cape,
and are all strikingly different in character and often in key.
The game consists of sneaking the protagonist back on stage
in a new way each time. Sometimes, as here, a chain of
trills, a cadenza, a fermata (there are no less than five fp
chords) prepare his return. Two more new themes (each
repeated)--minor arpeggios and chromatic octaves--appear
now, then hesitate, pause like actors who have forgotten
their lines, and on dashes Ron, for another brief scene.
Still a sixth theme, cantilena in E♭, enters, breaks into a
trill, and the ubiquitous Ron sneaks a LH entrance, only to
be brushed aside by Mme C. who likewise trills, but is not
allowed a cadenza, for Ron himself has the last flourish,
and bow. Cherchez la forme! Mod

Sonata in E♭, K 282. Most unusual in having for the
first movement a songful adagio (molto). To balance this
WAM writes two very rococo menuetti, and a lighthearted
allegro.

Sonata in G, K 283. The author's favorite. The
allegro has the winsomeness of a stately minuet. The
adagio could have served as a pathetic aria for Donna Anna
or the Contessa; and the presto, in spite of its intricate
form, has enormous brio. Mod

Sonata in D, K 284. The allegro must be orchestrated for the dramatic dynamic contrasts, the tremolandi,
the contrast of flute and oboe solos with bold tutti. The
Rondeau en Polonaise is rather disappointing. The Theme
and Variations are so fine and so long--12 in all, including
the lengthy adagio, and a cadenza--that they could well serve
as a separate program number. Mod Dif

Sonata in C, K 309. Written on a visit to Mannheim,
where he heard the famous orchestra, this too has the character of a symphony. The rondos grow longer and more
teasing, though this is marked grazioso. Mod Dif

Sonata in a, K 310. The Mozart player will have
discovered how limited the key system is (no sonatas or concertos in more than four sharps or flats); also that works in
minor keys are rare (only two sonatas) and usually superior.
This one has a fervor of restrained feeling in the outer move-

ments that anticipates Beethoven. The expressive andante
rises in its middle section to tragic grandeur. Mod Dif

Sonata in D, K 311. This rather large-scale work
saves its best effects for the final rondo, which is the longest and the best of its movements, with a cadenza before
one of the rondo reappearances. It must be presto possibile,
and must have the verve of a comic opera overture. Mod
Dif

Sonata in C, K 350. A well-balanced sonata, with
three attractive movements. The opening allegro (observe
the moderato) suggests the subtlety of the Figaro music,
with many chormatic passing tones, surprising modulations
and a coda of its own. The fine andante has an unusual harmonic scheme: F-f-A♭-f-F. The closing movt must not be
too fast, and has surprises in the form of a close, further
close, and final close. Mod

Sonata in A, K 331. Here the variations appear in
the first, instead of the third movt, and are too well-known
to need comment, as is the closing rondo alla Turca. The
Menuetto is rather like some of Bach's sarabandes, too
free and full of feeling to be a dance; more of a romanza.
Mod

Sonata in F, K 332. There is much of the rococo
dance about this allegro. The patience required for the over-
elaborate adagio (a Haydn heritage), is rewarded by the fine
finale, allegro (quasi presto, if you can cut it). Mod

Sonata in B♭, K 333. Another large-scale mature
work. In the closing rondo another "concerto cadenza" cam-
ouflages the reappearance of our friend Ron. Mod Dif

Sonata in c, K 457. Only one sonata dates from the
middle years, but it is possibly the greatest, paving the way
for Beethoven in its use of the tragic c minor, and in its
profundity-in-simplicity. Leashed fury seems to underlie
the whole allegro, even in the brief bitter-sweet wisps of
song. Profundity of restrained despair plumbs the depths of
the descending Adagio; and the forced gaiety of the finale has
the hermetic torsion of a mind on the brink. A reading of
some of the pitiful begging letters of WAM at this period
provides the image. Dif

Sonata in C, K 545. This is the familiar sonata

facile, usually tossed off by students. Music was for WAM an escape, not an outpouring (the great c minor is the exception); and he must have got kicks from writing this one. Mod-E.

Sonata in B♭, K 570. Einstein calls this small gem "perhaps the most completely rounded of them all, the ideal of his piano sonatas." The dull Alberti-basses of the early works give way, in the last two, to subtle, delicate counterpoint. Mod-E.

Sonata in D, K 575. The last of the sonatas is a large-scale work, written two years before his death. The "fanfare" movement in 6/8 is followed by one of the most deeply-felt adagios, and a closing allegretto that is worthy of the concertos. Mod-dif.

Fantasia in c, K 475. Several other fine works are usually published in a separate album of "pieces," though this fantasia appears with the Sonata in c. It is a fine stately full-fledged piece in several connected movements, and there is no need to couple it with the sonata, a surfeit of largesse. Mod

Fantasia in c, K 396. An even larger work, in a large allegro form, demanding precise mathematical division of beats by the performer, but having for the hearer, the effect of a free uninhibited improvisation, Baroque in its grandeur, if well played. Dif

Fantasia in d, K 397. A fine introduction to Mozart, for the sensitive student, this is much simpler, but perfectly formed in three linked movements, with enough of the romantic and the exhibitionist to make it more appealing than the more subtle sonatas. Mod-E

Rondo in D, K 485; Rondo in a, K 511. These games people played in the rococo age are too refined and subtle for most modern ears. (The sonata rondos are better, and best of all are the concerto rondos, where the whole orchestra gets in on the fun.) The second of these is the best, in fact very fine, though the pianist will have more fun than his friends. Mod Dif

Allegro in g, K 312. Missing from most collections, but found at the back of the Schirmer volume of 12 Pieces is this superb allegro in the rare key of g minor, brief but

well-developed in Mozart's late rarefied style. Since it
lacks other movements it can well be played with the minuet, adagio, and gigue in the same collection, as a concert
group. (The Romanza in the Schirmer book is by Franz
Bendel, q.v.)

    Minuet in D, K 355. This dance is really a Romanza
(MM quarter note = c 120) and is mature WAM, expressively
chromatic, even venturing pungent dissonant chord clusters,
subtly resolved. Mod E

    Adagio in b, K 540. Perhaps the most profoundly
moving of all Mozart's movements, this is a large-scale
slow allegro, with developments, return, coda, all used for
intense personal expression. The piano is not, alas, a string
quartet, so don't moon over it too long. Mod

    Gigue in G, K 574. Written after a visit to Leipzig,
this lighthearted 3-v fugue is a tribute to Bach, but pure Mozart,
of the finest vein. (MM dotted quarter = c 90). Mod

    Variations. There are 17 or 18 sets of variations,
mostly on popular operatic arias of the day, and mostly inferior. These grew out of the custom, still prevalent in
Liszt's time, of improvising in public on a tune requested
from the audience. Most of them might better not have been
written down. Only the set on "Unser dummer Pöbel Meint"
is of concert calibre; and it is over-extended. Like Beethoven, WAM wrote his finest variations on the themes of his
own, as movements of sonatas or chamber music.

MUSGRAVE, THEA (GB), 1928- .

    This composer of numerous chamber works with piano
has two solo works.

    Sonata (1956). An early work in free harmonic style,
secco, linear, often two-part, but with one voice in 3rds un-
derlining the dry calligraphic quality. Propulsive rhythmic
drive. Dif

    Monologue (1960). Unique concept, a seven-part dra-
matic scena for piano alone. Opens with a crepescular recitative, non-tonal but anchored in B♭. The sombre mood is
maintained in an ostinato allegro. There is a brief contra-

puntal section a turbulent, climactic cadenza, and a brief
recapitulation of the opening recitative with its B♭ pedal.
Mod Dif

NAKADA, YOSHINAO (Jap), 1923- .

One of the more than 125 composers in Japan writing
for piano (see Dornan). Though the piano has been manu-
factured, taught and played there for almost 100 years, and
many performers are beginning to win international recognition, few compositions have more than local interest, and
few are available outside the country. The publications of
Ongaku no Tomo Edition are available through TP.

"Time" Suite for Piano (1952): Prelude, Harpsichord, Piano, Etude, The Toyopet. The title is indicative
of an obsessive need to "catch up" with the West. The
time-lag is considerable, and most of these well-written
works might have come out of Europe in the first two decades of the century. The most attractive is the last, which
vividly characterizes the little car in a bi-tonal moto perpetuo, full of Stravinsky and Bartók devices, hammered altered chords in irregular meters providing both a percussive
driving rhythm and a "modern" sound to round out the suite.
Mod

Light and Shadow: High-Light, A Story of Ocean,
Girl Playing the Koto, Electronic Calculator, Dirge, Machine. The time gap narrows somewhat here, with the use
of a tone-row in both "A Story of Ocean," and "Electronic
Calculator." YN seems more at home in the sombre diatonic Dirge and the wistful "Girl Playing the Koto." There
is a modal quality to the last, but the composer misses a
fine chance to use the unique Japanese pentatonic, and the
sweeping arpeggios so characteristic of that instrument.
Mod

Sonata (1949). Almost every one of the 125 Japanese
composers has done his "duty sonata" and the results are only slightly duller than those ground out by young Western
composers, before they find the light. We get either correct form with forced modulations and uninspired melodies
as in YN's case; or free-wheeling original works for which
the composer is too indolent or ignorant to find a suitable
title. Mod

NAPOLI, JACOBI (It), 1911- .

Second generation Italian opera composer, who followed his father as director of Naples Conservatory, now
Director at Milan.

Polka-Galop (1967). Unique use of traditional dances
in bitonal harmony with original keyboard figures, free-
wheeling, building to a climax through sheer speed. Mod
Dif

NELHYBEL, VACLAV (Czech), 1919- .

Czech composer now living in New York, specializ-
ing in chamber music for brass.

Four Pieces for Piano. It is well he tells us these
four pieces are "for the piano," as there might otherwise be
some doubt. The intrada fanfares sound rather like a brass
transcription, complex in rhythm and highly dissonant; the
second movt proves that it is for the piano by being called
"Sonata" and ranging the length of the keyboard in wild
thrusts; the "Cantata" might better have been a choral work;
to clinch the point, that uniquely keyboard movement, the
virtuoso Toccata, closes. Mr. Nelhybel has now done his
duty by the piano, and may return to his proper métier.
Dif

NIELSEN, CARL (Den), 1864-1931.

Danish composer slowly winning favor for his well-
wrought symphonies and concertos, wrote little for piano.

Suite, Op 45. This work is uneven and unpianistic.
Nos 2, 4 and 5 are in a flowing cantabile style, viable on
the keyboard, if not highly original. The others seem to
need orchestration for their tremolandi, hammered octaves,
cork-screwing passage work. III is a Molto adagio e patetico
which might be powerful if its harmonic and melodic materials were more original. Six begins toccata style, but soon
calls in trombones, flutes and percussion. Dif

Chaconne, Op 32. "Gritty sonorities, convincingly

earnest and unsensuous" (J. Gibbs in Pelican KM).   Dif

Theme and Variations.   Large-scale set, technically demanding but more pianistic than other works.   Contrasting key tonalities (major-minor) add musical interest.   Dif

NIEMANN, WALTER (Ger), 1876-1953.

This scholarly musicologist was also a prolific composer (over 180 opus numbers) of rather mediocre piano music, programmatic or picturesque, often with a pseudo-Oriental flavor (he seems to have been an arm-chair traveller).

Three Sonatas: Romantic, Northern, Elegiac.   Teutonic scholarship and keyboard facility joined hands here, but the muse of inspiration was absent.   Large-scale, derivative, typically romantic 19th century.   Mod

10 Schwarzwald Idyls, Op 21; 10 German Dances, Op 26; Old Greek Temple Dances, Op 51; Old China (5 pieces) Op 62; The Garden of Orchids, Op 76; Bali Suite, Op 87; Barrel Organ, Op 107.   Best are the short pieces with dance rhythms, or descriptive effects.   Bird of paradise (Op 76) has avian imitations: The Singing Fountain and Mirror Lake (Op 95) are fluid and rippling.   The Balinese Cock-Fight is a dashing Toccata, the Porter's March, ponderous and plodding; Chinese Quarrel and Ricksha Ride full of ersatz Oriental effects, produced by using pentatonic scale harmonized in 4ths and 5ths; Barrel-organ quotes a Verdi aria over a drone bass.   All are pianistic; many, trivial.   Mod

NIN, JOAQUIN (Cuba-Sp), 1883-1949.

Pianist, collector and editor of Caribbean and Spanish folk-music and early keyboard classics, has several works for piano, not highly original but attempting to fuse Spanish idiom with a more modern harmony.

Iberian Dance (1925).   Neo-classic linear writing stemming from Soler, but fresh and vivacious.   Mod

Mensaje a Claudio Debussy (1929).   One of many
tributes to Debussy this large-scale habanera is lush and
lachrymose (de Falla's guitar homage is better).   Mod

Three Spanish Dances (1938).   Authentic flavor of
guitars, castanets, wailing melisma in free cadenzas, and
vigorous stomping dance, but difficult and not pianistic.
Dif

Sonata Breve (1934).   Nin's concerts featured early
sonatas by Soler, M. Albeniz, and Scarlatti, which he also
edited.   This neo-classic three-movt work is an outgrowth,
lean, sinewy and rhythmic, with tonal-dissonant harmony.
Mod

OLSEN, POUL ROVSING (Den), 1922- .

Composer-ethnomusicologist (research in Greenland)
has a piano and orchestra concerto and a sonata.

Op 35 Medardus, Suite for Klavier (1956).   A seven
note theme unifies the four varied movts: Impromptu,
Dance Barbaro, Meditation, Marche Interrompue.   Bartok-
derived work.   12 min, pianistic.   Mod Dif

Op 38, Five Intentions (1957).   Short serial studies,
in contrasting tempi, manipulating the row for more Bartók
ian effects.   Moderate difficulty.   (Peters pub)

ORNSTEIN, LEO (Rus-US), 1892- .

One-time "bad-boy of music" turned teacher.   He
played, along with other contemporary music of the 20s and
30s, his own works, now largely forgotten.   There are fou
sonatas, but the dance and program items are more interesting.

Wild Man's Dance, Op 13:2 (1915).   Product of Cubism and neo-primitivism this is unmitigated in its battering
of the keyboard with undistinguished and undistinguishable
clumps of notes.   Dif

A la Chinoise, Op 39 (1928). Might bear the same

title as the above, as there is little Chinese about it, and
it carries the polytonal keyboard onslaught a stage further.
Dif

PADEREWSKI, IGNACE JAN (Pol), 1860-1941.

Once a household word, mispronounced in homes
around the world, Paderewski left a few recordings of his
fabulous playing, and quantities of compositions, by which
he hoped to be remembered.   Two of his concertos have recently been recorded, but his name as a composer is rarely to be seen even on student recitals.   At his debut in London in 1890, the critic (one G. B. Shaw) wrote of him as an
"immensely spirited young harmonious blacksmith who puts
a concerto on the piano as upon an anvil and hammers it
out with an exuberant joy. "   But when IJP introduced some
of his own music, Shaw howled that a law should be passed
forbidding pianists to play their own works.

Chants du Voyageur: Minuet in G, Melodie in B,
Nocturne in B♭.   The elegant rococo dance in this set is
still hammered out with joy by young harmonious black-
smiths.   The other two have a quiet lyric charm.   Mod E

Variations and Fugues, Op 11, 23.   Variations IJP
could turn out, but not themes to vary, nor fugues.   Praised
by Hutcheson and Lockwood in the 40's, they are not mentioned by Kirby or Gillespie, writing in the 60's.

PALESTER, ROMAN (Pol-Fr), 1907- .

Another Pole who followed Chopin's footsteps to Paris
where his symphonies, operas and chamber music have been
heard.

Preludes.   Ten pieces to be played separately or together, neo-classic and basically diatonic but contemporary
in sound; pianistic but technically demanding.   Several are
slow and poetic, others exuberant and sparkling.   Both effective and affective.   Mod Dif

PALMER, ROBERT (USA), 1915- .

Successful composer of choral and chamber music,
has several sonatas for two pianos and four hands, and two
for piano solo.

Three Preludes (1941). Rather massive and formidable works, contrasting irregular meters (17/16, 11/4) with
a flowing cantabile movement between two propulsive ones,
freely dissonant. Dif

Three Epigrams (1958). More refined writing, all
three using a small tight motif, sometimes framed in octaves, sometimes above broken-chord figures. The shifting
meters are more confusing than helpful, but the sound has
a distinctive shape. Mod

Toccata Ostinato. Martellato chord study requiring
velocity and endurance. Angular and acerb. Mod Dif

PALMGREN, SELIM (Fin), 1878-1951.

Minor composer-pianist-conductor. There is little
of the rugged North in his music, but much fanciful imagination. His music is pianistic in a 19th-century idiom,
with mildly innovative figures and harmonies. He wrote
two sonatas, three suites, a Fantasia, 24 preludes, and a
Ballade with variations, almost none of which are available
in print or on records. A few small piano pieces have
earned immortality for their charm.

May-Night. Three-page atmospheric piece, with effective use of 9th chords, pedal effects. Mod E

Bird-song. Unique piece to add to your aviary.
Two pages, without bar-lines, the two hands playing unison
scale figures pp legatissimo, three octaves apart, punctuated by rolled chords. Mod Dif

The Swan. Similar to May-Night. Requires large
hand. Mod E

The Sea. Rolling arpeggios in the bass, with a
slower wave of melodic line, doubled in octaves and transferred to the bass for an impressive closing climax. Four-
page. Mod

The Dragon Fly. Broken octave moto perpetuo, leggiero. Mod

The Pin Wheel. Arpeggio study, allegro volante,
the two hands dividing the figures. Written throughout on a
single staff. Mod

PANUFNIK, ANDRZEJ (Pol-GB), 1914- .

Distinguished conductor-composer, who experiments
with microtones and new notation.

Six Miniature Studies. Contrasting set in contemporary keyboard idioms, ranging from the witty and brilliant
to the moody and sonorous. Mod

PAPINEAU-COUTURE, JEAN (Can), 1916- .

Distinguished Canadian composer - educator writes in
a style combining tonality and row-engendered textures.

Mouvement perpetuel. French studies (with N. Boulanger) are apparent in this lucid writing, with fluent LH
part. Mod Dif

Rondo (1951). A martellato figure alternates with
lyrical episodes, freely chromatic. Mod Dif

Suite (1959). Larger work: two Bagatelles in genial
scherzo style preceded by a free prelude, and cantabile aria.
Mod Dif

Etude in B♭ (1959). Large-scale virtuoso work exploring keyboard patterns in polytonal harmony. Dif

PARADISI, DOMENICO (It), 1710-1792.

Spanning the century of transition from polyphony to
homophony and harpsichord to piano, DP wrote 12 keyboard
sonatas which have an easy grace and charm, and sound
well on the piano. All are in two-movts, binary form, the

first often a full-fledged allegro, the second a lively dance.

Sonata No 6, in A. The second movt toccata is a brilliant moto perpetuo, often appearing alone. The opening vivace 3/4 has three fine lyric themes neatly linked with modulatory passages and properly developed. Mod

Sonata No 10 in D. Similar in structure and thematic material to No 6. The lively second movt is in d minor. Mod

Also recommended are No 1 in G and No 3 in E.

PENTLAND, BARBARA (Can), 1912- .

Canadian pianist, educator and composer whose numerous chamber works are in a Schönbergian serial technic.

Studies in Line (1949). Effective use of four permutations of the row in four sketches: "The first fluctuates like a graph; the second goes in circles; the third is level and tranquil as a straight line; and the last is zigzag." (Illustrated!) Mod Dif

Dirge (1961). Sombre, portentous piece achieving mood and sonority through polytonality and dissonant contrapuntal writing. Mod

Toccata (1961). Vivacious motor movt interrupting with a brief calm adagio the driving propulsion of its row-derived lines. Mod Dif

PEPIN, CLERMONT (Can), 1926- .

Three Pieces (1951-1955). Pianist-composer, his three early pieces are eminently playable, while exploring rhythmic and melodic devices, tonally anchored, but freely chromatic. The third, called Danse Frénétique begins with "boogie-woogie" bass, with chordal melody, then reverses the figures, subsides for a lyric passage, without losing its forward drive, and closes climactically. Mod Dif

PEPPING, ERNEST (Ger), 1901- .

Best known for his sacred choral music, EP has also written chamber music, four piano sonatas and various
pieces.

Sonata No 1 (1937).   Neo-classic three-movt work in
an amiable, euphonious style, traditional but pianistic.   Mod

Sonata No 4 (1948).   Similar to the others, but broader in scope.

12 Fantasias (1949).   Harking back to Telemann (who
wrote three dozen) these one-movt works explore a variety
of moods in a turn-of-the-century style.

PERAGALLO, MARIO (It), 1910- .

Distinguished Italian composer who attempted the difficult task of writing operas and cantatas in dodecaphonic
idiom.

Fantasia (1953).   Based on permutations of a row, a
difficult but pianistically effective work.   Dif

PERSICHETTI, VINCENT (USA), 1915- .

Most generous to the piano, VP writes in a confirmed
neo-classic style, pianistic, distinctive and with a somewhat
acrid harmony.

Poems for Piano (1939).   Two books of 11 short
pieces on lines from modern poets, Eliot, Millay, Unter-
meyer, etc.   Humor and sentiment alternate in original and
imaginative pieces.   Should be heard.   (E-V pub)

Five Sonatinas (1940-50); Six Sonatinas (1950-54).
Short formal transparent two- or three-movt works, varying
from 2-v inventions to Viennese rondos, allegros, fugues,
all with a modern asperity of harmony.   Good replacement
for worn out 18th-century sonatinas.   Mod E

11 Sonatas (1939-65).   Large-scale three- or four-

movt works, classic formally but highly original and varied.

Sonata No 3 (1943).   Declaration, Episode and Psalm,
chordal and melodic with grandiose close.   Mod Dif

Sonata No 4 (1949).   Meaty, variegated work, lengthy,
thoughtful; requires good legato finger-work, octaves, drive.
Dif

Sonata No 5 (1949).   Lighter, with a songful Berceuse,
ebullient finale.   Mod

Sonata No 7 (1950).   Grazioso, meandering folksy
moderato; brief light-textured linear middle; fast playful
finale.   Mod

Sonata 11.   A 20-min one-movt work in five sections,
marked risoluto, articolato, sostenuto, leggero and conclusi-
vo.   Non-metrical throughout, but rich in contrasting rhythms;
sonorous colorful pedal effects.   Requires powerful drive,
endurance.   Highly dissonant.   Dif

PHILLIPS, BURRILL (USA), 1907- .

Educator and composer of chamber and orchestra
works.   His neo-classic style effectively exploits American
rhythms.

Three Divertimenti.   Miniatures contrasting three
styles: Fancy Dance, Homage to Monteverdi (properly polyphonic); Brag.   Mod

Toccata.   Boogie-woogie bass provides an ostinato
under well-deployed melodic and chordal patterns, with canonic imitations and augmentation.   Brilliant and not difficult.
Mod

A Set of Three Informalities: Blues, Scherzo, Sona-
tina.   Melancholy chordal Blues, bi-tonal rapid scherzo; the
Sonatina is best in a neo-Romantic style with brilliant close.
Mod

Five Various and Sundry (1961).   19th-century composers would have called these preludes or intermezzos.
Somewhat more free harmonically than earlier sets.   The

pieces, which could be played separately, are called Dialogue, Tide-Mark, Music at Night, Jubilation. Mod

PIERNE, GABRIEL (Fr), 1863-1937.

One of many French petits maîtres who found time, between teaching at the Conservatoire and playing organ at churches to grind out numerous compositions. Almost all of these facile, shallow works are justly forgotten.

Pour mes petits amis. An attractive children's march is still heard occasionally: Marche des petits soldats de plomb. Mod E

Etude de Concert. Long brilliant concert waltz, introducing some interesting keyboard patterns and hemiola rhythmic shifts. Mod Dif

Variations in c, Op 42. Bravura work, highly regarded by GP's contemporaries, suggested for revival by recording artists in desperate need. Its complexity requires four staves, and performance requires good octave grip and endurance. Dif

PIJPER, WILLEM (Neth), 1894-1947.

Eminent Dutch music promoter, administrator and composer of chamber works. Championing new music, his works are experimental and transitional in style. Most enduring are the chamber works, though there are three sonatinas and a sonata for piano.

Sonatinas Nos 2, 3. Light genial neo-classic works experimenting with polytonality (but basically whole-tone) jazz and irregular rhythms. Musically difficult and rather undistinguished. Mod

Sonata (1930). Atmospheric, lugubrious adagio molto (with Debussy-like pedal-points) framed by non-symmetrical allegros. Anticipates much later and better work. Mod

PINTO, OCTAVIO (Braz), 1890-1950.

Brazilian architect and amateur composer, married the pianist Guiomar Novaes.

Scenes Infantis (1932). Music that can be either enjoyed or played by gifted children. Named after children's games and activities, the six pieces contrast finely a variety of moods, with simple but pianistic devices. Should be played as a set. Mod E

Dança Negreira. Brilliant moto perpetuo, with quirky syncopations. Sounds more difficult than it is. Mod

Marcha de Pequeña Polegar [Tom Thumb]. Scherzo in march-time, staccato. Mod E

PONCE, MANUEL (Mex), 1886-1948.

Considered the father of Mexican classical music, MP is known the world over for his song, Estrellita. His historic importance surpasses the quality of his works, seldom heard outside Mexico. The early salon music style gives way to greater complexity, after study in Paris following World War I. There is little Mexican flavor in his piano music.

Dos Etudes (1928). Early works, graceful, pianistic and shallow. Mod

Four Pieces (1929). Neo-classic dance suite, exploring bitonality, pentatonic scales, etc. Mod

Gavota (1941). Post-Paris style, more elaborate, yet lyrical and effective. Mod

Tema Mexicano Variado. Traditional variations, well-developed, on a genial folk-song. Mod

POOT, MARCEL (Bel), 1901- .

Critic, educator, one-time director of Brussels Conservatory, wrote utilitarian music in a traditional style.

Suite. Neo-classic treatment of four traditional
movts: prelude, fughetta, passacaglia and toccata.

Etude (1951); Variations (1952); Ballade (1958).
Several pieces written for student or contest use are still
attractive and playable, in a conservative style, with emphasis on developing technic. Mod

PORTER, QUINCY (USA), 1897-1966.

Sonata (1930). Well-known educator and composer of
chamber and symphonic works, his single piano sonata,
though early, is still pleasant to play and hear. Mildly dissonant, the three movements follow the classic F-S-F
form, the first and last melodious and lively, the middle in
a free improvisatory style. Not long. (CFP pub) Mod

POULENC, FRANCIS (Fr), 1899-1963.

The most popular member of Les Six, FP wrote for
piano throughout his lifetime with little change in style.
How much is enduring, how much salon trifles? He had a
facile gift for melody, though the same tunes keep turning
up, as do rhythmic motifs in his favorite 4/4. His keyboard writing lies well under the hand and there is little
bravura. His harmony is opulent, often banal and sentimental. He loathed rubato, liked fast tempos, and loved
lush pedalling. The late works, without key signatures, are
difficult to read; but most are only moderately difficult to
play. Perhaps the finest keyboard writing of FP is found
in the ensemble works: Concerto for two Pianos; Sonata
for Four Hands; Concerto Champêtre for Harpsichord and
Orchestra. There is much to enjoy.

Trois mouvements perpetuels (1918). These early
works remain the most popular, now in their 47th edition.
The first and last require a large band, and the third must
be very fast. Mod

Suite in C (1920). Longer than the Trois Mouvements,
these are equally good. Presto, Andante, Vif. Mod Dif

Trois Pièces (1928): Pastorale, Hymne, Toccata.
The first and last of these are FP at his best; the contrasting Hymne, less inspired. Pastorale (not to be confused
with the less attractive Pastourelle) is ternary, with a grave,
melancholy pavan at the center, opening and closing with a
wailing melisma over sinuous harmonies, calme et myster-
ieux, and slow (60 seems better than the 72 = quarter note
indicated). The genial and dashing Toccata begins 160, and
gathers speed. Much is staccato, and several passages are
marked très sec. Though no pedal is marked, it should be
used lavishly on all other parts, where a broad cantabile is
woven into the busy patter of chords. Mod Dif

Presto in B♭ (1934). Written for Vladimir Horowitz,
this is similar to the Toccata above, though harmonically
less interesting. Mod Dif

Huit Nocturnes (1938). The mature FP, more wide-
ranging in keyboard style and harmony. They may be
played as a set, (20 min) or separately. Four have program titles. There is nothing of the morbidly melancholy
about these; more of the bland cheerfulness of Fauré's Impromptus. "Bells of Malines" is impressionistic, "Phantom
Ball" a nostalgic waltz, "Moths" a fluttering bit of Chin-
oiserie (Presto misterioso). Mod

Les Soirées de Nazelle (1936): Preambule, Variations, Cadente, Final. This half-hour suite of "Evenings
at Nazelles" is considered by Friskin and Freundlich the
finest of FP, a summation of all his keyboard styles. It can
be shortened with an optional cut in the "portrait" variations. Mod Dif

12 Improvisations (1941). Uneven in quality and ranging from simple student pieces (Nos 2, 12) to more mature,
witty, sentimental brilliant numbers. Mod E

PROKOFIEV, SERGE (Rus), 1891-1953.

One of the most important 20th-century composers,
both for the quantity and quality of his piano oeuvre, and for
his influence on a generation of younger men. Precocious in
his development as a pianist and as composer, he early
found a distinctive idiom, and adhered to it unswervingly,
during a varied life as concert pianist in Europe and Amer-

ica, and as composer in the USSR where he defied attempts
to control his creativity. The elements of his unique piano
style are: (1) a virtuoso keyboard writing that makes full
but never impossible demands of the performer; (2) use of
classical dances and movements, freely treated; (3) a harmony basically tonal but highly devious; (4) a predilection
for duple meters in incisive rhythmic motifs, wide-ranging
but often basically diatonic, chromatic or chordal, and bearing a strong family likeness; (5) triple meters reserved for
broad contrasting lyric themes or movts, and compound
meters in percussive, propulsive chordal patterns, at fantastic speed. Add to this a constant background of derived
contrapuntal lines and figures, and a wry humor, and you
have a unique mix.

Sonata 1, Op 1 in f (1909). This product of the 18-
year old student of St. Petersburg Conservatory, with its
Tchaikovsky-Rachmaninoff aura, is understandably romantic.
A one-movt work in a broad pianistic style, not yet distinctive. Mod Dif

Four Etudes, Op 2 (1909). Technical studies were
de rigeur in the Conservatory, a famous piano-player factory;
and SP did his duty by them--3rds, scales, octaves, the
whole panoply--but his heart was not in them (as Chopin's
was). Dif

Four Pieces, Op 4 (1910) Reminiscences, Elan, Despair, Suggestion Diabolique [Temptation]. Here the real
SP stands up to be counted, and the seeds of all later works
are planted. His fantastic technic and sinuous melodic line
are at the service of music ends, ranging from the expression of nostalgia and despair, to uninhibited animal spirits,
and devilish laughter. The last piece has become a popular
concert encore, and is the best of the many portraits of
Mephisto. Mod to Dif

Toccata, Op 11 (1912). Exciting and hugely difficult
work, modelled after Schumann's, requiring stupendous drive
and endurance. V Dif

10 Pieces, Op 12 (1913). For pianists unable to cope
with the granitic Sonatas, these offer all the same material
in miniature. Marches and gavottes, with their strong
shapes, are favorites of SP. The three-page March is staccato throughout, moving from pp to ff, with two episodes
that slither through four keys, returning to f minor at the

end. The Gavotte is similar, but so interlaced with counter-
themes and octave doublings that it loses its spontaniety and
is clumsy. The Mazurka has a quartal melody, and the
Prelude (in the middle) is marked "for Harp or Piano."
Two puckish Scherzos are highly characteristic. Mod

    Sarcasms, Op 17 (1912-1914). The irony of this set
is more apparent in the title than in the five pieces, which
carry chromatic explorations and rhythmic motifs a stage
farther. One of the less attractive sets. Mod

    Sonata 2, Op 14 in d (1912). Large four-movt work,
still essentially romantic, but exploring bi-tonality and employing SP's own keyboard tricks. Lyric first movt; contrasting scherzo, with melody embedded in a texture of
double-note figuration; highly chromatic andante, typical
furioso finale. Mod Dif

    Visions fugitives, Op 22 (1915-1917). Determined
not to be trite and call his works merely Pieces or Preludes, SP comes up with another innocuous title, for a set
of 20 short, lyrical, yet discrete and finely-wrought sketches
containing some of his finest writing. There is no key sequence and many are written without signatures, baffling to
analyze, but always sounding inevitably right. They often op-
en with a foreign chord and a melodic motif that studiously
avoids the key which they later explore and end with. The
"Fleeting Visions" range from meandering pastorales, nostalgic dance movements sparkling with knuckle-breaking
ornamentation, bitonal flute-harp duets, to moods marked
inquieto, giocoso, ridicolosamente. The entire 20 can be
played as a set (25 min) or a group selected. Rubinstein
played ten, ending with No 14, Feroce, which anticipates
(in 2 pages) many of the sonata finales. Mod

    The Thing in Itself, Op 45; Thoughts, Op 62. Two
rather abstract and abstruse sets of pieces suggest a meta-
physical strain in SP, which he, fortunately, did not often
inflict on pianists. The first takes its title from Kant's
concept of "Ding an Sich." For the explorer, not the performer. Dif

    Two Sonatinas, Op 54. More intimate and restrained
than the sonatas, these are also somewhat laconic and ambiguous, both for player and for hearer. Short three-movt
works (modelled after Ravel); the first, in e minor, is better. Mod

Sonata No 3 in a, Op 28 (1917). Within the scope of the advanced student, this brilliant one-movt work is a macrocosm of SP's piano writing. The opening theme, tempestoso, hammered out at formidable speed, carefully avoids the tonic in its striding theme, and it is only on page 2 that the key is established. A brief episode based on this material bridges to a lyrical Moderato semplice e dolce second theme in C, a quiet canonic duet over a gently flowing tenor. A five-page development combines this highly diverse material in a masterful way, doubling themes in octaves over mounting triadic scales, spreading chords across the entire keyboard. The opening tempestoso returns, but in place of the second theme, a new development serves as coda, with a bold "quasi tromba" theme added to fill it out. Mod Dif

Sonata No 6 in A, Op 82 (1940). Sonatas 6, 7 and 8 were written during World War II and are all of virtuoso calibre, often appearing on concerts. They are tough nuts to crack. The mere reification of the score is a formidable task, followed by the chore of surmounting the manual problems; imagination must then be given full rein to discover and project the richly complex musical content. The mastering of such a work is deeply satisfying, and a sympathetic performance is sure to communicate. Dif

Sonata No 7 in Bb, Op 83 (1942). In No 7, as in No 3, a slow lyric second theme affords relief from the percussive urgency of the movement (allegro 6/8), and provides a rich palette of contrasting colors for the powerful build-up to follow. The andante middle movement (in E) reverses the pattern, with an animato core, though the big triple beat is maintained throughout. The brash, biting finale, 7/8 precipitato, is extremely difficult but electrically exciting. Dif

Sonata No 8 in Bb, Op 84 (1944). Equally demanding, but less inspired, No 8 is cyclic, the finale rounded off with reminiscences of earlier movements. Dif

Sonata No 9 in C, Op 103 (1947). Less brilliant, this combines neo-classicism and an almost Wagnerian romanticism. There is also a tenth, dating from his last year and left incomplete. It sounds faded and pale, with only flashes of the colorful master. Of the five concertos, the third is most popular.

RACHMANINOFF, SERGEI (Rus-USA), 1873-1943.

Here composer and pianist were sometimes at odds, and the music suffered. SR has given us a large corpus of piano solo music which the centennial year of his birth gives occasion to review. His output was limited by the demands of his concert appearances (the highest opus is 45), and when inspiration flagged, the Russian master fell back on keyboard antics which he alone could project. His own playing had enormous brio, dazzling technical perfection, a wide scale of touch effects. In playing his own music, another character seemed to take over, lavishing emotion with wild abandon. Try playing along with his records, and you find it almost impossible to anticipate the extremes of accelerando and ritardando, crescendo and diminuendo. Though pages of his writing look much like Fauré, the sound of the Russian's music is intensely personal and romantic, beside the cool iridescent objectivity of the Frenchman. Writing at the same time as Scriabin, Debussy, Ravel and Ives, Rachmaninoff's Tchaikovsky-inspired 19th-century opulence makes him an anachronism; but what a gorgeous anachronism. He wrote well for orchestra also, and the works in which he combined the two stand at the peak of his oeuvre.

Five Pieces, Op 3: Elegy. It is significant that the first published piece is an Elegy, for SR had an obsession with death. One almost expects to hear the Dies Irae intoned (as in the Rhapsody and Isle of the Dead). Instead the Chopinesque opening broadens into a sweeping Tchaikovskian line, with lush harmonization. Mod

Prelude in c#. SR was never allowed to stop playing encores until he had favored the audience with this early all-time hit. It is a powerful and expressive piece, in spite of the beating it takes. Mod Dif

Polichinelle. The mood of gloom gives way to one of puckish high spirits, and introduces trilled-chords, a broad singing melody in octaves with inner fingers busy weaving harmonic arabesques. The other two pieces in Op 3 are called Melodie and Serenade and are less attractive. Mod

Humoresque, Op 10:5. Similar to the above, this requires a fine rhythmic sense, and a crisp staccato touch, but otherwise is not taxing. Mod E

Moments Musicaux, Op 16.   In these early etudes, the emphasis is on technic rather than content, in spite of the name.   SR's fabulous keyboard facility here works itself out in excessively complex writing, preparing the way for the later, much finer sets of preludes.   Nos 3 and 5 are in slow tempi and easier, but uninspired.   No 2 is a good introduction to the fluid LH style, and a good work-out for anyone preparing to play the Concerti.   No 4 in e♭ the best of the set, has an even more complex LH, with the RH joining in at cadences, and doubling for the fff climaxes, prestissimo yet!   No 6 is a glorified Czerny exercise on the C major triad.   Dif

10 Preludes, Op 23 (1904).   One of the great prelude sets, these continue the tradition of Chopin, though on a larger scale, and with technical demands matching the Chopin Etudes.

Prelude No 1 in f♯.   Only the first and last in the book are moderately easy.   Here SR has found his own voice, and the Largo, opening in a shy, tentative way, builds to a single fine climax, then trickles to an end, with one of those rapping chordal closes that so often suggest a signature-tune on the composer's polysyllabic name.   Mod

No 2 in B♭.   Sometimes called SR's "Revolutionary," this prelude is indeed an etude, a brilliant tour de force on the tonic scale and chord of the key.   The hammered, up-thrusting chordal motif is answered by a down-rushing scale figure.   The mid-section drops to pp for a lyric duet that becomes a trio in SR's most lavish style.   The eight-meas coda is yet another ingenious var on the scale and tonic chord.   Requires rhythmic incisiveness and drive, to convey its joi de vivre.   Dif

No 3 in d.   A fine staccato chord study, this has more the character of a polonaise than that of the minuetto marked by SR.   A long coda begins with a pedal-point on d, with a 3-v canonic passage above.   Mod Dif

No 4 in D.   Serenity is the mood of this prelude, with the simple nocturne-like opening soon evolving into a complex ensemble of melody, counter-melody, canons, chiming treble echos.   One of the best.   Mod Dif

No 5 in g.   Almost as popular as the c♯, this military prelude (another staccato chord study) has awkward har-

monic sequences that manage to sound right. The eight-
meas chordal episode on page 2 is majestic, after the mysterious opening; and the broad second theme over a V^7 arpeggiated bass has its own canonic duet and is eloquent.
Touch and time require subtlety. Mod Dif

No 6 in E♭. The next two make a fine pair, this
one a first cousin of the famous Second Piano Concerto lyric theme. The andante must be teneremente, molto rubato.
Mod Dif

No 7 in c. There is little melody in this, but it is
SR at his joyous best, with broken-chord sequences rising
and falling in jets of purling sound. Allegro (molto); advanced technic needed. Dif

No 8 in A♭. A worthy successor to Chopin's best,
this sparkling prelude is allegro vivace, over in 2-1/2 min,
and is built on a single figure. Dif

No 9 in e♭. Like Chopin's double-note study in the
same key, this is fiendishly difficult for the player, and not
one of the most attractive to listen to. (Highly rated by
Culshaw.) Dif

Prelude No 10 in G♭. The shortest and simplest,
this adagio has SR's best features, a cantabile melody,
sensuous harmony, and a glorious four-layer-cake ending.
Mod

13 Preludes, Op 32 (1910). By including the early
hit in c♯ with the ten of Op 23, SR makes up, with the 13
in Op 32, the standard 24 in all major-minor keys. Though
very diversified, many of these lack the "first fine careless
rapture" of the earlier set.

Prelude No 1 in C. Brilliant and difficult three-page
study. The quiet closing chord sequence is as unique as the
ending of that "greatest Hit" in c♯. Dif

No 2 in b♭. A compound rhythm (9/8, 12/8) with a
dotted triplet figure rocking away from a chord and back
again becomes a frequent motif in the late works. Rises to
a brilliant crest with fancy arabesques above the chordal
roll. Requires sensitive nuance to avoid monotony. Mod

No 3 in E. A Beethoven fate motif hammered out in

octaves answered by rippling figures, is also exploited in
several late preludes and etudes. It does not compensate
for the lack of a melodic line. Mod

No 5 in G. An exquisite lyric with a single theme,
but unique variations, transitions and coda. One of the best.
Mod

No 7 in F. The monotony of the rather trite rhythmic figure in this quiet number is made up for by a pleasing
duet between soprano and bass. Simpler. Mod

No 8 in a. Similar to No 3, this three-page study
is effective. Mod Dif

No 10 in b. Inspired by a romantic painting by Böck-
lin called "The Return," this is built on the rocking triplet,
and the major-minor slide. An intense work requiring an
imaginative performer. Mod

No 11 in B. The same rhythmic motif in a less
solemn mood, this eschews all ornamentation and display.
Its restrained mood is too subtle for popular appeal, but a
pleasure to recreate. Mod E

No 12 in g#. A brilliant and expressive short prelude that must be taken very fast to allow for the frequent
broad rubatos. Three highly original themes and a finely
developed accpt figure. Dif

No 13 in Db. Enormously complex and difficult, this
is a summation of the prelude ethos, with hints of thematic
quotes from several, including "the hit." Never less than
three or four motifs are worked into the tissue of sound, and
a gloriously hammered chord climax, in Scriabin's best manner, makes a fine finish. Dif

Variations on a Theme of Corelli, Op 42. The great
piano and orchestra variations, Rhapsody on a Theme of
Paganini, is Op 43 (really a fifth concerto); and these seem
to have been a trial-run in the form. There is an earlier
set, Op 22, which is seldom played, because the theme
(Chopin's Prelude No 20 in c) is so perfect that the variations seem redundant. The La Folia in d, which Corelli and
many others varied (see C.P.E. Bach) is eminently suitable.
Twenty Variations and a coda use all SR's finest keyboard devices to produce a brilliant, well-rounded work (15-20 min).

After No 13, SR introduces an intermezzo, a richly ornamented Baroque recitative with lute-like cadenzas, modulating to D♭.   A mood of serenity is evoked by the sudden lift
to major.   A scherzo then leads to an agitato (back in d)
and swells to a grand chordal variation.   The closing coda
spins out the theme in a series of arabesques over luscious
melting harmonies, purified at the end to a simple d minor
chord.   A worthy successor to the great variations by Beethoven, Schumann and Brahms.   Dif

17 Etudes Tableaux, Op 33, 39.   Perhaps the celebration of the centennial of SR's birth will see reinstated
these grand works, so long regarded as merely a redundant
extension of the two books of preludes.   Idiomatically they
are closely related, but these are true concert studies,
written when SR was beginning to win fame as the greatest
keyboard virtuoso of his day.   No one who ever heard his
electrifying playing (or watched that grim, gaunt face under
the convict haircut) will ever forget it.   He was perhaps the
last of the great performing composers, and the sheer joy
in playing, as distinguished from the ideal pleasure of listening, sets the etudes apart.   It is heartening to find them
listed as requirements for the Van Cliburn contest 1973,
side by side with the etudes of Chopin and Liszt.   What other composer could offer such a choice?

Etude No 1 in f.   A colorful march, not excessively
long or difficult, with staccato bass ostinati striding down
the keyboard, under a sustained melody, enriched with the
familiar shifting inner voices, and ringing upper chimes.
Mod

No 2 in C.   The old-fashioned penman's push-pull
figure (used in the g♯ Prelude) provides a delicate shaded
background for the exquisite calligraphy of the melodic line,
which reappears above slow rolled chords, under a halo of
trills, for a Chopinesque coda.   Mod Dif

No 3 in c.   More a nocturne than an etude, this
three-page piece makes us wonder what painting inspired
such a stark yet moving threnody.   The unique title, "Tableaux," suggests both a narrative and a picture.   The central tranquillo is almost wholly diatonic, and after a brief
anguished chromatic passage, più mosso, agitato, ends with
the crystalline clarity of C major.   Mod

No 4 in d.   Falling 4ths and 5ths form the intervalic

material for this brilliant staccato study. To be played pp, except for two crescendi with leaping octave chords. Mod Dif

No 5 in e♭. A joyous virtuoso etude, presto, with chromatic passages purling over a rough and rocky LH pattern of constantly shifting rhythms and harmonies. Dif

No 6 in E♭. Here SR eschews the broad melodic line for a striking series of hammered tonic triad figures, accumulating power with each repetition. Allegro con fuoco, this requires a keen rhythmic sense and great endurance of the joyous blacksmith. Dif

No 7 in g. A mournful cantabile melody unites this etude, wreathed with broken chords, and broadened into triads for cadences. The four-page study builds to a cadenza climax, then, after a brief returning of mourning, ends with a minor scale passage, fff. Mod

No 8 in c♯. A bold declamatory work with five distinct themes that tend to fall apart at the seams, though SR combines them all in a powerful coda. The major-minor wail, so pervasive in SR, colors this unique etude. Four pages. Dif

No 9 in f. Another bumptious rabble-rouser, unflagging in its propulsion, but totally devoid of melody. The sheer excitement of flying fingers in lush harmonies (with two meas straight out of Scriabin) calls for bravos, this time for the pianist, not the composer. Dif

No 10 in a. This quiet lento has a lyric line, but lacks a contrasting theme, and the melody is too tenuous for such extended treatment. Mod

No 11 in f♯. An exuberant work-out for both hands. Odd metrical groups add piquancy to the highly original figuration which winds into a cadenza before doubling into staccato chords. Dif

No 12 in b. Time signature is omitted here for greater freedom, though there is powerful rhythmic drive in this staccato chord study, senza ped. The look of the page is familiar, but the sound is fresh and bold. Dif

No 13 in e♭. Best known of the Etudes, this big

appassionata movement combines the grand manner with a
fine epic song theme.   Its relentless martellato and its
three mighty climaxes leave both player and hearer exhausted and purged.   Makes a fine group with the E♭ (No
6) and one in c, either No 3 or No 15.   Dif

No 14 in a.   Bold, highly original Etude in 3/4, allegro.   A short spurt of chromatic scale tears it open, ties
together its varied sections, and slams it shut at the end.
Dif

No 15 in c.   SR's obsession with death is apparent
throughout his oeuvre, and this etude is a grand funeral
hymn.   The opening lugubre is a death march; and the second theme, lamentoso, rises to a cry when doubled in octaves.   A beautiful chordal passage recalls the three-part
choruses for boys' voices in SR's Russian Mass setting.
Yet a fourth passage in e♭ builds to monumental proportions, with the dead march, the lament and the chant all
blending at the end.   Sublime.   Dif

No 16 in d.   Similar to No 10 (8th notes in 9/8
throughout) this lacks a distinctive melody, but has the familiar opulent harmony.   Mod

No 17 in D.   As in the preludes, the ultimate one attempts a summation, with material gathered from all the
others for a new paean of joy.   And, like the last prelude,
it does not really succeed in its impossible goal.   Dif

Two Sonatas.   The sonatas may also be heard during
the centennial year, giving a chance to know and evaluate
them.   If they had been written 100 years ago, instead of
70, the archeologists would already be programming them,
for none of the forgotten 19th-century sonata makers equalled
them.   (Who, after Beethoven, did write great sonatas?)
Culshaw dismisses these with a short paragraph, finding the
first superior to the second, but both inferior and formidably
difficult.

Sonata No 1 in d, Op 28.   Neither sonata has any of
the broad singing themes of the concertos.   The first, which
takes about 35 min for its three movts, seems obsessed with
the tonic triad, and built on a series of cadences all resolv-
ing to it, often over a pedal-point or ostinato also occupied
with I or V chords.   The second movt has ravishing harmony, but
is too drawn out and the exuberant D major finale, when it fin-

ally arrives, is anti-climactic. V Dif

Sonata No 2 in b♭, Op 36. Sonata No 2 is in two
sections, and takes 20 min. Though it too lacks grand
themes, its lines are clearer, its contrasts sharper. It is
not complex; merely very busy. "Too many notes," SR ad-
mitted; but it is a gorgeous sound when reified by a Horowitz, able to give it a sculptured, high-relief quality. Most
pianists will be too absorbed in catching all the notes to
give it the range of dynamic and tempo nuance that might
bring it to life. V Dif

Song Transcriptions. SR followed in Tchaikovsky's
steps with numerous fine Art Songs. The familiar wordless
vocalise has been transcribed for almost every known instrument or combination, including two pianos, and an orchestra version (by SR).

The Lilacs; Daisies. His own transcriptions of two
songs are fine and simple enough for players who cannot
cope with the technical demands of the bigger works. (B&H
and CF pub respectively.) Mod E

RAFF, JOSEPH JOACHIM (Swi-Ger), 1822-1882.

Long remembered only for his "celebrated Cavatina,"
this assistant to Liszt has recently been exhumed, and a
suite and concerto recorded.

Suite in d, Op 91. Along with the nostalgic Cavatina, so characteristic of the late cabbage-rose Romantic
period, this has a bold and original fantasy and fugue, a
fine set of virtuoso variations, and a very plodding march.
Mod Dif

RAMEAU, JEAN PHILIPPE (Fr), 1683-1764.

This French contemporary of Bach, Handel, and D.
Scarlatti wrote over 50 pieces for keyboard solo, all dating
from before his fame as an opera composer and theorist.
Though written before the invention of the fortepiano, they
adapt well, being resonant and spacious, often built on long
sweeping arpeggio figures. The most authentic edition is

that of Durand edited by Saint-Saëns. Since the music was
written for the large concert clavecin with two manuals and
couplers, and since the custom of the day was to embellish
and register freely and colorfully, the experienced pianist
should not hesitate to add octaves and ornaments on repeats.
The definitive biographer, C. Girdlestone, deplores this
practice, and particularly excoriates an edition by Hans
Huber (CFP pub) now out of print. Actually (except for the
two spurious pieces) it is not bad, and does for the piano
very much what the contemporary of Rameau would have
done with the music on his clavecin.

First Book of Pieces for Clavecin: Prelude. Ten
pieces in A or a minor make up this collection, some of
which are quite fine. The opening Prelude is in bar-less
notation, like some of Bach's toccatas. A JPR feature is
the connection of important melody notes in treble or bass,
with rapid down-rushing scales. A gigue in 12/8 (presto)
rounds off the movement. Mod. Also in Bk I:

Sarabande I, II, Gavotte, Venitiènne. The clavecin
pieces fall into pairs. Best are the two sarabande and the
Gavotte, which can be played with the Venitiènne as trio,
contrasting major and minor and the square dance-step with
the lilting barcarolle (the first use of this dance in classical music?) Mod

Second Book of Pieces. The second volume is made
up of two sets of 12 pieces; the first, in E major and minor,
the second in D. Also in Bk II:

Gigue & Rondeau, I, II. The minor one is plaintive,
and the major sprightly, and both must be played quite fast,
JPR tells us. Mod. Also:

Le Rappel des Oiseaux. Of the many suggestive
titles this is the best: 'The Bird's Assembly," or "Fall-in,
Birds." The aural image can evoke both a bird and a bugle,
with its ornamented fanfares (some on augmented 4ths and
dim 7ths) in strict military rhythm. The pianist may imitate the clavecinist by repeating the sections sotto voce, una
corda. Mod Dif. Also:

Rigaudon I, II and Double in E. Here one uncovers
the inspiration for Ravel's delightful Rigaudon (though he
dedicates it to Couperin). These must be very lively,
snappy, and très sec. Mod Dif. Also:

Musette & Rondeau in E. This short work in 3/4,
E major, has its own variations and DC, and is one of the
most delightful of the set, with or without Hans Huber's accretions. It pairs well with either the foregoing, or the
following. Mod. Also:

Le Lardon. This brief minuet in which RH plays
triads on the beat while the LH inserts a broken-chord triad on the after-beats is meant, according to Girdlestone,
to suggest "inter-larding" of a beef-roast with strips of bacon
(Richard Strauss might have studied this bit of musical real-
ism). It is the theme of P. Dukas' monumental Variations.
Mod E. Also:

Tambourin in e. The most famous single piece, this
is found in many anthologies. Its dissonant bagpipe bass
chords have an affinity with Scarlatti's moorish sonatas, and
the accented ornaments suggest clacking castanets. Mod Dif

For the insatiable explorer, the second half of Book
II (in D-d) has several choice items: Les Niais de Sologne,
with two sets of brilliant variations; Tourbillons; Les Cy-
clopes.

Third Book of Pieces: Gavotte with Six Doubles in a.
This takes neat handling of ornaments, imaginative coloring
of its rather angular lines, and a crisp clean touch to make
it brilliant. Often anthologized. Mod. Also in Bk III:

Sarabande in A. A short work, but grave, stately
and grand. Also:

Menuet, I, II in g. Another attractive contrasting
pair, dainty and introverted. Also:

La Poule. "The Hen" is far more than a humorous
encore number, anticipating in its development of a single
simple figure many of Beethoven's technics. Light, dry,
brittle; but pull out the steps for the climax, with octave
doublings. Mod Dif

RATHAUS, KAROL (Pol-USA), 1895-1954.

Four Sonatas. Composer-educator whose larger
works have received performances. His sonatas are post-

romantic in style, often contrapuntal in texture, pianistic
and well structured, but rather undistinguished. Mod Dif

        Five Pieces, Op 9.   Varied studies in metrical
motifs, flowing and linear. Mod E

        Ballade, Op 40.   A folk-tune over a bagpipe bass, in
an extended and diversified series of variations. Mod

        Three Polish Dances, Op 47.   Like Szymanowski,
KR is at his best with native dance forms.   These three extended works are a vivacious Oberek, with reposeful mid-
section; lyric Kujawiak full of "zal"; a complex mazurka
linking several themes.   Require drive and advanced technic. Dif

RAUTIO, MATTI (Fin), 1922- .

        Suita per Piano (1951).   Lighthearted conventional
suite, mildly dissonant, pianistic.   A Czerny-style prelude
(à la Debussy); quaint dance intermezzo; rhythmic ostinato
in quirky rhythms spread over the keyboard; misterioso interlude; percussive but melodic close. Mod

RAVEL, MAURICE (Fr), 1875-1937.

        Though his total oeuvre for piano is small, the qual-
ity of MR's music is uniformly high.   Occasionally he reflects the same influences as Debussy--Impressionism, Satie,
the clavecin--but he is more the keyboard virtuoso, displaying a joi de jouer that stems more from Liszt than from
Chopin.   Unlike Debussy, his structure is often formal, even
classical, and he has a strong beat, sometimes Basque in
origin.   His admiration for Gershwin and his brief tour of
New York jazz spots are reflected in works like the fine
Concerto in G and the orchestra Bolero.   None of his piano
music is easy, and many works require concert pianism.

        Pavane pour un Infanta defunta (1899).   Familiar
through its many transcriptions (MR orchestrated many of
his own piano works) this grave, stately evocation of an imaginary Iberian ritual, though one of the simpler of the
pieces, is difficult to project on the piano.   The opening

combines cantabile and plectrum in such a way as to rule
out use of the damper pedal and make sostenuto difficult.
Other sections require much use of both pedals, for dynamics ranging from pppp to ffff. Based largely on a harmony
of parallel 7th and 9th chords, the melody throughout is inspired, and must sing. Mod

Minuetto Antique. Earlier than the Pavane, this is
similar, but melodically insipid, chordally awkward, and
over-extended. Mod

Jeux d'Eau. The brilliant premiere of this tour de
force almost caused a riot in Paris, because the 26-year
old composer had just been refused the Prix de Rome. In
no way an imitation of Debussy's water music (which it preceded) it is a perfectly rounded sonata allegro. Its opening
uses fluid arpeggio figures in 4ths, a broad soaring arc of
melody for a second theme, leaping 5ths, clashing non-chord
tones and a very playful and watery cadenza. The title does
not mean "The Fountain," but "Playing Water," and the epigraph says: The River God laughs at the water, which
tickles. A good work for the aspiring virtuoso, as musical
problems are few, but technical problems abound. Dif

Sonatine (1905). Though he used this title only once,
MR was an elegant master of this classic form. The four-
page opening movt (modéré) is a perfect allegro, with repeated exposition. The principal theme, which bears a re-
semblance to Debussy's earlier Reverie, introduces MR's
unique device of an octave melody, played with the hands
overlaid, the melody with the outside fingers, while the inner fingers work away at rhythmic and harmonic figures. It
is subdued and melancholy. The mouvement de minuet which
follows provides a contrasting mood, teasing and playful, yet
nostalgic. It ends with a coda that widens over the keyboard
from a pp echo to a grand Db climax. These two moderately easy movts are rounded off with a dazzling virtuoso
anime, which is at the same time a perfect allegro, using
thematic intervals from both the other movements. Wide
nuance and subtle rubato are all meticulously indicated. One
of the finest examples of the small sonata ever written, for
those who can compass it. (Good new ed by GSch.) Mod
to Dif

Miroirs (1905). Appearing the same year as Debussy's
set with the similar title, Images, these five following pieces
reflect the Symbolist poets and the Impressionist painters'
efforts to capture moods of nature.

Noctuelles. "Moths" flit in delicate flickering figures, with a meandering melody in irregular measures. A chordal passage in the lower register, sonore ed espressivo, adumbrates the nocturnal mood; then a Ravelian cadenza in broken 4th and 7th chords, and the moths flutter away in a chordal trill. Dif

Oiseau Triste. The finest of the set, MR here eschews virtuosity for haunting mood-evocation. The "sad birds" are heard in two simple motifs of a falling 3rd, and a single note repeated, above an ambivalent and mournful harmony of swaying triplet figures. A fluttering passage rises to f, suggesting birds in a cage (though MR suggests a torpid jungle), and yet another cadenza, bitonal and leggierissimo leads to an ending "somber and distant." Technically easy, but musically subtle. Mod Dif

Une Barque sur l'Ocean. Brilliant keyboard writing, Ravel revelling in fast finger-play, this is less imaginative and evocative than the others of the set, the harmony less daring, and the form aimless and over-extended. Dif

Alborado del Grazioso. Here the keyboard virtuosity is joined by the French wit and Spanish fire of this mestiso Parisian. Each must make his own story for the "Jester's Dawn Song"; but, once he has mastered its formidable rhythmic and technical difficulties, must give it a mood at once sardonic and joyous. Alone at dawn, on a Spanish tower, the minstrel tries out tunes, steps and quips for his trade; but pauses to soliloquize on his fate. The slow recitativo, with its light clicking castanets on the fermata, has the exaggerated melancholy and rubato of moorish flamenco; but the jeu d'esprit of the jester will not be smothered, and breaks out in the exhibitionism of glissandi in 3rds and 4ths, and a dazzling coda. Full mastery of the keyboard is needed here. Dif

La Vallée des Cloches. Another slow mood-picture, MR using all his devices of syncopated bell-tones, chiming fourths, with a broad octave melody passing from left to right hand with harmonies that, though now a bit jaded, once were daringly original. Mod

Gaspard de la Nuit (1908): (1) Ondine. These three poems for piano carry virtuoso pianism to still greater heights, yet remain truly poetic. In Ondine, the pianissimo chord trills, keyboard-spanning arpeggios, cascades of 3rds and 4ths, melodies in double rolled octaves, must be so fluid as always to evoke this water mileu of the doomed water-sprite, Ondine.   V Dif

(2) Le Gibet.   Played throughout with una corda and without rubato, misterioso.   The chiming off-beat octaves of Miroirs here are enriched with long pedal points, melodies in 9ths.   After the 1st page, 3 staves are required to score the wide-meshed, tiered strands of sound. Problems are musical, not technical.   Mod

(3) Scarbo.   Dedicated to the late Rudolf Ganz, this third piece of the Gaspard de la Nuit is another virtuoso movt: 3/8 shifting to 3/4 and back for an accelerando close; repeated notes, racing scales, and arpeggios in 32nd notes abound.   Dynamics range from a whisper to a shout, as the scherzo evokes a Jacques Callot-like harlequin.   Vir

Le Tombeau de Couperin (1917).   This tribute to the first great French composer has little to do with Couperin, and is far removed from the dainty clavecin; but the suite form gave MR a chance to group six large pieces in some of his favorite classic forms.   With the exception of the second, all are MR at his best.   26 min.

(1) Prelude.   This shimmering introduction, swift and delicate, rises in two great surges of sound.   The broken-chord-prelude style uses close-position under-the-hand figures with sharp mordents providing accents for the bell-like melody notes.   Dif

(2) Fugue.   Few modern composers have succeeded in this difficult form.   MR's simple five-note fugue theme in e minor is too undistinguished to make the 3-v writing absorbing, though as quiet contrast between the first and third numbers, it serves well.   Mod

(2) Forlana.   This early Italian equivalent of the giga makes lively use of the compound rhythm (6/8), dotted groups alternating with steady 8ths and longer chords.   A trio section introduces an iambic beat.   But it is the elusive wistful harmony of unresolved 7ths and 9ths, and the lacey ornamentation that give this dance its great charm.   Mod

(4) Rigaudon.   In this fourth piece of the Tombeau de Couperin suite, MR makes an ancient Provençal dance in duple meter a flashy brilliant pair for the dainty forlana.

Each section opens and closes with flourish and a snap; and though bristling with 9th chords, the harmony always re-solves to cheery C major or minor. Mod Dif

(5) Menuet. A favorite dance of MR, this is the simplest of the Tombeau (nothing faster than 8th notes, al-legro moderato). Its spell comes from the modal harmony, surprise cadences, hypnotic Musette, and high tinkling ro-coco melody. Mod

(6) Toccata. One of MR's most brilliant virtuoso pieces, often played separately from the other five in the suite. Into the rapid-fire staccato, martellato chord writing two lilting tunes are woven. The small opening chords grow into fistfuls as the movement broadens, peu à peu, and the coruscating harmonies resolve to a brilliant E major ending.

Valses Nobles et Sentimentales (1911). A charming "rehearsal" for the large orchestral La Valse, this chain of eight dances is airy, fey, dashing, pensive by turn, the set linked by recurring themes. Distinction is lent to their lighthearted grace by MR's unique harmony. Mod

Minuet sur le Nom de Haydn. Lightweight anniver-sary piece. Debussy's is better. Mod E

RAWSTHORNE, ALAN (GB), 1905-1971.

This composer of two piano concertos and numerous chamber works left three piano works in traditional forms and conventional keyboard idiom, basically tonal but verging on non-tonality.

Bagatelles (1938). Suite form is popular among con-temporary British composers. This is lighthearted, as the title implies, containing an allegro in Scherzo style, alle-gretto, a barcarolle; presto non assai; lento. Mod

Sonatina. Larger four-movt work. Sober, quiet alle-gro misterioso; lento; allegretto con malinconia; allegro con brio. When the melancholy has become almost too weighty, the last movement bursts into a brilliant, brash finale. Ma-ture; not excessively difficult. Mod

Ballade (1968). Big 12-min virtuoso work in one

movt. Modelled after Chopin, it is original, with quartal polytonality, dramatic and lyric sections alternating. Dif

REGER, MAX (Ger), 1873-1916.

Prolific composer who will probably be remembered for his organ works. His quantities of piano pieces, ranging from one-page character sketches to 50-page fugues are in a style that might be called Ende vom Lied, the dead-end of a tradition carried on too long. Rachmaninoff did the same thing, but the warm personal emotion that keeps his music alive is lacking in these scholarly lucubrations.

Improvisations (1895). Eight short expressive sketches in the manner of Brahms, whose eloquent swansong, Op 111, dates from the same time. Mod

Fünf Humoresken, Op 20; Sieben Fantasiestücke, Op 26; Sechs Burlesken, Op 58. When MR forgets the classroom, and moves out-of-doors, he is better. The second is a gypsy dance, and others are lively. The humor also comes through in some of the Fantasias: Scherzo, Humoresque, Caprice. Mod

Sei Intermezzi, Op 45; Silhouettes, Op 53. Here a heavy-handed virtuoso style alternates with an equally heavy funereal mood. Dif

Four Special Studies for LH Alone. Musical and technical problems abound but are rewarding to solve. Recorded by Paul Wittgenstein, the one-armed Apollo to whom we owe so many fine LH works. Dif

Variations and Fugue on a Theme of Bach, Op 81. Gargantuan work embedding in its massive slab many fine nuggets. Vir

Variations and Fugue on a Theme of Telemann, Op 143. We may, perhaps, give thanks that the Sonata form did not attract MR. His variation style relates to free-fantasy, and this set is more diatonic and classical than the Bach. But those impenetrable, interminable fugues! Vir

REICHA [REJCHA], ANTON (Boh-Fr), 1770-1836.

Piano Works. This contemporary of Beethoven, friend
of Haydn and Salieri, teacher of Liszt is currently represented on records only by chamber music. For the benefit
of pianists and record companies bored with those old-fashioned pieces by Beethoven, Mozart, et al., let it be mentioned that AR wrote numerous works for piano, a volume
of which has just been brought out by G. Henle Editions.
For comments, read Dussek, Clementi, Hummel, etc.
(GHEd pub) Mod

REINAGLE, ALEXANDER (GB-USA), 1756-1809.

America's first classical composer was of Scots-Ger-
man ancestry, and migrated from London, where he knew
J. C. Bach. Active in Philadelphia during its years as U.S.
capital, he imported the first pianos.

Sonata in E: Allegro, Adagio, Rondo. A graceful
three-movt rococo work in the manner of the Bach sons.
Well-structured, pianistic allegro with three attractive contrasting themes linked with purling scales and effectively developed. Adagio is properly pathetic, and explores the piano's potential for sonorities in arpeggios, recitativo, cantilena. Closes with a superb rondo, with vivid themes well
articulated. Mod

Sonata in D. Allegro is similar to above, but over-
extended. The minuet and gavotte must have titillated
Martha Washington and the senator's wives. Mod

RESPIGHI, OTTORINO (It), 1879-1936.

One of Italy's few modern symphonic composers, OR
is extensively recorded, his Suites of Pines, Fountains, and
Birds of Rome holding their own with French Impressionists.
For piano he wrote little and not fluently.

Ancient Airs and Dances (III sets). Interesting use of
ancient forms dating from the Renaissance, but much more
effective in the orchestrated version. Mod

Three Preludes on Gregorian Melodies. Through the
centuries plain-song has provided composers with a thesaur-
us of melodies. What OR does with them however is too
elaborate and florid to be useful. Dif

Nottorno. His best piece, a mesmeric melody above
gently tapping chordal background. Mod

Study in A♭. The same interlocking-chord device,
more brilliantly exploited. Mod

REZSO KOKAI (Hun)

Quattro Improvvisazzioni Hungarian rhapsodic expression seems to be the composer's intention in these four
improvisations, though the complexity of the texture miti-
gates against much spontaneity. Tonal and rather conventional, they are wide-ranging, with a fast staccato scherzo,
a melodic chordal slow movt and a powerful percussive
fourth movt. Dif

RHEINBERGER, JOSEF (Ger), 1839-1901.

Seldom has a mere piano teacher risen from such
humble beginnings to such heights: titles, honorary degrees, academy membership. JR looked on his composing
as a secondary interest, but wrote over 200 pieces, of which
a cantata, a piano concerto and a sonata have been recorded.
His organ music is still available and played occasionally.

Sonata in f♯, Op 184, "Romantic." For a contemporary of Brahms, Tchaikovsky, Dvorák and the young Debussy, JR was decidedly conservative. This large four-
movt work (his last) is bold and pianistic in its use of romantic clichés. The fine second theme of the allegro justi-
fies the title better than the Romanza, which might have been
written by Weber, 100 years earlier. The brilliant finale
keeps the pianist very busy, but offers few surprises or
pleasures for the ear. Mod Dif

RIBARI, ANTAL (Hun), 1926- .

All'Antica Suite (1969).   This composer of symphonic and chamber works has one suite for piano.   Traditional
to the point of conventionality, this four-movt suite is pianistic and well-sounding.   Two fast percussive movts with
varied meters alternate with somber harmonic sections.
Mod

RIEGGER, WALLINGFORD (USA), 1885-1961.

One of the first serious composers in the U.S. to
become interested in jazz and film-music.

Finale from "The New Dance."   The "Finale" represents an early pre-dissonant style, featuring jazz and modern rhythms with a flashy ending.   (B&H pub) Dif

Toccata (1957).   This is the last number in a didactic
work, called "New and Old," which introduces the student to
serial technics, dissonant counterpoint, polytonality, etc.
with helpful notes.   The 12th study is called "Fourths and
Fifths" in the book (black keys against white); and the Toccata has an added climactic ending.   (B&H pub) Mod to E

RIETI, VITTORIO (It-USA), 1898- .

Sonata in A♭ (1967).   Better known for his orchestral
work, VR often uses Spanish, Latin and jazz rhythms.   This
three-movt work is non-tonal but pianistic.   Rhythmic novelty
enhances the leisurely first movt, and the lyric second.   The
fast finale is a rumba.   Mod

RIVIER, JEAN (Fr), 1896- .

Sonata (1971).   The successful composer of seven
symphonies and numerous concertos and overtures wrote one
piano sonata.   More a suite than a sonata, the five-movt
work is a blend of Impressionism, and lucid French linear
writing in a free-ranging tonality.   The movts are titled:
Fluid, Incisive, Concentrated, Supple, and Violent.   Euphoni-

ous, colorful and bravura.   Mod

ROCHBERG, GEORGE (USA), 1918- .

It is pleasant to find a modern composer with a sense
of humor.   The Symphony No 3, premiered in 1970 (Nos 1
and 2 are already recorded), uses recognizable quotes from
Bach, Mahler, Ives and others much as "found objects" are
used in Pop Art and contemporary sculpture.

12 Bagatelles (1952) (TP).   An 11-min serial work of
great interest to the analyst and pianist, with wide variety
of rhythmic melodic and harmonic motifs, repeated often
enough to be recognizable.   The pages have the look of a
fine, free-hand design.   Directions for the page-long pieces
are worthy of Scriabin, ranging from drammaticamento e
con un tempo libero, through satirico, giocoso, intenso, and
con un sentimento di destino, to passionatamente.   Unfortunately, the one ultimate and indispensable criterion of music, that it sound well, is not fulfilled.   Like abstract art,
which has now said its say and bowed out, serial composition, capable of communicating to a point, as GR and others
have shown elsewhere, may also have wound down.   (TP
pub)   Mod

Sonata-Fantasia (1958).   Large virtuoso work in serial technic, freely treated, pianistic, well-deployed.   (TP
pub)

Nach Bach, Fantasy for Harpsichord or Piano (1967).
This work, dedicated to I. Kipnis, is intended for harpsichord but, since it also sounds well on piano, is included
here.   It is a long way "after Bach," but the old man would
have enjoyed the free improvisatory style.   It begins with a
12-tone row, and uses frequent 12-note or 6-note groups
(unrelated to the original 12) in a Bachian arpeggiated style,
with many fermati and trills.   A page in the middle (fast
fff, marcatissimo) is clearly 4/4 e minor though the composer tries to keep it a secret.   A passage that would have
amused old JSB has a broken-chord figure in the bass,
gradually rising chromatically, under a similar chromatic
sequence in the RH, marked "bravura, begin at a moderate
speed and gradually increase to prestissimo, wild!" (with
a footnote that this is "approximate, and the player may
form his own pattern").   This leads to a very Bachian pas-

sage, "sweeping gestures, gloriously broad, but don't drag,"
which sounds like the opening of the E minor Partita. The
old B-A-C-H theme finds its way in too, and it's all good
fun; but also good music. (TP pub) Dif

Prelude on Happy Birthday (for almost two pianos)
(1969). Premiered at Oberlin 20th Festival of Contemporary
Music, April 1970.

ROREM, NED (USA), 1923- .

Ned Rorem has had remarkable success as a composer of art songs. He has written in larger forms; and is
himself a fine accompanist with a fluent technic. Judging
from the works for solo piano which he has written thus far,
he is a little like Stravinsky, whose imagination completely
deserted him when faced with a keyboard; only with Rorem,
it is the absence of a poem which leaves him unable to con-
ceive an original melody, or rhythmic motif.

Toccata (1949). The Toccata is in b minor, with two
key changes, 8/8 with the 8ths hammered out in a 3-2-3
patter throughout its seven pages. It is marked clear, fast,
and hard, detached and cold, which it certainly is. At MM
152 = quarter note, I finished in 3:35, though on the title
page, it says "Duration: 19 min." A sales gimmick? The
nicest thing about it is the Larry Rivers drawing (with one-
and-a-half eyes) inside the cover. (CFP pub 1960) Mod

Three Barcarolles (1949). More French "Chansons
sans paroles" (helas!). Three undistinguished movements
in 6/8 time. For comments, see above anent song-writers
without words. (CFP pub) Mod

Spiders, for Harpsichord (NYC, July 1968 heat wave).
A beautiful piece to look at, especially the cover, which is
all black, with white letters. Why the publishers (B&H)
should have felt obligated to print this bit of heat therapy is
a mystery. Dif

Seconde Sonate pour Piano (1950). Large four-movt
work in neo-classic style, pianistic with some original figuration, light, lucid and French. The allegretto (f minor?)
is so ambiguous harmonically and the contrasting themes are
so undistinguished that the form is nullified. The scherzando

is quite delightful, and should be published as a separate
piece, to rescue it from oblivion. The moderato is pure
Poulenc, out of Ravel, and might have sounded fresh in the
20's, with its sentimental music-hall tune, and harmonization in parallel 7ths. The fourth movt is allegro molto, but
even the presto impossibile tempo at which it is played by
Katchen fails to conceal its melodic, harmonic and rhythmic
poverty. Two more sonatas, Nos 1 and 3, but both dated
1971, have appeared. The first is 20 pages for $3.50; the
second, 26 pages, for $5. No doubt there will soon be an-
other salacious diary explaining the numbering and delay in
publication; and, let us hope, another record album, with
NR's nice nose on the cover, and his fleet-fingered accom-
paniments to a new song cycle. (B&H pub)

ROSSINI, GIACCHINO (It-Fr), 1792-1868.

   Five Original Piano Pieces: Etude, Siberian Dance,
Capriccio, Gifts, Souvenir to My Wife. "Sins of my Old
Age," the famous opera composer called his instrumental
works, songs and piano pieces. Since he was only 37 when
he "officially retired," he was not all that old. The piano
pieces have a fresh, quaint, good humored quality that
makes them a pleasure to hear and play. There is an entire volume of piano pieces in the "Quaderni Rossiniani"
published by the Rossini Foundation. More available are
the five recently edited by Soulima Stravinsky and published
by CFP. Mod

ROUSSEL, ALBERT (Fr), 1869-1937.

      Late-starting but prolific composer remembered for
his exotic ballets. His early career in the navy took him
to Vietnam, India, Africa. His symphonic and chamber music are more idiomatic than his piano works.

      Suite, Op 14 (1910). Lengthy and difficult, relating
more to Saint-Saëns than to Debussy. The thick, almost
turgid, texture is relieved by dynamic contrasts, long crescendos, and rhythmic contrasts. The four movts are: prélude, siciliènne, bourrée (the best), and ronde. Dif

      Sonatine, Op 16. A Lisztian one-movt work, cyclic,

with a scherzo passage replacing the development, and a slow passage leading to a rondo, with illation to the opening modéré.   Dif

Petit Canon Perpetuel.   This novelty might find a place in some of the music marathons of the day.   The player is to repeat the short, lyric (but tricky) canon, an octave higher each time, until he reaches the limit of the keyboard.   Mod

ROZSA, MIKLOS (Hun-USA), 1907- .

Sonata, Op 20 (1951).   Serious composer who made a name first in films; recently premiered violin and piano concertos.   His Sonata is a large-scale thick-textured poly-tonal work.   Difficult and dissonant.   (B&H pub) Dif

The Vintner's Daughter (12 Variations on a French Folksong).   Well written, pianistic, and euphonious with splashes of dissonance.   Brilliance and introspection alter-nate.   Mod

RUBINSTEIN, ANTON (Rus), 1828-1894.

For today's youth, the name Rubinstein can mean on-ly one person, the great Polish-American pianist, possibly the greatest (ask Artur), now approaching 90, and playing the grand concertos and classics better than ever.   For their grandparents, however, it would be one of two almost equally talented Russian brothers, though Anton, who barn-stormed Europe and the U.S.A., was much more famous than Nicolas who stayed in the Moscow Conservatory.   Anton's playing was so dazzling that his compositions were hailed as masterpieces when he executed them, but forgotten as soon as he died.   He is now being revived, and three con-certos, and the Ocean Symphony are available on records, as well as numerous piano pieces.   His four sonatas have yet to be disinterred.   Most of his music is arrant trash; some has good musical content, slapped together in slip-shod fashion.

Barcarolles, Nos 1 to 6.   AR was fond of this form, and these are mong his more original pieces.   Mod Dif

Six Etudes, Op 23. No 1, the "Staccato Etude," was for many decades a war-horse for every virtuoso. Others might be revived. Very taxing. Dif

Album of Portraits. The "celebrated" Kammenoi Ostrow, once found in all albums of "best loved" piano favorites, is one of the portraits. Mod

Melody in F, Op 3. The saxophone, harmonica, Hammond Organ, the vibes have so exhausted this item that the original piano version sounds anemic. E

Six Preludes, Op 24. The first, in f minor, is much fresher than the famous Melody in F. AR later wrote fugues for these, but don't bother to look them up. Mod

Etude on Wrong Notes. This is amusing for its commentary on what was "wrong" a hundred years ago, and is also a brilliant study, demanding a huge hand. Dif

Miscellaneous Pieces, Op 93. For the record, there is a rattling ballade called "Leonore" and variations on "Yankee Doodle." Those who can never get enough of that tune might program these with Gottschalk's "L'Union." Mod

Theme and Variations in G, Op 88. Rated by Lockwood and Josef Lhevinne among the great variations, "worthy of a place beside Bach, Beethoven, Mendelssohn, Brahms." 40 min. Dif

RUBINSTEIN, BERYL (USA), 1898-1952.

Two Etudes. BR was a music educator, pianist, composer. The etudes are well written, pianistic, and modern. Both are fast, the first titled "Will o' the Wisp," the second, "Whirligig." (OxU pub) Mod Dif

Sonatina in c♯ (1929). Neo-classic yet original three-movt work, of moderate length and difficulty. (OxU pub) Mod

Three Dances (1930); Gavotte, Sarabande, Gigue. Large-scale neo-classic suite: graceful Gavotte in double notes. Pompous majestic chordal middle movement with contrasting linear trio; brilliant propulsive close, well written for piano. Mod Dif

12 Definitions. Sketches in etude and prelude style, contrasting dance rhythms, moods, keyboard figures. Varied and attractive. Mod to Dif

RUDHYAR, DANE (Fr-USA), 1895- .

This Hollywood-based painter, poet, Hindu philosopher and astrologer, whose original name was Daniel de Chenneviére, composed in a cosmic Scriabinesque style, adding a keyboard exuberance of his own. Three piano pieces are remarkably advanced for their time and bear comparison with many contemporary works.

Paeans (1927). The bold piano sonorities featured in this three-part work (Hymns of Triumph) are polytonal, but basically triadic with harmonic resolutions. The first is rhythmic, with scattered small-chord-clusters, a serial-sounding melody, bass tremolos, massive hammered chords, a tight four-note motif (B-A-C-H, or D-A-N-E?) The second part anticipates Messiaen in its sonorities, its square melodic phrases punctuated by harped chords. DR is fond of booming basses, and features them in the third part, after a quiet opening over an E♭ pedal-point. 7 min. Dif

Stars (1925). The astrologer begins di lontano, with delicate treble nebulae, an accompanied UFO melody, also in alt, a chordal passage and a return, all within 3 min. Evocative and communicative. Mod

Granites (1929). DR has not only enriched the repertoire with some unique titles, he has also produced here five richly-resonant and pianistic if somewhat ingenious works. Few pianists may wish to work up the volcano necessary to shape them. The five sketches contrast well the ponderous bass gongs, flying chordal appogiatura figures, and static tonal fragments. Dif

RUGGLES, CARL (USA), 1876-1971.

Evocations (1937); Four Chants for Piano. American

maverick composer receiving belated recognition for early
experimental works. His only work for piano solo waited
over 30 years to be heard (1971). The four pieces are as
short as Schönberg's early piano pieces, and as significant
in their setting. The title is apt, as the spare 4ths and
5ths, the bold dynamic swells to crashing climaxes, and the
lingering dissonant "after-notes" do seem to evoke the austere Vermont home of the composer, and the struggle that
life entails. An appreciative analysis of the pieces is found
in Mellers. Dif

RUST, FREDRICH WILHELM (Ger), 1739-1796.

Most famous member of a family of musicians, this
contemporary of Haydn wrote 48 sonatas during a busy career as music director at Dessau. A son, Karl Wilhelm,
taught piano in Vienna and was praised by Beethoven for his
Bach playing. A grandson, Wilhelm, contemporary of
Franck and Brahms, composed, "plugged" Bach, and taught
composition and counterpoint. He also brought out an edition of the by then forgotten sonatas of Grandpa Willi, which
he "improved" considerably. A copy of this came into the
hands of d'Indy in Paris, a generation later, who unsuspect-
ingly published them "for their advanced ideas anticipating
and influencing Beethoven and other 19th-century composers." Now they are again being plugged by a record
company, with no mention of the extensive rewrite job of
WR the III, or the additions and alterations which musicologists have discovered in them (see Grove and Shedlock). A
good project for some doctoral candidate would be to clarify this problem from extant manuscripts in Dessau and Berlin, and give us a new and authentic edition, by FWR I.

Sonata in Db (1777). The most remarkable thing
about this is its choice of key, one never used by Haydn,
Mozart or Beethoven, though popular with 19th-century romantics. The three-movt work is otherwise rather commonplace. FWR's version of the Alberti-bass used a broken octave with 4th or 5th between, instead of the Italian's 1-5-3-
5, 1-6-4-6. Mod E

Sonata in G. Another three-movt work with brilliant
fast outer movts and a songful middle. These are so advanced for their day, with chromatic sequences, rare modulations (the second Allegro theme is in d) that the tampering

of grandson Willi seems apparent. What are heralded as
prophetic anticipations of Beethoven thus turn out to be
echos. Fine forgery, though. Mod Dif

   Sonata in C. This two-movt work would also appear
to be by the two Wilhelm Rusts, a century apart, with dull
repetitious passage work giving way to a sprightly rondo,
into which is introduced, after a soulful recitative, a great
c minor fugue almost worthy of C. Franck or J. Brahms.
(Perhaps someone should look into those eight piano works
said to have been written by WR the III himself?) Mod Dif

   Sonata in f. Another bold, imaginative three-movt
work, in cyclic form, all movts derived from the same
germ-motif. Hmmm! Mod Dif

   Sonata in d (1788). This boasts a coda that is a
beautiful pastiche of Mozart's d Fantasy and Beethoven's
"Moonlight."

   Sonata in D (1794). Even more suspect is this old-
fashioned work, with its quaint minuet. For a second movt
it has a big Romantic "Wehklage" (Lamentation) in b, said
to have been "sketched" by FWR on hearing of the drowning
of his talented eldest son. It is as lush and morose as a
Brahms Lied (and very similar). Mod

RUTINI, GIOVANNI MARCO (It), 1723-1797.

   12 Sonatas, Op 1, 2. Worthy of revival are the
works of this Italian composer for the early forerunner of
the fortepiano. They are mostly in three-movts, the second
a brief intermezzo or minuet between lively opening and
closing. Homophonic, with fresh, graceful themes. Finger
dexterity required for the fast movts. Try No 2 (with opening largo) and Nos 5 and 6. Mod

SAINT-SAËNS, CAMILLE (Fr), 1835-1921.

   Throughout a long and active life as pianist, critic
and composer, CSS resisted all modern trends. His Second
Piano Concerto remains his finest work, though the suite for
two pianos and orchestra, published after his death (Carnival

of Animals) has good numbers.

Six Etudes, Op 52.   Possessed of a phenomenally
clear, crisp touch, CSS wrote numerous studies to help other pianists.   No 3 is an effective prelude & fugue.   No 6
is a brilliant Concert Valse, worthy of an occasional hearing.   Dif

Six Etudes, Op 135.   This set is for LH alone, and
develops muscle and musical sense at the same time.   The
Neo-classic Bourrée, No 4 is attractive.   Mod

Six Etudes, Op 111.   Virtuosity is the goal here.   An
Algerian motif is the theme of the brilliant closing Toccata.
Dif

Caprice on themes from Gluck's Alceste.   Frenchi-
fied Liszt, this lengthy work contains a fine theme and variations (3/8 time), which is often lifted out for a solo.   Mod
Dif

SAS, ANDRES (Fr-Peru), 1900-1967.

This Franco-Belgian ethno-musicologist spent his mature life in Peru, collecting folk music, on which many ballets, orchestral works, and his piano suites are based.

Aires y Danzas del Peru, I, II (1930, 1945).   Imaginative keyboard setting of a variety of songs and dances, in
diverse meters; basically tonal using dissonance and bitonality for effects.   Mod

Himno y Danza (1935).   Tribute to ancient Inca culture, the opening is ritually majestic; the dance, furioso
over a cam-like bass.   Mod Dif

Suite Peruana (1936); Sonatina Peruana (1946).   Two
more classical forms using ethnic material for rhythmic and
melodic motifs.   Some originality; much that is simply Pan-
American.   Mod

Sonata, Op 46.   Four-movt work in neo-classic style
with brilliant keyboard-spanning staccato allegro; lyric, canonic slow movement; third movt in triple meter is capricious
and lilting; closing rondo has two strongly contrasted epi-

sodes.   Well-crafted, pianistic.   Mod

SATIE, ERIK (Fr), 1866-1925.

"Turn these pages with an amiable thumb and a smile,
for they are works of pure whimsy." This advice of ES provides a good approach to the numerous piano works of this
master, so much discussed, and so little played. The recent revival of interest in him has produced three complete
recordings of his works, and several new publications.
Like Scriabin, who has undergone a similar death and
transfiguration, the extra-musical elements often draw attention away from the music. In Satie's case, the witty, enigmatic titles and commentary, often irrelevant and confusing,
are best left (like the titles of abstract painting), to be explored afterward. The music itself is simple, lucid, cool,
fragmentary and brief, often in sets of three short pieces.
Melodies are original and straightforward, chordal or diatonic, with occasional "quotes" or programmatic imitations.
Harmonies, subtly altered and full of mild surprises, are
imaginatively laid out in original keyboard figures. A "petit
maître," expressing himself in small subtle, refined, understated pieces, eminently worth exploring. Milhaud's prophecy, that Satie might have to wait fifty years to be appreci-
ated, seems accurate.

Ogives (1886). Three austere Preludes ("Gothic
Arches") expressing Satie's early admiration for Gregorian
chant. Mod E

Trois Sarabandes (1887). ES was a true antiquarian,
and this ancient dance form is revived in another triptych,
maintaining the slow triple rhythm with sustained second
beat, but exploring new harmonies. Pleasant to play, but
outshone by its off-shoots in the music of Debussy and Ravel. Mod E

Trois Gymnopédies (1890). Best known work of ES,
these sound well in some of the many transcriptions. Their
hypnotic swaying movement suggests "...the tracing of some
graceful arabesque by naked boys dancing under an early
morning Grecian sky" (Meyers). They should be played in
a set, for all three reflect varied facets of the same theme;
and, like Andy Warhol's underground movies, achieve their
soporific effect by sheer monotonous repetition. Mod E

Trois Gnossiènnes (1890).   A similar triad of nostalgic minor pieces meant to evoke the buried ancient capital of Crete.   The meter here is duple, with a ppp throughout; the first somewhat quicker with a firm beat, and subito
f chords; the second slightly slower, with a winding triplet
melody, suggesting Middle Eastern melisma; the last a new
melody above the same swaying trance-dance rhythm.   Mod
E

Prélude de la Port Héroique de Ciel (1894).   Considered by Friskin and Freundlich "one of the most successful
pieces stemming from his religious, mystical period."   ES
was an ardent Rosicrucian.

Pièces Froides (1897).   The airs and dances of this
early set manage to produce a cool blend of liturgical melisma and gentle ancient dance rhythms.

Veritables Préludes Flasques (1912).   Fifteen
years elapsed before ES produced his finest piano music, ten suites, mostly of three-movts.   Satie becomes the
"satyr of satire," with his abundant quips and weird titles,
which he forbids the player to read aloud during performance!   The "flabby" is no doubt a jibe at the amorphous
quality of much Impressionist music.   These, however, are
bold and martial, or taut and wiry, with lyric melodic lines.
Mod

Descriptions Automatiques (1913).   Probably the first
music written without meter, bars or key signatures, all
three are slow, but discrete, and very lucid, lighthearted,
lilting, with quotes from popular songs.   The LH ends "light
as an egg," with the RH, "heavy as a hog."   Mod

Embryons desséchés.   Delightful three-movt suite,
even without the nonsensical descriptions of three imaginary
crustaceans.   The first is a perpetuo moto, with abrupt in-
terruptions.   This animal purrs frequently, and the pianist
is instructed to play one passage "like a nightingale with a
toothache."   The coda repeats the G major chord 18 times.
The slow chordal middle movement is a spoof of the funeral
march, with the father urging the weeping family to listen
to "the celebrated Mazurka of Schubert," which is Chopin
(in a warped mirror).   A toccata "à la chasse" closes, with
quotes from "Malbrouck s'en va-t-en Guerre," and a "Required
Cadence (by the composer)" which lampoons Beethoven's symphonic endings with a page of tonic-dominant resolutions,

hammered out.   Mod to Dif

     Croquis et Agaceries d'un Gros Bonhomme en Bois
(1913).   The satire of this amusing set is directed at Mozart (the Turkish Rondo), Chabrier and Debussy.

     Chapitres Tournés en Tous Sens (1913).   The com-
mentary on the "Chapters Turned Every Which-Way" reads
like black humor; but again the three contrasting sketches
have a musical integrity independent of the text.   The first
(which might be called Chatterbox) natters away in ceaseless triplets (written mostly on one staff) with attempts to
"get in a word edgeways," and a coda in which "the husband falls dead of exhaustion."   The slow mid-movement is
Sisyphus stumbling about under his stone, the meandering
harmonies dotted with fermati as he hesitates, and ending
with a loud crash.   The "Grumbling of the Aged," carries
out a legato-staccato, chord-vs-melody dialog, with its own
bold ending.   Mod

     Sports et Divertissements: Chorale, The Swing, The
Hunt, Italian Comedy, The Chivaree, Hide and Seek, Fish-
ing, Yachting, Swimming, Carnival, Golf, The Octopus,
Horse Racing, Puss in the Corner, Picnicking, The Water
Chute, Tango, Sleighing, The Flirt, Fireworks, Tennis.
Four more similar suites date from 1914.   One, the largest
and musically finest of all, is a multi-media product pre-
senting 20 one-page sketches, complete with quips, hand en-
graved from ES' own calligraphy, in an out-size limited edition folio, with 20 color prints.   The music was in fact commissioned to illustrate the prints, and a performance combining music, commentary and projected prints makes an interested "happening."   Editions Salabert has now brought out
a facsimile edition in standard format (without the prints).
The music stands well on its own, though the titles help.
After a solemn tongue-in-cheek Chorale, with delightful
chordal cadences the sketches follow the adventures of a
sexy flapper through courtship, marriage, fun and games at
the sea, picnicking, sleighing, golfing, dancing, and end with
a tennis ball, landing in a cup of coffee.   Each piece is
made up of three or four very pianistic yet poetic figures,
usually ending with a surprise cadence.   Except for some
wide-ranging arpeggios and a couple of sweeping scales, the
technical demands are slight.   But the interpretive capacity
of the player is taxed to the limit.   Mod

SAYGUN, A. ADNAN (Tur), 1907- .

10 Etudes on Aksak Rhythms. Bartók's magnificent piano works on central European folk-melodies and rhythms have sparked many fine composers to explore their native heritage with results like this bold set of virtuoso studies. The complex rhythms are explained. The Middle-Eastern "wailing-chromatic" melisma adds another exotic element. For the explorer. Dif

Sonatina, Op 15 (1957). Three-movt work combining ethnic and classic elements, pianistically. Both rhythmic and melodic patterns of the allegro are distinctive; adagio uses repeated bass figures; closing Horon uses native 7/8 rhythm (2-2-3, 2-3-2, 3-2-3) Eastern scale, and dissonant harmony. (SMP pub) Mod

Anadolu'Dan, Op 25 (1957). From a suite called "Anatolia," these dance-inspired sketches are easier than the etudes, but just as piquant. Mesli (9/8, 2-2-2-3); Zeybek (9/4, slow 4+5); Halay (4/4 followed by 10/8). Mod

SCARLATTI, DOMENICO (It-Sp), 1685-1757.

Although the court of Spain, where DS spent 40 years of his life composing, playing, and teaching Queen Maria Barbara, had some of the new-fangled pianos, Scarlatti, like Bach, preferred the harpsichord. For the last 30 years, however, pianists have become increasingly aware of the riches contained in the 550 sonatas he wrote, and familiarity with a number of them is urged for all serious students of the piano. Other musicians sometimes call the music of DS "pianist's piano," not only because, like Chopin, DS wrote almost exclusively for the keyboard; but also because the technical resources of his instrument were exploited for as wide a range of musical expression as possible.

For years DS was known only through a highly edited romantic collection of a handful of his poorest works; or in a monumental collection of all 550 sonatas edited by Allessandro Longo, who arbitrarily arranged the short binary pieces in suites of four key-related works, and gave them L numbers. Recently Ralph Kirkpatrick, in a definitive study of DS, revised the order chronologically, and gave new K numbers to them. Mr. Kirkpatrick published a selection of 60 of his favorites in two vols (GSch). A facsimile re-

production is also available, for libraries and collectors,
in 18 vols (at \$15 a vol, pub JRC).   For the pianist who
wants more than the 60 Kirkpatrick selected, Heugel of Paris has just brought out an 11-vol ed of the complete 550,
in the K chronology.   The Longo-Ricordi is still available
(through BM), with 50 sonatas in each of the 11 vols, and
a thematic index in each.   A good selection of 35 is offered by CF, in two vols, though the thematic index is a
masterpiece of obfuscation.   The 24 selected by J. Friskin
for the two-vol JF ed are among the most popular, but
contain neither K nor L numbers nor dates or sources.

The GSch two-vol ed of 60 (hereafter known as DS-
60K) would be ideal for students if it only had a thematic
index in place of some of the nonsense in the introduction
(for harpsichordists only, and reprinted in both volumes).
A list of the best of these is given herewith, with both K
and L numbers for cross-reference.   Most of them require
a fast tempo, and good finger technic.

Sonatas in DS60K: VI D 4/4 K29, L461.   A good introduction to the 2-v presto style, with repeated notes in
alternate hands, a melodic line over LH chords, often with
dissonant 2nds and 7ths, suggesting Spanish flamenco guitar.

XI c 3/4 K84, L10.   DS's arpeggio style, quite brilliant, even at allegro moderato tempo.

XIII D 3/8 K96, L465.   A popular favorite.   Pianists must remember the terraced dynamics that substituted
for shading on the harpsichord, and use pedal and echo effects for the many repeated passages.   (JF)

XIV G 3/8 K105, L204.   One of the many sonatas
in which velocity is essential.   DS wrote for a fast Queen!

XIX C 3/4 K132, L457.   One of the greatest.   A
moderate tempo; DS60K indicates cantabile.   I suggest
maestoso.   A trill in meas 43-44 RH is effective.   The dissonances are quite startlingly modern.

XXI a 2/4 K175, L429.   This has LH "grapes" (as
one student called chord-clusters) of six notes within the octave.   Avoid editions like CF and GR in which the editor
has arbitrarily deleted many of these notes, which "must
have been effective on the harpsichord, but on the modern
piano produce only unpleasant hardness."   The editor had
obviously not yet encountered Ives or Boulez.

XXIX G 3/4 K259, L103.   One of the slower more
melodious ones.   (JF)

XXXVII G ¢ K394, L275.   An unusual and effective
one, with a Bachian arpeggiated fantasy in the middle, some
canonic imitations, a bagpipe trio.

XLIII g 3/8 K626, L128.   Attractive slow number
with fermata dividing the phrases; simple, expressive.

XLIV G 4/4 K427, L286.   A good companion for the
above, this is presto possibile, and ends each section with
a chordal exclamation point, ff.

XLV C ¢ K460, L324.   Beginning with a Bachian
fugue theme, this long moderato study illustrates the differ-
ence between the two contemporaries.   A counter-melody or
chordal accompaniment in DS, but never fugal writing.

XLVI C 3/8 K461, L8.   Attractive and popular; good
pair for previous one.

LI D 6/8 K492, L14   A favorite to be found in most
collections; spirited, but with a Spanish poignancy not unlike
the Polish "zal."   (JF)

LIV C 12/8 K513, LS3.   This late one is in two
movts, a slow Pastorale, suggesting Christmas music; and
a dashing Presto.

LVII F ¢ K518, L116.   Boldly rhythmic late work,
with dissonant chords under a duet theme.

LVIII f 3/8 K519, L475.   Lively, good to couple with
the above; Scarlatti at his best.

Other Sonatas: E 3/4 L23.   This stately andante
comodo has the elegance of a courtly polonaise, with trumpet
fanfares.   (JF & CF pub) Mod E

b 2/4 L263.   Somewhat simpler in texture, without
any scary hand-crossings or sweeping scales.   Good for a
start.   Mod E

E 2/4 L375.   Long considered "the" recital sonata of
DS (along with the following slow one, which was trans-
posed into e to match!) this is a real virtuoso piece requir-

ing velocity, accuracy, a fine touch control and wide dynamic range. (CF & JF pub) Dif

d 6/8 L413. Slower, legato, pastorale in character.
The same ornaments, trills, scales, leaping basses that are
elsewhere used for brilliance here serve expressive ends.
(CF & JF pub) Mod E

Bb 3/4 L396. Another dancy piece, it is harder
than it looks, and must not begin too fast, for after DS has
had his fun swapping hands, he doubles from 8ths to 16ths,
sweeping up the keyboard in arpeggios, and down in scales.
(CF & JF pub) Mod Dif

a 2/4 L430. Brilliant showpiece, rather shallow
and not too difficult, with some nice grapes for the LH.
(JF & CF pub) Mod

A ¢ L345. Dashing virtuoso piece, with a stirring
beat (presto), and treacherous leaps. In part II the RH
plays a quiet undulating figure, modulating down the scale,
while the LH crosses at reckless speed to provide both bass
and treble melody. Definitely written before Maria Barbara
(or DS) took on "embonpoint." (JF / CF pub) Dif

C 6/8 L104. Staccato study with all the tricks of the
trade, and only one fast scale. The player needs the imagination to vary the many repetitions and make the ornaments
titillating. (CF & JF pub) Mod

c 4/4 L352. One of the few in minor key, with a
more lyric melodic line, which later flowers into arabesques,
and adds a second line, played by the LH above the RH, but
at a leisurely tempo. Mod

b 3/4 L33. A quiet, expressive, 3-v sonata (with
no surprise runs or arpeggios). (CF & JF pub)   Mod E

G 12/8 L387. A favorite of Myra Hess, which she
played prestissimo, leggerissimo, with a breath-taking combination of verve and delicacy. Found in the Myra Hess Album (B&H pub) along with L33.

SCHARWENKA, XAVIER (Ger), 1850-1924.

This founder of three conservatories was recently disturbed in his well-earned sleep by recordings of two of his showy concertos and numerous pieces.

Polish Dance in e♭, Op 3:1.   Long a favorite on student recitals.   Mod E

Staccato Etude in E♭, Op 27:3.   One more of these; difficult and unimaginative.   Mod Dif

SCHEDRIN, RODION (USSR), 1932- .

Sonata (1962).   This composer's works range from popular ballets ("Hump-backed Horse") to this complex keyboard work.   Conventional in use of sonata form, but contemporary in its use of chord-clusters and free dissonance. The texture is often so thick as to be turgid.   Lengthy variations in contrapuntal style lead to a driving percussive rondo finale.   (MCA pub)   Dif

Toccatina (1966).   Short, dissonant, difficult, this is a true toccata in its use of touch patterns, some wide-ranging, some with hands overlapping.   (MCA pub)   Dif

SCHÖNBERG, ARNOLD (Aus-USA), 1874-1951.

This composer looms so large as an innovator and revolutionary that the sheer beauty of much of the piano music is overlooked.   This is due to the fact that students become acquainted with his pieces as "examples" for analysis, rather than as music for performance and enjoyment.   They are also neglected in the concert hall because of the welter of works they have spawned, many of which surpass them in both their vices and their virtues.   Though AS was not a pianist (and his other music is more representative), the six works are all remarkably pianistic, and produce a sonority that is still fresh, rich and satisfying.   Every serious pianist should attempt some of them.   The technic ranges from the moderately difficult to the very difficult; and all pose problems of musical interpretation.   James Friskin's "humble suggestion" that one first play the "melodic content" of each piece is not as simplistic as it sounds; for the melody is there, usually picked out with accents, marcato, sustained notes. Though AS topped the list in Swann polling of "Composers I like least," there are four complete recordings of his piano music, so somebody must like it.

Three Piano Pieces, Op 11 (1908). Stemming from the period of his first exploration of new atonal harmonic organization, these basically romantic pieces are among the freshest and most original. Since the music was meticulously edited (by the composer in 1942), the player needs only follow directions sympathetically to achieve the Expressionist ideal of a highly-charged emotional work in a distorted form. Familiarity with the Expressionist painting of Schönberg, Kokoschka, Munch, Nolda and others will be more helpful than the many harmonic and formal analyses found in textbooks. No 2 (7 min) builds to a powerful climax, with up-thrusting chord phrases under descending trills. No 3 anticipates much contemporary writing with its brevity, its velocity, its new keyboard figuration, its dynamics ranging from pppp to ffff in three pages; but is still largely expressed in standard keyboard patterns. Dif

Six Little Piano Pieces, Op 19 (1911). Further exploration of the same ideas, in miniatures (all are one-page, except the two-page No 1) refined, more atmospheric than emotional. Simple but subtle. Mod

Five Piano Pieces, Op 23. Equally succinct but more complex in texture, each miniature is a highly unified whole (only the closing waltz is built on a 12-tone row), yet loses none of its expressive spontaneity through compression and complexity. Dif

Suite for Piano, Op 25 (1924): Praeludium, Gavotte with Musette, Intermezzo, Minuet with Trio, Gigue. A case of pupil influencing master, the classical suite form used here was possibly the result of AS's work with Alban Berg, whose opera, "Wozzeck," is a tour de force of classic forms welded into a magnificent drama in serial technic. All five pieces are derived from the same 12-tone row, which gives an aural kinship to them; but the tracing of this row is a purely academic exercise, of little help to player or hearer. Though the dance rhythm is sometimes elusive, it gives character, and the pieces have a wonderfully varied and winsome sonority. Mod Dif

Two Piano Pieces, Op 33a, b (1932). Two serial
works continuing the process, making the utmost use of the
row, for expressive ends. The second uses the Schönbergian arc over a webbing of intricate patterns. More difficult
and less rewarding than the earlier sets. Dif

SCHUBERT, FRANZ (Aus), 1797-1828.

The best approach to the piano music of FS is, as
in the case of Brahms, by way of the Lieder, which no
sensitive musician can fail to respond to. Unfortunately,
whereas with Brahms the same qualities carry over into the
wordless piano music, in the case of Schubert this is not
true. A 3-min song that delights or moves to tears is blown
into a 15-min sonata movt that leaves us feeling very ho-
hum.

There seems to be a movement afoot to canonize FS
as a piano composer; and more and more of his works are
being forceably fed to students and audiences. We are told
that instead of the 11 sonatas which have been quite suffi-
cient in the past, we may soon be required to listen to 22,
when they are all "reconstructed." So far nobody has made
the misguided effort to revive the many stillborn operas
which stole so much time from FS's short life. One could
wish that the remaining piano works might also remain
buried.

Their virtues and faults are obvious. Nobody denies
the long graceful cantabile lines, nor the frequent brief tranquillo chordal passages, so satisfying the first time they appear. There are also those exciting and uniquely Schubert-
ian scales that go soaring up the keyboard over a fixed hammered bass chord. But the long melodies are incapable of
sonata treatment because of their very perfection, and developments become endless sequences of repetitions. In the
andantes the serenity becomes soporific on sixth hearing.
The same figures that so vividly underline the poetic text--
broken-chord basses, galloping scales, unison triadic motifs
in half-notes--here become monotonously dreary. The pages
of octave gallopades in that dotted rhythm that plagued Schumann's manic years (and Beethoven's deaf ones) are always
marked fff, reminding one of the rhetoricians rule that if
you have nothing to say, you should say it very loud.

Much is made of the "chains of fantastic modulations." On analysis, they resolve to a series of six to
eight sequential repetitions, moving chromatically, or key-

cyclically, each repetition containing a V^7, dim^7, tonic.
Totally absent are the euphoric surprises produced by the
rich, unpredictable chromaticsm of Schumann or Chopin
(whose Concert No 1 appeared only two years after FS's
last sonata). The slow movement of D959 in A described
by D. Matthews (Pelican Keyboard Music) as "invaded by a
cataclysmic passage of bravura recitative in which key as
such ceases to exist." This page (Kalmus p 200) consists
of six meas in D major, 10 meas in c♯, 16 in G♯, four in
f♯, etc., and each section contains only the three chords
named above. It will take more than such verbalization to
raise this master of the miniature Lied, of intimate ensemble music for two or more friends, and of the symphony,
into a first-rank piano solo composer.

The correct chronological order of the Sonatas has been
established by Otto Deutsch, and the now standard D numbers and old opus numbers are hereby given, for those for
whom Schubert sonatas are their cup of tea. Only the 11
completed ones appear here (consult the grave-diggers for
the others). D 537 a Op 164; D 568 E♭ Op 122; D 575 B
Op 147; D 664 A Op 120; D 784 a Op 143; D 845 a Op 42;
D 850 D Op 53; D 894 G Op 78; D 958 c Op Post.; D 959
A Op Post.; D 960 B♭ Op post. The first three were written
when FS was 20; the last three, the year he died. All au-
thorities agree that D 960 in B♭ is the greatest. Hutcheson also recommends D 845 in a, and D 784 in a. Friskin and Freundlich concur, and also praise D 850 in D.
The present writer likes best D 664 in A, because of its
"heavenly brevity."

D 760 "The Wanderer Fantasy." Of quite a different
character from the Sonatas is the "Wanderer" Fantasy, both
because of its virtuoso character and because of a cyclic
unity of movements. Written on commission, the intimacy
of Schubert's "music for friends" here gives way to a complexity similar to that of Hummel's concert music. The unity is provided, significantly, by a song theme, the melodic
or rhythmic motif of which appears in all four "movements."
Though continuous, the work contains distinct sections,
marked allegro con fuoco ma non troppo, in C major; adagio
in the unexpected key of c♯--the real heart of the work; a
presto in A♭ in scherzando style; and a closing allegro.
Liszt attempted to turn this work into a concerto, to make
up for the rather surprising absence of a work in this form;
but it remains most effective as a brilliant piano solo. Dif

Ländler, Op 171, 172: Duets. It is not surprising

that the finest works of Schubert are the "music for friends,"
the art songs, the four-hand music, the smaller solo works,
intended for a musical evening; and the dances (Ländler,
waltzes, minuets.) After all, once FS left the paternal nest
he never had a home of his own, and spent his short life
living under the roof of one friend or another. Mod

Four Impromptus, Op 90. A good introduction to
Schubert, each of these has its own character, sufficiently
contrasting that they can be played successively, though the
reptitions within each piece make them taxing and tiresome
at times. The second and fourth are rapid etudes, but with
contrasting lyric sections. The third is an Andante (correctly written in six flats, not in G), a fine exercise in cantabile playing. Mod

Six Moments Musicaux, Op 94. All of these are
good, and range from easy to moderately difficult, two to
three pages in length. No 2 has a stately sarabande character; No 3 in f minor is a kind of Turkish march; No 4,
a study in staccato-legato figures; No 5, a dance-like chord
study; and No 6 has the simplicity and lyricism of his finest songs. E to Mod

Four Impromptus, Op 142. These four, like the Op
90, seem to have been intended as a set and in fact have
more unity than some of the works bearing the name of
sonata. No 1 is a well-developed allegro in f minor--the
rondo in the same key; the second is a majestic Sarabande,
with a contrasting broken-chord trio; and No 3 is an attractive set of variations on a theme (a little over-extended, ev-
en without repeats). Mod

SCHUMAN, WILLIAM (USA), 1910- .

Distinguished award-winning composer of symphonic,
choral and ballet music, has two for piano.

Three-Score Set (1943). Brief triptych (20 meas in
each piece) contrasting a flowing linear style with bi-tonal
chordal passage, and a running linear staccato scherzo.
Mod

Voyage (1954). Better known in its orchestra version
as a ballet by Martha Graham, the five large pieces are

freely tonal and strongly rhythmic. The titles, derived from the ballet are: Anticipation, Caprice, Realization, Decision, and Retrospection. Mod Dif

SCHUMANN, CLARA [née Wieck] (Ger), 1819-1896.

Women's rights are giving Clara's compositions a hearing nowadays. They prove, what we have always known, that she was a magnificent pianist, married to a remarkable composer, whom her long career as a performer and teacher helped to establish. Her concerto has recently been dusted off and recorded, along with these pieces.

Two Scherzi, Op 10, 14 Variations on a Theme of Robert Schumann; Four Fugitive Pieces. These might all pass for Robert's work, except that they lack the sparkle and exuberance which lifts his music above the vast flood of German romantic music. The short genre-pieces, brief and fleeting, are best.

SCHUMANN, ROBERT (Ger), 1810-1856.

This late-starting, short-lived composer has left more works for piano than most any of his contemporary Romantics. This is partly because both RS and his wife, Clara, were pianists, though RS did not, like Chopin, confine his composing to his instrument but also wrote copiously for voice, ensembles and orchestra. His piano works are collected in seven vol published by Kalmus, based on manuscripts edited by Clara, who outlived him by 40 years. Vol VII contains the great Concerto in a, and two lesser, but interesting, concert pieces for piano and orchestra. The best music is found in the early works, and Vol V and VI contain only a few items of interest. The literary background of RS and a literary gift almost the equal of his musical one account for the picturesque fantasy that is so much a part of his best work. His critical writing, though there is much nonsense in it, helped launch such worthies as Chopin and Brahms.

Variations on the name ABEGG, Op 1. His first opus introduces us at once to one of RS's games, "musical anagrams," with a tune spelled out from a name. Though

immature, angular and sometimes unpianistic, the variations
are musical and still playable. His unique new piano style,
avoiding broken chords, scales, etc., is already in evidence.
Mod Dif

Papillions, Op 2. Another game of the youthful RS
was to imagine his friends in costumes and masks, as char-
acters in Commedia del Arte (or in one of the romantic nov-
els of his favorite authors, Jean Paul, or E. T. A. Hoffmann). Fortunately the original titles of the 12 sketches of
Butterflies got omitted from the printed edition; the miniatures are vividly contrasted, and need no picturesque names.
The "disappearing chord" (already used in ABEGG) here suggests the guests departing, one by one, after the strokes of
the clock. Good technic and pedalling essential, but not complex. Mod Dif

Etudes, Op 3, 10. These books, written under Paganini's diabolical spell and as a protest against Czerny's
dreariness, can be passed over, since Liszt and Chopin did
this sort of thing so much better. Technic per se had no
more interest for RS than keyboard exhibitionism. Dif

Intermezzos, Op 4; Impromptus, Op 5. These also,
though exploring many new devices and advancing RS's own
skill, may well be by-passed for the greater things to come.
Mod Dif

Davidsbündler Dances, Op 6. Seldom played because
of their great length (18 pieces), these contain much fine music. Here he "acts out" in well diversified keyboard sketches the fantasies that he has been writing out in his influential music magazine; and the two aspects of this split personality are vividly characterized in sound. The David's Band
of his lucubrations consisted of his friends and fellow-musi-
cians who under the joint leadership of the suave and gay
Eusebius and the sensitive poetic Florestan (RS's pen names)
were to put down the anti-musical Philistines of the world.
Mature musicians will find much of interest to explore here.
Dif

Carnival, Op 9 "Little Scenes on Four Notes." One of
the mountain peaks of piano literature, this demands both
technical mastery and profound musical feeling. The contrasting personalities of the guests must all be made clear;
they include, besides the twin hosts, Eusebius and Florestan,
Chopin (in an exquisite miniature nocturne); Paganini himself

madly sweeping the strings of his bow; gentle Clara (and
other bolder girl-friends); and sundry others, costumed as
Harlequin, Pierrot, Pantalon-Columbine, who dance, promenade, whisper sweet nothings, unmask, and finally join in
a march against "the Philistines." The game of anagrams
is also played throughout, the "four-notes" of the title,
taken from SCHumAnn's own name (SCHA) and the name of
the village of ASCH, occurring in every one of the 20 pieces,
and giving to the suite a unity which the 12-tone row seldom
bestows. The audience, as well as the performer, needs
musical maturity, and some clue to the fun that is going on.
Dif

Grand Sonata No 1 in f#, Op 11. RS does his duty
by the sonata with three works, like Chopin, Mendelssohn
and Brahms. Like them, also, the sonatas do not represent the composer's best; for the necessity to expand, extend, repeat and connect his fine ideas was not natural for
RS and the works are overburdened with dull passage work.
Yet the many fine themes which they contain still make them
worth playing. No 1 (40 pages!) has a bold adagio introduction before the redundant allegro, where RS can think of
nothing better to do in the development than to repeat the
entire section a 3rd higher. The two-page andante cantabile
is a trifle lush, but fine piano writing. The scherzo and
intermezzo have real vitality and humor, with a "spoof" of
the courtly polonaise, as well as of operatic recitative. The
finale is intolerably long and repetitious, and judicious cut-
ting is essential. Already the jerky dotted figure that is to
plague so many bridges and developments appears. Dif

Sonata in f, Op 14. This 47-page work seems to
represent all the worst in RS, and is in fact rarely played.
The four-page "Quasi Variations" of the slow movt would
make a nice short piece, if not impacted in a sonata. Dif

Sonata No 2 in g, Op 22. The shortest of the sonatas, and a good concert number for the pianist with subtlety
and imagination to enliven the monotonous rhythmic patterns
of the outer movts. The second movt is one of RS's finest
cantabiles, and the scherzo is also vivid. The cadenza-like
coda requires great reserves of technic and endurance. Dif

Fantasia, Op 17. Like Chopin, RS's single work in
this form is one of his masterpieces. Freed from the allegro requirements, RS sets forth a family of related themes.
Into these he introduces a sad, quiet legend, which gathers

excitement in the telling, till it swings back to the grand opening apassionata. A bold swashbuckling march opens the middle movt (similar to the wonderful Piano Quintet) and recurs like a rondo, varied each time, till it finally closes with a dashing (and treacherous) leaping-chord coda. Unfortunately the panache with which this virile theme enters each time is dissipated by the series of fluttering, effeminate gestures with which it ends, and the long rattling ric-rac passages between. The Fantasia closes with a serene lento, and we heave a sigh of relief at being spared that compulsory closing sonata rondo. Dif

Synphonic Etudes, Op 13. Another of the all-time greats, this work is cumbered with an unnecessarily complex title and numbering system (Etudes en forme de Variations, XII Etudes symphoniques), with some of the 12 bearing two different numbers, as etudes and as variations. The 16-meas binary theme should be played adagio (not andante) and is a masterpiece in itself. It is followed by 12 profoundly poetic and boldly bravura pieces, some only remotely related to the theme, yet forming a magnificent structure culminating in another grand Goliath-slaying finale. It alone, of all the set, has flaws, being overextended with pages of pseudo-development galloping along in dotted-note passages; but redeemed at the end by the glorious lift of the theme from minor to major. Dif

Fantasiestücke, Op 12. This title, as well as that of Op 16, was suggested by the writings of Hoffmann, who was composer as well as novelist. Whereas the Op 17 Fantasia is actually a great three-movt free-form sonata, here we have Fantasy "pieces," eight of them, all very fine. They could well be played together, but each is also an entity. Some are simple enough for students (with imagination), others require a virtuoso technic. No 7, Dream Tangles, must be presto possibile. Evening, Soaring, Why?, Whims--the titles must not be taken too seriously. My favorite is In the Night, not a nocturne, but a ghost story, full of fine contrasting passages. For small hands, the Schirmer ed division of parts is helpful. Mod

Arabeske Op 18; Blumenstück, Op 19. Written on a visit to Vienna, these are avowedly salon music, written to titillate the ladies. After RS's death, Clara popularized them during her 40 years of teaching and concertizing. Mod

Humoreske, Op 20. Another large-scale work (29-

pages 28 min) RS regarded it highly and wrote Clara that
she would find "beautifully depicted in 'the great Humoreske'"
how he had laughed and cried while writing them in Vienna,
later ruefully admitting that it was rather a melancholy joke.
There is much of the best of first-period RS in the eight
linked, untitled pieces; perhaps taking a place above the abstract sonatas, but below the literary-program suites.

Novellettes, Op 21.   Another large opus, containing
eight separate pieces, each in ternary or rondo form, the
shortest five pages, the longest, 18.   They have little in
common (the odd name derives from Clara Novello, "because
she was also Clara," as RS wrote to Prof. Weick's daughter, the future Mrs. Schumann) except their boldness and
vigor.   No 1 can be played by an advanced student; but the
2nd requires the endurance and drive of a professional, and
is glorious to hear.   Nos 4, 5 and 6 are somewhat easier,
and are a waltz, a polonaise, and a rondo.   No 7 is the
shortest, but brilliant and effective.   The last is the longest
and most difficult--a virtuoso number.   Mod to Dif

Romance in F♯, Op 28:2.   This two-page gem consists of a black-key duet for thumbs, a 3-v canonic trio, and
modulations that range from D♯ to C major, and it maintains throughout a tender lyricism that earns it the title and
its popularity.   Mod

Nachtstück in F, Op 23:4.   This lacks the melancholy
of Chopin's nocturnes, but has a cantabile theme so songful
that it has become a favorite hymn; interesting technical problems with canons and rolled chords.   Mod

Prophet Bird, from Forest Scenes, Op 82:6.   Of the
late works, only the wistful Bird as Prophet has earned a
place in the repertoire.   Its pedal, fingering, ornamental
and interpretive problems are worth solving for the charming
miniature it is.   Mod

SCOTT, CYRIL (GB), 1879-1970.

A prolific composer with over 100 works for piano
who is almost entirely forgotten today.   Like his contemporary Scriabin, he dabbled in theosophy, but his musical style
is derived from French Impressionism, with little that is
original added.   There are two concertos, and three sonatas.
None of his music has been recorded.   His fin de siècle,

"mauve decade" style lingered on too long. His frank biography does much to explain his limited output and unchanged style.

Lento (from Two Pierrot Pieces). Lush languid short movement, (a Valse Lent) this has a pallid charm. Mod E

Lotusland. One of many exotic pseudo-oriental pieces, this has an attractive modal theme, melismatically treated, over a hypnotic drum-bass, and builds an effective climax. Mod

Danse Negre. Still a popular encore number, the brilliant short piece is in a flowing moto-perpetuo style requiring velocity and accuracy. Mod Dif

SCRIABIN, ALEXANDER (Rus), 1872-1915.

The centennial of Scriabin's birth saw a revival of his keyboard works in concert hall and on records; numerous experiments with technicolor light effects; articles about the philosophy, and a two-vol biography boxed and bound in Japanese silk, with more form than content. When all the brouhaha has died, we are left with a new awareness of a fine body of keyboard work, highly idiosyncratic and original yet eminently pianistic, and long neglected. The theosophy, incense, tepid poetry can be brushed aside, leaving 10 solid sonatas, 24 preludes, 12 etudes, and countless small pieces. Placed beside the works of his school rival and cousin, Rachmaninoff, these reveal a strong sense of form, a distinctive voice, a lyric gift, a command of keyboard technic the equal of his more famous cousin; and a questing mind that transformed his sound, throughout his short life, from an extension of the Russian post-Romantic to something highly original. The serious pianist can take or leave the egomaniac theosophy that sought musical expression, but he cannot ignore the experimental works it produced, some tenuous and transitory, some winged flights into new space. Only a few of the 24 preludes and later pieces are relatively easy; others demand full keyboard mastery.

Etude in c#, Op 2. Worthy of its model, Chopin, this work (more a prelude or nocturne than an etude) makes a fine distinction between melody, counter-theme and accompaniment, and requires subtle use of both pedals. Mod E

Prelude for LH in A, Op 9. While suffering from an overworked right hand, AS wrote these two charming masterpieces, the first a duet between thumb, as tenor, and fifth finger as bass. Mod E

Nocturne in D♭ for LH, Op 9. The nocturne is more of a concert etude, and has a bold melodic line over sensuous chords, hammered out in a manner that was to become a hallmark of AS. It has two cadenzas. Mod Dif

12 Etudes, Op 8. Taking up where Chopin stopped, AS produced 12 highly imaginative technical studies in which a musical experience must result from the mastery of specific keyboard problems.

Etude No 1 in c♯. AS's predilection for keys bristling with sharps (eight of the 12 etudes) makes his music difficult to read, but his natural pianism makes it highly playable. LH parts differ from Rachmaninoff's racing figures by their chordal character, often enclosing both melody, harmony and basic beat, while the RH taps out broken chord figures, as in Nos 1, 3 and 5, or brushes in swirling calligraphic lines, as in Nos 2 and 4. Allegro, but the very fast MM marks for the etudes and sonatas are, as AS laughingly confessed, not meant to be taken too seriously. Dif

No 2 in f♯. A capriccio, con forza, this unique etude is at the same time a traditional romantic, even melodramatic work, and a highly idiomatic example of the composer's use of striding triplets against irregular, undulating figures in 5ths, 6ths and 7ths, with the strong melody shared between the hands. Dif

No 3 in b. A fondness for original markings appears with this tempestuoso; also a habit of scoring that looks like one thing and sounds like another. To get the beat of this odd-looking 6/8, play first measures 17-27; then try the opening. Ternary form, with a cantabile counter-theme. Easier than it looks. Mod

No 4 in B. This two-page flowing piacevole, legato cantabile is harder than it looks, but rewards the labor with a lovely, lyric sound. Find the long line, and do not fragment it with excessive rubatos. Dif

No 5 in E. Most popular and frequently anthologized, this joyous etude should be marked alla breve, and sounds best at the brisk tempo marked by the composer: brioso, MM half note = 72 (you may compromise at half note = 50). The sensitive player will resist the temptation to linger over each measure, and fit the nuance and rubato to the big 4-meas phrase. A masterpiece. Mod Dif

No 6 in A. Less inspired, this study in RH 6ths is an obvious Chopin imitation. Mod Dif

No 7 in B♭. Flats, at last, modulating to the relative major for a grand choral mid-section. This fine etude, presto tenebroso agitato, sotto voce pp (and very fast), looks harder than it is because of AS's habit of putting the meas bars in the wrong places (learned from Schumann?). If this were written without an up-beat, it would be simple to read; and if the correct LH fingering is found, it lies well under the hand. Dif

No 8 in A♭. Take the lento quite slowly (tempo rubato, 8th notes in 3/4), for the second theme is poco più vivo, and ends with a variation in 16th notes. The easiest. Mod E

No 9 in g♯. This etude is a grand large-scale study with octaves in both hands, the left pounding out triplets under a bold rapping RH theme. In the second page, where the hands reverse roles, the enharmonic modulations, while hard to decipher, sound eminently right, and soar to a jubilant codetta. The meno vivo continues the octave exercise, but is mystic and as subtly evocative as a Monet cathedral. A return of the Alla ballata declamatory opening rounds off this fine study. Dif

No 10 in D♭. A RH study in chromatic running 3rds, staccato and legato, over a simple flowing left (note-for-note) accompaniment figure. Resounding octaves provide a brief climax. Very effective if played moto perpetuo. Mod Dif

No 11 in b♭. This andante cantabile etude is more in the nature of a prelude, and its problems are musical, not technical. Pleasing. Mod

No 12 in d♯. Returning to sharps for another of his "greatest hits," AS writes an etude at once so technically complex and dramatically brilliant that it deserves its fame.

Only for virtuosi or advanced students.   Dif

    24 Preludes, Op 11. This set of preludes is clear-
ly Chopin-inspired, even using the major-minor key cycle,
up through sharps, down through flats, but many sound a
distinctly new note, and even the most derivative are original enough to be a welcome addition to the post-Romantic
repertoire.

    Prelude No 1 in C. One of the most original, the
concept is Chopin's single-motif one-page form, but the five-
note over-the-bar figures in both hands, with a displaced
RH figure for phrase punctuation, is decidedly new. A subito pp in the middle starts the climax that widens into octaves in each hand for the close.   Dif

    No 2 in a. AS was fond of the valse and mazurka,
and this simple accompanied melody might fit either form.
Mod E

    No 3 in G. A brief breezy number, vivo   MM half
note = 200 with RH triplets against LH eighths throughout.
Mod

    No 4 in e. This prelude is an expressive lento solo
for LH, with RH playing slow chords and counterpoints.
One-page, pp throughout.   Mod E

    No 5 in D. A simple chord sequence in 4/2 over a
fluid accompaniment, repeated four times, each repetition
enhanced with varied melodic ornamentation, chromatic harmonic shifts, and rolled chord expansions.   Andante cantabile.   Mod

    No 6 in b. Simple 2-v canon, both hands playing oc-
taves, with surprise modulations and rhythmic variations
adding up to an attractive easy but brilliant piece.   Mod E

    No 7 in A. A simple accompanied melody (rather
undistinguished) is expanded with wide-ranging octaves and
wide chords, before subsiding ppp.   Effective if played vivo.
Mod Dif

    No 8 in f♯. Similar to Prelude No 3, but less in-
spired.   Mod E

    No 9 in E. Chopin would have been proud to have

written this one-page andante, and the sensitive pianist will find much pleasure in working out its subtle pedalling, phrasing, rubato. In both this and the following, AS discovers a new surprise ending, with a single tone held over from a staccato chord, to lead to the closing cadence. Mod

No 10 in c♯. Another inspired piece in simple a-b-a form (20 meas). Into a mesh-work of highly original chord figures played pp, a three-note alto motto sounds, four times, like a cry. After the serene 4-meas section in E major, the chord figures take up the alarm in a passage marked fff, then vanish in broken phrases, with the lone alto c♯ singing on. Mod

No 11 in B. Vigorous allegro with a 6/8 lilt, some interesting figuration and chord progressions. Mod

No 12 in g♯. A quiet 2-v andante prelude in 9/8 that is fresh and appealing. Mod E

No 13 in G♭. Lento, similar to No 9, but less original. Mod E

No 14 in e♭. A brilliant and effective octave study, presto in 15/8. This consists of three groups of five 8th notes in each measure, and the player must avoid dotting the RH quarters, thereby turning it into a banal 4/4. Broadens to a keyboard-spanning climax capped with six hammered tonic chords fff in the bass. Dif

No 15 in D♭. Chaste and limpid, this fey lento prelude, which never ventures off the diatonic scale, begins with a flowing 8-meas duet (for two recorders), which is then repeated as accompaniment to a simple slow treble melody (for flute). The base has a few bars of solo with the other two tootling away, before a II-V-I cadence in whole notes. Nice. Mod E

No 16 in b♭. Left and right play unison parts throughout this subtle and curious prelude, marked misterioso (una corda, sotto voce). Measures of 5/4 and 4/4 alternate, and a Wagnerian trumpet motif sounds over a sinuous winding figure. Mod

No 17 in A♭. This 12-meas gem should be marked 6/4, not 3/2. It develops a single cadential figure through four repetitions. Mod

No 18 in f. Brilliant octave toccata pitting LH triplets against RH chords and even notes then reversing it (the
bar lines are again misplaced). Sounds more difficult than
it is, with its presto fff coda. Mod

No 19 in E♭. A distinguished work, with drive and
intensity, this prelude is more difficult to read than to play.
2/4 Affettuoso, with a five-note figure wreathing the strong
triplet melody. Mod

No 20 in c. One-page Apassionato with theme derived from No 19, with which it could be paired. Mod

No 21 in B♭. Hushed, reposeful number, given distinction by two short melodic motifs, separated by rests,
and a meter alternating 3/4, 5/4, 6/4. Mod E

No 22 in g. The lento preludes (Nos 9, 13, and 22)
all follow the same pattern, a long cantabile line (all in
eighths, 3/4, minor keys) later broken into short, urgent
restless phrases, with a "dying fall." Mod E

No 23 in F. A vivacious vivo. Must have a strong
LH beat to keep its shape. Mod Dif

No 24 in d. A brilliant "curtain-ringer," this final
prelude of Op 11 is much easier than it sounds. The 8ths
must always be equal, to convey the breathless quality produced by alternating 6/8, 5/8. An accurate LH is needed
for the hurtling LH octaves of the finale.

The Prelude continued to intrigue AS throughout his
life, and many other attractive ones may be enjoyed, if
available (some are anthologized). Recommended are: Op
13:6 in b♭; Op 15:2 in F♯; Op 16 (all five have qualities);
Op 27:1,2; Op 67 (late style).

Five Preludes, Op 74. The very last published piano
work before his early death is a set of five short, diversified preludes, all having the ambiguous unresolved harmony
of his late style, with many slow half-step trill motifs. For
pianists for whom the sonatas are "too much," all the same
material is found here, in miniature. The difficulties are
musical, not technical and the extravagant titles help interpret them. No 1 is "sadly shredded"; No 2, "slow, contemplative"; 3, "like a cry"; 4, "slow, vague and indecisive";
5, "proud, belligerent." Mod Dif

Three Pieces, Op 45: Feuille d'Album; Poème fantasque; Prélude. Representative of his early style, the first of these, andante piacevole, is an exquisite miniature which was a favorite of both the pianist and his audiences. The Fantastic Poem introduces the new quartal harmony (notes in 4ths), the sighing chromatic quavers, and a tapping theme. The Prélude returns to more conventional harmony, with a charming arpeggio flutter for phrase punctuation. Mod

Scherzo in C, Op 46. The three-page presto in ternary form has little of the humorous about it, but has an exhilarating up-sweeping theme, and a fine contrasting chorale. Mod

Fantasia in b, Op 28. Large-scale concert work, embodying all AS's finest early period keyboard devices in a spontaneous and exuberant form, as well organized as a sonata allegro. Dif

Poème Tragique, Op 34. Another big concert study in ternary form, more ecstatic than tragic. The opening 12/8 (12 chords to the meas) is marked festivamente, fastoso, but must not be started too fast, as there are numerous più allegro sprinkled along the way. The contrasting second theme (4/4) has a rumbling bass worthy of Rachmaninoff, and a theme that is "irate and fiery." When the tempo primo returns, with the tremolo chord figure in the RH, the player is kept very busy. Requires sure-footed fingers, but otherwise uncomplicated. Mod Dif

Vers la Flamme, Op 72. Fine short work in late style (5 min) with its ambivalent irresolute harmony based on quartal chords and unresolved 9ths. Raymond Lewenthal's description is so vivid, it makes the music anticlimactic. He writes, " 'Toward the Flame' begins in utter darkness, and moves inexorably toward dazzling, blinding light.... Two muted themes appear, slow, almost inarticulate; mysterious forces begin to stir, and they develop ... come to life and glow. Then, over a molten sea of LH arpeggii and RH trills, the second theme sounds a clarion call. A few bars before the first theme reappears in final satanic glory, a sinister Morse code-like motif begins to flicker high up like a signal from outer space, with the persistency of the Chinese water-drop torture, at first faintly, then growing louder until it fairly screams for recognition and the whole world blows up in one final holocaust." Scriabin would have liked the prose, and the explosion.   Dif

   10 Sonatas.   Not since Schubert had a composer written this many sonatas for piano; and nobody but Prokofiev
has followed suit.   Among the 10 are three or four that have
now taken their place in the concert repertoire.   Many appeared for the first time during the Scriabin centennial year;
and some are of more interest historically than musically,
the early ones showing the struggle to adapt the form to his
keyboard ideas and the late ones, the struggle to shape it
to his mysticism and changed idiom.   As early as 1940
Lockwood was making a plea for more attention for the sonatas, and his book has helpful analyses of Nos 2, 5, and
9, representing the three periods of AS's style.

   Sonata No 1 in F, Op 6.   Earlier than the preludes
and etudes, this four-movt work belongs in the experimental
category, and can safely be by-passed; more Brahms than
Scriabin.   Many romantic and modern composers wrote one
similar work, after which they gave up.   Dif

   Sonata-Fantasie in g#, Op 19.   Two-movt work similar to many of the etudes, the first in allegro form; the
second a moto perpetuo, à la Chopin (last movement of the
Funeral March Sonata).   See Lockwood.   Dif

   Sonata No 3 in f#, Op 23.   This work opens prom-
isingly, drammatico, with a bold two-note bass motif leaping from dominant to tonic, answered with a graceful arching theme in the RH.   The allegro, however, is disappoint-
ingly structured, with a weak second theme and the principal theme returning too often.   The other three movts exploit either the bass motto or the arching answer, which
could give a cyclic unity, but instead is monotonously repetitious.   The rigid 4-meas phrase throughout also palls.   A
large-scale work (25 to 30 min) good for an occasional airing.   Dif

   Sonata No 4 in F#, Op 30.   Here the real Scriabin appears in a finely wrought two-movt work.   The three-page andante reveals the mystic, with restless tenuous harmony under a
plaintive but clear melodic line, enhanced when repeated by
trills and softly chiming chords, quietiasimo, dolcissimo,
ending on a lingering 9th.   The prestissimo volando opens
with the same chord expanded into a dashing allegro first
subject, with a broad chorale for contrast.   A true development combines these and the mystic theme in growing ardor,

for a jubilant return.   For coda, the opening andante is repeated, but over hammered chord clusters in a style AS
was to make his own, exploiting sheer repetition and volume
of sound in an overwhelming way.   The coda is marked fff,
focosamente giubilioso.   Dif

Sonata No 5 in F#, Op 53.   This great work is perhaps the crest of Scriabin's oeuvre.   Its highly original harmonic fabric, rhythmic complexity, wiry sinuous melodic
line, while set forth in traditional sonata allegro structure
(a single movt, with introduction), communicate the curious
compound of the sensuous and spiritual, and above all the
questing mind of the composer.   Lockwood's analysis is
recommended, but one cannot refrain from listing some of
AS's own directions: impetuoso con stravaganza; languido;
accarezzevole; misterioso affannato; quasi trombe ff imperi-
oso; con una ebbrezza fantastica; presto tumultuoso esaltato.
Dif

Sonata No 6, Op 62.   Lest you give thanks that the
multiple-sharp key signatures have gone, take note that the
music bristles with accidentals, and time signatures change
several times to a page.   In spite of this, the big allegro
shape remains (and the boring 4-meas phrases).   The directions read like a ballet scenario, starting with mysterious
sighs, a dream that takes shape, surges, ends in a deliri-
ous dance.   Odd that so little of Scriabin is danced, while
so much of Stravinsky is.   For the explorer.   Dif

Sonata No 7, Op 64; Sonata No 9, Op 68; Sonata No
10, Op 70.   No 7 is called the "White Mass" and No 9 (the
"Black" by this curiously color-conscious composer.   If
pure devotion was intended by the first, and evil magic dese-
cration by the second, the hearer will find it hard to detect.
No 7 is perhaps the most complex, requiring four staves to
write in places.   No 9 is simpler, as is 10.   The problems
are musical and interpretive, if the music is to avoid ob-
scurity and monotony.   Dif

SEARLE, HUMPHREY (GB), 1915- .

Successful author and composer of opera, ballet and
chamber music; has written little for piano.

Sonata (1951).   Massive one-movt work in tribute to

Liszt, successfully proving that it is impossible to write a
sonata in serial technic. The flamboyant keyboard passage
work is totally at variance with the non-tonal melodic line,
which attempts a dramatic declamatory stance, on a 12-
tone-row. Since the essence of a sonata is key-contrast,
and since serial work totally eschews key-tonality--nay,
avoids it like the plague--such works had better settle for
Fantasy or Piece for a title. Even properly labelled, this
is too much of a pastiche to merit serious attention. Dif

     Prelude on a Theme by Alan Rawsthorne. SH has
moved on to a post-Webern serial style in this wispy, muted,
fragile birthday piece. Mod

SEROCKI, KAZIMIERZ (Pol), 1922- .

     A Piacere (1970). Aleatoric work from a Polish
composer who has "progressed" from free-tonality in sonata
form to music of chance. In three sections of 10 "structures," called suggestions, to be played a piacere, never
twice the same. Copious notes and directions provide a
guide. Not excessively difficult for the avant-garde player.
(EBM pub) Mod Dif

SESSIONS, ROGER (USA), 1896- .

     This veteran composer and educator's works are
serious, original, and challenging for both player and hearer.
Their complexity sometimes verges on the impenetrable and
they become practically unplayable.

     Sonata No 1 (1930). The four contrasting sections of
this one-movt work are in traditional S-F-S-F pattern, and
the piano writing is idiomatic, though complex and difficult.
Basically tonal, though experimenting with textures. The
toccata-like drive requires mature technic and musicianship.
Dif

     From My Diary (1937-40). Neither tonal or serial,
this suite has the random quality of diary jottings, though
each of the four pieces is well organized. Structural lines
are strong but blurred by fussy passage work. The four
pieces again alternate S-F-S-F; the third a quiet misterioso;

the fourth, ff pesante using black against white chord-clumps. Mod Dif

Sonata No 2 (1946). Music for musicians (mere pi-anists stay away!) this is rated by some as one of the finest sonatas of the century. Its three movts (allegro con fuoco; lento; misurato e pesante) explore new rhythms and key-board patterns in a texture dense and opaque, relentless in its avoidance of recognizable tonality. Might sound well as a chamber work with the complexity clarified by contrasting timbres, and a division of labor. Not for the timid. Dif

Sonata No 3 (1968). Carries complexity to the point where note-reading and key-grasping become almost insur-mountable obstacles. Alternates a dense serial polyphony with brief relief in delicate pointillistic passages or a Schön-bergian arch. The frenetic tempo required in the thick moto perpetuo makes it practically impregnable. Devoted students of the master have recorded all three sonatas. V Dif

SGAMBATI, GIOVANNI (It), 1843-1914.

Italian pianist, conductor-composer.

Vecchio Minuetto Gavotte in a. Fond of classical dances, SG wrote a graceful minuet, once quite popular; and an attractive gavotte. Mod

Toccata in A♭. More brilliant, this is a moto per-petuo chord study. Mod

Melody (from Gluck's "Orpheus"). The exquisite flute solo from the "Elysian Fields" is effective transcribed as a lento piano solo. Good opening number. Mod

SHOSTAKOVICH, DIMITRI (USSR), 1906- .

This prolific composer, considered the Dean of Soviet Musicians, is rather an enigma to much of the world. He appears to be either a second Grieg, grinding out one dreary opus after another in the hope of matching his early success-es, Symphonies I and V (Symphony No 14 was Op 135); or a

great genius, frustrated by the necessity of conforming to
a constricting ideology. Let us by-pass this issue, and ex-
amine the piano works for their intrinsic worth.

Three Fantastic Dances, Op 5. Light, charming,
pianistic youthful works. Good for students. Mod E

Sonata No 1, Op 12 (1926). Large-scale cyclic one-
movt work; highly chromatic themes, non-key-anchored,
with dissonant chords used percussively. It has the emotional intensity of early Schönberg and the virtuoso keyboard
writing of early Prokofiev. Dif

24 Preludes, Op 34 (1923-33). The key cycle of
Chopin's preludes is followed, short pieces in a wide variety of styles, many lacking in originality. The "wrong-
key" dissonance which seems fortuitous and gratuitous in a
tonally oriented set, detracts. The best is the one-page e♭
No 14, a sombre pesante adagio that rises to a powerful climax, then subsides. No 15 is a gay waltz, more attractive
in a violin transcription, as is also No 10. The two-part
fughetta in e (No 4) is admired by some, and anticipates Op
87. The fleet D major (No 5) is a dashing etude in velocity,
and No 24 a gay (Prokofiev) gavotte. Mod

Sonata No 2, Op 64 (1943). This dreary 60-page
work illustrates the unevenness of DS' work. The first
movement has the RH diddling on "Alberti-bass" figures,
while the LH plays a heavy triadic theme linked with five-
finger figures, on adjacent white keys. There are two more
such movts. Mod

24 Preludes and Fugues, Op 87, Vol I, II (1950).
The idea of a tribute to Bach on the bicentennial of his
death as well as the desire to prove that the old forms were
still viable (it had already been done by Paul Hindemith at
Yale, with his "Ludus Tonalis," seven years earlier) are
laudable. Opus 87 is inevitably compared to the Well-Tempered Clavier, but it has much more affinity with "The Art
of the Fugue." It is an enormous work, over 200 pages, in
two vol; and appears to have been written neither in a bland
popular style to meet a bureau's approval, nor in an arti-
fically dissonant style for concert use (in spite of Freundlich's prophecy, it is rarely heard); but rather, like Bach's
last work, for the composer himself. Hence it is often profoundly expressive (especially in the many lengthy adagios)
and in spite of superficial plagiarisms remarkably original.

The "Chaplinesque parody" which some purport to find is, I suspect, unintentional. For the conservative pianist, the preludes offer hours of pleasant keyboard rumination; and for the inveterate fugalist, fields of delight. For the keyboard athlete, there is little to challenge him, and few of the works seem suited for performance. Too many are based on a single four- or five-note figure, which in the hands of Bach or Chopin might have fascinated us for three or four pages, but here is extended for eight or ten, to the point where monotony sets in.

Prelude and Fugue No 2 in a. No 2 (the Chopin key-cycle is followed, rather than the Bach chromatic order) is one of the few short ones with a dashing etude-like prelude and rhythmic fugue. Mod

No 3 in G. Another short one with dramatic declamatory unison figures alternating with high melisma; a fast running fugue. Mod Dif

No 4 in e. A chorale variation for prelude, with a long meditative fugue. Mod Dif

No 5 in D. A graceful, light prelude, and a scherzando fugue. Short. Mod

No 12 in g#. One of the long adagio preludes, but a very imposing one with a passacaglia theme developed. The fugue is more dissonant and asymetrical than most.

No 14 in eb. Very Russian adagio (two pages) with a Moussorgskian theme and tremolo. Fast 3-v Fugue. Dif

No 16 in bb. One of the nicest of the preludes, andante with flowing cumulative variations. The fugue (a seven-page adagio) has a theme of fascinating rhythmic complexity, ranging from half notes to 32nds and sounding like an Oriental ululation. Dif

SIBELIUS, JAN (Fin), 1865-1957.

Finnish composer whose seven symphonies and many orchestral tone poems achieved enormous popularity during the decades between the wars. He wrote over 100 piano pieces, most of which were pot-boilers and are negligible.

Only two or three are heard today.

Romance in D♭. A popular recital piece, this has a broad sentimental melody, and is pianistic. Mod E

From the Land of a Thousand Lakes, Op 46. These 10 sketches attempt to emulate Grieg, but lack the lyric charm, freshness and originality.

Three Sonatinas, Op 67. There is an early sonata, turbid and unpianistic. These are lighter, more explora- tory. No 1 is genial and innocuous. No 2 has three move- ments all derived from a single motif, using linear imita- tion, rhythmic variation with some originality. Mod

SINDING, CHRISTIAN (Nor), 1856-1941.

Sonata, Op 91; Fatum Variations, Op 32. A piano concerto and a sonata by this prolific and mediocre succes- sor to Grieg remain mercifully undisturbed in their grave; but a number of CS's pieces are recorded.

Six Pieces, Op 32: Marche Grotesque. Effective pianistic alternate-hand staccato chord study. Mod E

Rustle of Spring. Still charms on first hearing, and is fun to rustle at. Mod E

SMALLEY, ROGER (GB), 1943- .

Piano Pieces I-V. The five pieces by Mr. Smalley, British musical-activist, are anything but small in their technical demands. There is no reason why the pianist-dog should not learn new tricks, and there are many to try here: dynamic shifts in rapid succession, in the low register; thick meaty contrapuntal passages in displaced tone-rows ranging over the entire keyboard. Serial and non-tonal throughout. For the explorer. V Dif

SMETANA, BEDRICH (Czech), 1824-1884.

Leading figure in the folk-renaissance of the ancient Czech folk culture, BS imbued his many small piano works with this spirit. The story is told that the national dance of the country, the polka, was first danced by Bedrich's father, on the occasion of the child's birth. It was raised to an art form in the opera, "The Bartered Bride," and in the many piano dances of BS. (pub by Artia and Bärenreiter)

Three Poetic Polkas, Op 7; Three Salon Polkas, Op 8. Great variety and pianistic ingenuity within the meter of the lively, but highly rubato 2/4, with pick-up. Mod

Czech Dances I, II. Sometimes called "Souvenir de La Bohême" or "Bohemian Dances," these are in the same style as the above, but more taut and brilliant. Mod

By the Seashore, Concert Etude. Virtuoso tone-poem, producing restless surging ceaseless waves built on arpeggios of g♯ and e chords superimposed, under a broad tragic melody. Fine concert work. Dif

SMITH, HALE (USA), 1925- .

Evocation. One of Cleveland's many musical sons, this black composer-educator now teaches at the University of Connecticut. This serial work, well titled, is finely derived from the opening statement, with vivid contrasts of mood, through dynamics and rhythm, with hints of a jazz beat. Dif

SOLER, ANTONIO (Sp), 1729-1793.

One of the richest finds to be added to the repertoire of classical piano solo music in the last 15 years is the body of music left by Padre Soler, court musician at the Escorial. Known previously by only a half dozen pieces in collections, Soler now emerges with more than 180 works-- largely discovered, edited and recorded by Frederick Marvin. Thirty-six of them have been published (Mills) in four vols and more are promised. Contemporary with Haydn's works, these

belong to the period of transition from harpsichord to piano,
and carry over the finest of harpsichord devices, while adding a lyric, sustained line that is distinctly pianistic. Much
is made of repeated echo phrases in the harpsichord terraced dynamics manner, with rich and unique bird-call ornamentation, plaintive harmonic sequences, and the dissonant
guitar-chord effects of D. Scarlatti, his older contemporary
at the Spanish court. Almost all are in Scarlatti's binary
form, with a group of related but contrasting themes introduced in the first half, some with abrupt transitions, some
with extended codettas, and the second half developing this
material in sequences modulating widely, but gravitating
back to the tonic for the close. After Scarlatti's 500, it
seems a miracle that the form could yield such a quantity
of fresh and original material. There are also minuets,
rondos and polaccas from AS's late period, as yet unpublished; and ten large sonatas for two keyboards, which sound
well with various combinations of organ-piano-harpsichord.
The Marvin numbering has now become standard.

Nine Sonatas, Vol I: M1 in c. Lively allegro in
3/8, opening with a bold descending octave scale, answered
by a strumming V-IV passage, with elaborate transitions and
codas.   The unusual phrase lengths add to the charm: 5-4-
3-3-4.   Mod

M2 in c. This adagio largo (2/4, but four beats to
the meas) is in the 18th-century pathetic style, and full of
delightful surprises. The second theme is three-part writing, introducing one of AS's favorite devices, a grace-note
ornament on the dim 7th, that has the sound of a birdcall,
as do many of his other trills and ornaments. Six distinct
themes follow each other, and are finely wrought into a
shapely movt. Pairs well with M1 or M3. Mod

M3 in g. Marked allegro, it is played presto by
Frederick Marvin in his recording of the complete sonatas.
Two-and 3-v writing, alternating arpeggios, stair-stepped
passages, accompanied broken-chord figures. Still a new
device introduces the second half, arpeggios alternating with
solid chords. Requires good technic and bravura style.
Mod Dif

M4 in c; M5 in C. A cantabile 4/4 and allegro et
spiritoso assai 3/4; not quite up to the first three, but well
above the average in this prolific period of keyboard writing,
and containing some fine passages. AS was not very adven-

turous in choice of keys, using the same five or six repeat-
edly. Mod

M8 in d; M9 in D. Both marked andante, the minor
one is a plaintive song with a haunting sequence of modulations. No 9 is a stately dance, with a passage that mounts
through three, four and five sharps to end in the key of a
minor. The lengthy coda exploits the V-I resolution with
scales and arpeggios. Mod

12 Sonatas, Vol II: M10 in C. A brilliant toccata
(molto allegro) lines up four showy keyboard figures, repeating each with contrasting dynamics, and puts them (and the
pianist) through their paces. Technically demanding. Dif

M11 in c; M12 in c. Two more in the Padre's favorite minor key, both expressive, though quite different. No
11 is 3/8 allegro presto, though Marvin plays it more like
an andante, with much nuance on the upward-downward chain
of trills. No 12 is andantino C, with a fugal theme that
never develops, but leads to slow arpeggios with avian ornaments. Mod

M13 in B♭. Allegro spirituoso in 3/8 with the form
and character of a playful rondo. Not as easy as it looks.
Mod

M14 in E♭. This begins with the limpid scale figures of a rococo sonata allegro, but soon piles on ornaments
till it ends in lavish baroque style. Mod Dif

M15 in D♭. The rare key leads us to expect something unusual, and we are rewarded with a series of discrete
themes, some gravely paced, some sweeping the keyboard in
bold panache. Mod

M16 in b. Large-scale virtuoso work, with brilliant
and difficult passages of rapid hand crossing, leaping chords,
racing scales and arpeggios. Dif

M17 in e. One of the most unique and expressive,
this adagio has four distinct themes, the first two in 5-meas
phrases, the third a chromatic sequence leading to the mournful coda. Chains of trills and exquisite modulations make up
a short development, with the return of the coda, in e.
Mod

M18 in F♯. This large work is really 2-in-1, equivalent to a pair of the others, its elegant cantabile with its
shimmering trill passages followed by a brilliant allegro
(presto) octave study.   Mod Dif

M19 in f♯.   One of the best, with unpredictable developments and a Spanish tang.   Both Scarlatti and AS pushed
the device of repeated figures to the point where they become
almost as excruciating as the Chinese water-drop torture,
but with a sure instinct for judging at exactly what point to
change the pattern.   Mod Dif

M20 in g; M21 in g.   Two very distinctive sonatas in
the same key.   No 20 is cool, delicate, classical.   No 21
alternates a brilliant prestissimo with a languid cantabile,
which spills over into trills, then a cadenza.   Large hands
help.   Dif

13 Sonatas, Vol III: M23 in c; M24 in c.   The later
books begin to sound repetitious.   Two in this vol are outstanding.   The cantabile in c is marked to be followed by the
next, allegro (like M7 except that here they have two numbers).   Mod

Fandango.   This unique tour de force is indeed a work
sui generis, a 10-min keyboard solo in an authentic dance
form, using throughout a 2-meas basso ostinato, on three
chords in d, relieved only occasionally by a 6- to 8-meas
passage in F, building through sheer velocity and melodic
variation a tremendous climax, culminating, like the original
folk-dance, on an unresolved V^7 chord.   Bach's d min Chaconne does a similar thing for violin; and Ravel, using another Spanish dance, the Bolero, builds excitement with almost exactly inverse means, a relentlessly unvarying beat and
a steady crescendo produced by the addition of instruments,
as more and more dancers join the soloist.   Whether the
Padre's instrument was the piano or the harpsichord, the
achievement is equally impressive.   The accelerando poco a
poco sin al fin is intensified by a steady increase of the number of notes from two to six-to-the-beat, alternating passages
of arpeggiated figures with chromatic scales, folkloric counter-themes, and syncopated drum-chord figures.   First published and recorded by Mr. Marvin in 1957, it has recently
been published by Samuel Rubio (UME-AMP), who has also
recently brought out several of the sonatas (the version favored by Alicia della Rocha).   This edition, "revised and
transcribed for harpsichord," differs from Marvin's mostly

in its (unauthentic) resolution of the final chord; and in its seemingly authentic use of melodic minor for the ostinato, rather than the harmonic used by Marvin. Early descriptions of the dance mention the flatted 7th and 6th in the descending cadential approach to the final dominant. Harpsichordists have the advantage over pianists of being able to couple manuals and add octave registrations for the buildup; but pianists can have fun doing it through sheer speed. Demands drive, endurance, accuracy. Dif

SPINNER, LEOPOLD

Inventions, Op 13 (1967). Five pieces in post-Webern serial style, disjunct, pointillistic "eye-music." Scraps of melody are strewn over the page (with a plethora of accidentals, and no doubt some accidents) the hands wandering and pouncing from one end of the keyboard to the other. (B&H pub) Dif

STARER, ROBERT (Aus-USA), 1924- .

Composer of chamber music and operas, born in Vienna, educated in Jerusalem Conservatory from the age of 14, now teaching in New York.

Five Caprices. Well named, the five short character pieces explore moods and techniques: a melody-playing with chords adagio espressivo, a 2-v invention, a singing andantino, a staccato toccata. Melodic and rhythmic motifs are imaginative, but the prevailing non-tonality may be a deterrent for some. Mod Dif

Lullaby for Amittai. Quiet one-page piece, melodic, pianistic, free harmonic shifts, but reposeful. Mod

Prelude and Toccata (1946). Opening cantabile over shifting chords, varied rhythmic patterns in a driving toccata. Mod Dif

Sonata (1949): Allegro, Andante, Frivole. Big work, traditional in form, original in content, requiring power, legato melody-line. Brilliant finale. Demands mature musicianship. He also has a Sonata No 2. Dif

STEVENS, HALSEY (USA), 1908- .

This music educator, Bartók biographer and composer of symphonies and brass chamber music has written three piano sonatas, and numerous smaller works.

Sonata No 3 (1948). Three-movt, neo-classic, freely chromatic, pianistic and fluent. All movts are based on a germ-motif stated at the beginning. Introspective slow middle movement, followed by bright dashing finale. Mod Dif

Toccata (1948). Light, evanescent work, featuring shifting rhythms in a chromatic texture. Mod

Nepdalszvit (1950). By-product of HS's monumental study of Bartók these eight Magyar dances use melodies collected by Bartók in a fresh, original, yet lively and authentic manner. Mod Dif

STEVENSON, RONALD (GB), 1928- .

Passacaglia on DSCH for D. Shostakovich (1967).
This Op 70, by a relatively unknown composer, is 141 pages in length, and requires 1 hour 20 min to perform. It seems to be a modern attempt at a Kunst der Fugue or Fantasia Contrapuntistica (Busoni). Like the latter work, it has been played by John Ogdon, which means that it is practically unplayable by anyone else. Its three big sections are all derived from the notes D-E♭-C-B, signifying Dimitri. (Shostakovich wrote his own modern counterpart to Bach in his Op 87.) In this gargantuan encyclopedia of neo-Baroque technical devices, a few pages here and there reveal outstanding musical quality. Any artist of integrity, it seems, would have followed Sibelius' advice and "cut away the surplus," leaving something of worth in a viable form. Take it away, Dimitri (and John); it's all yours. (OxU pub) Dif

Peter Grimes Fantasy (1971). There is also a large fantasy on themes from Benjamin Britten's most popular opera. Dif

STILL, WILLIAM GRANT (USA), 1895- .

The first black musician to conduct a symphony, WGS wrote extensively for orchestra and numerous choral and opera works. His piano music is less important, rather derivative and dated, but pianistic and attractive.

Three Visions: (1) Dark Horsemen. Genre pieces in the 19th-century Romantic manner, tonal but exploring new harmonies. The first has a galloping urgency that recalls both Schumann and Schubert. Mod

(2) Summerland. American white composers owe so much to their unknown black counterparts, that it is gratifying to find a black composer writing a piece which, if it only had words, could have been a song by that nice rich white Jewish boy, George Gershwin. Mod

(3) Radiant Pinnacle. The extravagant title belongs to a rather low-key work in flowing 8ths, with ambiguous harmony, an occasional spicy jazz beat, and one rather low hill, for climax. Mod

Seven Traceries. These brief nostalgic miniatures are too dated in their skillful keyboard figures on 9ths and augmented chords to have much appeal. Mod

STOCKHAUSEN, KARLHEINZ (Ger), 1928- .

Acknowledged leader of the plugged-in turned-on school of electronic composition, KS has shown little interest in the piano of late, though he wrote 11 piano pieces in the 50's which continue to be thorns-in-the flesh for pianists. One wishes more composers had the integrity of Rouault, who is reported to have burned several hundred early paintings, after he found his style. There is much more rewarding music for serious pianists and musicians, and these pieces can safely be left for musicologists and composers to break their teeth on.

Piano Pieces, Nos 1 to 11. Nr 2 (KS's designation for Op 2) contains pieces 1 to 4, and is 12 pages long. The others are all published separately, and range from 5 pages (No 8) to 45 (No 6). Few will wish to go beyond the first four, and only Nos 2 and 3 are technically within the range of the normal, non-computerized pianist.   Dif

STRAIT, WILLARD (USA), 1930- .

Structure for Piano. Commissioned to write the surprise number, released at the 11th hour to eliminate incom-
petent contestants for the Second Van Cliburn Quadrennial,
WS produced this toccata-style solo, knotty with rhythmical
and digital problems, but musical and brilliant. The "structure" is not simple, five distinct but linked sections following the introduction. Freely chromatic and polytonal, its
texture is woven of traditional keyboard idioms, and most
any contestant able to play the rest of the required repertoire must have found it cold turkey to play; but tasty.
Could be included on any menu. Dif

STRAVINSKY, IGOR (Rus-USA), 1882-1971.

Musical innovator who, like Picasso, seldom repeated
himself, was acclaimed "the greatest" at the time of his
death. He has made little contribution to piano solo literature, but added some valuable ensemble pieces. His prodi-
gious gift for invention seems to have deserted him when
faced with a keyboard.

Four Etudes, Op 7 (1908). These large chunks of
unpianistic, homogenous granite may safely remain buried,
for the youth of AD 2071 to unearth. Dif

Sonata (1924). Short, light three-movt work, promising much, but ultimately disappointing. An amorphous first
movement in flowing 8ths is followed by an arioso in ornamented Baroque style, and a short moto perpetuo. The total effect is nugatory. Mod

Trois Mouvements de Petrouchka (1921). Since this
ballet was originally conceived as a piano concerto, these
are good to have; but are meant for pianists with brobdingnagian hands, and phenomenal technic. Dif

Serenade en la (1925). Neo-classic work in three
movements, called Hymne, Romanza, and Cadenza finale. In
spite of the fine ideas, monotony and ultimately boredom set

in after page two.   Mod

SURINAC, CARLOS (Sp), 1915- .

Successful Spanish composer of popular orchestral
works evoking ancient Iberia.

Trois Chansons et Danses Espagnoles.   Well written
and pianistic, in a conventional style.   The familiar hemiola
duple-triple shift is a rhythmic feature.   No 3 has the rhapsodic histrionic character of flamenco.   Mod

Sonatina.   Three-movt neo-classic work, charming
if not highly original.   The allegro is both agitated and lyrical; the andantino is languidly melancholy; the finale is a
cheerful scampering rondo.   Mod

SWANSON, HOWARD (USA), 1909- .

The Cuckoo (Scherzo) (1949).   Bewitching little gem,
built on the falling third, with a filigree of birdsong.   Fleet
finger control.   Can be played una corda and senza ped
throughout.   (Wein pub)   Mod

Sonata (1950).   Nineteen-page three-movt work by this
successful black composer of symphonic works.   Written
without key signatures, the music is basically tonal, with
much chromatic alteration.   The work suffers from a lack
of contrast, in rhythm and keyboard figuration, all movements built on similar motifs in a homogeneous texture.
The genial third, an A-B-A allegro vivo is best.   (Wein pub)
Mod

SYDEMAN, WILLIAM (USA), 1928- .

Sonata (1970).   This successful contemporary composer of chamber music has now done his duty by the sonata
form and for the piano, and can go back to "the things he
does so well."   This is a drawing-board work written with
utmost disdain for the keyboard, human hand, and ear.
Period.   (ECS pub)   Dif

SZALONEK, WITOLD (Pol), 1927- .

Mutanza per Pianoforte (1971). Established Polish
composer here adopts the avant-garde approach to the piano
which ignores the keyboard, and uses the harp, soundboard
and case as a source for exotic new sounds. These graphed
procedures are carefully explained in a lengthy introduction,
and include tapping the strings with metal rods and balls,
stroking with a nylon hairbrush, plucking and damping with
plastic sticks. "Grating sounds of differing length, color
and texture" are also called for by rubbing the soundboard
with a nylon cork. No doubt as much fun to watch as to
hear, though it needs a Chico Marx for full effect; and 18
min of it seems a bit much. One is tempted to ask, Why
pick on the piano with the whole battery of orchestral percussion available? The really imaginative composers, like
Harry Parch, have invented new instruments for their new
sounds. (Ch pub) Dif

SZALOWSKI, ANTONI (Pol-Fr), 1907- .

Contemporary Polish composer of orchestral and
chamber works writes in a genial French neo-classic style,
tonal but spiced with dissonance.

Suite for Harpsichord or Piano. Three-movt lightweight work, alternating linear and homophonic writing, sonorous but lucid and transparent. Moderato, tranquillo, animato. (Aug pub) Mod

SZYMANOWSKI, CAROL (Pol), 1883-1937.

One of the few Poles to follow in Chopin's steps as
a composer (there have been many pianists) CS is more
akin to Scriabin in harmony and experimentation. Though
championed by Rubinstein, and admired by Lockwood, his
works have not become popular. Many are extremely difficult, and passionately emotional.

Four Etudes, Op 4. Of these, No 3 in b♭ is best,
with a fine moody canzone con dolore in octaves, above a

harmonically opulent bass, with fragmentary counter-themes, sweeping ornamental scales and arpeggios, a wide dynamic range. Mod Dif

Three Sonatas. The first two of these are written in the post-Romantic Scriabinesque manner; the third in an experimental late style. Sonata No 2, highly complex and difficult, is analyzed in detail by Lockwood. Dif

Metopes, Op 29. Fascinated by the antique, CS titled these after three Greek legends represented in sculpture. Though thick-textured, the effect is tenuous and fragmentary. Dif

Masques, Op 34. Mediaeval comedy provides these three works with programs; see above for style. Mod Dif

12 Etudes, Op 33. The late style, bitonal, unresolved, and meaty. A set of 12 concert works, highly diversified and imaginative, and musically effective once the technical obstacles have been mastered. Recommended are No 3, a vivacious two-page toccata; No 5, an expressive andante (four lines only) that is highly chromatic but basically E♭; No 6, a Scriabinesque chord-study; the espressivo No 8; and the brilliant moto perpetuo finale. Dif

50 Mazurkas in 5 Vol. In the dances the formidable barrier of technical complexity is lowered, and an authentic Polish zal comes through the dissonant and surprising harmonies. The first four have recorded by Rubinstein, and are beautiful modern offshoots of Chopin's root. Dif

TAJCEVIC, MARKO (Yug), 1900- .

Seven Balkan Dances. This Yugoslav folk music authority and choral composer has written seven brilliant piano pieces based on Serbian melodic and rhythmic patterns, very pianistic, varied and attractive. Mod Dif

TAKACS, JENO (Hun), 1902- .

Hungarian pianist who has taught in Manila and Cairo and composed a Philippine Suite and Nile Legend for

orchestra, wrote several piano pieces, of which this available work is representative.

Toccata (1948). Brilliant four-min recital piece,
basically tonal with bitonal passages. (Uni pub) Mod

TAKAHASHI, YUJI (Jap), 1931- .

Chromomorphe No 2 (1964); Metathesis (1968); Rosace
No 2 (1968). Phenomenal Japanese pianist rivalling David
Tudor in his reifying of the most obscure contemporary scores
(Cage, Xenakis) in which style he also composes. Recently
his piano works have employed computer programming of
piano sounds according to pitch, density, intensity, distribu-
tion. The visual experience of a performance is much more
rewarding than the aural; so don't bother to get the records.
There is no reason why this kind of noise cannot be produced just as efficiently by the computer itself; but it would
not be as picturesque.

TAKATA, SABURO (Jap), 1913- .

Graduate of Tokyo Academy has become a successful composer with numerous chamber works. Himself not
a concert pianist, he has written well for the instrument in
a traditional tonal style in, for example, his two sonatas.

Five Preludes (1949). These are his most repre-
sentative work, combining impressionist and program ele-
ments in a fluent keyboard texture of considerable variety.
The titles of the pieces give an idea of the style: "By the
Dark Blue Marsh"; "The Sunlight Dances in the Wind";
"The Wild Pigeon"; 'Down in the Blue Valley"; "Mountains
Fading into the Twilight." The pieces evoke the Orient with-
out actually incorporating Japanese material. Mod

TAKEMITSU, TORU (Jap), 1930- .

Two Lentos (1950); Piano Distance (1960); Corona
for Pianist (1962). Prize-winning festival-featured avant-
garde composer, now represented on records by 10 works,

mostly electronic. His early Two Lentos caused a sensation in Japan by their unorthodox juxtaposition of two slow
movts, expressive but freely non-tonal. More recent works
(Asterism, Arc) combine piano and orchestra with electronic sounds. Piano Distance, an amorphous improvisory disjunct work exploring various piano sonorities and involving
the breathing of the pianist, was premiered by Y. Takahashi in Manila at the Festival of Musics of Asia in 1966.
It is said to seek "an expression similar to that found in
the Noh play" [Ueno]. In Corona for Pianist, TT collabo-
rated with a designer to produce a work printed on five colored squares of paper, the music written in two concentric
circles, and placing great reliance on the performer's creativity, taste and temperament.

TALMA, LOUISE (USA), 1906- .

    Sonata No 1 (1943). Chalk up another success for
Women's Liberation. The Sonata No 1 was a prize winner
in 1947. Large-scale 3-movt work, pianistic, varied chordal largo introduction; first movt is a driving allegro molto
vivace. Second movt is chordal and melodic in chamber-
music style in quartal harmony. Presto finale in toccata
style with much use of ostinato, repeated note figures with
irregular rhythms, building to a finish. (CF pub 1948)
Mod Dif

    Six Etudes. Chopin-inspired but contemporary in free
tonality, they are virtuoso studies on six technical problems.
No 2 develops velocity; No 3 is a legato study, with use of
sostenuto pedal; No 4 develops accuracy in leaping chords;
all require endurance and control. (GSch pub) Dif

    Alleluia, in form of Toccata (1947). Highly original
5-min work. Introductory declamatory section in octaves on
a two-note motif leads to a rapid joyous allegro vivace,
largely in two voices, one a sort of boogie-woogie bass of
light staccato eighth notes, while the other does detached
four- to five-note motifs (Al-le-lu-i-a). It has the look (but
not the sound) of a Scarlatti sonata. Sustained cantabile
middle. All these combine in an exciting climax with the
added fun of a superimposed jazz beat. Probably meant to
be played with the quiet Pastoral Prelude. (CF pub) Dif

TANSMAN, ALEXANDRE (Pol-Fr), 1897- .

One of many Poles who, like Chopin, lived out their
lives in Paris, AT writes in an eclectic style incorporating
elements from Chopin to Debussy, Gershwin to Stravinsky.
His enormous output includes much teaching material. There
is little assimilation of the many disparate styles, and most
of the music sounds derivative.

Sonatine Transatlantique (1930). His most popular
piece, this has been orchestrated and choreographed. It
uses jazz and popular rhythms throughout, with a slow blues
and spiritual, between movements called Fox-trot and Charles-
ton. Mod

Trois Préludes en Formes de Blues. A Gershwin-
esque attempt to blend early "soul" music and classic form.
Mod

Quatre Préludes. Another Blues number opens this
set, followed by a tribute to Ravel. The third owes much to
Scriabin. A moderato, moving from deciso to grazioso is
the fourth. Mod

Mazurkas, Books I and II. An atavistic urge to express the Polish zal has produced two uneven sets of dances.
E to Mod

Intermezzi (1940) Quatre Series. Exploration of a
more dissonant harmony, in 24 studies of moderate length,
more than average difficulty. AT's tune-mongering extends
even to his own works, No 21 of this set doubling as slow
movement for Sonata No 4. No 19 is a tribute to Charlie
Chaplin. Mod Dif

Trois Ballades (1941). The title only is borrowed
from Chopin. The three large-scale works are more complex and acerbic than earlier AT. Dif

Suite dans le Style Ancien. Here AT has a go at
classic dance forms, in a pseudo-Bach style, including a 4-
v choral-fugue. Mod

Sonata No 3; No 4. The third is lighter, easier,
more French; the fourth, Teutonic in its chromaticism, in-

tensity of expression, and complexity.   Mod Dif

TCHAIKOVSKY, PETER I. (Rus), 1840-1893.

The enormous success of a piano concerto does not
guarantee that a man will be a first-rate piano composer.
PIT was much more at home with symphonic and ballet music than at the keyboard. (There are two other concertos,
both with qualities.) Most of the piano pieces are pot-
boilers, written in haste for a deadline, technically simple
and rather pedestrian.

The Seasons, Op 37. Ground out, one a month, for
the publisher, this set of 12 has yielded two that are still
played: a June Barcarolle has fluid charm; the November
Troika is lively.   Mod E

Song Without Words, Op 2:3; Romance, in f, Op 5;
Humoresque in G, Op 10:2; Chanson Triste in g, Op 40:2.
Good recital material for the advanced child.   The Humor-
esque is an attractive staccato study, with a contrasting
Russian choral passage.   Mod

Six Pieces, Op 19: Scherzo humoristique; Nocturne
in c#; Theme and Variations in F.   The pieces in this set
are longer and more demanding, and three have musical interest.   The PIT of the symphonic scherzos and ballets can
be heard in the No 2; and the master of the long melodic
line in the Nocturne.   In No 6, both the theme and the variations are attractive, flawed only by a weak ending.   Mod
Dif

Sonata in G, Op 37a.   A devoted keyboard genius can
occasionally bring this angular, sprawling work to life.   PIT
was always plagued with the problem of linking his themes;
and the moments of beauty are often lost between the stitch-
ery of the seams.   Four-movts.   Dif

Dumka, Op 59.   A fresh and attractive work, in spite
of the monotonous harmony, this captures the bucolic charm
of a "Russian Country Scene," and gives the pianist some
fun and games (10 min).   Mod Dif

TCHEREPNIN, ALEXANDER (Rus-USA), 1899- .

Prolific composer-pianist whose cosmopolitan background seems to militate against his forming a style of his
own.   Born in St. Petersburg, son of a composer-conductor, AT has lived in Paris, Shanghai, Tokyo, Chicago and
New York, teaching, publishing, performing and producing
a third generation of composers (see below).   His music,
much of it written for specific pupils or occasions, is fluent, pianistic, sometimes piquant and original, reflecting
its milieu, but more often superficial and derivative.   A
few of the more characteristic works are listed below.

10 Bagatelles, Op 5.   Two- to three-page pieces of
great variety and moderate difficulty, possibly the best of
AT.   They have been arranged by the composer with orchestra accompaniment.   Mod

Eight Preludes, Op 9.   Similar to the Bagatelles,
effective and attractive.   Mod

Chinese Bagatelles, Op 51:3.   Twelve short simple
pieces (in 12 keys) mostly 2-v, using the anhematonic pentatonic (avoiding fa and ti).   Though only two use actual Chinese melodies, all have an authentic air, and are fresh and
attractive.   AT avoids the pitfalls of the pseudo-Oriental by
harmonizing this essentially monodic music with 4ths, 5ths,
unisons and octaves, with occasional 2nds to suggest percussion, street noises, etc.   Mod E

Five Concert Studies, Op 52: Shadow Play; The Lute;
Homage to China; Punch and Judy; Chant.   These also reflect the China visits, but are more brilliant concert works
(perhaps played by Mme. Tcherepnin, née Lee Hsien-Ming).
What they gain in brilliance, they lose in authenticity and
charm.   No 1 is the most effective.   No 5 is a setting of
the ancient "Fisherman's song."   Mod Dif

Show-Case (1946).   From the Paris years, five longer pieces suggested by glass animal figurines.   The 1st
two, Greyhounds and The Cow, seem to belong to the pentatonic Chinese series; others are more programmatic: Crabs,
The Frog, The Weasel, The Deer.   Mod Dif

Songs without Words, Op 82 (1953).   These sound

like youthful compositions réchauffé for publication. Five
pleasant, pianistic 19th-century pieces, with a Moussorgskian melancholy (and Russian sub-titles). AT has also written
six piano concertos, and a suite for harpsichord.

TCHEREPNIN, SERGE (USA), 1941- ; and TCHEREPNIN,
IVAN (USA), 1943- .

The sons in the third generation of this dynasty of
composers have turned to electronic music. "Light Music
with Water" (1970) by Ivan T, who teaches at Leland Stan-
ford University, is for four instrumental groups, four sound-
activated strobe lights, electronic accessories and prepared
tape. Ivan's "Four Pieces from Before" (1957-62), written
while a teenager, and privately published by a fond parent,
are not representative. Neither are the three student essays, in serial writing, by Serge, now composing for films.

THOMPSON, VIRGIL (USA), 1896- .

Influential critic, author, autobiographer (Virgil
Thompson), VT will probably be remembered for his operas
with texts by Gertrude Stein. His simplistic music texture,
homophonic, triadic, diatonic, is sometimes straightforward,
sometimes satirical, though the humor is almost as innocuous as the music.

Five Two-Part Inventions. Uninventive two-part writing, tonal with splashes of dissonance and humorous allu-
sions to Bach. Mod

10 Etudes. More inventive than the above, these ex-
ploit various keyboard effects such as: Repeating Tremolo,
Tenor Lead, Fifths, various types of glissandi, For the
Weaker Fingers, Oscillating Arm, and Ragtime Bass. Mod

Four Sonatas. Short, lightweight neo-classical works,
described as "witty, nonchalant and delightful" by Gillespie.
Mod E

Portraits, Vol I, II, III and IV. A few of these 40
works (10 in each book) will go a long way, as the "sitters"

soon begin to look alike. The "wrong-note" Portrait of
Picasso, subtitled "Birds and Bugles" is representative,
with its bi-tonality, humor through interminable repetition
of an inane figure, waltzes and marches superimposed, with
white-key scales and black-key chords. Perhaps intended
to "serve Picasso right" for making musicians look so square
and ugly. Mod

THORNE, FRANCIS (USA), 1922- .

A rara avis among composers--philanthropist of muni-
ficent music grants, and recognized avant-garde composer.

Eight Introspections (1966). Pianistic miniatures
(each two pages) moody or ebullient, highly dissonant. (EBM
pub) Mod Dif

TIPPETT, MICHAEL (GB), 1905- .

Successful neo-classic composer of works for chorus
and instruments, MT has two sonatas for piano.

Fantasy Sonata (1938). Two-movt, tonal work opening with variations contrasting clear linear part writing with
succulent harmonic passages richly woven; followed by a
taut, propulsive finale, relating thematically to other parts.
Mod Dif

Sonata No 2 (1962). Single movement modified rondo
form, stating and developing a series of episodes in varying
meters, in a linear, freely chromatic, but lean and objective
style, eschewing effusive expression. Mod

TOCH, ERNST (Aus-USA), 1887-1964.

Brilliant autodidact musician who began his career
winning Mozart and Mendelssohn prizes in Vienna and finished
it winning the Pulitzer Prize in Hollywood. Besides film music and Symphonies (No 3 won the Pulitzer in 1955) he wrote
three large experimental piano sonatas, and numerous suites.
His best pieces are in a light, bright staccato style that soon

becomes obsessive and undistinguished. If one may venture
a pun, Toch seems always to be writing Toc-catas. Tempos
are fast and a good finger technic is mandatory.

Burlesken, Op 31. Three toccati, all in 2/4 without
key signature, but generously peppered with flats and sharps.
Obviously composed at the keyboard, where ET's hands keep
straying back to the same busy patterns, occasionally varying the steady rat-tat-tat of 16ths with brief 8th or quarter-
note motifs. No 3 is called The Juggler and the coda is
quasi xylophone, molto martellato, over a tremolo bass. A
very fast tempo helps. Dif

Caprichetti, Op 36. Five brief sketches, two quiet
one-page andantes separating the busy ones. Neither key nor
time signatures. Mod Dif

Profiles, Op 68. Six pieces, similar to the above.
Mod Dif

Ideas. The title seems to be carried out mostly in
the names and markings. No 2 is "A Black Dot Dances in
My Closed Eye." The "ideas" in the music are jejune, tired
and overworked. Mod

Sonata, Op 47. Here the toccata (quasi) leads off in
the first movt, though the third might well be another. After a quiet genial Intermezzo, that hammering starts up
again. When it becomes almost unbearable, the coup de
grace is given with a quiet coda. Dif

Three Little Dances, Op 85. No 1 is written for
black-key pentatonic scale, in a graceful flowing style; No 2
uses only white keys, in a rustic, bumptious dance; the third
gives equal time to whites and blacks, in a vigorous chromatic movement. Mod Dif

Reflections, Op 86. At the age of 75 one is entitled
to reflect. Contemporary looking, without time or key signatures, the five one-page sketches are only mildly dissonant. Mod Dif

TRAVIS, ROY (USA), 1924- .

Conductor and composer of chamber music.

Five Preludes.   Pianistic works in free-tonality,
gratifyingly short and listenable.   Martial first; lyric second;
third grazioso; undulating boat-song; boisterous close.   Recital.   Mod

TREMBLAY, GILLES (Can), 1932- .

Phases et Réseaux (1956-58).   Avant-garde Canadian
who more recently has combined electronics and instruments,
here explores, with great imagination and originality, piano
sonorities alone.   Rhythmically and melodically amorphous,
the "phases" hammer out simple bass intervals (an augmented 4th), then let the overtones resound through various pedal
and keyboard devices.   The second work, "Networks," carries the same technic further, expanding the overtones into
arabesques and figures, high in the treble range derived from
the booming bass fields of sonority.   A pupil of Messiaen
and Martinot, his most recent work suggests a return of impressionistic evocations, with the title "Le Sifflement des
Vents Porteurs de l'Amour" (flute-percussion, 71).   Dif

TRUBITT, ALLEN (USA), 1931- .

Six Philippine Folk Songs for Piano Solo.   From that
melting pot in the Pacific, Hawaii, comes a set of arrangements, simple enough for teaching, but artistic enough for
a program needing an international touch.   Freely harmonized with dissonant and quartal chords, counter subjects,
melo-rhythmic basses, they are contrasting and evocative.
(SMF pub)   Mod E

TUPAS-GIRON, BENJAMIN (Phil), 1930- .

Brilliant Filipino pianist-teacher, student of Myra
Hess, has two compositions for piano: one is Elegy (1955).

Toccata (1956).   Spirited virtuoso study with RH ro-
tating on octave-4th figures, LH overlapping and crossing to
provide bass pedals and a lilting, syncopated bi-tonal melody motif.   (ACH pub)   Dif

TURINA, JOAQUIN (Sp), 1882-1949.

Spanish composer who wrote copiously for piano, in a casual, semi-popular salon style. His more than 25 suites of pieces almost all bear Spanish place names, and many use dance or folk-song rhythms and melodies. The keyboard writing is fluent, facile and undistinguished. A few representative works from the long list are named here.

Sonata romantica Sobre una Tema Española (1905). An attempt at a large-scale 19th-century keyboard work, using the Spanish song, "El Vito," as thematic material for the opening set of variations, and also for the scherzo and finale. Requires mature technic. Dif

Sanlúcar de Barrameda, Op 24 (1922). Described by JT as a pictorial sonata, this is possibly his best work. Its three movts are scenes: I, "In the Tower of the Castle"; II, "Portrait of a Woman"; III, "The Beach" and "The Fisherman." The last movt begins with an atmospheric introduction; then builds an impressive 4-v fugue on a Spanish theme. Brilliant, well-structured and pianistic (about 20 min). Dif

Danzas Gitanas I, II (1930-35). Ten Spanish Gipsy dances (in 2 vol), of moderate length and difficulty, but lacking the authenticity and keyboard distinction of "the three." Mod

El Circo Suita (1931). Typical of the many suites, this has six numbers. A jaunty two-page chordal Fanfare opens the circus, and serves as coda. The jugglers is moto perpetuo, 6/8 in two-finger-typist style, with a brief suave melody. After a brief quote from the Fanfare, the bareback riders appear, a vivo 3/8. The Trained Dog attempts a clumsy gavotte; Clowns is alternately lively and pseudo-sad; Trapeze Artists suggests aerial acts with arpeggios and trills. Mod E

VALEN, FARTEIN (Nor), 1887-1952.

Norwegian composer who, working in isolation, arrived at a style similar to serialism, using tone-rows in a

polyphonic texture. His melo-rhythmic motifs are not strong
and original enough to make his works significant.

Sonata: The Hound of Heaven (1941). The program
idea, classical form and experimental idiom fail to crystal-
lize into a viable work. Good for an occasional hearing.
Dif

Variations, Op 23. A row and its backward version,
stated in single notes, forms the theme, followed by 12 variations that intensify to a climax, and terminate in a quiet
coda. Dif

Prelude and Fugue, Op 28. Two-v prelude, freely
chromatic. Extended 3-v fugue in the style of a Bachian
gigue. Dif

VALLIER, JOHN (GB)

Variations on John Peel (1964). Pleasant surprise
to find a familiar tune treated in a traditional form. Twelve
variations range from the playful to the wistful, the boisterous to the brilliant and exhibitionist. Long but effective.
(Gal pub) Mod Dif

VILLA-LOBOS, HEITOR (Bra), 1887-1959.

Prolific and exuberant composer, his researches in
native folk song and dance led him to determine to write only
music based on these sources. In spite of this limitation,
he has greatly enriched the piano repertory, evolving his
own eclectic idiom. Rubinstein and Guiomar Novaes introduced abroad works which have now become standard repertoire. There are many books of children's pieces, based on
folk song. The following sets are all concert material.

The Three Maries (1939): Ainitah, Alnilam, Mintika.
Legend as well as folk scales imbue these with charm and
humor. Contrasting lyric and fast staccato chord passages.
Mod

Cirandas (1926). Sixteen pieces in virtuoso style,
based on folk material. Seven or eight are outstanding, and

can be played separately.   Mod Dif

Prolo do Bebe [Baby's Dolls], Book I: ' Porcelain
Doll, Paper Doll, Clay Doll, Rubber Doll, Wooden Doll,
Rag Doll, Punch, Witch Doll. Written to entertain Octavio
Pinto's children, these are all deservedly popular for their
pianistic and musical quality.   Chiming fragile effects are
achieved with pedal points and ornaments in the first.   The
Clay Doll is a sultry samba, with complex counter rhythms.
The Rubber Doll is full of bounce, freely rubato.   The Rag
Doll sounds plaintive and simple, and is a highly complex
blending of four motifs.   Most popular of all, Punchinello
is a brilliant breathless moto perpetuo, guaranteed to call
for an encore.   Bruxa, the Witch Doll, is alternately threatening and pleading, and builds a fine climax for the set.
Impressionistic, yet distinctly Villa-Lobos.

Prolo do Bebe, Book II: Paper Bug, Cardboard Cat,
Rubber Dog, Glass Wolf.   The nine pieces in the second set
of dolls are more difficult and less spontaneous--an idea
carried too far.   The animal titles have little to do with the
music, though there is a sort of animal spirit of irrepres-
sible exuberance.   Most are in a Latin duple rhythm with
busy figures suggestive of bongo drums, against two, three
or four melodic and harmonic themes and chords.   The first
four are best, all combining a plaintive theme and brilliant
keyboard writing.   The Rubber Dog is in 11/8 time with
measures of 6 and 7/8, a Lisztian cadenza, and a series of
barks for coda.   The closing piece (Glass Wolf) is a wild
virtuoso toccata.   Dif

Floral Suite: Summer Idyl, Singing Lass, Joy in the
Garden.   Rubinstein popularized the last of these.   A sense
of high-spirited joy permeates the dance-like movement.   The
first two are more lyrical, though the second builds a climax.   Mod Dif

Alma Brasileira (Choros No 5).   Few composers have
succeeded in being at the same time nationalistic and regional, and universal in appeal.   HVL's unique keyboard style
enabled him to raise his material to the level of a fine art.
This is a lament, with a plaintive cantabile theme above purling broken-chord figures.   Mod Dif

Dansa (Bachianas Brasileiras, 4).   The large set of
"Brazilian Bachiana" is unique with works for eight 'cellos
and soprano, chorus and brass, etc.   This vigorous dance

uses all VL's best devices, a folk-theme over flowing figures, dissonant bass ostinato, fiery coda.   Mod Dif

Rudepoema.   This lengthy "Rough Poem," written for
Rubinstein, is indeed rough on the pianist, extremely difficult, but musical, though somewhat amorphous.   It was later
orchestrated.   Dif

VOLKMANN, ROBERT (Boh), 1815-1883.

Variations on a Theme by Handel.   A contemporary
of the great first generation Romantics, RV spent his life
teaching and composing in Prague.   Though most of his piano pieces are negligible miniatures in the genrestück style
of Schumann and Mendelssohn, his large set of variations on
Handel's Harmonious Blacksmith might well be recorded and
performed by the new generation of Romantics.   They add a
lush harmony to Handel's classic tune, a great variety of
character and ornamental variations, and an interminable
finale.   Dif

WALKER, GEORGE (USA), 1922- .

Works by this black American composer-pianist-edu-
cator include chorus and song settings.   His keyboard music
is all pianistically idiomatic, finely structured and large-
scale.   (GMP pub)

Sonata No 1 (1953): Allegro feroce.   The first sonata
is basically c♯, though the harmony is freely chromatic and,
in the first movt, often quartal.   A bold single-note theme
doubles into octaves then speeds up into rapid figures, well-
deployed, to bridge to a lyrical and richly contrapuntal second theme.   The strong rhythm is varied by shifting meters;
the development builds to a fine frenzy in unison octaves,
which also provide a climactic coda.

Moderato (second movt).   Six variations on a Kentucky
folk song, "O Bury Me Beneath the Willow," form a superb
middle movt, able to stand alone as a program item.   Highly imaginative and contrasting, the short sections include inverted canonic imitations, powerful martellato octaves, an
espressivo with bell-like pedal-points, folk-dance and toccata
styles.

Allegro con brio (third movt). In the stunning last
movt, a ringing c♯ octave approached by minor 2nds above
and below forms the first motif; for a second theme, another
folk tune, dancey and lilting. The short movt ends bravura.
Demands full technic and musicianship. Dif

Sonata No 2 (1960). More taut and finely-wrought,
this four-movt work takes less than 10 min to play. Whereas the first used quartal intervals and chords, the melodic
motifs in all movts here are major-minor 3rd figures, giving it an organic unity carried out by a return of the opening theme for finale.

Adagio non troppo (first movt). Though the first
movt is laid out as a theme (g) of 4-meas with 10 variations (also mostly 4-meas) and coda, the ear is unaware of
divisions, and hears a continuously unfolding line with wonderful diversity and very idiosyncratic keyboard figures,
like a passacaglia that conceals its repetitions. The mood
is urgent and portentous.

Presto (second movt). Jazzy syncopation suggesting
a barn-dance contrasts the second, with brief disjunct figures, staccato-legato, joining for a long melodic line.

Adagio (third movt). A broad, moving cantabile,
5/4, in the tenor is answered by a plaintive arabesque in
the treble, all parts doubling and multiplying for the ff climax; the ending fades to ppp, but maintains the range from
resounding bass to chiming treble.

Allegretto tranquillo (fourth movt). A theme in G,
related to the presto opens the fourth quietly, but quickly
builds to a whirlwind, with the portentous opening theme and
octave arpeggios for coda. Dif

Spatials (1960). This effective 3-min work is a set
of six variations organized entirely on a tone row. It appears six times in the statement, the rows overlapping like
run-on lines in free-verse, to form linear, 2-v, chordal
motifs. The first variation uses the retrograde row, relating to the statement in general movement of voices and shape
of motifs. Two of the brief variations introduce a sustained
voice; and all except the last two, which are linked, end with
a cadence--sometimes delayed, sometimes carried over and
surprisingly resolved. Dif

Spektra (1970).   In a free fantasia form, this 3 min
30 sec piece explores piano color and dynamic intensities in
a series of rapid arabesques ranging over the keyboard like
UFOs (and requiring five staves for notation on the last
page).   Chords form distant constellations, with delicate
tremolo clouds, static messages tapped on a single key.
Amorphous, but heartening in its demonstration that there
is still life in the old keyboard, without resort to gadgets.
Dif

WARD, ROBERT (USA), 1917- .

Opera composer, bandmaster, educator and editor,
RW has one published piano work that makes us want more.

Lamentation.   This fine elegiac four-page 4-min work
builds from a d minor opening to a powerful histrionic climax, then subsides.   Tonal but original and pianistic.   A
good slow program item.   Mod Dif

WARD-STEINMAN, DAVID (USA), 1936- .

Three Lyric Preludes (1969).   Eminent California
composer of chamber music has just published these.
Marked "for keyboard instrument," there is a footnote suggesting organ or piano, thus introducing at the same time
an aleatoric element and a revival of a Renaissance and
Baroque practice.   The simple linear-chordal texture seems
to require organ color, and the long pedal-points, a pedal
bass.   They are marked Moderately fast, Very slow, and
Not too slow, and much dynamic contrast and rubato are indicated.   The last gathers momentum and volume for a climax with a scale and chords of the 9th, and a coda using
two-octave white-key chord clusters, pp.   Mod

WEBER, BEN (USA), 1916- .

Established composer of chamber and symphonic
works, has a concerto and several solo works.

Five Bagatelles (1939).   Brief sketches experiment-

ing with tone-rows, pianistic and expressive. No 1 is a 2-
v study, scherzando; No 2, an elegiac Canzonetta; then a
2-v presto; an intense climactic adagio No 4; and a driving
finale marcato. Mod Dif

Suite No 2, Op 27. Four-piece set of highly contrasted serial pieces--imaginative, pianistic, well-deployed
--though the presto finale requires accuracy in large skips
in tricky rhythms. Mod Dif

Fantasia (Variations). A serial work that manages
to sound tonal, this unique set of seven variations continues
with an interlude, and a passacaglia with five more variations and a free fantasy for close. Effective and affective;
8 min. Dif

WEBER, CARL MARIA von (Ger), 1786-1826.

The piano was still new when CMvW wrote, and his
works combine classic form, expressive content, and a new
"Spiel-Freude" (playing-joy) that demands good technic.
Less original and inspired than those in whose shadow he
lived--Haydn, Beethoven and Schubert--and harmonically inhibited, with pages of V-I chords, his once popular works
are now enjoying a revival.

Invitation to the Dance, Op 65. Once a ubiquitous
program number, this series of varied waltzes with the
imaginative opening "invitation," has brilliant keyboard writing, flawed only by the persistent I-V harmony. Mod Dif

Momento Capriccioso, Op 12; Rondo Brillante, Op 62.
An early and a late work, showing how little the composer
developed harmonically. The first anticipates the staccato
spriteliness of Mendelssohn's fairy music. In the second
the monotony of harmony and repetition are offset by brilliant keyboard figures.

Sonatas No 1 in C, Op 24; No 2 in A♭, Op 39. No
1 is a large-scale four-movt work, well unified, contrasting
declamatory and dainty writing, with CMvW's favorite moto
perpetuo finale. Rated the best of the four sonatas by Ogdon (Matthews). Friskin and Freundlich place No 2 first for
its nobility, lyricism and brilliance. Both Mod Dif

Sonata No 3 in d, Op 49; No 4 in e, Op 70. The
sparkling closing rondo of No 3 is often played separately.
All of the sonatas improve after the first movt. No 4 has
a rippling, purling Minuetto, a pensive andante, and a dashing tarantelle. Both Dif

WEBERN, ANTON von (Aus), 1883-1945.

This Schönberg disciple, who carried his guru's 12-
tone non-repeating weapon to the point of diminishing returns,
had an enormous fascination for composers of the 60's, who
formed a cult, convinced that there was an Ultima Thule
still unmapped. Fortunately AvW had the sense to write only one piano piece, realizing that his "maximum use of minimal material" extended to non-repetition of timbre and range
was best served by a motley assortment of 12 instruments,
one for each gun. If tenors are singers with resonance
where their brains should be, most pianists are machines
with switchboards where their minds should be, sometimes
with a large or small soul attached. For these player-
pianos--par'n me, piano-players--the "post-Webern" school
of composition has little appeal, a fact which may account
for the 19th-century revival of the 70's, as well as for a
new trend toward aural-manual oriented composition.

Variations, Op 27 (1936). This rather charming and
innocuous three-movt suite is over in 5 min 35 sec. The
three movts are clearly defined, even the row in its prime
and retrograde forms is sharply etched in the first, which
is quiet, introspective and has a surprisingly ternary sound.
Bold bright rhythmic patterns stand out in the middle passage. The last movt is linear, with varied versions, introducing chordal punctuation, and a quiet coda, restating the
row. Pianists with only a switchboard mind, and musical
sensitivity, need not be deterred. Those with curious minds
may wish to study the countless analyses of AvW's process
(Matthews, Salzman, et al.). Mod

WELLESZ, EGON (Aug-GB), 1885- .

This distinguished professor at Oxford University will
probably be remembered more for his musicological writings
than for his compositions. He was a prolific composer, and

piano music from various periods of his long life reflects his researches and surroundings, though adding little that is viable to the repertoire.

Five Epigrammes, Op 17 (1913). Five contrasting sketches, elegant and pianistic in the manner of R Strauss and Reger, though No 3 is more experimental. Called "Vision," it reminds us that this is the time and place of origin of Freudian psychology, which influenced Expressionist and Surrealist painters. Mod

Five Idylls, Op 21 (1917). Impressionist mood pictures with narrative elements, in a dissolving harmony. Mod

Five Dance Pieces, Op 42 (1927). The musical milieu has changed, with the arrival of Schönberg, Bartók and Stravinsky, and these works explore dissonance and polytonality in a linear style similar to Hindemith. Mod

Triptychon, Op 98. Serial technics and dissonant counterpoint are the scholar's interest here. Mod

Studies in Gray, Op 106 (1970). The composer succeeds in creating a monochromatic effect, through vague, uniform melodic and harmonic motifs, lacking definition or direction. Mod

WILLIAMSON, MALCOLM (Ausl), 1936- .

This prolific Australian composer has been most successful with chamber music, operas, symphonic works. Has a piano concerto, and three sonatas.

Sonata (1956). Brief three-movt tonally-anchored pianistic. Pithy linear and chordal writing with contrasting slow movt between two fast outer ones, which use wide-spaced chords, dissonant counterpoint, shifting rhythms. Like Ravel's Sonatina, MW's three movts all employ the rising or falling 5th motif. Dif

Five Preludes (1966): Ships; Towers; Domes; Theatres; Temples. Beautiful paper music, with pages that look as interesting as Debussy, written on three staves; and intriguing titles. However the static chords (often only

tonic-6/4), the unrelated successions of tonic triads in a
1920's syncopation, the bare octaves and quartal chords are
largely lacking in any aural appeal, though evidently intended
to be impressionistic.   Add to this the absence of any technical challenge to the player, and one understands why young
pianists are digging up those 19th-century war-horses, the
3 R's (Rheinberger-Ries-Rubinstein) or the 3 H's (Herz-
Hiller-Hummel).   (Wein pub) Mod

WÖLFL, JOSEPH (Aus), 1773-1812.

Re-entry into the hall of fame is being sought for
this once admired piano virtuoso and rival of Beethoven, by
the Society for Forgotten Music (founded by the late Vernon
Duke).   He is variously claimed to have written 30, 58 and
125 piano sonatas, during his brief career in Salzburg, Vienna, Paris and London.   He seems to have been a facile
improvisor; his works are of very uneven quality.   One published by William Newman is imposing, and gives the impression of a man born too late, with a fluent gift for counterpoint in an age when that was despised.

Sonata in c précédé d'un Introduction & Fugue.   A
dramatic four-line adagio (similar to Mozart's Fantasy, K
475) provides thematic material for a 4-v fugue that is both
correct and musical, and for a shapely allegro, with rather
inert harmony.   Here and in the adagio the music stirs from
time to time when JW starts off with a promising counter-
theme or canon; then, suddenly remembering that this is a
sonata, drops back into a hum-drum chordal-figure style.
A few chances for his contrapuntal skill crop up in the lively rondo, and one of the episodes derives from the Introduction.   Mod

Sonata in d, Op 33:2.   Shorter, three-movt work in
18th-century style, light in texture.   The andante has a
fresh lyric quality, and the closing alla polacca may be taken
to indicate the uninhibited way in which JW treated the sacred Sonata form.   Mod

Sonata in E.   An 11 min, three-movt work, similar
to the above.   Mod

WOLPE, STEFAN (Ger-USA), 1902-1972.

Distinguished chamber-music composer whose works reflect his Russian-Palestinian background, and successive interest in jazz atonality, and serialism.

Dance (in form of a chaconne) (1941). Short dissonant work, driving and propulsive. Dif

Passacaglia (1936). Lengthy serious work linked by eight-meas ground-bass, exploring chromatic harmony on all intervals from minor 2nds to 9ths. Dif

Pastorale. Quiet linear work, freely non-tonal but cantabile. Mod

YARDUMIAN, RICHARD (USA), 1917- .

Composer of several symphonic works, a violin and a piano concerto, weaves Middle Eastern color from his Armenian ancestry into his rather monochromatic music.

Three Preludes (1945). Brief atmospheric sketches in simple linear and chordal style, titled The Wind, The Sea, The Sky. Mod

Chromatic Sonata (1947). This three-movt work alternates passages of dance music in irregular Eastern meters with a choral movt and figures derived from the ululating cantillation of narrative song. Mod

Prelude and Chorale (1949). Two brief contrasting sections using the same qualities and elements. Mod

ZATMAN, ANDREW (USA), 1945- .

I resent the "b" in the next entry's name, which prevents AZ from being the last. He is the youngest composer represented, and if he continues his dual pianist-composer career, may one day wish to renounce these youthful works as "formative." It may be that among the next generation of composers, who so obviously have firm roots in the past, some will fulfill Thomas Mann's Prophecy.

24 Preludes (1965). The Chopkin key-cycle still attracts, though AZ acknowledges a debt to Shostakovich, Stravinsky and Poulenc. They range from introspective nocturne-like pieces to vigorous bi-tonal marches, a whirling saltarello, a minuet, a gigue. All are pianistic, but the opening and closing ones are most exciting.

Sonata No 2 (1967). More a sonatina than a sonata, though this 11-min work uses sonata-allegro form in all three movts. Thematic material is finely contrasted and well developed, and if there are echos of Harris and Hindemith, still they are good models. Mod

ZBINDEN, JULIEN-FRANÇOIS (Swi), 1917- .

Swiss musician interested in both serious and entertainment music, has concertos for piano and orchestra, for double-bass and O, and one for jazz-band and strings called Jazzific.

Four Solitudes, Op 17 (1955). Complex, contrasting set, dissonant yet expressive. Dif

CHRONOLOGY OF COMPOSERS

birth	17th Century	death
1683	Rameau, J. P.	1764
1685	Bach, J. S.	1750
1685	Handel, G. F.	1759
1685	Scarlatti, D.	1757

	18th Century	
1706	Galluppi, B.	1785
1710	Arne, T.	1778
1710	Alberti, D.	1740
1710	Bach, W. F.	1784
1710	Paradisi, D.	1792
1714	Bach, C. P. E.	1788
1723	Rutini, G. N.	1797
1729	Soler, A.	1783
1732	Haydn, J.	1809
1735	Bach, J. C.	1782
1739	Dittersdorf, K.	1799
1739	Rust, F. W.	1796
1749	Cimarosa, D.	1801
1752	Clementi, M.	1832
1755	Grazioli, G. B.	1820
1756	Mozart, W. A.	1791
1756	Reinagle, A.	1809
1760	Albeniz, M.	1831
1760	Dussek, J. L.	1812
1769	Asioli, B.	1832
1770	Beethoven, L.	1827
1770	Reicha, A.	1836
1773	Wölfl, J.	1812
1776	Hoffmann, E. T. A.	1822
1778	Hummel, J. N.	1837
1786	Weber, C. M.	1826
1791	Czerny, K.	1857
1792	Rossini, G.	1868

1793	Hünten, F.	1878
1794	Moscheles, I.	1870
1797	Schubert, F.	1828

19th Century

1803	Herz, H.	1888
1806	Arriaga y Balzola, J.C.	1826
1809	Mendelssohn, F.	1847
1810	Bürgmuller, N.	1836
1810	Chopin, F.	1849
1810	Schumann, R.	1856
1811	Hiller, F.	1899
1811	Liszt, F.	1886
1813	Alkan, C.	1888
1813	Heller, S.	1888
1814	Henselt, A.	1889
1815	Volkmann, R.	1883
1817	Gade, N.	1890
1819	Schumann, C.	1896
1822	Franck, C.	1890
1822	Raff, J.	1882
1824	Smetana, B.	1884
1828	Bargiel, W.	1897
1829	Gottschalk, L.	1869
1829	Rubinstein, A.	1894
1833	Bendel, F.	1874
1833	Brahms, J.	1897
1835	Saint-Saëns, C.	1921
1837	Balakirev, M.	1910
1837	Jensen, A.	1879
1839	Moussorgsky, M.P.	1881
1839	Rheinberger, J.	1901
1840	Tchaikovsky, P.I.	1893
1841	Chabrier, E.	1894
1841	Dvořák, A.	1904
1843	Grieg, E.	1907
1843	Sgambatie, G.	1914
1845	Fauré, G.	1924
1849	Godard, B.	1895
1850	Scharwenka, F.X.	1924
1851	D'Indy, V.	1931
1854	Janáček, L.	1928
1854	Moszkowski, M.	1925
1855	Liadov, A.K.	1914
1856	Sinding, C.	1941
1857	Chaminade, C.	1944
1857	Elgar, E.	1934

1859	Liapunoff, S.	1924
1860	Albeniz, I.	1909
1860	Paderewski, I. J.	1941
1861	Arensky, A.	1906
1861	MacDowell, E.	1908
1862	Debussy, C.	1918
1863	Delius, F.	1934
1863	Pierne, G.	1937
1864	d'Albert, E.	1932
1864	Nielsen, C.	1931
1865	Dukas, P.	1935
1865	Glazunoff, A.	1936
1865	Sibelius, J.	1957
1866	Busoni, F.	1924
1866	Satie, E.	1925
1867	Granados, E.	1916
1868?	Joplin, S.	1917
1869	Roussel, A.	1937
1870	Godowsky, L.	1938
1872	Scriabin, A.	1915
1873	Rachmaninoff, S.	1943
1873	Reger, M.	1916
1874	Ives, C.	1954
1874	Schönberg, A.	1951
1875	Ravel, M.	1937
1876	Falla, M. de	1946
1876	Carpenter, J. A.	1951
1876	Hofmann, J.	1957
1876	Niemann, W.	1953
1876	Ruggles, C.	1971
1877	Dohnanyi, E.	1960
1878	Palmgren, S.	1951
1879	Bridge, F.	1941
1879	Grovlez, G.	1944
1879	Ireland, J.	1962
1879	Respighi, O.	1936
1879	Scott, C.	1970
1880	Bloch, E.	1959
1880	Medtner, N.	1951
1881	Bartók, B.	1945
1881	Miaskovsky, N.	1950
1881	Valen, F.	1952
1882	Dett, R. N.	1943
1882	Grainger, P.	1961
1882	Kodaly, Z.	1967
1882	Malipiero, G. F.	
1882	Stravinsky, I.	1971

1882	Turina, J.	1949
1883	Bax, A.	1953
1883	Casella, A.	1947
1883	Nin, J.	1949
1883	Szymanowsky, C.	1937
1883	Webern, A.	1945
1884	Griffes, C.	1920
1885	Berg, A.	1935
1885	Riegger, W.	1961
1885	Wellesz, E.	
1886	Ponce, M.	1948
1887	Bauer, M.	1955
1887	Toch, E.	1964
1887	Valen, F.	1952
1887	Villa-Lobos, H.	1959
1888	Alexandrov, A.	
1890	Ibert, J.	1962
1890	Martin, F.	
1890	Martinu, B.	1959
1890	Pinto, O.	1950
1891	Prokofiev, S.	1953
1892	Castro, J.M.	1964
1892	Honneger, A.	1955
1892	Jarnach, P.	
1892	Milhaud, D.	
1892	Ornstein, L.	
1893	Mompou, F.	
1893	Moore, D.	1969
1894	Pijper, W.	1947
1894	Moeran, E.	1951
1895	Castelnuovo-Tedesco, M.	
1895	Castro, J.J.	1968
1895	Hindemith, P.	1963
1895	Rathaus, K.	1954
1895	Rudhyar, D.	
1895	Still, W.G.	
1896	Rivier, J.	
1896	Sessions, R.	
1896	Thompson, V.	
1897	Ben-Haim, P.	
1897	Cowell, H.	
1897	Porter, Q.	1966
1897	Tansman, A.	
1898	Bacon, E.	
1898	Eisler, H.	
1898	Elwell, H.	
1898	Gershwin, G.	1937

1898	Harris, R.	
1898	Riete, V.	
1898	Rubinstein, B.	1952
1899	Auric, G.	
1899	Casadesus, R.	
1899	Chavez, C.	
1899	Hernandez Moncada, E.	
1899	Poulenc, F.	1963
1899	Tcherepnin, A.	

20th Century

1900	Antheil, G.	1959
1900	Barraud, H.	
1900	Bush, A.	
1900	Copland, A.	
1900	Fuleihan, A.	1970
1900	Halfter, R.	
1900	Křenek, E.	
1900	Sas, A.	1967
1900	Tajcevic, M.	
1901	Apostel, H.	
1901	Beck, C.	
1901	Crawford, R.	
1901	Jelinek, H.	
1901	Pepping, E.	
1901	Poot, M.	
1902	Eckart-Gramatte, S.	
1902	Takacs, J.	
1902	Wolpe, S.	1972
1903	Blacher, B.	
1903	Berkeley, L.	
1903	Chavez, C.	
1903	Giannini, V.	1966
1903	Duke, V.	1969
1903	Kadosa, P.	
1903	Khachaturian, A.	
1903	Lopatnikoff, N.	
1904	Dallapiccola, L.	
1904	Kabalevsky, D.	
1905	Bacevicius, V.	
1905	Halftter, E.	
1905	Jolivet, A.	
1905	Menasce, J.	1960
1905	Rawsthorne, A.	
1905	Tippet, M.	
1906	Caturla, A. G.	1940

1906	Creston, P.	
1906	Egge, K.	
1906	Fuga, S.	
1906	Shostakovich, D.	
1906	Talma, L.	
1907	Badings, H.	
1907	Palester, R.	
1907	Phillips, B.	
1907	Rozsa, M.	
1907	Saygun, A. A.	
1907	Szalowski, A.	
1908	Babin, V.	1972
1908	Bosmans, A.	
1908	Carr, A.	
1908	Carter, E.	
1908	Ferguson, H.	
1908	Messiaen, O.	
1908	Stevens, H.	
1909	Castro, W.	
1909	Swanson, H.	
1909	Haufrecht, H.	
1910	Barber, S.	
1910	Holzman, R.	
1910	Peragallo, M.	
1910	Schuman, W.	
1911	Ardevol, J.	
1911	Bergman, E.	
1911	Bowles, P.	
1911	Hovhaness, A.	
1911	Menotti, G. C.	
1911	Napoli, J.	
1912	Bate, S.	1959
1912	Cage, J.	
1912	Jelobinsky, V.	1946
1912	Moncayo, J.	1958
1912	Pentland, B.	
1913	Archer, V.	
1913	Bettinelli, B.	
1913	Britten, B.	
1913	Dello Joio, N.	
1913	Takata, S.	
1914	Fine, I.	1962
1914	Kubik, G.	
1914	Malipiero, R.	
1914	Palmer, R.	
1914	Panufnik, A.	

1915	Alexander, H.
1915	Diamond, D.
1915	Lee, D.
1915	Persichetti, V.
1915	Searle, H.
1915	Surinac, C.
1916	Babbitt, M.
1916	Binkerd, G.
1916	Ginastera, A.
1916	Papineau-Couture, J.
1917	Ward, R.
1917	Harris, L.
1916	Weber, B.
1917	Kay, U.
1918	Bernstein, L.
1918	Gramatges, H.
1918	Kasilag, L.
1918	Rochberg, G.
1918	Yardumian, R.
1918	Zbinden, J. F.
1919	Bentzon, N. V.
1919	Kirchner, L.
1919	Nelhybel, V.
1920	Fricker, P.
1920	Le Montaine, J.
1921	Bergsma, W.
1921	El-Dabh, H.
1922	Fiala, G.
1922	Campos-Parsi, H.
1922	Foss, L.
1922	Hamilton, I.
1922	Henze, H. W.
1922	Serocki, K.
1922	Thorne, F.
1922	Walker, G.
1923	Chou, W. C.
1923	Matsushita, S.
1923	Mennin, P.
1923	Nakada, Y.
1923	Rorem, N.
1924	Aitken, H.
1924	Laderman, E.
1924	Lees, B.
1924	Starer, R.
1924	Travis, R.
1925	Berio, L.
1925	Boulez, R.

1925	Hoffmann, R.
1925	Mayer, W.
1926	Arizaga, R.
1926	Feldman, M.
1926	Henze, H.W.
1926	Kurtag, G.
1926	Kohn, K.
1926	Morel, F.
1926	Pepin, C.
1926	Ribari, A.
1927	Angerer, P.
1927	Beckwith, J.
1927	Castaldo, J.
1927	Joubert, J.
1927	Matriano, S.
1927	Szalonek, W.
1928	Cummings, R.
1928	Helps, R.
1928	Musgrave, T.
1928	Stevenson, R.
1928	Stockhausen, K.
1928	Sydeman, W.
1929	Crumb, G.
1929	Hoddinott, A.
1929	Mayuzumi, T.
1930	Strait, W.
1930	Amram, D.
1930	Blackwood, E.
1930	Halftter, C.
1930	Heider, W.
1930	Moroi, M.
1930	Takemitsu, T.
1930	Tupas-Giron, B.
1931	Bussotti, S.
1931	Takahashi, Y.
1931	Trubitt, A.
1932	Goehr, A.
1932	Schedrin, R.
1932	Tremblay, G.
1934	Durko, Z.
1934	Mathias, W.
1934	Maxwell Davies, P.
1936	Bennett, R.R.
1936	Cardew, C.
1936	Ward-Steinman, D.
1936	Williamson, M.
1937	Del Tredici, D.

1939	McCabe, J.
1940	Chambers, S.
1941	Tcherepnin, S.
1943	Smalley, R.
1943	Tcherepnin, I.
1945	Zatman, A.

BIBLIOGRAPHY

Aguettante, Louis. La Musique de Piano. Paris: Albin Michel, 1954.

Apel, Willi. Masters of the Keyboard. Cambridge: Harvard University Press, 1947.

Bach, Carl Philipp Emanuel. Essay on the True Art of Playing Keyboard Instruments. (Transl. by Wm. Mitchell.) New York: W. W. Norton, 1949.

Baker's Biographical Dictionary of Musicians. 5th ed. New York: G. Schirmer, 1971.

Bauer, Marion. Twentieth Century Music. New York: Putnam, 1947.

Blom, Eric. Mozart. New York: E. P. Dutton, 1940.

_____, ed. Grove's Dictionary of Music and Musicians. 5th ed. London: St. Martin's, 1970.

Blom, Eric and J. A. Westrup, editors. Mussorgsky. 1st ed. New York: Crowell-Collier, 1962.

Boncourechliev, Andre. Schumann. (Transl. by Arthur Boyars.) New York: Grove Press, 1959.

Bourniquel, Camille. Chopin. New York: Grove Press, 1960.

Bowers, Faubion. Scriabin. 1st ed. 2 vols. Japan: Kodansha International, 1969.

Broder, Nathan, ed. Contemporary Music in Europe. New York: W.W. Norton, 1965.

Broder, Nathan. Samuel Barber. New York: G. Schirmer, 1954.

Butler, Stanley. Guide to the Best in Contemporary Piano Music: An Annotated List of Graded Solo Piano Music Published Since 1950. Volume I: Levels 1 through 5. Metuchen, N.J.: Scarecrow Press, 1973.

_____. Guide to the Best in Contemporary Piano Music .... Volume II: Levels 6 through 8. Metuchen, N.J.: Scarecrow Press, 1973.

Cage, John. Silence. 1st ed. Cambridge: Wesleyan University Press, 1961.

Contemporary Music of Japan '72. Ongaku No Tomo Sha
    Corp. , Kanguraza 6-30, Shinjuku-ku, Tokyo, Japan.
Cowell, Henry and Sydney. Charles Ives and His Music.
    New York: Oxford University Press, 1955.
Culshaw, John. Rachmaninov. New York: Oxford Univer-
    versity Press, 1950.

Dale, Kathleen. Nineteenth-Century Piano Music. New
    York: Oxford University Press, 1954.
Demuth, Norman. Ravel. London: J. M. Dent, 1947.
Dornon, Eleanor K. Japanese Piano Music. Sendai, Japan,
    1972. (Unpublished.)

Einstein, Alfred. Mozart: His Character, His Work.
    (Transl. by Arthur Mendel and Nathan Broder.) New
    York: Oxford University Press, 1951.
_____. Music in the Romantic Era. New York: W. W.
    Norton, 1947.
_____. Schubert: A Musical Portrait. New York: Ox-
    ford University Press, 1951.
Eschman, Karl. Changing Forms in Modern Music. Bos-
    ton: E. C. Schirmer, 1945.
Ewen, David. The World of Twentieth-Century Music.
    Englewood Cliffs, N. J. : Prentice-Hall, 1969.

Friskin, J. and I. Freundlich. Music for the Piano. New
    York: Rinehart, 1954.

Gal, Hans. Johannes Brahms. (Transl. by Joseph Stein.)
    1st ed. New York: Knopf, 1963.
Geiringer, Karl. Johann Sebastian Bach. New York: Ox-
    ford University Press, 1966.
_____. The Bach Family. New York: Oxford Univer-
    sity Press, 1971.
_____. Brahms. New York: Oxford University Press,
    1934.
_____. Haydn: A Creative Life in Music. New York:
    W. W. Norton, 1946.
Gillespie, John. Five Centuries of Keyboard Music. Bel-
    mont, Cal. : Wadsworth, 1966.
Girdlestone, Cutbert. Jean-Philippe Rameau: His Life and
    Works. London: Cassel, 1957.
Gottschalk, L. M. Notes of a Pianist. New York, 1964.

Hinson, Maurice. Keyboard Bibliography. Cincinnati:
    Music Teachers Association, 1972.
Hoover, Kathleen and John Cage. Virgil Thompson. New

    York: Thomas Yoseloff, 1959.
Hutcheson, Ernest. The Literature of the Piano. 2d ed.
    New York: Knopf, 1949.

Jacob, Eduard Heinrich. Felix Mendelssohn and His Times.
    (Transl. by Richard and Clara Winston.) 1st ed.
    Englewood Cliffs, N. J. : Prentice-Hall, 1963.

Kirby, F. E. A Short History of Keyboard Music. New
    York: The Free Press, 1966.
Kirkpatrick, Ralph. Domenico Scarlatti. Princeton, N. J. :
    Princeton University Press, 1953.

Lang, Paul Henry, ed. The Creative World of Mozart.
    New York: W. W. Norton, 1963.
Lockspeiser, Edward. Debussy: His Life and Mind. Vol.
    1. New York: Macmillan, 1962.
Lockwood, Albert. Notes on the Literature of the Piano.
    Ann Arbor, Mich. : University of Michigan Press,
    1940.
Loesser, Arthur. Men, Women and Pianos. New York:
    Simon & Schuster, 1954.
Loggins, Vernon. Where the Word Ends: The Life of Mor-
    eau Gottschalk. Baton Rouge, La. : Louisiana State
    Press, 1958.
Lubin, Ernest. The Piano Duet. New York: Grossman,
    1972.

Maisel, Edward M. Charles T. Griffes. 1st ed. New
    York: Knopf, 1943.
Marek, George R. Beethoven: Biography of a Genius.
    New York: Funk and Wagnalls, 1972.
           . Mendelssohn. New York: Funk and Wagnalls,
    1972.
Matthay, Tobias. Musical Interpretation. Boston: Boston
    Music Co. , 1913.
Matthews, Denis. Keyboard Music. Harmondsworth, Eng-
    land: Penguin Books, 1972.
Mellers, Wilfred. Music in a New Found Land. New York:
    Knopf, 1966.
Meyers, Rollo. Erik Satie. London, 1948.
Moldenhauer, Hans. Duo-Pianism. Chicago, 1951.
Monrad-Johansen, David. Edward Grieg. (Transl. by
    Madge Robertson.) New York: Tudor Pub. Co. , 1945.

Newman, William S. The Sonata in the Baroque Era. Chap-
    el Hill, N. C. : University of North Carolina Press, 1959.

_____. The Sonata in the Classic Era. Chapel Hill,
N.C.: University of North Carolina Press, 1963.
_____. A Selected List of Music Recommended for Pi-
ano Students. 2d suppl. Chapel Hill, N.C.: University of North Carolina Press, 1967.

Puchelt, Gerhard. Verlorene Klänge: Studien zur deutschen
Klaviermusik 1830-1880. Berlin: Verlag Robert Lie-
nau, 1970.

Rorem, Ned. Music from Inside Out. 1st ed. New York:
G. Braziller, 1967.
_____. The New York Diary. New York: Braziller,
1967.
_____. The Paris Diary. New York: Braziller, 1966.

Sablosky, Irving L. American Music. Chicago: Univer-
sity of Chicago Press, 1969.
Salzman, Eric. Twentieth Century Music: An Introduction.
Englewood Cliffs, N.J.: Prentice-Hall, 1967.
Schauffler, Robert Haven. The Life and Works of Robert
Schumann. New York: Henry Holt, 1945.
Schmitz, Robert E. The Piano Works of Claude Debussy.
New York: Duell, Sloan and Pearce, 1950.
Schneider, Marcel. Schubert. (Transl. by Elizabeth Por-
ton.) New York: Grove Press, 1959.
Scholes, Percy A. The Oxford Companion to Music. 9th
ed. London: Oxford University Press, 1955.
_____. The Concise Oxford Dictionary of Music. Lon-
don: Oxford University Press, 1964.
_____, ed. Dr. Burney's Musical Tours in Europe.
London: Oxford University Press, 1959.
Schönberg, Harold C. The Great Pianists. New York:
Simon & Schuster, 1956.
Schweitzer, Albert. J.S. Bach. (Transl. by Ernest New-
man.) London: Adam and Charles Black, 1964.
Scott, Cyril. Bone of Contention. New York: Arco Pub.
Co., 1969.
Shaw, G.B. Music in London. 3 vols. London: Constable,
1932.
Shedlok, John S. The Pianoforte Sonata. New York: Da
Capo Press, 1964.
Slonimsky, Nicolas, ed. Baker's Biographical Dictionary of
Musicians. 5th ed. New York: G. Schirmer, 1965;
and 1967 suppl.
Smith, Julia. Aaron Copland. New York: E.P. Dutton,
1955.

Stevens, Halsey. Bela Bartók. London: Oxford University
    Press, 1953.
Stravinsky, Igor, and Robert Craft. Themes and Episodes.
    New York: Knopf, 1966.
Stuckenschmidt. Arnold Schönberg. New York: Grove
    Press, 1959.
Suckling, Norman. Fauré. New York: Pellegrini and
    Cudahy, 1951.

Thompson, Oscar. Debussy, Man and Artist. New York:
    Tudor Pub. Co., 1940.
Thompson, Virgil. Virgil Thompson. New York: Holt,
    Rinehart & Winston, 1966.
_____. American Music Since 1910. New York: Holt,
    Rinehart & Winston, 1970.

Ueno, Akira. Contemporary Japanese Piano Music. (Transl.
    by Eleanor Dornon.) From articles appearing in "Mu-
    sicanova" [a pianists' journal]. Sendai, Japan, 1972.

Watson, Corinne and Jack M. A Concise Dictionary of Mu-
    sic. New York: Dodd, Mead, 1965.
Weinstock, Herbert. Chopin: The Man and His Music. 1st
    ed. New York: Knopf, 1949.
Wierzynski, Casimir. The Life and Death of Chopin.
    (Transl. by Norbert Guterman.) New York: Simon &
    Schuster, 1971.